The Heart of Hell

The

THE SOLDIERS' STRUGGLE FO

Civil War America

PETER S. CARMICHAEL, CAROLINE E. JANNEY,
and AARON SHEEHAN-DEAN, *editors*

This landmark series interprets broadly the history and
culture of the Civil War era through the long nineteenth
century and beyond. Drawing on diverse approaches
and methods, the series publishes historical works that
explore all aspects of the war, biographies of leading
commanders, and tactical and campaign studies, along
with select editions of primary sources. Together, these
books shed new light on an era that remains central to
our understanding of American and world history.

Heart of Hell

POTSYLVANIA'S BLOODY ANGLE

Jeffry D. Wert

upton at the Salient

THE UNIVERSITY OF NORTH CAROLINA PRESS CHAPEL HILL

© 2022 Jeffry D. Wert
All rights reserved
Set in Miller and Stymie by Westchester Publishing Services
Manufactured in the United States of America

The University of North Carolina Press has been a
member of the Green Press Initiative since 2003.

Library of Congress Cataloging-in-Publication Data
Names: Wert, Jeffry D., author.
Title: The heart of hell : the soldiers' struggle for Spotsylvania's
Bloody Angle / Jeffry D. Wert.
Other titles: Civil War America (Series)
Description: Chapel Hill : University of North Carolina Press, [2022] |
Series: Civil War America | Includes bibliographical references and index.
Identifiers: LCCN 2021054796 | ISBN 9781469668420 (cloth) |
ISBN 9781469668437 (ebook)
Subjects: LCSH: Spotsylvania Court House, Battle of, Va., 1864.
Classification: LCC E476.52 .W45 2022 | DDC 973.7/36—dc23/eng/20211116
LC record available at https://lccn.loc.gov/2021054796

Jacket illustrations: *Front*, Thure de Thulstrup, *Battle of Spottsylvania* [sic]
(Boston: L. Sprang & Co., 1887); *back*, Alfred R. Waud, *The Toughest Fight Yet*
(May 12, 1864). Both courtesy of the Library of Congress
Prints and Photographs Division.

To Gloria, Jason, Kathy, Rachel,

Gabriel, Natalie, and Grant

with love.

Contents

Maps

Preface

At 4:35 A.M. on Thursday, May 12, 1864, twenty thousand officers and men of the Second Corps, Union Army of the Potomac stepped forth. Ordered by General-in-Chief Ulysses S. Grant to lead a major offensive, these veteran troops advanced toward a bulge (often referred to as a salient) in Confederate defenses outside of Spotsylvania Court House, Virginia. Ahead of them, their foes in the Army of Northern Virginia maintained a tenuous position behind earthworks.

Battle-tested as both armies were, neither side could anticipate the hellish ordeal that would unfold over the next day. But for weeks they had speculated around campfires about when once again they would meet their old foes on battlefields. In this, the conflict's fourth spring, the war's end seemed as elusive as it had in the previous three. Although Union forces had won critical victories at Gettysburg, Pennsylvania, and at Vicksburg, Mississippi, in the summer of 1863, two major Confederate armies remained in the field, standing defiantly in Virginia and in Georgia. As the officers and men anticipated, active campaigning resumed with warm weather and the drying of roads during the first week of May. Union offensives went forward against both Confederate forces, with coordinated movements that had been planned and ordered by Grant, appointed commander of federal forces with the rank of lieutenant general two months earlier.

In Georgia, Major General William T. Sherman led three armies south toward Atlanta, against General Joseph E. Johnston's Army of Tennessee. In Virginia, meanwhile, the offensive consisted of a three-prong advance—one, south up the Shenandoah Valley toward rail connections; a second on Bermuda Hundred between the James and Appomattox rivers toward the Confederate capital of Richmond; and the main operation in central Virginia against General Robert E. Lee's redoubtable Confederate host. Each of these offensives, each forthcoming engagement, each advance or retreat unfolded against the backdrop of the fall's presidential election in the North.

Grant accompanied Major General George G. Meade's Army of the Potomac in its confrontation with Lee's Army of Northern Virginia, pitting the conflict's greatest generals against one another. In their letters and diaries during the early spring, soldiers in both armies awaited the historic meeting between the pair, arguing who would be the victor. Both commanders, however, faced difficulties. Within days of the campaign's outset, Grant witnessed firsthand the army's leadership, which was plagued by cautiousness characterized by a deeply held attitude of avoiding defeat instead of attaining victory. This attitude had been the army's history and its curse, ingrained seemingly into the army's soul by its second commander, George B. McClellan. Grant soon determined that he would have to direct the operations personally if he was to exorcise McClellan's ghost.

For Lee, the difficulties were far graver. His battle-tested veterans—arguably the war's finest—would have to wage a struggle against a force nearly twice its size. The army's combat prowess suffered from a depleted officer ranks, particularly at the rank of major, lieutenant colonel, and colonel. Furthermore, Lee had mounting concerns with the capabilities of corps commanders Richard Ewell and A. P. Hill. Lee understood also that his army would likely be waging a defensive struggle in the impending campaign, whose direction rested with his opponent.

It took time for Grant and Lee to take the measure of each other. The long-awaited encounter began in the so-called Overland Campaign on May 4, when the Federals crossed the Rapidan River, moving south and east. It had been exactly ten months since the Rebels had begun a retreat after their defeat by the Yankees at Gettysburg. Since then, these foes had met in a pair of indecisive operations—the Bristoe Campaign in October 1863 and the Mine Run Campaign in November. The first major clash came on May 5, in a blinding struggle in the Wilderness of Spotsylvania. On this day and the next, the opponents fought each other in a series of attacks and counterattacks. By nightfall on May 6, the armies remained on the battlefield. Unlike in the past, the Federals went forward, not back, the next day. To Grant, there was to be no retreating, and he directed the army toward Spotsylvania Court House on the roads to Richmond. There, on a rainy Thursday, began a dark future: land scarred by entrenchments, doomed assaults, and daily bloodletting that those in the ranks endured in an unending nightmare from North Anna to Cold Harbor to the many battlefields of Petersburg.

The armies remained outside of the crossroads village of Spotsylvania from May 8 until May 20. By the time they departed, the nature of warfare in the Overland and future campaigns had been altered. Both armies had erected fieldworks in the Wilderness; in fact, the first extensive use of such works in Virginia had been by Lee's troops during the Mine Run Campaign. At Spotsylvania, however, the entrenchments of logs and dirt extended for miles. Behind them Confederate defenders repulsed enemy frontal assaults on May 8 and 10. Attacking in linear formations, Grant's Union troops staggered and recoiled before the rifle and cannon fire from behind the man-made defenses.

A breakthrough occurred on the evening of May 10, when a dozen Union regiments, led by Colonel Emory Upton and stacked three regiments across in four lines, penetrated a section of the salient at the northern limit of Confederate lines. When reinforcements failed to appear, Confederate reserves drove back Upton's troops. But Upton's tactical use of a deep column and its limited success convinced Grant to undertake a larger and similarly arrayed attack on the salient, which its defenders had dubbed the "Mule Shoe." So, in the morning darkness, fog, and rain of May 12, veteran infantrymen of the Second Corps charged.

By the time the combat had ceased at roughly three o'clock on the morning of May 13, upward of 55,000 fellow Americans from both armies had been drawn into the relentless and merciless fury. For some twenty-two hours, amid downpours of rain, and separated in many places only by hastily assembled logs and dirt, the foes killed and maimed one another in a struggle without parallel in the four-year conflict. Total casualties amounted to 17,500 killed, wounded, captured, or missing, the highest number incurred in a single day in the eastern theater from Gettysburg on July 3, 1863, to Appomattox and the war's end on April 9, 1865. But as is so often the case, such statistics fail to capture the brutality of the battle and its effect on those who endured it and recorded their memories.

For the tens of thousands of Yankees and Rebels who fought at the Mule Shoe salient, the ceaseless nature of the combat and the nearness of their enemies surpassed anything in their previous experience. As a Union chaplain put it afterward, "Combine the horrors of many battlefields, bring them into a single day and night of twenty-four hours, and the one of May 12th includes them all." The struggle was Civil War combat at its most grievous personal level, waged often at the length of a rifle barrel along hundreds of yards of parapets and adjoining traverses.

A return trip to the battlefields in and around Fredericksburg and Spotsylvania, Virginia, ended for me at the Mule Shoe's famous "Bloody Angle." Standing at the bend in the eroded works, I was reminded of the fury that had engulfed the ground on that memorable day, one of the worst for combatants in all of American military history. What struck me was that for all the previous works that have recounted the military history of the Overland campaign and its epic battles, one cannot fully appreciate the place of this fight in the war's history without immersing oneself in the words of those who endured it. The broad histories of campaigns and battles often belong to the generals, but in many ways, the story of the Mule Shoe belongs to the privates, corporals, sergeants, and company and regimental officers, Northerners and Southerners, whose words resound through time in graphic and even harrowing descriptions of their shared ordeal. I decided then that their profoundly compelling stories should have a retelling.

Jeffry D. Wert
May 10, 2021

The Heart of Hell

{ 1 }

We Must Whip Them

Major David W. Anderson of the 44th Virginia knew that the sounds coming toward him through the darkness of night might indicate enemy troops on the march. A farmer from Fluvanna County before the war, the thirty-five-year-old native Virginian had been in Confederate service for nearly three years. On this night of May 11–12, 1864, outside of Spotsylvania Court House, Virginia, the veteran major was serving as officer of the day and responsible for the command's security. Experience told him that the "steady rumble" he heard meant something, perhaps an ill wind blowing in with a new day's dawn.[1]

Fellow officers and enlisted men shared Anderson's concern. A staff officer described the sound as a "subdued roar or noise, plainly audible in the still, heavy night air, like distant falling water or machinery." Skirmishers from Colonel William A. Witcher's brigade, posted along a farm lane roughly five hundred yards to the front, reported that there must be thousands of Yankees beyond the woods to the north. Music from Union bands drifted through the cold, steady rain into Confederate lines as if it were an advance requiem.[2]

The Confederate soldiers belonged to Major General Edward Johnson's division of the Second Corps, Army of Northern Virginia. They manned a bulge or a salient in the army's lines, which the men thought resembled a horse or mule shoe. Such a defensive formation invited attacks and, on the day before, May 10, a dozen Union infantry regiments, stacked in four lines, breached the salient's western face, penetrating deeper into it and capturing prisoners and cannon. Confederate reserves repulsed the Federals and resealed the wide gash in the Confederate works.[3]

The Rebels and their foes, members of the Union Army of the Potomac, had been fighting each other in this new campaign for seven consecutive days. They were old enemies, killing and maiming each other at terrible places—the Cornfield at Antietam, along the stone wall below Marye's Heights at Fredericksburg, and across the farmers' fields and orchards at

Gettysburg. But this past week of combat had had a different character to it, an unrelenting bloodletting that seemed to portend a darker road ahead.

Were the sounds then, as Anderson and his comrades increasingly believed, the massing of Federal infantry and artillery for another assault? With each passing hour toward dawn, the Confederates became more concerned that the Yankees would be coming. "There was," recalled a Rebel skirmisher, "a nameless something in the air which told every man that a crisis was at hand." This infantryman and his fellow veterans could not have known in the early morning's darkness the magnitude of the crisis that would soon engulf them. More than a crisis, however, loomed over the salient, for a hellish fury was to be unleashed, the depths and duration of which had not been witnessed before in this fearful conflict.[4]

The Union Army of the Potomac and the attached Ninth Corps began crossing the Rapidan River in central Virginia on May 4, 1864, initiating a long-anticipated spring campaign. Altogether, the army was a powerful force, with 119,000 officers and men. An accompanying newspaperman called them "the Grand Army," adding, "It is a compact, self-reliant, veteran host, conscious that it is able to deliver mightier blows than ever before, knowing that there will be blows to take as well as blows to give."[5]

South of the river, awaiting them, were the 66,000 members of the Confederate Army of Northern Virginia. A certainty to the forthcoming campaign's outcome imbued their ranks. "I think you may confidently expect a glorious issue in the impending campaign," a lieutenant had assured his sister two days earlier, "a campaign between right and wrong, we are backed by an army of good and true men, the other by a bunch of lawless outcasts and mercenaries." A fellow officer put it more bluntly in a letter home, "We only wish for a chance to slaughter" the Yankees.[6]

The approaching confrontation between the old nemeses had had an inevitability for weeks, if not months. As the Federals forded the Rapidan on May 4, it had been ten months to the day since the Confederates had undertaken their retreat from the battlefield at Gettysburg, Pennsylvania. The withdrawal ceased by the end of July 1863, in the region drained by the Rappahannock and Rapidan rivers. An interlude of sorts in active operations followed, extending through autumn 1863 and into winter and spring 1864.[7]

Before winter brought cold and inclement weather, however, both armies—General Robert E. Lee's Rebels and Major General George

G. Meade's Yankees—undertook offensive movements. Lee advanced against the Federals in mid-October in the Bristoe Campaign, which brought the opposing forces to the outskirts of Washington, D.C. Prodded by the Union administration, Meade led his army across the Rapidan River in the Mine Run Campaign at the end of November. Both operations proved indecisive, with the armies settling into winter quarters for the next five months.[8]

Confederate winter camps sprawled across the countryside south of the Rapidan and Rappahannock rivers. Shortages of rations and fodder for animals plagued the army throughout the winter months. At one point, Lee admitted to a general, "The question of *food for this army* gives me more trouble and uneasiness *than every thing else combined.*" He was forced to disperse his cavalry units and artillery batteries across the various counties because of a lack of feed for the horses and mules.[9]

Letters by officers and men to home folks reflected the hardship in their camps. A Georgian informed readers in a newspaper, "Rations are short now, but there is little complaint made." Occasionally, the men received coffee, sugar, and rice, which reminded "us of home before the war." A Virginian told his wife, "The officers have been reduced down to same rations as the privates and it is issued to them just the same as it is issued to us." Another soldier recalled: "Coffee and sugar were priceless luxuries. Bread and bacon were worth risking life for. A pair of shoes from a dead man." Folks tried to alleviate the shortages with packages of foodstuffs and clothing items.[10]

Shortages in the army and stark conditions at home, related by loved ones in letters, drove many to desert. Loosened restrictions on furloughs lessened the problem but did not cease the outward flow. "Running away from the army is not fine work," argued a member of the 11th North Carolina. "We are soldiers, and we have to stay as long as there is any war." Thousands of men reenlisted, however, while recruits, or "new issue" as veterans dubbed them, joined the army.[11]

The tens of thousands who remained in the ranks, performing their soldiery duties, had been steeled by past hardships and adversity. The reasons they had enlisted earlier still held as motivation—duty, honor, God, defense of home and family, and the cause of independence. They had a shared legacy of battlefield prowess and an "unconquerable spirit." Another reason in the estimation of a North Carolinian was "Determination" to see the war through to the end.[12]

Perhaps nothing kept them in the field with all the shortages and concern for families at home more than a profound belief in the army's commander. "With unbounded confidence in Gen Lee, and men enough," asserted a Virginian, "we fear not the issue." Colonel Clement Evans of the 31st Georgia said of Lee and his men, "He is the only man living in whom they would unreservedly trust all power for the preservation of their independence." The bond between Lee and the army's rank and file had been forged at Second Manassas, Antietam, Fredericksburg, Chancellorsville, and even Gettysburg and remained unshakable.[13]

The men had always appreciated Lee's concern for their welfare, and the lack of food and clothing during this winter tested their commander's administrative abilities more than ever. It appears that the effects of an illness in March 1863 still lingered, weakening him. "I feel a marked change in my strength since my attack last spring at Fredericksburg, and am less competent for my duty than ever," he confided to a son. Lee had suffered from some sort of heart problem, likely angina pectoris, the inflammation of the membrane around the organ.[14]

A Confederate officer returned to the army in the spring and recounted: "I was struck by the change in General Lee's complexion. When I saw him the year before, his skin was a healthy pink. Now it was decidedly faded. He had aged a great deal more than a year in the past twelve months." The officer noted, "But he sat on Traveller [the general's favorite horse] as firmly as ever."[15]

The burdens of army command, however, required Lee's daily attention. Headquarters consisted of a handful of small tents pitched on a steep hill two miles northeast of Orange Court House. Lee relied heavily on a small personal staff of highly capable officers—lieutenant colonels Walter H. Taylor, Charles Marshall, and Charles S. Venable—to attend to the paperwork and myriad details of the administration of an army. Despite his words to his son about his stamina, Lee spent many hours at a desk, in meetings with subordinates, or examining on horseback the army's defenses along the rivers.[16]

From headquarters Lee contemplated the strategic landscape before him, recognizing that the situation had changed since fall 1863. "We are not in a condition, & never have been, in my opinion, to invade the enemy's country with a prospect of permanent benefit," he informed President Jefferson Davis on February 3, 1864. "But we can alarm & embarrass him to some extent & thus prevent his undertaking anything of magnitude against us." It was a frank assessment and, in turn, a subtle admission that Lee's opponent might dictate the struggle's future course.[17]

Since Lee had assumed command of the army on Sunday, June 1, 1862, outside of Richmond, with the Union army at the doorstep of the Confederate capital, he had adopted an aggressive offensive strategy. As Davis's military adviser, Lee had witnessed the results of the government's passive defensive strategy during the winter and spring of 1862. Union armies and navy had captured forts and cities—Nashville and New Orleans—had won battlefield victories, and stood poised to capture Richmond and thus end Confederate hopes for independence.[18]

By the war's second spring, then, Lee understood that the conflict had become a struggle between two democratic societies. Each side's war effort depended upon the support of its respective populaces, their willingness to accept the casualties and sacrifices necessary to achieve ultimate victory. Lee believed that the Confederacy's limited resources could neither sustain a long conflict nor result in an overall military victory. Confederate independence could only be obtained in a political settlement with the Union administration. In turn, Lee directed his strategy against the consent and support of Northern civilians.[19]

In Lee's judgment, a protracted conflict doomed the Confederacy. The North's vast agricultural and industrial resources, combined with a deep reservoir of manpower and a network of railroads, could sustain its military forces in prolonged campaigns across the geographic vastness of the Confederacy. Time was a relentless enemy of the Confederates. If their opponents remained steadfast in support of the cause of the Union, the struggle's outcome seemed inevitable.[20]

To stay that powerful and darkening shadow of Union military might from descending across the Confederacy, Lee acted, adopting an aggressive offensive strategy. If the Confederates were to break the will of the Northern populace to wage war, they had to win a series of battlefield victories, killing and maiming enemy soldiers. It was a matter of waging an unblinking war, searching for a victory of annihilation. Against formidable odds and "those people," as he called the enemy, Lee led forth his army on a road not taken by others.[21]

The Army of Northern Virginia's strategic victory in the Seven Days Campaign at the end of June 1862 secured the Confederate capital and drove the foe down the Virginia Peninsula. More important, the victory changed the course of the war in the East, giving Lee the strategic or operational initiative in the theater. For nearly the next two years, the Confederate commander shaped the contours of campaigns, achieving victories at Second Manassas, Fredericksburg, and Chancellorsville. His army held the field at Antietam but suffered a crippling defeat at Gettysburg.[22]

The three-day engagement in Pennsylvania seriously impaired the offensive capability of Lee's vaunted army. The Confederates incurred

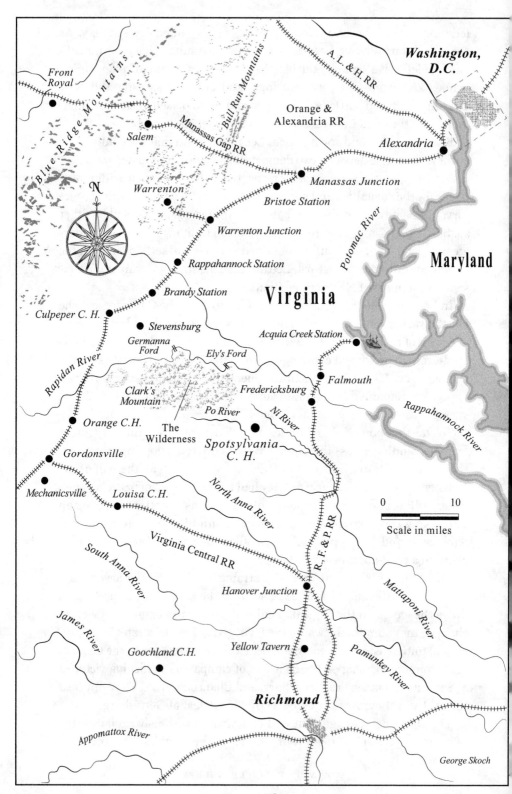

Eastern Theater

28,069 killed, wounded, or captured, a staggering casualty rate of nearly 39 percent. The engagement decimated Lee's officer ranks. Nine generals were killed, seriously wounded, or captured, while approximately 150 colonels, lieutenant colonels, and majors at the regimental level were casualties. "Gettysburg was more than a defeat," declared Jennings Cropper Wise, the historian of Lee's artillery. "It was a disaster from which no army, in fact, no belligerent state, could soon recover."[23]

Despite the terrible casualties and other hardships, the Confederates remained a resilient command. It took time but, to the extent possible, the army healed. Recovered wounded men returned to their regiments, while recruits and draftees added to the ranks. Critically, an unconquerable spirit endured, binding them together as a formidable enemy.[24]

By early spring 1864, then, Lee still considered seizing the initiative with an offensive movement when the weather permitted. To President Davis, Lee had stated that all he expected to accomplish was to "alarm & embarrass" the enemy, but he told Major General Henry Heth that another advance across the Potomac River into the North was "to be our true policy." It was now, however, an unrealistic strategic goal. The shortages of food and forage prevented such an undertaking against an opponent with nearly a two-to-one numerical advantage.[25]

Lee had witnessed the changing nature of Civil War combat during the Mine Run Campaign at the end of November 1863. His army manned miles of fieldworks that convinced George Meade that frontal assaults would be costly and futile. The Confederates' extensive use of fieldworks or entrenchments was a harbinger of tactics in the forthcoming campaigns.[26]

For Lee, a defensive strategy and tactics best served the cause. The early romantic notions of warfare had disappeared long ago in a cauldron of blood on many battlefields. In the war's fourth spring, the Confederacy simply had to endure, to conserve manpower, and to outlast the North, by inflicting more grievous casualties on the Federals and by maintaining strategic stalemates in both the eastern and western theaters. Overhanging military operations this year was the presidential election in the free states in the fall. If the Northern populace believed final victory remained elusive and if the sacrifices and carnage were at last not worth the struggle, President Abraham Lincoln's reelection campaign might fail.[27]

Lee understood the possible implications for Confederate independence if Lincoln were defeated at the polls. Through the enemy press he had watched closely the section's political climate, the mounting war weariness and dissent. For two years, with audacity and skillful movements, Lee had eroded Northern civilians' willingness to sustain the administration in Washington and to continue accepting the war's cost. As long as Rebel armies still stood defiant and in the field, the Union president's second term and the conflict's final outcome remained in doubt.[28]

While circumstances and the likely advance of their foes precluded a new offensive strike, Lee and his army were proven masters of defensive warfare. On April 3, the commanding general summoned his aide Walter Taylor into his tent, where they speculated about possible enemy movements. At the end of the conversation, Lee declared, "but Colo[nel] we have got to whip them, we must whip them and it has already made me better to think of it."[29]

A special train from Washington, D.C., stopped at Brandy Station in Culpeper County, Virginia, on the morning of March 10, 1864. Around the depot on the Orange and Alexandria Railroad sprawled campsites of the Army of the Potomac. As a cold, late winter rain fell, Lieutenant General Ulysses S. Grant stepped from a car and walked toward the station, where the army's commander, Major General George G. Meade, welcomed him. The pair of soldiers had not seen each other in nearly two decades.[30]

The generals rode to Meade's headquarters, a tent pitched on a spur of Fleetwood Hill roughly a mile and a half from the depot. On the previous day, in a ceremony at the White House, Grant—the victor at forts Henry and Donelson, Shiloh, Vicksburg, and Chattanooga in the West—received his commission as lieutenant general. Congress had authorized the rank and, after being assured Grant had no political aspirations in 1864, President Abraham Lincoln appointed him general-in-chief of all Union forces. Only George Washington had held a comparable rank.[31]

"I was a stranger to most of the Army of the Potomac," Grant wrote in his memoirs. "I might say to all except the officers of the regular army who had served in the Mexican War." Months earlier, as Grant's name appeared more frequently in newspapers, Meade's wife had asked her husband about him. "It is difficult for me to reply," answered Meade. "I knew him as a young man in the Mexican War, at which time he was considered a clever young officer, but nothing extraordinary. He was compelled to resign some years before the present war, owing to his irregular habits. I think his great characteristic is indomitable energy and great tenacity of purpose."[32]

Grant's "irregular habits" referred to intemperate use of alcohol. Another officer and fellow West Pointer saw Grant in Mexico and claimed at the time "he was drunken & dirty to the last extreme." He also suffered from migraines, which could be debilitating at times. Tedious duty at various posts in the antebellum army and separation from his family worsened the problem until he resigned his commission in the spring of 1854. Seven years of failed civilian endeavors followed, with poverty a seeming constant presence in the life of the Grant family. But then the war came, revealing in Grant an aptitude, if not a genius, for a warrior's calling.[33]

Meade and others soon learned what Grant's subordinates in the West had witnessed. The new general-in-chief was a relentless enemy. "He habitually wears an expression as if he had determined to drive his head through a brick wall, and was about to do it," as Lieutenant Colonel Theodore Lyman of Meade's staff described Grant. "The art of war is simple enough," contended Grant. "Find out where your enemy is. Get at him as soon as you can. Strike at him as hard as you can and as often as you can, and keep moving on."[34]

"Moving on" could exact a price, a fearful toll in blood. Grant understood warfare's appetite for souls and accepted it. Amid the turmoil of a battlefield under the most trying of circumstances, he possessed an inner stillness, habitually chewing or smoking a cigar and calming others. A woman in the capital saw him and observed that "he walked through a crowd as though solitary." A former comrade remarked during the war that Grant "is not distracted by a thousand side issues, he does not see them. He sees on a straight line."[35]

Unlike the magnetic George McClellan, "Little Mac" to the army's old rank and file, the lieutenant general lacked a commanding physical bearing. Of medium height, spare and strongly built, he walked stoop-shouldered, usually wearing a plain uniform. Lieutenant Colonel Rufus Dawes of the 6th Wisconsin, having seen Grant, wrote home, "He looks like a very common sense sort of a fellow—not puffed up by position nor to be abashed by obstacles." Lyman noted that Grant's face "has three expressions; deep thought; extreme determination; and great simplicity and calmness."[36]

Meade informed his wife that the general-in-chief was "very civil" in their initial meeting outside of Brandy Station. "I think I told you I was very much pleased with General Grant," Meade added in a subsequent letter. "In the views he expressed to me he showed much more capacity and character than I had expected." During their private conversation, Meade "offered to vacate command of the Army of the Potomac, in case he [Grant] had a preference for any other," and Meade stated that he would be willing to "serve to the best of his ability wherever placed."[37]

Grant replied to Meade, assuring the army commander "that I had no thought of substituting any one for him." "This incident," Grant wrote in his memoirs, "gave me even a more favorable opinion of Meade than did his great victory at Gettysburg the July before." As the discussion proceeded, Grant indicated that he would have his headquarters with the army. The general-in-chief had planned originally to conduct Union operations from the western theater but, once he arrived in the capital, he thought otherwise. "It was plain," as he put it later, "that here was the point for the commanding general to be. No one else could, probably, resist the pressure that would be brought to bear upon him to desist from his own plans and pursue others."[38]

Grant's presence with the army, however, would complicate command matters between the two generals and their staffs. The general-in-chief, not its commander, would direct the army's movements. In his subsequent report, Grant argued, "I tried, as far as possible," to let Meade retain independent command, issuing only general instructions and "leaving all the details and execution to him." While Meade proved to be, in Grant's words, "the right man in the right place," the lieutenant general admitted in his memoirs, "Meade's position afterwards proved embarrassing to me if not to him."[39]

Meade grasped the import, in part, of Grant's decision; Meade told his wife, "So that you may look now for the Army of the Potomac putting laurels on the brows of another rather than your husband." For the present, however, Grant had impressed Meade, and he was a professional soldier, a man bound to the demands and sacrifices of duty. "You may rest assured he is not an ordinary man," Meade wrote of the general-in-chief, adding later, "I intend to give him heartiest co-operation."[40]

Grant and Meade boarded a train on March 11, traveling to Washington, where they dined with President Lincoln at the White House on the next evening. From the capital, Grant journeyed to Tennessee and spent a week or so organizing command arrangements for spring offensives in the East and the West. Meade remained in the city, testifying once more before the congressional Joint Committee on the Conduct of the War, whose members, mostly Radical Republicans, had launched investigations into the Chancellorsville and Gettysburg campaigns.[41]

Former generals in the army, led by Daniel Sickles and Abner Doubleday, testified before the committee, alleging, in Sickles's words, that Meade had "intended to retreat from Gettysburg." The army commander had been dissuaded from doing so by his senior officers, particularly Sickles himself. Doubleday echoed Sickles's false charge. In truth, the self-serving members wanted to replace Meade with the Radicals' favorite, former commander Joseph Hooker. The hearings, which Meade called a "hullabaloo," lasted into April. Although other generals in the army testified in support of Meade's conduct, his reputation had been stained in public.[42]

For the past eight months Meade had been battling, not Congress, but Lincoln, Secretary of War Edwin Stanton, and then general-in-chief Major General Henry W. Halleck. The president had believed—wrongly—that Meade had allowed the Confederates to escape into Virginia after Gettysburg without engaging the Rebels in another battle. With a flooded Potomac River at their backs, the Confederates manned two parallel lines of entrenchments on ridges around Williamsport, Maryland. Meade planned a reconnaissance-in-force or an assault for July 14, but Lee's army had crossed the river during the preceding night.[43]

When Lincoln learned of the enemy's escape, he canceled preparations for a cabinet meeting. He was profoundly disappointed, and Halleck wired Meade of the president's "great dissatisfaction" over events along the Potomac. Meade replied within hours, "I feel compelled most respectfully to ask to be relieved from command of the army." Halleck answered that Lincoln's reaction to Lee's escape "was not intended as a censure" and "is not deemed as sufficient cause for your application to be relieved."[44]

The dispute strained the relationship of the president and the army commander for the rest of the war. Lincoln questioned Meade's willingness to engage Lee; Meade bristled at the president's interference from a distance. Through the rest of the summer and fall, the administration prodded Meade to take the offensive against the Rebels. He did so during the last week of November in the Mine Run Campaign. When Meade decided that an assault on the enemy's works would be too costly and likely to fail, he ordered a retreat, ending active operations for 1863. Meade expected to be removed from command.[45]

Among the army's rank and file, the judgment of Meade's generalship differed from that of Washington officials. All that the men had wanted was a fair fight on a fair field against their opponent, and Meade had given that to them at Gettysburg. Undoubtedly, many expressed dissatisfaction and disappointment about the Rebels' escape into Virginia, with one of them stating a common reaction: "I do not think Lee will ever be caught up in as tight a place again." Conversely, most praised Meade for not attacking the Confederates in their works behind Mine Run, moving a

Massachusetts sergeant to assert that Meade's "conduct in the last campaign has fastened his name firm in the hearts of those who compose this army."[46]

Meade had earned promotion and the troops' respect on battlefields. Wounded at Glendale on June 30, 1862, he had served as brigade and division commander of the hard-fighting Pennsylvania Reserves before leading the Fifth Corps. He admired George McClellan and shared his social and political conservatism but had managed to avoid the army's internal politics. Lincoln had appointed Meade to command of the army on June 28, 1863, three days before the engagement at Gettysburg. The president took a risk on Meade at such a momentous time with the Confederates in Pennsylvania, but Lincoln had learned in the aftermath of Chancellorsville that Meade had the support of the army's senior leadership.[47]

The president had selected a man Lincoln barely knew, but an honest man and a thorough, professional soldier. Like Grant, Meade usually wore a plain uniform over his tall, thin frame. An officer claimed, "it would be rather difficult to make him look well-dressed." A corporal thought that Meade "might have been taken for a Presbyterian clergyman, unless one approached him when he was mad." He had an irritable disposition when conducting the routine of army command and possessed a volcanic temper when angered. When not busy, he could be kind and agreeable, but few in the rank and file witnessed that side of him.[48]

With Meade, the army's officers and men awaited the resumption of operations with favorable spring weather. Blustery winds, snow, and cold temperatures marked the winter months. The Union campsites dotted the landscape in Culpeper and Fauquier counties, a region that was, according to a soldier, "a desolate looking place/war has swept over the fields of this state and left its mark here." Fortunately for the Yankees, harvests from farms and products from factories flowed south on the Orange and Alexandria Railroad, meeting the army's voracious daily needs.[49]

When not on picket duty along the rivers, drilling, or standing for inspections, the men huddled in their huts, with two topics garnering much conversation. The War Department offered thirty-day furloughs and states promised bounties if veterans in three-year regiments reenlisted as Veteran Volunteers. Many, if not most, of their enlistments were to expire in April and May. A regiment could qualify for the furloughs if three-fourths of its members, present and absent, signed up a second time. In the end, roughly twenty-eight thousand veterans extended their enlistments and went home for thirty days.[50]

During the winter's final days, Meade and Secretary of War Stanton finalized plans for a major reorganization of the army. Meade had commanded seven infantry corps and a cavalry corps at Gettysburg. With the dispatch of the Eleventh and Twelfth corps to Tennessee in September 1863, the infantry corps had been reduced to five during the Bristoe and Mine Run campaigns. In turn, Meade advocated the disbandment of the First and Third corps, whose ranks had not recovered from the serious casualties incurred at Gettysburg.[51]

In a meeting Stanton told Meade, "there were several officers in my army that did not have the confidence of the country, and that I was injuring myself by retaining them." Meade responded that he did not know whom the secretary meant but would not object if they were removed from command. The official reorganization was announced in General Order No. 115 on March 23.[52]

Units of the First and Third corps were assigned to the Second, Fifth, and Sixth corps, commanded respectively by major generals Winfield Scott Hancock, Gouverneur K. Warren, and John Sedgwick. Stanton had wanted to transfer Sedgwick to command in the Shenandoah Valley, but Meade objected, and Lincoln intervened by selecting Franz Sigel for the post. Sigel was an important figure among German Americans, a critical bloc of voters for the president in the forthcoming election. The next day, Stanton removed Major General Alfred Pleasanton from command of the cavalry corps. "I suppose the result will be a pretty general sweeping out," Meade had predicted to his wife in February. It had been an overdue, if not necessary, cleansing.[53]

"We do not like the change a bit," grumbled Captain William Orr of the 19th Indiana, a regiment in the disbanded First Corps. The captain was surely not alone in this reaction to the reorganization. Officers and men of the Third Corps believed Meade had chosen them because of his intense dislike of their former popular commander, Daniel Sickles. They held an "indignation meeting," while some members erected a tombstone to the corps's demise in a "mock cemetery." Meade allowed the troops in the two corps to retain "their badges and distinctive marks." Major General Andrew A. Humphreys admitted, however, that after the corps's disbandment and the merger of the units into "other organizations their identity was lost and their pride and *esprit de corps* wounded."[54]

Grant rejoined the army the day after the reorganization order had been issued. His return prompted a soldier in the 149th Pennsylvania to inform his parents, "General Grant intends doing something very large this summer i hope that he may have success the troops have great confidence in him and will fight better under him than any other general." A few days later Theodore Lyman of Meade's staff observed: "Grant seems to have impressed people. He is plainly sharp."[55]

Grant and spring weather brought forth fresh stirrings in the Union camps, especially during April. Drills increased, volleys of musketry rolled across the landscape as soldiers shot at targets, and divisions and corps passed in review before Grant and Meade. The general-in-chief welcomed Major General Ambrose Burnside and the Ninth Corps from Tennessee. As the army's former commander, Burnside outranked Meade in seniority, so Grant designated the corps as an independent command, with Burnside reporting directly to Grant. In early April, Major General Philip H. Sheridan reported to the army from the West. Grant had selected Sheridan to succeed Pleasanton as head of the cavalry corps.[56]

The general-in-chief designated May 4 as the beginning of Union offensives across the Confederacy. In the West, the main thrust would be with Major General William T. Sherman's three armies—110,000 troops into Georgia toward Atlanta. In Virginia, two secondary movements—one in the Shenandoah Valley under Lincoln's choice, Major General Franz Sigel; the other up the James River to Bermuda Hundred, a broad expanse between Richmond and Petersburg, under Major General Benjamin F. Butler.[57]

Meade's army and Burnside's Ninth Corps—119,000 officers and men— would cross the Rapidan and advance on the Army of Northern Virginia. Grant's instructions to Meade were "wherever Lee went he would go also." After the war, Grant explained, "To get possession of Lee's army was the first great object," adding that "Lee, with the capital of the Confederacy, was the main end to which all were working."[58]

The army's rank and file had been awaiting the day. Experience taught them that the struggle ahead would be difficult and bloody. Whatever roads the men followed, if they succeeded, the final one led them home. "All are expecting hard fighting and have coolly made up their minds to it," wrote a surgeon in late April. "They don't cheer and shout as they did two years ago . . . but they are all the better soldiers for it and have confidence that they have a general, though not superhuman, has a strong will, good sense, and power to do as he thinks best. I think he is more than satisfied with this army, and knows they will fight."[59]

On May 2, as the Federals completed preparations for the movement, an officer predicted that the army "has obtained a grip upon the throat of the Confederacy, a grip that will not be relaxed until treason gasps and dies." Two days later these Yankees filed into columns that seemed to stretch for endless miles in ribbons of blue, heading toward "Old Bob," their nickname for Robert E. Lee.[60]

Brigadier General Edward Porter Alexander, chief of artillery, First Corps, Army of Northern Virginia, had witnessed the war from the beginning at First Manassas. He had fought on all the major battlefields in the East and had seen war's terribleness and pageantry. Recounting years later, the brilliant artillerist still was moved by what he had experienced on April 29, 1864. "No one who was present could ever forget the occasion," Alexander professed.[61]

A pair of infantry divisions and an artillery battalion of the First Corps had assembled for a review in a pastoral valley near Gordonsville, Virginia. Led by Lieutenant General James Longstreet, these veteran foot soldiers and gunners had been away from the army for seven months, having been transferred in September 1863 to Georgia, where they arrived in time to be decisive in the Confederate victory at Chickamauga. Since then they had been repulsed in an attempt to capture Knoxville and had endured a difficult winter in East Tennessee. They had rejoined their comrades in the army a week earlier.[62]

Generals Lee and Longstreet and their staffs entered the one-hundred-acre field through large square gateposts, halting on a knoll. An observant soldier thought the army commander "had aged a great deal more than a year in the past twelve months." A bugle sounded a signal, and Alexander's cannon fired. Lee removed his hat and then, as Alexander remembered, "we shout & cry & wave our battleflags & look at him again. For sudden as a wind, a wave of sentiment such as can only come to large crowds in full sympathy . . . seemed to sweep over the field. Each man seemed to feel the bond which held us all to Lee. There was no speaking, but the effect was that of a military sacrament, in which we pledged anew our lives."[63]

Alexander joined the entourage on the knoll and remarked to Charles Venable of Lee's staff, "Does it not make the general proud to see how these men love him?" "Not proud, it awes him," replied Venable. Finally, before them the First Corps veterans passed in review. They were arguably the army's finest combat troops. A Georgian in the ranks put it well afterward: "All were certainly glad to see General Lee. And I expect he was glad to have us again under his Banner."[64]

Days before the review, Walter Taylor, Lee's chief of staff, stated in a letter, "Old Pete Longstreet is with us and all seems propitious." With

Stonewall Jackson dead almost a year, no subordinate compared to Longstreet as a tactician and as a corps commander. An Alabamian called him Lee's "right-hand man," while a staff officer noted, "The reputation that Longstreet had as a fighting man was unquestionably deserved." As night darkened the blood-soaked battlefield at Antietam, Lee had greeted him, "Ah! Here is Longstreet; here's my old warhorse."[65]

At Gettysburg, Longstreet had objected to Lee's plan to resume the offensive on the second and third days. Longstreet voiced strong opposition to the assault on Cemetery Ridge on July 3, warning that Pickett's Charge, as it became known, could not succeed. He oversaw the preparations for the attack but not with his usual skill and thoroughness. His judgment had been correct, but decades later he confessed that Gettysburg became "the sorest and saddest reflection of my life for many years."[66]

Now, however, with the prospects for a renewal of fighting perhaps only days away, Lee and the army, as Taylor wrote, welcomed back Longstreet and his veterans. But Lee's reservations about the performances of his other two corps commanders—lieutenant generals Richard S. Ewell and Ambrose Powell "A. P." Hill of the Second and Third Corps, respectively—had been mounting. Both of them had faltered at times during three days at Gettysburg. By October 1863, Major Thomas H. Carter, an artillery officer, confided to his wife, "Ewell & Hill are poor concerns."[67]

Hill had been plagued with recurring health problems and appeared frustrated, if not overwhelmed at times, with the responsibilities of command. He had allowed units of the corps to stumble into a bloody repulse at Bristoe Station on October 14, 1863. Ewell had performed well in the early phases of the Gettysburg Campaign and initially on July 1, but then he wavered, uncertain or unwilling to act. A serious wound at Groveton on August 28, 1862, and a subsequent amputation of a leg perhaps had drained some of the fire out of him.[68]

On May 2, Lee gathered corps and division commanders on Clark's Mountain, an eminence that offered a broad vista of the countryside north and south of the Rapidan. Weeks earlier, he had told a staff officer that "he wanted every man at his post that we had hard work to do this year." On this day, according to Ewell, Lee "gave it as his opinion that the enemy would cross by some of the fords below us, at Germanna or Ely's." Brigadier General William N. Pendleton, the army's chief of artillery, met with Lee the next day; Pendleton informed his wife later that the army commander "is well & in Capital spirits."[69]

Lee's mood reflected his men's morale and their willingness to meet the Yankees on another field. Rumors of an impending battle had been floating through the camps for weeks. "We are all getting ready to meet the Yankees. . . . The boys seem to be anxious for the fight," claimed a Mississippian in a typical letter. Colonel Gilbert Jefferson Wright of Cobb's Legion told his wife, "I think we are ready for *Mr. Yank* now when ever he may think proper to come." Private Henry Brown of the 27th Virginia professed. "How long this war will last is not known to Eny on Earth & though it is to be hoped that this Campaign will end it, at least it is the opinion of many that the time is not fare off wich will end the war."[70]

Many of the Confederates welcomed the confrontation between Lee and the Union's acclaimed commander, Grant. "If Grant advances upon *us* . . . I will almost wager my heart that he gets such a thrashing as he has never before carried," declared a North Carolinian. A Georgian believed, "Our troops is in fine health & spirits & all feel confident of whipping Grant." A soldier in the 47th Virginia predicted that the Federal general-in-chief "will doubtless follow in the foot steps of his illustrious predecessors and walk the plank into obscurity after his first engagement with Uncle Bob Lee." Colonel Clement Evans assured his wife, "I am not at all uneasy about the result of an engagement."[71]

Lee's nearly sixty-six thousand officers and men then awaited the approach of their opponent, whose numbers were almost double their own. But, as one Rebel put it, "the soldiers ar in very high spirits & all seam to bee confiden of success this summer." A North Carolinian informed newspaper readers back home, "There is no use disguising the fact, the main armies of the North and South are concentrated on the banks of the Rapidan, and here will be the final tilt on a grand scale."[72]

On May 1, in a letter to his wife, Lieutenant Colonel Alexander S. "Sandie" Pendleton, Ewell's chief of staff, predicted that one of the war's bloodiest battles would be fought somewhere near in forty-eight hours. The young officer had been Jackson's adjutant and knew well the dangers of and the price exacted by this fought-over region. Pendleton went on, lamenting, "The green shores of the Rapidan River would be stained by the blood of thousands. It is sad to think of it; the soil, in calm reflection, recoils from the contemplation of the ghastly spectacle."[73]

{ 2 }

The Deeply Hated Wilderness

Local folks called it simply the Wilderness. It was a forbidding expanse of tens of thousands of acres along the southern bank of the Rapidan River, spanning the counties of Orange and Spotsylvania in Virginia. The Wilderness was, in the words of Confederate soldiers, "a boundless forest," with "undergrowth almost impossible to penetrate." Intertwined bushes filled gullies and crowned knolls, while "noticeably stunted" oaks, pines, cedars, alders, and willows created a vast darkening blanket in the spring and summer months.[1]

"Here and there," noted a Confederate artillerist, "I saw a few cleared little patches, with a live hut in the center of each, that looked dismal, dilapidated, forlorn, and ought to be forsaken." It had been a hard place to claw out a living. Few roads crisscrossed the region, but the main two—Orange Turnpike and Orange Plank Road, running parallel—connected Orange and Culpeper counties with Fredericksburg.[2]

Both armies had fought within the Wilderness's confines during the Chancellorsville and Mine Run campaigns in the spring and fall of 1863, respectively. A Pennsylvanian who had been there described it as "the deeply hated Wilderness." Confederate artillery commander E. Porter Alexander claimed, "The Wilderness was our favorite fighting ground," for it negated the Federals' superiority in artillery. A Southern staff officer likely spoke for many in both armies when he declared, "Never have I fought on a more unsatisfactory battlefield."[3]

Toward the "unsatisfactory battlefield" came both armies on May 4, 1864, a day in which "all nature seems smiling this spring morning," as a Virginian put it in his diary. Union General-in-Chief Ulysses S. Grant and Major General George G. Meade, the army commander, planned to pass beyond the Confederates' right flank to clear the Wilderness and then to offer battle on open ground with their numerically superior force. Grant and Meade's strategy depended initially on the passage through the wooded region before the Rebels, as they had a year earlier, entangled the Federals again in an engagement there.[4]

The blue-coated infantry and artillery units marched after midnight, crossing the Rapid Anne, the stream's original name, at Germanna and Ely's fords. An officer noted the "purple violets, in great plenty" along the roads from the fords. By evening the Second and Fifth corps had entered the Wilderness, while the Sixth and Ninth corps and the army's ponderous wagon train remained strung out to the rear. Convinced that Robert E. Lee would keep his veteran troops west of Mine Run, Meade unwisely had ordered a halt to the day's movement. Underestimating the aggressive Confederate commander was, however, a dangerous proposition.[5]

Captain Porter Farley, a New Yorker in the Fifth Corps, remembered: "All was quiet. An ominous silence was our only welcome." At another campsite, an infantryman pried the skull of a Chancellorsville corpse from a shallow grave and remarked to his messmates, "That is what you are all coming to, and some of you will start toward it tomorrow."[6]

The enemy who would fulfill the morbid veteran's prediction of impending death was approaching from the west on the turnpike and plank road. Confederate signalmen on Clark's Mountain had detected the enemy movement at first light, relaying reports to army headquarters outside of Orange Court House. Uncertain of the Federals' objective, Lee hesitated initially to react. Before noon, however, he ordered Lieutenant General Richard Ewell's Second Corps east on Orange Turnpike and Lieutenant General A. P. Hill's Third Corps east on Orange Plank Road. An hour or so later, Lieutenant General James Longstreet received instructions to follow with the First Corps, whose camps lay farther to the west around Gordonsville. Longstreet's two infantry divisions and artillery battalions started marching at 4:00 P.M.[7]

"Privates, as well as officers, were well aware of what they were doing, and where they were going," recounted a Rebel of the march. *"In a general way, they knew what was going on, and what was going to go on, with the strangest accuracy."* A comrade wrote home later to a newspaper, contending that when they had headed north toward Pennsylvania in June 1863, they had done so with "a general burst of merriment," but on this May 4, "a quiet determination pervaded the line."[8]

Lee left his headquarters late in the afternoon, following Hill's columns before halting for the night at New Verdiersville. Lee wired President Jefferson Davis, "But it is apparent that the long threatened effort to take

Richmond has begun, and that the enemy has collected all his available force to accomplish it." Meanwhile, Lee's chief of staff, Walter Taylor, wrote to Ewell with directions for the next day: "If the enemy moves down the river, he [Lee] wishes to push on after him. If he comes this way, we may take our old lines [at Mine Run]. The Genls desire is to bring him to battle as soon now as possible." Hill's troops, Taylor added, were on the plank road, with one division east of Verdiersville.[9]

Like a billowing summer storm in the distance, the confrontation in the "deeply hated" Wilderness developed slowly on Thursday, May 5, 1864. With characteristic boldness and odds of three to one against him on this day, Robert E. Lee drew the Federals into a battle on unwanted ground. Opposing skirmishers announced the storm's approach throughout the morning. It broke about 1:00 P.M., initially enveloping the woods and sixty-six-acre Saunders's Field beside Orange Turnpike before shifting south to the thickets and trees alongside Orange Plank Road. Here amid the Wilderness's entangling mysteries, the fury lingered all through Thursday and on until nightfall on Friday, May 6.[10]

A Yankee remembered the onset of it all: "Suddenly, these hitherto quiet woods seemed to be lifted up, shook, rent, and torn asunder." Officers and men learned quickly that it was a place of "hell-like horrors . . . where desperate instinct replaced impossible tactics." Another soldier described it as "a blind and bloody hunt to the death, in bewildering thickets, rather than a battle."[11]

Saunders's Field and surrounding woods became a killing ground for the next several hours. Major General Gouverneur K. Warren's Fifth Corps troops initiated the Union offensive, attacking Richard Ewell's battle-hardened Confederates behind hastily built fieldworks in the woods along the western edge of Saunders's Field. The combat swelled and receded as a Yankee thrust met a Rebel counterthrust across the cleared acres and among the underbrush and trees. Volleys of musketry filled the woods with smoke, blinding men as opposing units stumbled into point-blank rifle blasts from their foes. The discharges ignited fires in the brush and matted leaves. One of Warren's men called it "a weird, uncanny contest—a battle of invisibles with invisibles." One of Ewell's men had a blunter description: "a butchery pure and simple."[12]

A member of the Fifth Corps, Lieutenant Abner Small of the 16th Maine, asserted that a soldier on a firing line in combat became indifferent to "the stiff disorder of the dead lying where they fell." "He resented it all,"

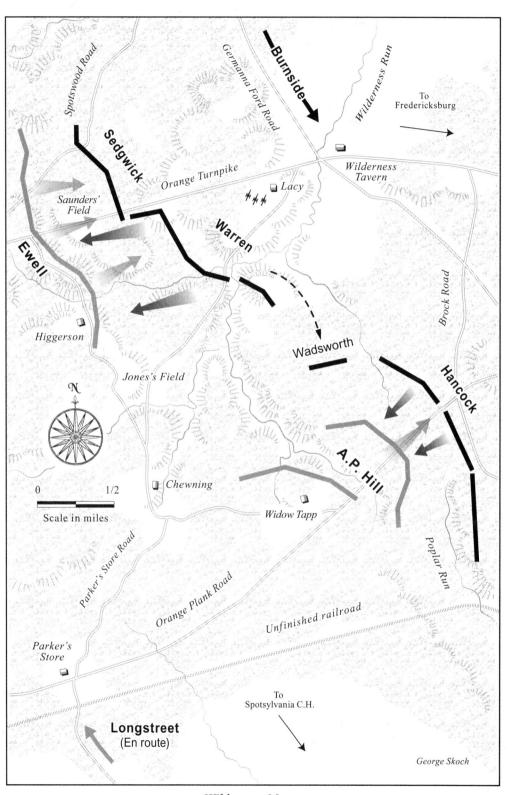

Wilderness, May 5

wrote Small, "and at times his resentment grew into a hatred for those who forced the whirlpool of war—a whirlpool that had soon engulfed him. He hated his surroundings and all that implied." He understood it "was cruelty," but "always in front of him was the enemy, a something which, the more he thought of it, the more he hated; and as likely as not he never quite knew why."[13]

If it were so, hatred walked the firing lines in Saunders's Field and nearby woods on this afternoon. When a Confederate counterattack routed one of Warren's divisions, the entire Fifth Corps line collapsed, with the shattered ranks fleeing eastward. In their place, in the woods north of Orange Turnpike, advanced a division of Major General John Sedgwick's Sixth Corps. One of the Yankees called the terrain the "awfullest brush, briars, grapevine, etc., I was ever in." If it were not hellish enough, Rebel skirmishers lit the undergrowth on fire before their oncoming foes.[14]

This attack by the Sixth Corps troops accomplished little more than the spilling of more blood. "It was impossible to see the enemy," stated a Federal, "and though we peered into the thick woods, we were fighting invisible foemen." After nearly two hours of killing and maiming, the Yankees withdrew, ending Union offensives along Orange Turnpike for the day. Ewell, his subordinate officers, and their stalwart infantrymen had waged a masterful defensive struggle. The fight had come to them and, as they had done so often in the past, they had prevailed, holding the ground.[15]

Three miles to the south along Orange Plank Road, meanwhile, the fighting had intensified. Hill's Confederate troops had reached the battlefield at the Widow Tapp farm. Lee had accompanied Hill's two infantry divisions and ordered an advance toward the intersection of Plank Road and Brock Road, where brigades of the Union Sixth and Second corps were either in position or en route to the vital crossroads.[16]

It was late in the afternoon, then, when Hill's veterans stepped forth across the open ground of the Tapp farm and into the woods. Suddenly, as if by mutual consent, the opposing ranks triggered volleys of musketry. "Never have I fought on a more unsatisfactory battlefield," grumbled a Rebel staff officer, adding that it was "almost a battle in the dark." A North Carolina infantryman claimed, "I never have seen and heard such musketry in my life; it looked like a man could not live."[17]

Hill forwarded reinforcements, as did his Union counterpart and Second Corps commander, Major General Winfield Scott Hancock. At the combat's worst, a dozen Federal brigades fought eight Confederate brigades. Twilight darkened the woods, which added to the confusion and grim struggle. "Death came unseen," recounted a Southerner, "regiments stumbled into each other's ranks guided by the cracking of the bushes. It was not war." A Northern officer thought, "The very trees seemed peopled by spirits that shrieked and groaned through those hours of combat." Finally, perhaps from exhaustion or the futility of it, the shooting ceased. At places among the trees, the opposing ranks were only "a biscuit's toss" away.[18]

Robert E. Lee had halted the Union army's offensive movement beyond the Rapidan River and had brought his opponent to battle on ground advantageous to the Confederates. It had been a risky gambit, confronting odds of more than three to one. Lee had done so, according to Charles Venable of the general's staff, because of "his profound confidence in the steady valor of his troops, and in their ability to maintain themselves successfully against very heavy odds."[19]

Despite the day's results, however, Lee's army faced a crisis at nightfall. With the arrival of Major General Ambrose Burnside's Union Ninth Corps on the battlefield, Ulysses S. Grant had his entire force in Lee's front. In turn, James Longstreet's two divisions and Major General Richard H. Anderson's Third Corps division had not yet joined the Confederate army. During the day, Lee twice sent a staff officer to Longstreet to hurry his march to the field. Longstreet assured one officer, "I shall be with him [Lee] at daylight and do anything he wants done."[20]

The Rebels' immediate danger lay in Hill's front on Orange Plank Road, where his pair of divisions, commanded by major generals Henry Heth and Cadmus Wilcox, were badly intermingled and within yards of the enemy. Heth and then Wilcox urged Hill, who had become ill with a fever and pain in the groin, to let them restore order in the ranks and to deploy on both sides of the road. Wilcox related in his report, "Hill told Heth to let his men rest as they were, that they would be relieved before day (so Heth told me)." Deeply concerned, Heth searched for Lee to plead his case but never located army headquarters. So he and Wilcox passed an "anxious" night, awaiting the appearance of Longstreet's troops.[21]

That night at Union headquarters, Grant decided to seize the tactical initiative. In his judgment, Meade and the army's senior commanders had waged the day's battle with a lack of aggressiveness. The general-in-chief intended to change that mindset by ordering an assault for the next morning. Hancock's Second Corps officers and men would undertake a frontal attack on the plank road, while Sedgwick's and Warren's troops confronted Ewell's Confederates along the turnpike. In support of Hancock, infantrymen from the Fifth and Ninth corps would advance into the gap between the roadbeds against Hill's left flank. The Federals would step forth at five o'clock.[22]

For the common soldiers and their officers, the night proved to be "hideous." Many of them slept where they had been when the fighting ceased, among the newly dead and the skulls of Chancellorsville's fallen. The fires that had been either kindled by musketry or deliberately lit spread, fueled by evening breezes. Hell must have seemed to be at hand as the smell of burning flesh and the screams of wounded men trapped within the flames haunted the hours. If they had not known before, the men learned that the Wilderness belonged to demons, not angels.[23]

A North Carolinian in Heth's division thought the Wilderness to be "a good place to die in" and remembered on this night, "the mournful, melancholy piping of the whipporwill; and many a poor fellow did breathe out his life in those gloomy shades, with the weird requiem of 'whipporwill' filling all the space of sound about him." A New Yorker witnessed "battle-field ghouls" who walked among the dead and rifled their pockets.[24]

At first light, minutes before 5:00 A.M., the Wilderness awakened to the sounds of musketry and men's shouts. On Orange Turnpike, Ewell's veterans tested the enemy's ranks and recoiled before the gunfire. On Orange Plank Road, fourteen Union brigades from Second, Fifth, and Sixth corps, upward of thirty thousand officers and men directed by Hancock, attacked the battered and disorganized ranks of Heth's and Wilcox's Confederate divisions. "We expected an attack in overwhelming numbers at the first flush of dawn," stated Colonel William Palmer, Hill's chief of staff.[25]

Heth's and Wilcox's troops never had a chance before the Federal onslaught. Rebel brigade after brigade, regiment after regiment dissolved with its members fleeing westward in a rout. Before long the Confederates emerged from the woods into the fields of the Tapp farm, where an artillery battalion opened fire on the oncoming Yankees. Hill was on the field, directing the fire of the guns and endeavoring to rally his shattered ranks. Present, too, was Lee, who was witnessing the shredding of his right flank and the "imminent" destruction of his army.[26]

Lee "was exceedingly disturbed," in Charles Venable's words, that Longstreet's two divisions had not reached the battlefield before the Union assault. But they were at hand, marching on both sides of the plank road. Longstreet met Lee while the veterans of major generals Charles Field and Joseph Kershaw shifted into a heavy skirmish formation on Longstreet's instructions. Officers and men of the First Corps

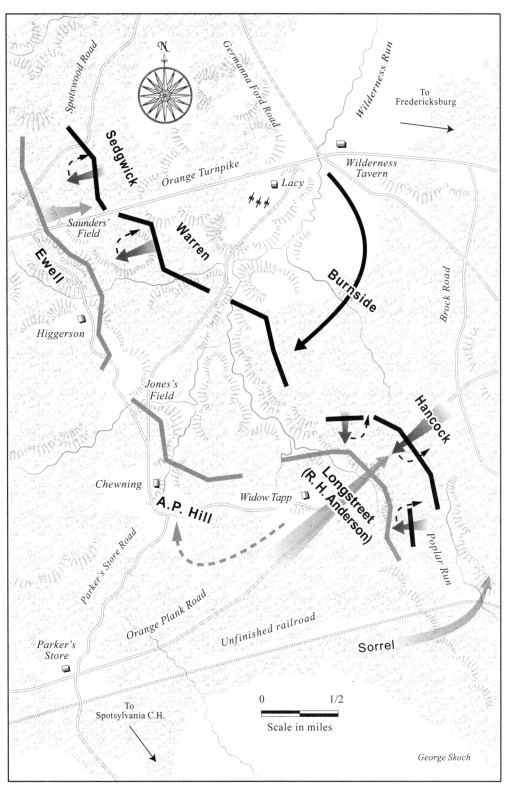

CHAPTER TWO

Wilderness, May 6

believed the army had not a better tactician on a battlefield than "Old Pete," as the soldiers called Longstreet.[27]

Lieutenant Colonel Moxley Sorrel, Longstreet's chief of staff, wrote years later: "I have always thought that the forming line, in the dense brush, under fire of the enemy, amid the routed men of A. P. Hill, and the beating of the enemy under these circumstances was the steadiest and finest thing the Corps ever did. To their chief was due that steadiness as always."[28]

The Federals were closing on Hill's cannon when Longstreet's men charged north of the road around the Tapp farmstead, where Lee met the famed Texas Brigade. The commanding general appeared "so excited, so disturbed" and rode forward with the Texans. The men shouted for him to "go back, General, go back." A captain took Traveller's reins and led Lee toward the rear. One of the Texans contended that they then "went in like devils."[29]

Longstreet's ranks triggered a volley of musketry, which "seemed to shake the earth itself." The Yankees staggered and then broke under what a veteran claimed was "one of the most destructive fires I was ever under." They rallied and counterattacked. But the Southerners came on like "a whirlwind," driving the enemy back toward Brock Road. Venable thought Longstreet's attack was "superb."[30]

A Mississippian boasted later of the May 6 attack, "Our brigade had done good fighting before, but I thought it reached a climax on that occasion." For the next two hours the foes fought amid the thickets and trees with neither side gaining an advantage. A lull ensued, and during it a Confederate engineer located an unfinished railroad bed that led beyond the enemy's left flank south of the road. Longstreet assigned four brigades to the attack, and they advanced about eleven o'clock. With his other units, Longstreet attacked north of the road.[31]

The Rebel assault shattered the Union flank, and Hancock's troops fled in "a general skedaddle" toward their fieldworks along Brock Road. Longstreet followed his advancing lines, riding with aides and other officers on the roadbed. In the smoke and confusion, some of his infantrymen fired into the mounted party, with a bullet striking Lee's senior general in the throat and right shoulder. The volley wounded others and mortally wounded Brigadier General Micah Jenkins. With Longstreet seriously injured, the Confederate attack lost momentum, and another lull in the bloodletting ensued.[32]

Three miles to the north along Orange Turnpike, meanwhile, the fighting remained stalemated. Neither Union corps commander, neither

Warren nor Sedgwick, had been willing to assault the Confederate field-works in the woods and behind Saunders's Field. A Federal soldier claimed that it would have been "next to madness" to attack the Rebels. When Sixth Corps troops tested the enemy ranks north of the turnpike, a fierce clash boiled forth, lasting an hour. So intense was the musketry, Ewell reported, that "the men's guns became so hot they could not hold them, & had to lay them down to cool."[33]

Late in the day, three Confederate brigades, led by Brigadier General John B. Gordon, struck the Sixth Corps's right flank among the trees north of the turnpike. "Unearthly screeching and yelling" announced the Rebels' presence as their attack shattered the ranks of two Union brigades. A Yankee "thought Hell had broke loose," with blue-coated soldiers fleeing in "wild confusion." Sedgwick arrived and rallied his men, and other regiments held firm, repulsing the enemy in the darkening woods. This settled it; neither side had more to give.[34]

Earlier, on both sides of Plank Road, Longstreet's two divisions undertook a final assault on the enemy works along Brock Road. The attack had been ordered by Lee, a fierce warrior and an implacable foe when he believed he had the enemy near a breaking point. On this late afternoon, on this fiendish terrain, against Union infantry and artillery behind field-works, this frontal assault was a bold endeavor, a desperate, if not forlorn, offensive strike.[35]

Emitting "a womanlike scream," Field's and Kershaw's redoubtable troops went in at four o'clock and into a cauldron of musketry and artillery discharges. The troops kept coming, however, to within thirty yards of the roadbed, "seeming confident that they would carry everything before them," according to a defender. When the underbrush ignited from the gunfire and the flames rolled over the log works, the Federal infantrymen fled rearward, creating a breach in the line. Into it charged the Southerners like "so many devils through the flames." A hand-to-hand struggle of point-blank gunfire and rifles used as clubs drove the Rebels out of the works. It was finished.[36]

Colonel Joseph N. Brown of the 14th South Carolina later described the reality of fighting in the Wilderness: "Lee's troops were as completely lost as the Federals. All alike were unable to see fifty, or in some places, even twenty yards in any direction. The men on each side fired into dark thickets and fell pierced by the musket balls from an unseen army." The blinding struggle in the forsaken landscape had fueled men's fears, as death seemed more random than ever before, unsettling even veteran troops.[37]

The combat among shadows had exacted a fearful toll. Dr. Horatio S. Soule, a Union surgeon who had tended to the battle's human wreckage, put it well in his diary on May 6: "This war is horrid." Federal casualties amounted to 2,246 killed or mortally wounded; 12,037 wounded; and 3,383 captured or missing—for a total of 17,666. Among the dead or dying were Fifth Corps division commander James Wadsworth and Second Corps brigade commander Alexander Hays. Slightly more than two hundred officers, including eight regimental commanders, had been killed or mortally wounded.[38]

Confederate losses totaled 11,502—1,936 killed or mortally wounded; 7,633 wounded; and 1,933 captured or missing. Among field officers—colonels, lieutenant colonels, and majors—thirteen had been killed or mortally wounded, thirty-one wounded, and eight captured. Three brigadiers were dead—John M. Jones, Leroy Stafford, and Micah Jenkins. Brigadier John Pegram and Edward A. Perry suffered severe wounds. The army's most grievous loss was the tragic wounding of James Longstreet by gunfire from his own troops. Ironically, he had fallen roughly four miles from where Stonewall Jackson had suffered a mortal wound from a volley by Confederate soldiers a year earlier.[39]

The carnage defined the battle's outcome. Neither side had won a decisive victory or even gained a tactical advantage. Both armies had waged successful defensive fights—the Rebels along Orange Turnpike; the Yankees at the intersection of Orange Plank Road and Brock Road. The forbidding terrain, lackluster performances by senior officers, leadership mistakes, and misfortunes characterized the struggle. A Union enlisted man had it right when he called the place "a wilderness of woe."[40]

For Lee, the two-day engagement renewed questions about the army's capabilities since Gettysburg. Its rank and file had shown once again their incomparable élan and prowess on a battlefield. With few exceptions, Ewell and Hill performed capably on both days. Lee and Hill bore joint responsibility for not addressing Heth's and Wilcox's concerns about the disarray in their units, which resulted in the rout on the morning of May 6. Only the fortunate arrival of Longstreet's troops arguably saved Lee's army from a crippling defeat, if not destruction.[41]

The incident with Lee and the Texas Brigade on May 6 indicated his increasing personal direction of matters on a battlefield. Gettysburg had decimated the army's officer ranks, particularly at the regimental and brigade levels. Lee had struggled to find capable replacements for those experienced officers. Longstreet's wounding compounded difficulties at the command level, for he would be away from the army for several months. In a postwar interview, Lee revealed an interesting judgment on the Wilderness, stating that the enemy attack on May 6 along the plank road "injured their [his men's] morale. He always felt afraid when going to attack after that."[42]

For Grant, the bloody engagement proved instructive. His estimation of Lee had risen, as the combative Virginian was a far more skillful opponent than Grant had encountered in the West. Lee's aggressiveness and determination matched that of the Union general-in-chief.[43]

Grant's immediate difficulties, however, lay within the Union army, with the ingrained caution among Meade and his corps and division commanders, a legacy of its former commander, George B. McClellan. Grant believed that the army's senior leadership had squandered opportunities to inflict serious damage upon the enemy or had dithered at critical moments. If he were to alter the mindset of avoiding defeat instead of achieving victory, he had to assume more personal direction of the army and to diminish the role of Meade. But it had been the general-in-chief, not Meade, who had imposed the awkward and cumbersome chain of command resulting from Grant's presence with the army.[44]

For those lying beneath the trees or beside the roads among their comrades, night likely came as a welcome visitor. The horrors of the previous night had abated. Lost soldiers stumbled through the darkness, searching for their regiments. Whip-poor-wills sang once more, and the dead shared a bivouac.[45]

{ 3 }

Sponsey Crania Burnt House

Spotsylvania Court House, Virginia, had a long-ago look about it in the spring of 1864. As the county seat, the village boasted a court house and jail, a hotel, a pair of churches, and several residences. But its heyday had been a century earlier when colonial Virginia's first iron furnace operated nearby. For the past few decades, the region had suffered economically, and the war had come close, first at Fredericksburg, then at Chancellorsville, and now at the Wilderness. In the early hours of May 8, 1864, however, the conflict—bringing history with it—was approaching the village's doorstep.[1]

The county seat, "a very small village" in a newspaper's description, lay roughly ten miles, as a crow flew, from the center of the Wilderness battlefield. A network of roads intersected or crossed at or near Spotsylvania Court House. In the words of another newspaper, the town was "a point where several roads converge like the radii of a man's outstretched fingers, and possessing under the circumstances eminent military importance." If the Federal offensive were to continue toward Richmond, it would head either east to Fredericksburg or more southward through Spotsylvania Court House, a place that a Yankee thought was called "Sponsey Crania Burnt House."[2]

Grant had decided to advance on Spotsylvania Court House on the evening of May 6. He had undoubtedly concluded that he would do so by the next morning, telling a staff member, Lieutenant Colonel Horace Porter: "We cannot call the engagement [at the Wilderness] a positive victory, but the enemy have only twice reached our lines in their many attacks, and have not gained a single advantage. This will enable me to carry out my intention of moving to the left, and compelling the enemy to fight in a more open country and outside of their breastworks."[3]

Believing that his opponent, Robert E. Lee, would retreat south, Grant instructed army commander George Meade, at 6:30 A.M. on May 7, to

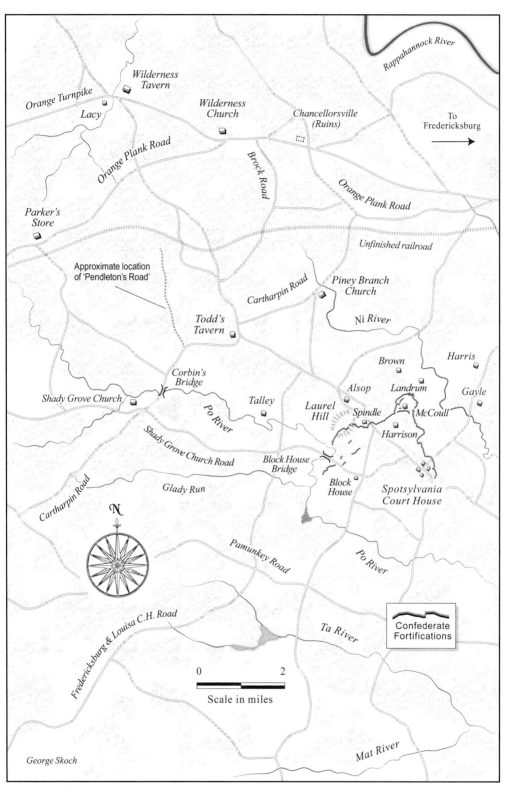

Spotsylvania Campaign

"make all preparations during the day for a night march to take a position at Spotsylvania Court House." In the order, Grant further directed the routes of march for the four infantry corps and the army's massive train of wagons. "It is more than probable," Grant added, that the Confederates would once more assault the Federal line at the Orange Plank Road–Brock Road intersection. If the Rebels came and suffered a repulse, the Yankees should counterattack "with our whole force." Grant wrote that a successful Federal attack "would necessarily modify these instructions" on a movement to Spotsylvania Court House.[4]

The Union commander needed information on enemy activity, a duty that fell to infantry skirmishers and cavalry units. Once again the woods, thickets, and clearings beside Orange Turnpike and Plank Road became a killing ground manned by the opposing skirmish lines. Probes and counterprobes characterized the action. A Federal infantryman described an effort to obtain intelligence on the Rebels: "The instructions were to feel and drive the enemy. The latter part of the direction was inserted more in hopefulness than as a command. It was easy to feel, but the driving was not so readily accomplished." The gunfire ignited the underbrush, casting a smoky pall across the landscape for the third day.[5]

On the armies' edges and along roads, Union and Confederate cavalry units clashed. The Wilderness, heavily wooded with a few clearings, had limited mounted actions during the two-day battle. But the need for current information brought more heated exchanges, particularly on roads leading south and east toward Spotsylvania Court House. Major General James Ewell Brown "Jeb" Stuart's Rebel horsemen repulsed the thrusts of blue-jacketed troopers under Major General Philip H. Sheridan. Men fell on both sides without acquiring much knowledge of their enemy's movements.[6]

By nightfall, despite the paucity of solid intelligence on the Confederates, Grant expressed more confidence in his belief that Lee would retreat during the night. Earlier in the day, Grant had remarked in his usual pointed manner to Meade, "Joe Johnston [the former Confederate army commander] would have retreated after two such days' punishment." According to Theodore Lyman of Meade's staff, Grant's assurance of the enemy's retreat "showed that he [Grant] did not yet fully take in Lee's obstinacy & the goodness of his army."[7]

In his memoirs Grant explained his rationale for the night march away from the Wilderness battlefield: "I wanted to get between his [Lee's] army and Richmond if possible; and, if not to draw him into the open field." The Federals started forth then toward Spotsylvania Court House at

8:30 P.M. Gouverneur Warren's Fifth Corps infantry led the march, east on Orange Turnpike and then a turn south on to Brock Road. John Sedgwick's Sixth Corps headed east toward Chancellorsville before angling southeast toward the destination. Winfield Hancock's Second Corps, Ambrose Burnside's Ninth Corps, and the army's wagon train trailed.[8]

Grant had hoped for a rapid march to the crossroads, but from the outset, the march unraveled. Jammed roads, exhausted soldiers, and the inevitable confusions and misunderstandings plagued the operation. Watching the infantry pass his battery, an artillerist thought: "The men seemed aged. They were very tired and very hungry. They seemed to be greatly depressed."[9]

Fitful starts and halts slowed the pace, undoubtedly eliciting strings of curses. While in the Wilderness, still burning fires brought choking smoke as the stench of carnage smothered the columns. The bone-weary Yankees stumbled on through the darkness. "So the exhausting march continued for hours," remembered a Pennsylvanian, "being the most cruel and aggravating kind of a night march to which tired soldiers could be subjected." A fellow infantryman claimed that men marched while asleep, "mechanically as it were, and were kept up at a perpendicular and under motion by their file covers."[10]

Grant, Meade, and their staff officers abandoned their field headquarters and joined the marchers on Orange Turnpike. It was likely after ten o'clock when the mounted party approached the intersection with Brock Road. Warren's veterans cleared the roadway, watching expectantly to see whether Grant continued east or headed south. When the general-in-chief turned his mount into Brock Road, the Fifth Corps soldiers threw their hats into the air and shouted "On to Richmond!" In the estimation of Grant's aide, Horace Porter, "The night march had become a triumphal procession for the new commander."[11]

Grant, Meade, and their staff members endeavored to silence the cheers, worried that the clamor might alert the enemy. But they could not, for in this army's storied, albeit tragic, history, this was one of those defining moments. The rank and file had endured the defeats and had waited for a commander who would lead them down a final road to victory and then to loved ones at home. Not only were they leaving the Wilderness, but they were marching away from the past, knowing that it meant more killing and maiming. One of them who could not forget that fateful scene wrote, "I do not know during the entire war I had such a real feeling of delight and satisfaction as in the night when we came to the road leading to Spotsylvania Court and turned to the right."[12]

The Union generals and their mounted party wove through the marching ranks, arriving at Todd's Tavern on Brock Road around one o'clock on May 8. Meade expected that Philip Sheridan's cavalrymen had cleared the road to Spotsylvania Court House as instructed. Instead, the army commander found the troopers of two cavalry divisions asleep in the nearby fields. Ahead in the darkness, Confederate horsemen barred the road, which at the time was known as Old Court House Road.[13]

Sheridan's apparent disobedience of orders infuriated the short-tempered Meade, who bypassed Sheridan and directed the two division commanders, brigadiers David Gregg and Wesley Merritt, to mount up and to proceed toward Spotsylvania Court House. Merritt's three brigades started about two o'clock on Old Court House Road, while Gregg's division guarded the right flank, angling southwest on Catharpin Road. Sheridan's third division under Brigadier General James Wilson was ordered by the cavalry commander to march on Fredericksburg Road and to pass through Spotsylvania Court House, securing a bridge over Po River below the crossroads village.[14]

Merritt's troopers had not ridden far from Todd's Tavern when they encountered Major General Fitzhugh Lee's Rebel horsemen. A nephew of the Confederate commander, Lee had two brigades and a battery of horse artillery with him. The Southerners fought doggedly until the vanguard of Warren's infantry appeared and replaced Merritt's troopers. Lee withdrew slowly to a ridge, Laurel Hill, which overlooked Old Court House Road and covered the approach to the village, about a mile to the southeast. Lee summoned reinforcements.[15]

To the west and south, meanwhile, through the hours of darkness, Confederate infantry and artillery units had been also on the march to Spotsylvania Court House. Like Grant, Robert E. Lee had wrestled with discerning the intentions of his opponent on May 7. He believed that the Federals would abandon the Wilderness, marching either toward Fredericksburg or Spotsylvania Court House. The former might indicate a retreat; the latter might presage an overland advance on Richmond.[16]

With his army farther away from the courthouse village than Grant's force, Lee instructed his artillery chief, Brigadier General William N. Pendleton, to clear a trail, wide enough for infantry, from the army's right flank in the woods below Orange Plank Road almost due south to Catharpin Road. From that point, the Rebels could march to Todd's Tavern on Brock Road or strike Shady Grove Church Road to Spotsylvania Court House. Pendleton's road or direct route would save miles and critical time and would give Lee strategic options once the Union movement was detected.[17]

Lee recognized the necessity of occupying Spotsylvania Court House before the enemy but was unwilling to commit his entire army until he knew with certainty the direction of the enemy's movement. Instead, he chose James Longstreet's two infantry divisions and three artillery battalions to march to the vital crossroads. The First Corps units manned the army's right flank and were next to the trail being constructed to Catharpin Road. Before Lee could prepare the orders, he had to assign a commander to the corps in place of the seriously wounded Longstreet.[18]

The Confederate commander brought Longstreet's chief of staff, Moxley Sorrel, to army headquarters at Parker's Store. Lee greeted the highly capable Georgian: "I must speak to you, Colonel, about the command of the First Corps." Lee went on, "you have been with the corps since it started as a brigade, and should be able to help me." Lee then offered the names of three major generals for Sorrel's thoughts—Jubal Early, Edward Johnson, and Richard H. Anderson.[19]

Early, replied Sorrel, was the most able of the three but would be the most unpopular choice with the corps's rank and file. Johnson was unknown as an officer to the corps; but about Anderson, the staff officer stated, "We *know him* and shall be satisfied with him." Lee thanked Sorrell and added as he departed, "I have been interested, but Early would make a fine corps commander." Sorrell expected that it would be the irascible Virginian.[20]

Later on May 7, Lee chose Anderson to command the First Corps temporarily. Anderson was the senior major general by date of commission in the army, but Sorrel's argument of his familiarity with members of the corps likely swayed Lee's decision. The forty-two-year-old South Carolinian and West Pointer had served under Longstreet during the campaigns in 1862. When the army had been reorganized after Chancellorsville, Anderson's division was assigned to the newly created Third Corps. Porter Alexander knew him well and wrote of him, "Gen. Dick Anderson was a pleasant a commander to serve under as could be wished, & was a sturdy & reliable fighter."[21]

Lee met with Anderson at headquarters, with the pair of generals likely studying a map. The Confederate commander ordered Anderson to march after nightfall toward Spotsylvania Court House. Lee stated further, "I wish you to be there to meet him [the enemy], and in order to do so, you must be in motion by three o'clock in the morning." Let the men rest until then, Lee commanded, but no campfires should be built. The infantry divisions would use Pendleton's newly cut trail, while the artillery battalions would march on a road from Orange Turnpike to

Shady Grove Road, where the two columns would combine at Shady Grove Church.[22]

Anderson joined the divisions of Joseph Kershaw and Charles Field in the woods south of Orange Plank Road. By nightfall, the underbrush and trees were on fire and, in Anderson's words, "burning furiously in every direction." He decided to begin the march hours earlier, ordering the troops to pack up and be prepared to step out at 11:00 P.M. Kershaw's veterans led the column south on the road carved through the forest by Pendleton, which was described as "narrow" and "frequently obstructed." With no place to stop and to rest because of the burning woods, the Rebels kept moving, reached Catharpin Road, and turned right, joining the artillery units on Shady Grove Road and finally halting roughly three miles from the courthouse crossroads at the locally known Block House Bridge. It was soon after daylight when Anderson allowed the men to rest in the open fields beside the road.[23]

Before long Jeb Stuart with his staff members and couriers passed Anderson's troops, riding north toward Laurel Hill, where Fitz Lee's horsemen were clinging to the ridge against the Yankees. Soon one of Stuart's couriers returned to Anderson with a message from the cavalry commander for artillery support. Anderson dispatched two batteries and followed them with a pair of infantry brigades from Kershaw's division— Colonel John W. Henagan's South Carolinians and Brigadier General Benjamin G. Humphrey's Mississippians. Shortly afterward a second courier met Anderson, reporting that Union cavalry had ridden into Spotsylvania Court House. The First Corps commander ordered Kershaw's final two brigades—Georgians under brigadiers William T. Wofford and Bryan Goode—to the village.[24]

Anderson accompanied the South Carolinians and Mississippians up Old Court House Road to the rear slope of Laurel Hill, where they were met by Stuart. Although Anderson was the senior officer, he relinquished command to thirty-one-year-old Stuart, who directed Henagan's men to the left and Humphreys's to the right. One of the infantrymen thought Stuart was "cool as a piece of ice, though all the time laughing." He ordered the foot soldiers, "Run for the rail piles. The Federal infantry will reach them first, if you don't run." Stuart then placed the two batteries into position.[25]

The Confederate infantrymen raced up the hillside, spilled over the crest, and manned the line of fence rails piled up earlier by Lee's dismounted troopers, who withdrew. To their front and down the slope lay the 312-acre farm of Sarah Spindle. A forty-year-old widow, Mrs. Spindle lived in the family's two-and-a-half-story wooden house with her children. The farm had 200 improved acres, an orchard, and outbuildings. In 1860, Mrs. Spindle possessed real estate valued at $3,000 and personal wealth of $14,600, primarily based upon eight male and nine female slaves. On this morning, the Spindles had sat down for breakfast when rifle and cannon fire resounded outside.[26]

Coming across the fields of the Spindle farm and up the rise were blue-coated veterans of the Fifth Corps, three brigades of Brigadier General John C. Robinson's division. The Rebels had won the race to the rails by the narrowest of margins, as some of the Yankees were within a hundred yards. "Hold your fire until the Federals are well within range," Stuart had admonished the riflemen, "and then give it to them and hold this position to the last man. Plenty of help is near at hand."[27]

The South Carolinians and Mississippians gave it to them, triggering volleys into the charging ranks. The Yankees staggered before the musketry and cannon fire but kept coming. At one point, the Federals reached the Rebel line held by the 3rd South Carolina beside the road. "For the first and last time in my warring," recalled a South Carolinian, "I saw two hostile lines lock bayonets." The Confederates repulsed the assaults, and Warren sent in a second division, under Brigadier General Charles Griffin. Colonel William F. Perry's brigade of Alabamians joined the struggle on Henagan's left.[28]

"We killed a heap of Yankees. . . . There was eighty-three Yankees killed in front of us. . . . I call that raking them down," bragged a private in the 3rd South Carolina. Warren sent in his final two divisions, and more Fifth Corps troops were heaped up before the withering enemy fire. After two hours or more, the Union commander halted the attacks, and his troops began erecting fieldworks north of the Spindle farm. During the action Confederate gun crews had fired deliberately into the Spindle farmhouse, igniting the structure and forcing Sarah Spindle and her children to flee their burning homestead.[29]

Throughout the fighting, according to an onlooker, Jeb Stuart was "sitting on his horse amidst a storm of bullets, laughing and joking with the men and commending them highly for their courage and for the rapidity and accuracy of their fire." Fitzhugh Lee's stubborn defense against superior numbers, Anderson's decision to march through the night, and his veteran infantrymen's and artillerists' fighting prowess, along with Stuart's leadership, prevented the enemy from reaching Spotsylvania Court House in force. To their rear, the Georgians had secured the village as Wilson's Union horsemen withdrew before the Rebel infantrymen.[30]

Robert E. Lee learned of the action at Laurel Hill about ten o'clock in the morning. The news confirmed for him that the enemy intended to either occupy or to pass through Spotsylvania Court House in a movement toward the Confederate capital. Lee reacted to the information by ordering Richard Ewell "to move on with your corps as rapidly as you can, without injuring your men. I will proceed to Shady Grove Church, and wish you [to] follow me on to that point." Once Ewell's Second Corps veterans cleared the Wilderness, A. P. Hill's Third Corps was directed to follow.[31]

While Lee had waited for reports from Stuart and Anderson, he was informed that Hill had taken ill, so sick with a fever that he could not sit up. One officer wrote in his diary that Hill had fainted. Lee relieved the stricken general of his duties and assigned Early to temporary command of the Third Corps. In turn, Lee placed John B. Gordon in command of Early's Second Corps division. A fellow brigade commander in the division, Harry Hays, outranked Gordon by date of commission as a brigadier. The commanding general resolved the issue by consolidating Hays's Louisiana regiments with Colonel Zebulon York's Louisianans in Edward Johnson's division. Lee cited the necessity for the consolidation and transfer as the two brigades "being so much reduced." Finally, Lee shifted Robert D. Johnston's North Carolina brigade from Robert Rodes's division into Gordon's as a replacement for Hays.[32]

Early led the Third Corps out of the Wilderness around three o'clock on the afternoon of May 8, using Pendleton's narrow trail through the woods. When the Rebel column approached Catharpin Road, it encountered a brigade of the Union Second Corps. An engagement ensued that eventually involved Early's leading division, two of Stuart's cavalry brigades, and two Federal brigades. Darkness ended the affair. About the same time to the northeast, a Union attack by the Sixth Corps on Laurel Hill resulted in another repulse.[33]

By nightfall on this Sabbath day, the two armies had converged on the farmlands and woodlots outside of the crossroads village. The movements toward it had begun in the darkness before midnight and continued even after night's return. Men still plodded through the blackness, giving shape to things to come.

Neil McCoull owned a 600-acre farm roughly two and a half miles northwest of Spotsylvania Court House. Called "Woodshaw Farm," the property consisted of 100 "improved" acres of corn and other grains and 500

"unimproved" acres of mostly woods. The fifty-four-year-old McCoull had prospered as a farmer, with real estate worth $4,800.00 and a personal worth of $3,600.00, including six slaves, in 1860. He shared the one and a half-story clapboard house with his three spinster sisters—Eliza, Mary, and Mildred or Milly.[34]

The dwelling and outbuildings, including a detached kitchen, sat on a slight rise, with oak and cherry trees surrounding the residence. A gate and fence framed at least the front of the house. A swale lay beyond the house to the north, where a spring supplied water for the family, slaves, and farm animals. Neighbors and townsfolk drank from "the crystal waters" of "McCoull's Spring" and often enjoyed a picnic by it.[35]

When the three-year-old conflict arrived in the neighborhood on May 8, Neil McCoull was away from "Woodshaw Farm," likely on business. The sisters had remained at home. Eliza was nearly seventy years old, with Mary five years younger and Millie twenty years younger. In 1860, the sisters had a combined personal wealth of $8,000. They surely heard through the darkness on this night the sounds of the tramp of thousands of men as they came on to their property. The war had twice visited the region, but now it had come to their front door.[36]

The visitors belonged to Robert Rodes's and Edward Johnson's divisions of the Second Corps, Army of Northern Virginia. They had been on the march for hours from the Wilderness and, by nightfall, were extending the line of their First Corps comrades. Rodes's troops led and filed into position first on the right flank of Joseph Kershaw's ranks. Johnson's men continued on without guides or lights. A North Carolina officer described it as "the most terrible march of the 8th," while a Louisiana captain declared, "It was the most fatiguing march I have ever made."[37]

After passing Rodes's line, Johnson's column ascended a rise, thickly wooded with oak and pine trees. In the distance to the north and west, enemy campfires glowed "considerably below the plane of our position," according to an officer. The deployment of four brigades on unfamiliar ground in the extreme darkness must have surely drew forth strings of curses. "The whole division was stretched out in some fashion," recalled a staff officer, "and was ordered to rectify the alignment and throw up breastworks." Most of the exhausted and hungry veterans ignored the instructions, lay down, and went to sleep. Behind them, 300–400 yards away, sat a farmhouse, where the McCoull sisters likely listened and wondered.[38]

By daylight on Monday, May 9, the Confederate line outside of Spotsylvania Court House zigzagged nearly four miles from the Po River to

Johnson's position on a brow of the wooded ridge. The line's left front, manned by the divisions of Charles Field and Kershaw, angled northeasterly from the river. From Kershaw's right, the line held by Rodes and Johnson ran due north before bending to the east and then south, creating a large salient or bulge. Brigadier General James A. Walker, commander of the Stonewall Brigade, explained: "The position thus taken by Johnson's Division was such as the fortune of battle gave it. It was determined for us by the enemy, more than by our choosing, and formed a sharp salient."[39]

Captain William W. Old, a Second Corps staff officer, noted later, "and when daylight appeared, it was found that General Johnson had only done the best he could have done under the circumstances." A salient or bulge in an army's lines possessed, however, natural weaknesses. It could be subjected to enemy fire on three sides. A Louisianan with Johnson understood, writing, "It was so liable to be enfiladed by artillery and would be a dangerous trap to be caught in should the line be broken on the left or right." Porter Alexander called it, "a piece of bad engineering, certain to invite an attack as soon as the enemy understood it."[40]

A Georgian depicted it as "an awkward and irregular salient to the northward." It was crescent-shaped or U-shaped, with soldiers describing it as a "horse shoe," a "mule shoe," and even an "acorn." The salient was more than a half mile deep and roughly 1,160 yards or less than three-fourths of a mile in width near the McCoull house, covering an area of approximately 250 acres. From Rodes's left flank to the end of Johnson's right flank the salient extended for more than two miles.[41]

Accompanied by the army's chief engineer, Major General Martin L. Smith, Second Corps commander Richard Ewell examined the salient position on the morning of May 9. An 1842 graduate of the military academy, Smith had been assigned to the duties less than a month before, on April 16. The mapmaker, Jedediah Hotchkiss, said of Smith, "he rides his horse as erect as a ramrod." The engineer had served in the western theater, commanding an infantry division and overseeing the defensive works at Vicksburg, Mississippi, before the city's surrender on July 4, 1863.[42]

In their inspection, Ewell and Smith likely noted that the terrain inside and beyond the salient consisted of "undulating ground, diversified by fields, pine thickets and patches of woods." Much of the interior of the "mule shoe" was covered with pine and oak trees, while the neighboring forests edged from 150 yards to more than 300 yards of its eastern and western faces, respectively. Opposite the apex or "nose" of the salient, a convex-shaped ravine extended several hundred yards to the north, a natural avenue of open ground for an assault.[43]

Ewell and Smith knew the tactical weaknesses of a salient, its vulnerability to enfilading artillery fire and the danger to defenders of a breakthrough on either side by enemy infantry. Both generals decided, however, that the Confederates must hold the low ridge or "slight eminence" occupied overnight by Rodes's and Johnson's troops. By maintaining the position, they prevented Union batteries from occupying the elevated ground.[44]

At some point, the army commander joined Ewell and Smith in the salient. Lee likely met the pair of generals during the morning. According to Charles Venable, Lee usually departed from the battlefield for his headquarters in the rear between nine and ten o'clock at night, but rose about three o'clock the next morning and rode to the front. Colonel Thomas T. Munford, a cavalry officer, saw Lee on May 9, writing in a letter, "Genl. R. E. Lee is in fine spirits."[45]

Lee's spirits evidently darkened as he inspected the large bulge in his army's lines. Meeting Ewell and Smith, he allegedly declared: "This is a wretched line. I do not see how it can be held!" Ewell countered by noting that Johnson's division held the higher ground and, if abandoned, it would be seized by the Yankees. Lee relented, ordering batteries placed in the salient as support for Rodes's and Johnson's veterans and directed Smith to construct a second line in the rear of the salient.[46]

While Lee and the generals conferred, the salient defenders resumed the construction of fieldworks. The weaknesses of a salient required more extensive works than had been built in the Wilderness. Although units had axes, they possessed few entrenching tools. Consequently, the Confederates used their bare hands, bayonets, tin cups, plates, and canteen halves for digging out a trench. With their axes, they hewed the oaks and pines, stripping them of the branches.[47]

One of the Rebels wrote that the men "worked like beavers. . . . Trees were felled and piled upon each other, and a ditch dug behind them with the earth out of it thrown against the logs." Private Thomas Gold of the Stonewall Brigade remembered: "A fence rail nearly gave us the foundation. We dug dirt with whatever we could, with our bayonets and one pick, and threw it up the best we could, and in a short time we had it breast high and thick enough to withstand bullets, if not cannon balls."[48]

The initial construction resulted in what another Confederate described as "a double row of stakes like a tomato trellis . . . filled in with poles and dirt." The log breastworks stood four feet high, with the ditch or trench two feet deep. In time, the men added a head log, placed on wooded blocks atop the works, with a firing slot. They also built steps upon which to stand in the trench. Outside the works, they constructed abatis of sharpened limbs, which pointed toward the front.[49]

To protect themselves from enfilading artillery fire, the infantrymen felled more trees, fashioned logs, and erected traverses, which ran perpendicular to the main works. Colonel Joseph N. Brown of the 14th South Carolina stated that these structures were "about twelve or fifteen feet long running backward, forming three sides, being open in the rear, forming pens, the sides to protect the flanks, the front facing north." Some were more than twenty feet long, with roughly forty feet between them. Each pen could hold eight to ten men, and the troops dubbed the area between the traverses "horse-stalls" or "hog pens."[50]

The trench and breastworks along the broad, flat apex ran in a rough straight line for around three hundred yards. At each end, the works bent southward, forming an east-facing and a west-facing angle. A grove of oak trees stood behind the apex and the angles in the works. Johnson's troops manned the works along the apex and down the eastern and western faces of the salient. Rodes's soldiers extended Johnson's left flank along the western face, connecting its ranks with First Corps units.[51]

Work on the second line of entrenchments ordered by Lee also began on the morning of May 9. John Gordon's Second Corps division had trailed Rodes's and Johnson's brigades during the night march, halting roughly three hundred yards south of the McCoull farmhouse. A quarter of a mile farther south, sitting on a knoll, stood "LaVilla," the home of Edgar and Ann Maria Harrison and their three children. It was a modest one-and-a-half story wooden farmhouse, built in 1860. The Harrisons had owned nine slaves before the war began. Edgar was serving in the 9th Virginia Cavalry and, when the Confederates appeared, Ann fled with the children.[52]

Gordon's fieldworks extended from west to east between the two farms. His veterans cut down trees and tore down slave quarters on the Harrison property for the construction. Peter Alexander, a correspondent with Lee's army, described the second line, noting that it "extends the angle, and which may be considered the base of the triangle covering the hill. Even this line is somewhat in advance of the direction of the general line."[53]

Colonel Thomas H. Carter, who commanded an artillery battalion and whose guns were rolled into the salient, shared Lee's concern about the bulge in the line. Carter called the salient "a wretchedly defective line . . . only kept because of the work done upon it, and the belief that our troops, entrenched, could never be driven out." Construction and improvements continued on the front and second lines and the traverses into the next day, when by noon, according to a staff officer, the "works were sufficient for protection."[54]

While the Southerners labored on the breastworks and traverses, they endured rifle fire from enemy skirmishers. Members of the Stonewall Brigade had conducted a reconnaissance to the north at daybreak, advancing more than a mile without encountering any Federal troops. Later that morning the Yankees appeared, and the opposing skirmish lines exchanged gunfire. While Ewell inspected the salient works, a spent bullet or minié ball had struck the general but did not hurt him. The sporadic musketry of skirmishers indicated a coming together of the old nemeses once again.[55]

In Lee's army, the arrival of Jubal Early's three Third Corps divisions on the battlefield completed the Confederate march from the Wilderness. Early's veterans had spent the night at Shady Grove Church before angling northeast toward their comrades. A. P. Hill remained ill and followed in an ambulance outfitted with a bed. Cadmus Wilcox's brigades led Early's column, moving east of Fredericksburg Road, guarding the army's right flank. Lee held the divisions of Henry Heth and William Mahone in reserve at the crossroads village.[56]

Beyond the Confederate lines, the officers and men of the Army of the Potomac had anticipated a quiet Monday, May 9. Before midnight on the previous night, George Meade had issued an order, "The army will remain quiet to-morrow, 9th instant, to give the men rest and to distribute ammunition and rations." Meade further directed, "Corps commanders will strengthen their positions by intrenchments." Like Lee, Meade had to bring forward all of his units to the battlefield.[57]

During the morning, Winfield Hancock's Second Corps came up from Todd's Tavern and extended the right flank of Gouverneur Warren's Fifth Corps's position opposite Laurel Hill south toward the Po River. On Warren's left, John Sedgwick's Sixth Corps troops strengthened their lines, conforming them to and opposite the western face of the salient. Farther east and beyond the salient, Ambrose Burnside's Ninth Corps officers and men began arriving by mid-morning, marching south on Fredericksburg Road.[58]

With both armies on the battlefield at last, digging earthworks, unlimbering batteries, and probing with skirmishers, the race for Spotsylvania Court House had ended. A Virginian put it well in his diary under this date: "Wonder what General Grant thinks of Master Bob today. Here he is right in his way to Richmond." And for the fifth successive day, killing and maiming marked the passage of time.[59]

The unrelenting combat had exacted other costs, fraying nerves and exhausting bodies. A crisis developed along the lines of the Union Sixth Corps when a division commander, Brigadier General Thomas H. Neill, began withdrawing his troops from the front. Sedgwick learned that Neill had "entirely lost his nerve" and was a "wreck from no fault of his, simply tension too great for him to bear." Sedgwick relieved Neill of command and halted the withdrawal.[60]

Sedgwick remained at the front among the troops, shifting units and bringing forward batteries. No general in the army had the affectionate regard of his officers and men more than this fifty-year-old Connecticut native and West Point graduate. His soldiers thought of him as "a father," while calling him "Uncle John." He had endeared himself to them with his concern for their welfare and his plain, unassuming manner. One of the men related, "It is even said that once when he attempted to draw his sword to lead a charge he could not do it, for it was rusted into the scabbard." In quiet moments when alone, he enjoyed playing solitaire.[61]

The Sixth Corps commander rode to the juncture of two branches of Brock Road north of the Spindle farm to redeploy the 14th New Jersey and to post a section of Battery A, 1st Massachusetts Artillery. It was around 10:00 A.M. as he dismounted from his horse at the edge of some woods. The shifting of the infantry and the posting of the cannon drew the attention of enemy sharpshooters. Bullets whizzed past, causing some men to dodge. Sedgwick reproved them, asking what they would do if the Rebels opened fire along their entire line, declaring, "They couldn't hit an elephant at this distance." When more bullets whined by and a sergeant fell to the ground, the general berated him, repeating, "They couldn't hit an elephant at that distance."[62]

Veterans knew the sound, the thud of a bullet striking flesh. Sedgwick staggered and fell in to the arms of his chief of staff, Lieutenant Colonel Martin T. McMahon. "The ball entered just below the left eye & passed through coming out at the base of the brain," as Captain Ned Russell described the general's fatal wound in a letter to his family. A surgeon examined Sedgwick but could do nothing. Staff members carried him to the rear and into an ambulance. Despite his aide's efforts to keep the general's fall quiet, word raced through the ranks, "Johnny is wounded."[63]

Sedgwick's death stunned the Federals. "We were perfectly astounded," asserted a Pennsylvanian. "We knew he was reckless and brave, but the thought that he would be killed never occurred to us." When informed of the incident, a dumbfounded Grant asked twice, "Is he really dead?" The Sixth Corps commander's body was laid in state on a rustic bier under a canopy of pine branches. Later, it was transported to Washington, arriving on May 11, and from there to Cornwall, Connecticut, for internment. Ned Russell professed, "Not one in the whole Army but speaks of him with respect."[64]

The fighting, however, did not stand still, even for the death of a popular major general. At Grant's urging, the Federals undertook reconnaissances against the Confederate flanks. Burnside's Ninth Corps units clashed with Rebel brigades along Fredericksburg Road, gaining little ground. At the western end of Lee's line, Hancock's Second Corps advanced south across the Po River. Enemy resistance and darkness halted the movement. Lee saw an opportunity to strike the isolated Union corps, dispatching the divisions of Mahone and Heth toward the Yankees for an attack the next morning.[65]

Grant had used two infantry corps in the reconnaissances because his cavalry divisions—ten thousand officers and men—had ridden south at daylight on an expedition against Jeb Stuart's horsemen. Meade and Sheridan had had a heated confrontation at Todd's Tavern on the morning of May 8, when Meade encountered the latter's troopers without orders and Brock Road held by the enemy. Meade's volcanic temper let loose, lashing the cavalry commander with "hammer and tongs." Sheridan replied with "expletives," blamed Meade for the situation, and then snorted, "if he could have matters his own way, he would concentrate all the cavalry, move out in force against Stuart's command, and whip it."[66]

Later that day Meade recounted Sheridan's insubordination and words to Grant. "Did Sheridan say that?" inquired the general-in-chief. "Well, he generally knows what he is talking about. Let him start right out and do it." Hours afterward, Meade issued the orders to "proceed against the enemy's cavalry." Leaving only one mounted regiment with the army, Sheridan departed on May 9; the column of horsemen stretched for thirteen miles. Around noon, Jeb Stuart led three thousand troopers in pursuit.[67]

In "Sponsey Crania Burnt House," meanwhile, Lee had his headquarters tent pitched near the square, brick Spotswood or Sanford Hotel, with its portico of four whitewashed columns. Across a road stood the one-and-a-half-story brick courthouse and jail, enclosed by a low brick wall. In one of the churches the Confederates established a signal station on the upper floor. For the observant, the war appeared to be lingering.[68]

{ 4 }

No Backward Steps

"The enemy hold our front in very strong force and evince a strong determination to interpose between us and Richmond to the last," wrote Ulysses S. Grant to Union chief of staff Henry W. Halleck in Washington, D.C., on the morning of May 10. Grant continued: "I shall take no backward steps. . . . We can maintain ourselves, at least, and, in the end, beat Lee's army, I believe." He requested more supplies and "all the infantry you can rake and scrape," perhaps ten thousand from the capital's defenses. He ended, "We want no more wagons nor artillery."[1]

The two days of fighting on May 8 and 9 near Spotsylvania Court House had yielded few tangible results, except for the mounting casualties. The Rebels blocked roads toward the Confederate capital, manning miles of earthworks. Little had changed since the collision in the Wilderness, the daily constant of death and wounds. Sergeant Edward R. Crockett of the 4th Texas undoubtedly captured the reality for the men in both armies when he scribbled in his diary, "We have to keep on watch continuously, our fare is rough & our duty hard & we are getting very tired."[2]

The Confederates ascribed the bloody stalemate to Grant. Major Eugene Blackford of the 5th Alabama declared to his sister, "Grant is the most obstinate fighter we have ever met." Walter Taylor, Robert E. Lee's chief of staff, said of the Union general-in-chief: "He alone of all would have remained this side of the Rappahannock after the battle of the Wilderness. This may be attributable to his nature, or it may be because he knew full well that to relinquish his designs on Richmond, even temporarily, w[oul]d forever ruin him & bring about peace."[3]

Blackford and Taylor had taken a fair measure of their foe. Unknown to them, Grant had defined himself and the campaign's ultimate end earlier when he had turned his horse south on Brock Road on the night of May 7. Now, three days later, "no backward steps" meant seeking an opportunity to break the deadlock on the route to Richmond. By midmorning, based on reports from the front, Grant decided to assault the

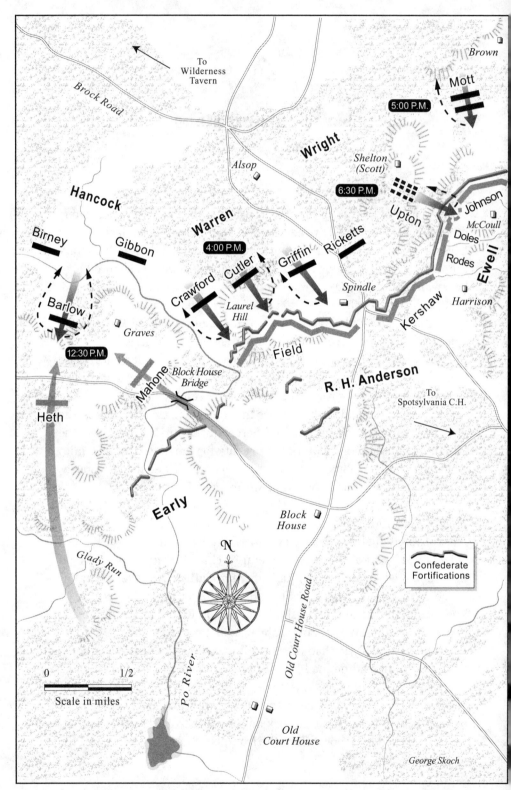

To
Wilderness
Tavern

Brock Road

Brown

Mott

5:00 P.M.

Wright

Alsop

Shelton
(Scott)

6:30 P.M.

Upton

Johnson

McCoull

Hancock

Warren

Doles

Rodes

Ewell

Birney

Gibbon

4:00 P.M.

Crawford

Cutler

Griffin

Ricketts

Barlow

Laurel
Hill

Spindle

Harrison

Graves

Field

Kershaw

12:30 P.M.

Mahone

Block House
Bridge

R. H. Anderson

To
Spotsylvania C.H.

Heth

Early

Block
House

Glady Run

N

Confederate
Fortifications

Po River

Old Court House Road

0   1/2

Scale in miles

Old
Court House

George Skoch

Union Assaults on Laurel Hill and Upton's Attack on Salient, May 10 enemy defenses on Laurel Hill with troops of the Second, Fifth, and Sixth corps. Such an offensive strike would require hours of preparation, so Grant scheduled the attack for 5:00 P.M.[4]

The general-in-chief had been informed that Lee had been shifting troops from the center of his line to the left opposite Winfield Hancock's Federals along Po River. Grant concluded that, if this information was accurate, Lee must have weakened the Laurel Hill position. To keep his opponent's attention along the river, Grant directed Hancock to keep one of his divisions south of the stream as if readying for an advance. Hancock chose Brigadier General Francis C. Barlow's four brigades. Around eleven o'clock, Hancock started his other two divisions, under brigadiers John Gibbon and David Birney, northward for the planned late afternoon assault.[5]

In fact, Lee had not been pulling units from the earthworks on or near Laurel Hill but had marched the divisions of Henry Heth and William Mahone from the reserve position at the crossroads village during the previous night. It was not long after noon when Heth's and Mahone's veterans advanced against Barlow's dangerously isolated ranks. Jubal Early had accompanied his Third Corps divisions and now directed the action. Barlow dispatched a courier with a message to Hancock, who rushed back to the river. In the estimation of Francis A. Walker of Hancock's staff, the situation was "already critical."[6]

"A defeat to our troops in such a situation, far from the rest of the army and with a river between them, would have meant something very like destruction," recounted Walker. Barlow's men fought stubbornly, hanging on for more than two hours. Hancock ordered them back across the stream, which "was, however, by no means an easy matter," Walker noted. The Rebels pressed forward, their musketry and artillery fire sweeping the ground as the Yankees retreated toward pontoon bridges.[7]

The 148th Pennsylvania fought a rearguard action, covering their comrades' flight. "Our last position referred to was altogether the most critical in which the Regiment was placed during the entire War," attested Colonel James A. Beaver. The Pennsylvanians escaped through burning woods, having lost about 175 killed and wounded. A member of Barlow's division claimed that the survivors abandoned 500 wounded comrades.[8]

Arrangements for the Union assault on Laurel Hill proceeded throughout the afternoon. Grant had assigned Hancock to command the offensive, but the crisis along the Po River pulled Hancock there. Fifth Corps commander Gouverneur Warren assumed leadership and convinced

Meade to allow the attack to go forward sooner instead of the planned hour of five o'clock. Warren designated two of his divisions and brigades from Gibbon's Second Corps division for the attack. Warren knew of Grant's and Meade's concerns about his generalship and evidently sought to redeem his reputation.[9]

A Union veteran remembered the moments before a charge, and it must have been similar for these Yankees as they stood before Laurel Hill: "Oh! It is an awful sight a host arming for battle. The packing of knapsacks, the examination of cartridges, the ringing of rammers in the muskets, to see that all is ready for the dread conflict, the orders of the officers, the hasty couriers and aides riding their horses to the utmost speed, the forming in ranks to *right face* and *forward march*!!! All tell of the *dead* work to come."[10] Into the field and woods of the Spindle farm stepped the Federals. From Laurel Hill, musketry and artillery discharges met them. The Confederates had strengthened their log and dirt works and edged them with abatis in front, making the position almost impregnable to a frontal assault. The blue-coated infantrymen kept coming, but they never had a chance. Some Yankees reached the crest and then disappeared while others went to ground to spare themselves. The gunfire ignited pine needles and underbrush, creating a hellish landscape like that in the Wilderness.[11]

The struggle—the insanity for those lying before Laurel Hill—went on for two hours. Their words said as much. "How we got through it all I don't know," professed a New Englander. A member of the renowned Iron Brigade admitted that it was "sure death to stand up there and a waste of powder to fire." Rebel gun crews tore bodies and trees apart with loads of double canister. One Confederate artillerist believed "our firing was probably never so destructive as on this day." An onlooker saw it clearly, describing Spindle's Field as a "dreadful scene."[12]

Finally, a man at a time, in pairs, by regiments and even brigades, the Federals gave it up, ebbing away. Angels prevailed briefly on this cursed ground as Lee's troops withheld their fire while their foes saved wounded and dead comrades from the flames. Too many, however, had fallen before the fires reached some of them. The misjudgment by Warren—perhaps blinded by a desire for redemption—resulted in a bloody debacle that shattered the troops' morale and engendered a festering ill will toward those responsible.[13]

Grant's designs for an army-wide offensive had been disrupted by clashes along the Po River and Warren's repulse. Undeterred, Grant ordered another assault by Second and Fifth corps units on the Confederate defenders on Laurel Hill. When division commander Samuel Crawford received the instructions, he said aloud with evident distress: "This is sheer madness. I tell you this is sheer madness, and can only end in wanton slaughter and certain repulse." When a sergeant heard the orders, he declared: "I could not imagine the possibility of ever getting back. Then the thought suddenly occurred to me: this is death."[14]

Crawford, the sergeant, and thousands more obeyed the general-in-chief and, as predicted, a tempest of madness and death swept across the ranks. Three Union regiments breached the works and charged toward a battery only to be beaten back. Most of the Yankees barely started before tumbling rearward, lashed by the Rebels' musketry and cannon fire. Laurel Hill's slope and crest had become a charnel house.[15]

Warfare suited Colonel Emory Upton. He embraced it with an evangelist's fervency and a scientist's objectivity. A native New Yorker, Upton was twenty-four years old in the spring of 1864 and three years out of the academy on the Hudson River. He had drilled recruits, had been appointed colonel of the 121st New York after the Battle of Antietam, and now served as a brigade commander in the Sixth Corps. A fellow officer wrote that Upton had "an ardent love for the profession of arms."[16]

Upton also possessed, in the estimation of Brigadier General James H. Wilson, "a patriotic sleepless ambition" and "the resolve to acquire military fame." Under his tutelage, the 121st New York became so proficient in drill and discipline that it acquired the nickname "Upton's Regulars." An unbending abolitionist and "despiser" of "all treason," he could be, however, arrogant and self-important. There could be no denying what Wilson stated about Upton: "His courage was both physical and moral, and therefore of the highest type. In the hour of battle he was as intrepid a man as ever drew a saber."[17]

It was this intense, enterprising colonel who had approached his division commander, Brigadier General David A. Russell, with a plan of attack on the afternoon of May 9. Upton had been at the forefront of a swift assault on an enemy bridgehead at Rappahannock Station, Virginia, on November 7, 1863. It had been a stunning Union victory. Upton's troops had overrun the Confederate works, using only their bayonets, not stopping during the advance to fire a volley, which was standard tactical practice. His units had charged on a narrow front as they had at Fredericksburg the previous May during the Chancellorsville Campaign.[18]

When he met with Russell, Upton proposed a similar tactical formation, with the regiments stacked in four lines, advancing rapidly without firing shots until they reached the enemy's works. Once they breached the entrenchments, the troops in the first line would fan out left and right, widening the breakthrough. The second line would deepen the penetration, while the third and fourth lines came up in support. Russell took Upton to Sixth Corps headquarters, where he presented the plan to Brigadier General Horatio G. Wright, who had succeeded the mortally wounded John Sedgwick.[19]

Although not the senior subordinate in the corps, Horatio G. Wright had been Sedgwick's preferred choice as a successor. Staff officer Theodore Lyman described him as an "unassuming, sturdy solid kind—never pyrotechnic" and "especially fitted to command infantry." A newspaper correspondent with the army wrote of the Connecticut native: "General Wright is the natural successor of the lamented Sedgwick, and none other would have been so well received by the corps. In social, personal temperament, and in military qualities he seems to bear a marked resemblance to Sedgwick himself."[20]

Wright endorsed Upton's scheme and later discussed it with Grant and Meade. Both commanders approved, but neither general possessed adequate intelligence on the nature and strength of the enemy's defenses and the disposition of Confederate units. Although the tactical formation differed from linear alignments, it remained a blind, frontal assault. Nevertheless, they authorized Wright to select a dozen regiments for the attack force and to assign a division to be ready to exploit a breakthrough. In turn, Wright assigned Russell to overall command of the operation. The attack force would advance from the Union center toward the opposing Rebel earthworks or a section of the salient.[21]

Wright met with Upton on the morning of May 10, informing the colonel that twelve regiments from the Sixth Corps had been assigned to his command. Earlier, Grant had shifted Brigadier General Gershom Mott's Second Corps division to the left flank of the Sixth Corps and placed it under Wright's direction. Mott's two brigades, Wright said, would support Upton's attack. Captain Ranald S. Mackenzie of the engineers "will show you the point of attack," concluded the corps commander. Wright's instructions had been verbal.[22]

In a postwar letter, Upton stated, "My interpretation of these orders was that the object of my assault was to break the enemy's line; that Mott would then move through the opening; and, forming at right angles to the works, would charge, continuing to roll up the enemy's flank." Upton did not confer with Mott about what was expected of each officer's role in the offensive strike.[23]

Sixth Corps chief of staff Martin McMahon showed Upton a list of the twelve regiments the aide had chosen for the attack. "Upton, what do you think of that for a command?" inquired McMahon. Upton looked at the assigned units and replied: "Mack that is a splendid command. They are the best men in the army."

The staff officer continued, explaining his duty, "Upton, you are to lead those men upon the enemy's works this afternoon, and if you do not carry them, you are not expected to come back, but if you carry them I am authorized to say that you will get your stars."

"Mack, I will carry these works," declared Upton. "If I don't, I will not come back."

The ambitious warrior mounted and, turning in his saddle, exclaimed: "Mack, I'll carry those works. They cannot repulse these regiments."[24]

The officers and men in the dozen regiments numbered upward of 4,500. Seven regiments served in Russell's division, including three from Upton's brigade, and the remaining five came from Thomas H. Neill's command. The men hailed from Maine, Vermont, New York, Pennsylvania, and Wisconsin—veteran soldiers with fine combat records. The previous autumn Upton had observed to his brother, "No soldier in the world can equal the American, if properly commanded."[25]

Captain Mackenzie conducted Russell and Upton to the edge of woods opposite the western face of the salient, where a slight bulge or "curve" protruded out from the main earthworks. Three regiments of Georgia troops, perhaps 1,350 officers and men, under the command of Brigadier General George Doles manned this smaller salient—later called Doles's Salient. Behind the Georgians, four cannon of the 3rd Richmond Howitzers provided support for the infantry. From the woodline, the Yankees needed to cross roughly 150 yards of open ground, break through abatis, and cross over the line of works into the trenches.[26]

Upton gathered the regimental commanders together and explained in detail the plan, assigning a role to each regiment. Three regiments in each line, twenty paces between the lines, Upton told them. Each soldier should load his rifle, but only the troops in the first line—Upton's own units, 5th Maine, 96th Pennsylvania, and 121st New York—would have their weapons loaded and capped, ready to fire. The command would rendezvous at a house owned by William D. Scott, rented at the time by a man named Shelton, located behind woods slightly more than a quarter of a mile from the Rebel works.[27]

Headquarters scheduled the charge for 5:00 P.M. in conjunction with the renewal of assaults on Laurel Hill. When they were delayed, Upton's attack was rescheduled for an hour later. The regiments rendezvoused at the Shelton house, and Upton led them on a woods road or path to the edge of the tree line across from Doles's Georgians. Here the Federals "formed for the charge," in Upton's words. The time approached 6:30 P.M. "I looked about in the faces of the boys around me," recounted a New Yorker, "and they told the tale of expected death. Pulling my cap down over my eyes, I stepped out."[28]

The Mainers, Pennsylvanians, and New Yorkers emerged from the trees. Across the open ground, a Rebel shouted to his comrades, "make ready, boys—they are charging." The Yankees began to run, cheering as they went. The Georgians triggered a volley and then a second one. The Federals reached the abatis, clawed their way through the stakes and entwined branches, and jumped on to the earthworks. Then, the Federals "left them have it." Upton had accompanied the first line and reported later that the enemy "absolutely refused to yield the ground."[29]

For a few minutes, the struggle in the trenches became a frenzy of killing and wounding. Yankee and Rebel alike wielded their bayoneted rifles, stabbing with them, swinging them as clubs, and even hurling them as spears. Upton's second line scrambled over the works and joined in the fighting. The Georgians fled rearward while Upton's first line filed left and right down the trenches, widening the breach. The Federals "poured through," exclaimed a Georgian, overran the four cannon of the 3rd Richmond Howitzers, and captured many Rebels, including George Doles, who lay down on the ground.[30]

Penetrating deeper into the main salient, the attackers struck the right front of Junius Daniel's North Carolina brigade, shattering its ranks. At the left end of the breakthrough, the Federals raked the flank and rear of the 2nd and 33rd Virginia of the Stonewall Brigade, sending them fleeing "in great confusion." "It was a crisis of dreadful suspense," exclaimed a Confederate staff officer, "and for a brief interval the worst fears prevailed."[31]

Richard Ewell had been at the Harrison house when Upton's regiments charged. He rode to the scene, meeting eddies of fleeing soldiers. He halted by Daniel's North Carolinians and tried to rally them, shouting: "Don't run, boys. I will have enough men here in five minutes to eat up every damned one of them." Even as he spoke, Confederate reinforcements were racing toward the breach—from the south, Stephen Dodson Ramseur's North Carolinians and Cullen Battle's Alabamians; from the east, Robert Johnston's North Carolinians and Clement Evans's Georgians. As Captain J. W. Williams of the 5th Alabama recorded, the Rebels "went in at a run." Behind them, a pair of Confederate batteries turned their guns on the blue-coated foes.[32]

Johnston rode ahead of his troops and met Ewell, Lee, and their staffs. Ewell was, wrote Johnston, "very much excited and entreating me to hurry up the Brigade." Lee had been with Ewell at the Harrison house when the enemy attacked. The army commander had spurred Traveller ahead, joining Ewell at the front and helping to rally their officers and men. "The General," noted Johnston of Lee, "was looking very calm and quiet and pointed out to me the line of works occupied by the enemy."[33]

Lee, Ewell, and their aides were less than two hundred yards from the fighting and under Union artillery fire from the guns supporting Upton's attack. One shell struck within fifteen feet of the army commander, plowed along the ground, and barely missed Traveller. "I look for him [Lee] to fall every minute," asserted a courier in a letter to his aunt the next day. Walter Taylor's horse was wounded twice, while Charles Marshall had a hole shot through his pants and a button clipped off his coat.[34]

Johnston's North Carolinians came up double-quick, halted, and strung out a line of battle. When they saw Lee, who was "greatly exposed," the officers and men refused to advance until the army commander withdrew to the rear. The incident rivaled the Texans' encounter with Lee on Orange Plank Road on May 6. Lee turned rearward, and the North Carolinians charged. Behind them came George H. Steuart's brigade of Virginians and North Carolinians.[35]

Loading and firing, pressing forward, veteran fighters from eight Confederate brigades closed in on the attackers. "The excitement of the advance . . . was beyond anything I have ever felt," Major Campbell Brown, Ewell's stepson and chief of staff, exclaimed in a letter to his mother. "I shouted till I was hoarse." In the Union ranks, all twelve of the regiments had entered the enemy works but had become entangled in a mass. "There was not a single unit under my control," Upton admitted later.[36]

The Federals fought stubbornly, clinging to the breach in the enemy line. The struggle was "the bravest fighting I ever saw," attested Captain Williams. "Not a Yankee bent his body that I could see, and I know our men stood perfectly erect, loaded and fired." A North Carolinian wrote in his diary, "It was an awful time for about thirty minutes." Upton ordered his men to retire outside of the works and "to hold the ground." The Union colonel expected reinforcements from Gershom Mott's Second Corps brigades.[37]

Mott's troops had advanced before Upton attacked, angling toward the apex of the salient. When they cleared some woods into open ground, Confederate batteries in the salient raked them with shellfire and canister. The Yankees reeled under the blasts and then broke in confusion to the rear. No one informed Upton of Mott's bloody repulse.[38]

"Night had arrived," Upton stated in his report. "Our position was three-quarters of a mile in advance of the army, and, without prospect of support, was untenable." He rode back to their starting point in the woods and met Russell, who ordered a withdrawal. Upton returned to the action, penned a retreat order, and had it sent along the line. Members of the three Vermont regiments refused until instructed to do so repeatedly by corps commander Wright. "This I assure you was galling to the pride of brave men," declared one of their officers, adding that he and many men cried while others voiced "unnumbered salvos of profanity."[39]

Upton estimated his losses at about 1,000 killed, wounded, and missing. The Mainers, Pennsylvanians, and New Yorkers of his brigade in the first line suffered 464 casualties, while the 49th Pennsylvania in the second incurred losses of 246, or a casualty rate of 52 percent. The Yankees captured 950 Confederate officers and men, and "several stands of colors." Upton reported, "Many rebel prisoners were shot by their own men in passing to the rear over the open field."[40]

Upton regarded the assault as a "complete success" but attributed the outcome to "the difficulty of combining the operations of two corps." Others were more pointed in their criticisms. Theodore Lyman groused that Mott's troops "behaved abominably." A fellow staff officer, Oliver Wendell Holmes Jr., declared, "Nobody did anything to speak of except 6th Corps."[41]

Tuesday, May 10, had been a difficult day for Union leadership and its rank and file. The assaults on Laurel Hill had been ill-conceived and wretchedly executed and had ended in costly failures. Veteran units either had refused to advance far or had gone to ground. Frontal attacks eroded morale, causing demoralization among the soldiers. The day had been the costliest since the Wilderness, with approximately 4,100 killed and wounded.[42]

Across the bloodstained ground behind the Confederate earthworks, Lee's officers and men had demonstrated their fighting prowess once again. They had punished the Yankees along the Po River, tore gaps in their foes' ranks in front of Laurel Hill, and undertook fierce counterattacks that recaptured Doles's Salient. Lee informed Secretary of War James Seddon, "Thanks to a merciful Providence our casualties have been small." The losses surely exceeded 2,000, if not 3,000. Doles's Georgians had begun the campaign, for instance, with roughly 1,560 officers and men but counted only 550 after Upton's attack.[43]

A Rebel courier who had witnessed the counterattacks against Upton's Federals claimed in a letter, "but it had not been that Gen. Lee was so close and rallied our men, the day would have been lost." The army commander and his aides had been fortunate that no one among the group had been killed or seriously wounded. The concern for Lee's safety and his irreplaceable bond with the army had been exemplified first by the Texans and then by the North Carolinians within five days.[44]

Before Lee returned to the army headquarters, he sat with Ewell and various Second Corps generals on the porch of the McCoull house. At one point, Lee turned to Robert Rodes and remarked, "General, what shall we do with General Doles for allowing those people to break over his lines?" "We shall have to let Doles off this time," responded Rodes, "as he has suffered quite severely for it already." Doles had escaped a Union prison by feigning death until his men and their comrades had driven the Yankees from the salient.[45]

Later Lee instructed Ewell, "It will be necessary for you to re-establish your whole line to-night." He conjectured that Grant might undertake a night attack "as it was a favorite amusement of his at Vicksburg." Lee and Ewell evidently had discussed holding the salient, for the army commander wrote, "I feel no apprehension on your part if the men do their duty." He urged Ewell to keep pickets alert during the night and to send out scouts toward the enemy's lines to the west.[46]

Earlier, shortly after the repulse of Upton's charge, a Confederate band played "Nearer, My God, to Thee." In the distance, a Union band followed with the "Dead March." A Rebel soldier wrote that he and his comrades remained "in fine spirits, and eager for the enemy to come."[47]

A sense of things, a dark reality, seemingly hung over some in the Federal ranks on Wednesday, May 11. One of Winfield Hancock's aides, Lieutenant Colonel Francis A. Walker, complained that since the Wilderness "everything had gone wrong with the Union army." In a letter on this day, a Second Corps brigade commander, Colonel Robert McAllister, confided to his wife: "This campaign beats all the rest in desperation and determination. God only knows the result."[48]

Six days of unrelenting combat, of random death brought by unseen sharpshooters, of futile assaults, and of woods and fields awash in carnage had marked the passage from the fords of the Rapidan River to the earthworks of Spotsylvania Court House. It could have appeared that both armies had descended into a foreboding nightmare of staggering cost and without an end. It could also have appeared that the descent would only deepen.[49]

Ulysses S. Grant, however, assessed the situation as promising on the morning of May 11. While eating breakfast, Grant was joined by Elihu B. Washburne, a friend and congressman who had been with the general-in-chief since the campaign's outset. Washburne was returning to the capital and suggested that Grant might want to write a note to the president. Grant demurred, explaining: "We are certainly making fair progress, and all the fighting has been in our favor. But the campaign promises to be a long one, and I am particularly anxious not to say anything just now that might hold out false hopes to the people."[50]

Later, in a dispatch sent at 8:30 A.M. to Henry W. Halleck, Grant wrote, expecting the chief of staff to share the message with Abraham Lincoln: "We have now ended the sixth day of very heavy fighting. The result to this time is much in our favor. But our losses have been heavy, as well as those of the enemy." Grant estimated his casualties at twenty thousand men, believing that the Rebels' "must be greater." Reinforcements, he hoped, "will be sent as fast as possible, and in as great numbers."[51]

"I am satisfied the enemy are very shaky," Grant continued, "and we are only kept up to the mark by the greatest exertions on the part of their officers, and by keeping them intrenched in every position they take." He reiterated his commitment to the ongoing campaign: "I am now sending back to Belle Plain [on the Potomac River] all my wagons for a fresh supply of provisions and ammunition, and propose to fight it out on this line if it takes all summer."[52]

The soldiers had come to call Grant the "silent man." An artilleryman said of him about this time, "I have seen Genl Grant a few times he is plain quiet looking man smokes no show." Writing to a hometown newspaper, a 5th Wisconsin soldier, who had charged with Emory Upton, maintained, "The army is well satisfied with Gen. Grant's plans and movements thus far, and is giving him its most entire confidence."[53]

Upton's breakthrough had convinced the general-in-chief that another assault on a massive scale with timely support could succeed in possibly ending the stalemate around the crossroads village. The army's senior leadership, however, knew little of the nature, shape, or extent of the Confederate lines on the enemy's right front and flank. Grant concluded that the farm of John and Elizabeth Brown, where Gershom

Mott's troops had started from on the previous night, could serve as the staging area.[54]

Grant dispatched Lieutenant Colonel Cyrus B. Comstock of his staff on a reconnaissance of the ground between Mott's division and Ambrose Burnside's Ninth Corps units posted east of Fredericksburg Road and south of the Ny River. Comstock's efforts yielded scant solid information on the enemy's dispositions and fieldworks. Mott offered limited knowledge of the terrain but advanced troops to the Willis Landrum house, which lay south of the Brown homestead and closer to the Confederate position. Rebel skirmishers contested the movement, and Mott withdrew. Comstock agreed with Grant that the Federals should use the Brown farm.[55]

"The result of the day's work on our front," wrote Lieutenant Colonel Horace Porter in his memoir, "was to discover more definitely the character of the salient in Lee's defenses on the right of his center." In his memoirs, Grant stated: "A salient was discovered at the right center. I determined that an assault should be made at that point." Both accounts, however, were written from hindsight, not reflecting accurately the writers' knowledge of the contours of Lee's lines at that time.[56]

Nevertheless, by three o'clock in the afternoon, Grant had "matured his plans," according to Porter, and sent instructions to George Meade: "Move three divisions of the Second Corps by the rear of the Fifth and Sixth Corps under cover of night so as to join the Ninth Corps in a vigorous assault on the enemy at 4 A.M. tomorrow." Warren and Wright should "take advantage of any diversion caused by this attack." Grant had "little doubt in my mind" that Upton's attack would have succeeded had it gone forward an hour earlier and "had been heartily entered into" by Mott and the Ninth Corps. Left unstated was that Grant expected the undertaking to be different on May 12.[57]

When Meade received Grant's orders, he summoned Hancock, Warren, and Wright to army headquarters. Details of the discussion went unrecorded, but no one at the meeting or at headquarters possessed firm knowledge of either the location of or the approaches to the Confederate position. In turn, Meade directed Hancock to march the divisions of Francis Barlow, David Birney, and John Gibbon after dark to a point between the left flank of the Sixth Corps and the right flank of the Ninth Corps, joining Mott's Second Corps brigades. Warren and Wright were ordered to make preparations for either a diversion or an attack in support of Hancock. Meade likely impressed upon the three generals the importance of this large-scale offensive to the general-in-chief.[58]

While Meade finalized matters, Grant issued orders to Burnside at 4:00 P.M. The instructions reflected Grant's mounting concern for the cautiousness, even the outright failures, of the former commander of the Army of the Potomac during the campaign. At times, Burnside had been immovable and seemingly incapable of directing even a corps. "You will move against the enemy with your entire force promptly and with all possible vigor at precisely 4 o'clock to-morrow morning," commanded the general-in-chief. Preparations should be completed "with the utmost secrecy, and veiled entirely from the enemy." In his earlier orders to Meade, Grant stated, "I will send one or two officers over to-night to stay with Burnside and impress him with the importance of a prompt and vigorous attack."[59]

Grant assigned Comstock and Lieutenant Colonel Orville E. Babcock to the duty. The Union commander also wanted them to conduct a thorough examination of the terrain toward the enemy works. Colonel Charles H. Morgan, Hancock's chief of staff, and two aides accompanied Comstock and Babcock. It had been raining most of the day, more heavily in the late afternoon. The five horsemen rode for hours, with Comstock "missing the way" and finally halting at Burnside's headquarters. Hancock's staff officers turned back, searching for the proposed staging area, which they located finally about dark.[60]

According to one of them, Major William G. Mitchell, they "made as careful a survey as possible before night." The three officers had crept forward until they encountered an enemy picket line. Staff member Francis Walker argued subsequently, however, that the "party had to select the positions for the column of attack, without learning much definitely regarding the extent and direction of the works to be assaulted." The staff officers reported their findings to Hancock as the rain kept falling.[61]

Private Asbury Jackson of the 44th Georgia wrote to his mother on May 11. A member of George Doles's brigade, Jackson had survived the attack by Yankees on the previous evening. The Georgian finished his letter home by probably repeating a camp rumor: "I forgot to say the prisoners captured last night were drunk, this is said to be the case throughout the lines. They wont fight when sober."[62]

Perhaps so, but inebriated or not, the enemy had broken through the Rebels' earthworks, overrun a battery, and fought their foes for an hour before being ordered back. Although the Confederates had sealed the breach with counterattacks by reserve units, the Union assault demonstrated the exposed nature of the salient. In the fighting's aftermath,

Robert E. Lee had instructed Richard Ewell to "rectify his line and improve its defenses."[63]

Improvements in the salient's defenses had been ongoing since their original construction. On May 11, the Confederates strengthened the earthworks and added more traverses, cleared more ground in front by cutting down trees, and fashioned more abatis with "limbs and branches interwoven into one another." Colonel Bryan Grimes of the 4th North Carolina boasted on this day, "We now have good breastworks and will slay them worse than ever." Stonewall Brigade commander James Walker thought the fieldworks were "apparently impregnable."[64]

The rain and occasional shots from Union sharpshooters hampered the labors. Some men recalled being soaked by afternoon thunderstorms. Danger from sharpshooters proved to be a constant throughout the day. At one point, Walker ordered Colonel William Terry of the 4th Virginia to select two hundred men and "to feel" for the Yankees beyond their skirmish line. Before Terry acted, the order was revoked. Morale among the salient's defenders remained high. "Our boys are in fine spirits," Captain John G. Webb of the 9th Georgia informed his father in a letter on this day.[65]

Late in the afternoon, General Lee came to the Edgar Harrison home, which Ewell used as his headquarters. With Ewell were Robert Rodes, the Second Corps's chief of artillery, Brigadier General Armistead L. Long, and their staffs. Reports from scouts, skirmishers, and signal officers in the upper story of a brick church near the village courthouse indicated a movement by the enemy. While Lee was there, a 4:30 P.M. dispatch arrived from his son, cavalry Major General William H. F. "Rooney" Lee. Referring to the units of Burnside's Ninth Corps, the message read: "There is evidently a general move going on. Their trains are moving down the Fredericksburg road, and their columns are in motion."[66]

If Grant were withdrawing and marching south, Lee wanted to pursue, either interdicting the movement or barring its route. Was the intelligence accurate, or were the Federals just redeploying units within their lines? During the previous night, while sitting on the porch of the McCoull house, Lee "playfully remarked" to the assembled subordinates, "I do not know which one of you may be called to the command of the army when I am gone. Until then you could not know the difficulties which beset the commander of an army, the greatest of which is to distinguish the true from the false reports which come from scouts."[67]

His son's dispatch evidently settled the matter. "Genl Lee had information which he considered reliable that Grant was moving his army somewhere else," wrote the army's chief of artillery, William N. Pendleton, two days later. Four days earlier, the Union commander had abandoned the Wilderness, moving south, so Lee had reason to conclude that his opponent was undertaking a similar movement. Lee ordered Ewell to evacuate the salient, withdrawing the Second Corps infantry divisions to the crossroads village. Ewell expressed concern for the men's welfare in the heavy rain, asking if they could remain under their shelters and leave in the morning. Lee acceded to the request.[68]

The army needed to be prepared to march, so Lee directed Long to pull out the Second Corps batteries from the salient. "This involved the removal before dark of such artillery as might embarrass or retard a withdrawal from the lines at night," Long explained in his memoirs. The gun crews "had to pass through a dense wood by a narrow and difficult road" to reach Spotsylvania Court House. The batteries limbered up and began rolling before dark.[69]

When Lee examined the salient and described it as "a wretched line" on May 9, the arguments for maintaining the position had been predicated on artillery batteries being posted behind the infantry. The guns began unlimbering that day and, by the morning of May 11, three battalions of Second Corps artillery manned the salient. Major Richard C. M. Page's four-battery battalion and Lieutenant Colonel William Nelson's three-battery battalion were posted to cover the apex and approaches to the left and right front of the salient, twenty-nine cannon in all. Lieutenant Colonel Robert A. Hardaway's five batteries of twenty guns were arrayed behind Rodes's infantrymen and swept the ground in front of the salient's western face. It had been one of Hardaway's batteries that Emory Upton's attackers had seized temporarily.[70]

In compliance with Lee's orders, Long withdrew Page's and Nelson's battalions, stripping the main sections of the salient of critical artillery support. Two batteries from Major Wildred E. Cutshaw's battalion moved forward from their reserve position, with eight cannon replacing twenty-nine. Major James M. Carrington's Virginia battery unlimbered near the Stonewall Brigade, with a pair of guns posted to fire to the left and "really straight down the fortifications," while the other pair unlimbered roughly twenty yards to the right to fire "straight down their front." Captain W. A. Tanner's Virginia gun crews deployed their four cannon to the southwest of and at a right angle to Carrington's crews.[71]

Carrington's artillerists shouldered their cannon into traverses, which one of them described as "oblong pens of logs, filled with earth, with openings left for the guns." They strengthened the works, but one of them stated later, "I remember that the men complained of the position and said that something was wrong as we were exposed to a cross fire on account of the federal line of battle."[72]

Colonel Thomas Carter had been assigned to "special direction" of Cutshaw's battalion. He had never believed that the salient was defensible, "so miserable was the shape." He had voiced opposition to staying there "all the day" on May 10, to Lee and Ewell. But, according to Carter, Rodes and Johnson, "having made their breastworks, insisted they could hold it." Carter decided to remain with Cutshaw's batteries in the salient and to spend the night with artillery chief Long.[73]

Like Carter, battalion commander Hardaway raised objections to the withdrawal of his batteries. "I told Gen. Rodes & Ramseur," Hardaway asserted in a postwar letter, "that if they would sustain me in a court martial, I would disobey orders and retain my artillery in position though I had orders to move at dark and Gen Lee had left the McCoul house and I could not communicate with him."[74]

Hardaway encountered Armistead Long and perhaps pleaded his case. Long told him that "he did not intend for the guns to be brought out until the troops left." Hardaway informed his battery commanders to remain in position until the withdrawal of Rodes's infantry, which had been planned for the next morning. Long's retention of Hardaway's and Cutshaw's batteries was perhaps based on the judgment that if the Yankees attacked again, it would be on Rodes's front.[75]

"The withdrawal of these guns was the one fatal Confederate blunder of this whole campaign," observed Porter Alexander, who kept his First Corps batteries with the infantry in the works on Laurel Hill. The reports of a Union retreat "proved erroneous," but Lee accepted their accuracy. Believing the reports to be true, he might have seen an opportunity to regain the initiative in the campaign and to strike the enemy while on the march. The removal of the artillery would have saved some time at the outset of the pursuit but, if he was mistaken about Grant's intentions, withdrawing the artillery incurred serious risk. Perhaps historian Gordon Rhea had it right, "Never had Lee made a more egregious miscalculation."[76]

When Lee rode away from the salient, he stopped at Henry Heth's headquarters in a church in the village. A sick A. P. Hill and other officers were with Heth when Lee arrived. They criticized Grant for attacking the Confederate earthworks and having his men "slaughtered." Lee countered, "Gentlemen, I think that General Grant had managed his affairs remarkably well up to the present." Then, turning to Heth, the army commander asserted: "My opinion is the enemy are preparing to retreat tonight to Fredericksburg. I wish you to have everything in readiness to pull out at a moment's notice, but *do not disturb your artillery*, until you commence moving. We must attack these people if they retreat."[77]

Hill interjected, stating, "General Lee, let them continue to attack our breastworks, we can stand that very well." Lee answered, "This army cannot stand a siege; we must end this business on the battlefield, not in a fortified place." With this done, Lee walked out of the church, mounted Traveller, and rode away in the darkness.[78]

{ 5 }

Near to Momentous Happenings

Whether he took time for reflection or not, Winfield Scott Hancock surely understood the import of the orders—for the second time in seven days the Second Corps, Army of the Potomac, had been designated to spearhead an assault on the stalwart Army of Northern Virginia. It should not have been a surprise that he and his officers and men had been selected for the critical offensive. Hancock was the finest corps commander in the army, and those who followed him arguably constituted the army's finest combat infantrymen.

A native Pennsylvanian and 1844 graduate of West Point, the forty-year-old Hancock had been, in a staff officer's estimation, "a kind of meteor on the battlefield." On May 5, 1862, at Williamsburg, Virginia, he had earned the sobriquet "Hancock the Superb," and on the war's bloodiest day, September 17, 1862, at Antietam, his performance moved Major General William B. Franklin to say of Hancock, "I never met a man who as a general officer, while under my observation, combined so well as he did the prudence which cherished the lives of his command, with the dash which was his distinguishing characteristic. . . . To be under his command, to know him . . . was to have a complete military education."[1]

At Fredericksburg, on December 13, 1862, when commanders stayed behind, he personally led his division up the long slope toward the stone wall at the foot of Marye's Heights. At Chancellorsville, on May 3, 1863, his division fought a rearguard action as he rode along the ranks "amidst this rain of shells utterly indifferent, not even ducking his head when one came close to him," said a Yankee. Promoted to command of the Second Corps in June, Hancock seemed to be everywhere on the southern end of the Gettysburg battlefield on the afternoon of July 2, 1863. He directed counterattacks, inspired wavering troops, and closed gaps in the lines, rendering a performance unmatched by any corps commander in the army in any previous engagement.[2]

"General Hancock is in his element and at his best in the midst of a fight," professed a lieutenant. A New Englander in the Second Corps believed, "Had General Hancock worn citizen's clothes his orders would have been obeyed anywhere, for he had the appearance of a man born to command."[3]

Hancock could sear a man's soul while issuing orders or reprimands with a string of curses. "He is a curious man," thought a surgeon, "will fret and scold and swear." The doctor went on, "He is one of the most singular men I ever saw, one moment swearing like a trooper at some unfortunate fellow who has incurred his displeasure, the next as affable and polite as though he had been brought up exclusively in a drawing room."[4]

Tall and physically imposing, the Pennsylvanian had been considered, in 1862, "the best looking officer in the army." Dr. Frank Dyer described him as "a fine-looking man," adding: "The gossip about his extreme simplicity is nonsense. He dresses as becomes his position, no more, no less." Hancock always wore a clean, white shirt under his uniform as if he were attending a military ball.[5]

Hancock had been seriously wounded during the afternoon of July 3, at Gettysburg, during the Confederate assault on Cemetery Ridge. A bullet struck the pommel of his saddle, driving a shard of a bent tenpenny nail into his thigh. He did not return to duty until January 1864. The unhealed wound, however, clearly drained him of strength and stamina. Theodore Lyman recorded in his diary in early April that John Gibbon, a Second Corps division commander, "feared Hancock could not keep the field, as his bone wound threatened to slough." The wound—perhaps osteomyelitis at this stage—required a surgeon's daily attention as it continued to discharge pieces of bone even as he led the corps in the campaign.[6]

Hancock had withstood the rigors of active campaigning, displaying his fighting spirit and prowess in the Wilderness and during the early days outside of Spotsylvania Court House. Now, with his orders in hand for a charge at 4:00 A.M. on May 12, he gathered three of his division commanders—Major General David B. Birney and brigadiers John Gibbon and Francis C. Barlow—at Second Corps headquarters around seven o'clock on the evening of May 11.[7]

Having seen this quartet of generals together two days earlier, a staff officer had portrayed them in a letter to his wife:

As we stood there, under a big cheery tree, a strange figure approached. He looked like a highly independent, mounted newsboy. He was attired in a flannel checked shirt, a threadbare pair of trousers, and an old blue kepi; from his waist hung a big cavalry sabre; his features wore a familiar sarcastic smile—it was General Barlow, commanding the 1st division of the 2d Corps, a division that for fine fighting cannot be exceeded in the army. There, too, was Gen. Birney, also in checked flannel, but much more tippy than Barlow; and stout Gen. Hancock, who always wears a clean *white* shirt (where he gets them nobody knows); and thither came steel-cold Gen. Gibbon, the most American of Americans, with his sharp nose and up and down habit of telling the truth, no matter whom it hurts.[8]

The thirty-nine-year-old Birney was the senior officer by rank of the division commanders. Son of renowned antebellum abolitionist James G. Birney, he had practiced law in Philadelphia, Pennsylvania, before the war. Commissioned colonel of the 23rd Pennsylvania, Birney commanded a brigade in the Peninsula Campaign, learning the trade under one of the army's most aggressive fighters, Philip Kearny. "His genius of command was especially conspicuous on this day," Kearny said of Birney at the Battle of Williamsburg on May 5, 1862. He succeeded the fatally wounded Kearny in command of the division in the Third Corps. Birney earned promotion to major general for his performance at Chancellorsville and, when Third Corps commander Daniel Sickles was wounded at Gettysburg on July 2, assumed temporary command of the corps.[9]

In Gettysburg's aftermath, controversies arose, culminating in hearings before the Congressional Joint Committee on the Conduct of the War in March 1864. Daniel Sickles, Abner Doubleday, and others publicly censored George Meade's actions during the three-day engagement. Birney appeared before the committee, providing testimony in support of his former commander, Sickles, and against Meade. With the reorganization of the army and the disbandment of the First and Third corps, unlike other critics of Meade, Birney remained in the army and was assigned to command of a division in the Second Corps.[10]

Dignified and rather aloof, Birney was not a popular individual among his fellow generals. Lyman claimed that he "had many enemies. . . . He was a pale, Puritanical figure, with a demeanor of unmovable coldness." A private who served under him offered a somewhat similar description of Birney: "He reminds me of a graven image and could act as a bust for his own tomb, being utterly destitute of color. As for his countenance, it is as expressionless as a Dutch cheese."[11]

Gibbon, when he had expressed concern about Hancock's stamina to Lyman, added that Birney as senior officer would succeed Hancock—"an undesirable result," in Gibbon's judgment. But Lyman had taken the measure of Birney as a soldier, arguing, "we had few officers who could command 10,000 men as well as he. . . . I always felt safe when he had the division; it was always well put in and safely handed."[12]

Like Birney, the twenty-nine-year-old Francis Barlow had practiced law before the war. His parents were Unitarians and Transcendentalists and, when they separated in 1840, his mother, Almira, took the children with her to Brook Farm, a transcendental utopian community. The family stayed at Brook Farm for only a few years. Known as Frank to family and friends, Barlow attended Harvard, graduating first in his class of 1855. "I never saw him thrown off his poise in any emergency," remembered a classmate, while another fellow student intimated that Barlow "was resolved to see things as they really were" and "spoke his thoughts without restraint, and with a singular and almost contemptuous disregard of consequence."[13]

When the war began, Barlow enlisted as a private in a three-month regiment but, after mustering out, was appointed lieutenant colonel of the 61st New York. His icy, earnest demeanor and reputation for harsh discipline earned the hatred initially of the New York volunteers. He led the regiment as colonel on the Virginia Peninsula and at Antietam, where he suffered a serious wound. His conduct brought promotion to brigadier general.[14]

By Gettysburg, Barlow commanded a division in the Eleventh Corps. In the fighting on the afternoon of July 1, he fell critically wounded as the Confederates swept the "damned Dutch" of the Union corps from the fields north of the town. In a letter to his mother six days later, he stated that the Rebels had been "very kind" to him and that a staff officer, Lieutenant Andrew L. Pitzer, had him carried first into some woods, laid on leaves, then later had him taken into a nearby house.[15]

That night three Confederate surgeons probed the wound, determining that the bullet had struck his left side below the arm pit, spiraled downward, cutting the peritoneum, and lodged in the pelvic cavity. They informed him "that there was very little chance for my life," gave him a dose of morphine, and departed. One of them returned the next day and repeated the assessment that the wound was mortal.[16]

Barlow's wife, Arabella, had accompanied the army on campaigns and, when she arrived at Gettysburg, she learned of her husband's wounding and capture. The Confederates agreed to her passage through the lines to care for Barlow. When the Southerners retreated, Union surgeons saw to the brigadier's treatment. With Arabella by his side, the recovery took months. On March 25, 1864, Barlow succeeded John Caldwell in command of a Second Corps division. Ironically, Caldwell had recommended Barlow's promotion to brigadier general after Antietam, but Caldwell had run afoul of Hancock and was assigned to court-martial duty in the capital.[17]

Theodore Lyman and Barlow had been classmates at Harvard and, when the staff officer saw his old friend, Lyman wrote, "It was odd to see Frank in his General's shoulder straps, the same old penny." Seeing his friend again weeks later, Lyman described Barlow as "a queer, lean figure, in a cap." Major Henry S. Abbott of the 20th Massachusetts asserted, "He [Barlow] struck me very favorably indeed." Another Union officer, writing on April 9, contended: "Barlow is a very brave man. Everything snaps in the Div. His old regt. hated him they hated anything, but he was the man after all they wanted to go up into a fight with?"[18]

The third division commander, John Gibbon, was Regular Army to the marrow of his bones and the depths of his soul. The thirty-seven-year-old Gibbon was born in Philadelphia, Pennsylvania, but his family moved to North Carolina when he was a young boy. Appointed to West Point from North Carolina, Gibbon graduated in 1847 with classmates Ambrose Burnside and A. P. Hill. Gibbon served with the army in Mexico and in Florida before spending five years as an artillery instructor at the academy. Although three brothers joined the Confederate army, Gibbon remained steadfast to the Union cause. After serving as a divisional chief of artillery, he was appointed brigadier general on May 2, 1862, and assigned to command of four regiments "from way down beyond the sunset."[19]

Gibbon had a prejudice against volunteers, but these officers and men from the West at the time—2nd, 6th, 7th Wisconsin, and 19th Indiana—had something to prove as soldiers to their eastern comrades. The new brigadier and the westerners clashed from the outset as he imposed strict discipline and implemented rigorous drill. A private confided, "You'll just feel that you hadn't better call him Johnnie." Gibbon wanted them to be as good as Regulars and authorized the issue of new uniforms of long blue frock coats and the tall, black Hardee hat of Regulars. The cost of the uniforms came from the men's monthly pay.[20]

The members of the brigade grumbled constantly about their commander until he led them into combat at Groveton in the Second Manassas Campaign, at South Mountain, and into the Cornfield at Antietam.

After these engagements, the men earned the nickname of the Iron Brigade and had emerged as the finest combat brigade in the army. Their Hardee hats became a distinctive badge of honor, as their foes called them "those damned black hats."[21]

Promoted to divisional command in the First Corps in November 1862, Gibbon suffered a severe wound at Fredericksburg. When he returned to duty in winter 1863, he was assigned to a Second Corps division, which he led at Chancellorsville and Gettysburg. A shell struck him on the shoulder during the Confederate assault on July 3 at the Pennsylvania crossroads town. He remarked later that surgeons told him the wound "would have been mortal, had it passed a quarter of an inch more to the left." He then said "dryly," "the quarter-inches are in the hands of God."[22]

Major Henry Abbott thought Gibbon to be "a splendid officer," while a staff officer described him as "cool as a steel knife, always, and unmoved by anything and everything." When Lyman first encountered Gibbon in spring 1864, he recorded in his diary: "He is an off-hand, soldierly man, of middle height, sharp nose, brown hair, and rather stern of aspect. He is remarkably outspoken." Few enlisted men likely would have believed that the "rather stern" Gibbon kept photographs of his children, his "babies," on his desk and, in quiet times, enjoyed a game of solitaire.[23]

Birney, Barlow, and Gibbon came, then, to the Second Corps headquarters around 7:00 P.M. Hancock informed the trio that reconnaissances had not yielded solid intelligence. They knew of a projecting angle in the enemy's works, but "the exact location was unknown." The corps commander possessed no information on Confederate numbers and the extent or strength of their position.[24]

The divisions of Barlow and Birney, supported by Gershom Mott's, would undertake the principal assault, with Gibbon's command posted in reserve, Hancock explained. Barlow stated after the war that Hancock provided no instructions on a plan, the formation of units, or "any matter material to the assault, I am absolutely certain." Barlow added that he was not criticizing Hancock, "whom I highly esteem and respect," but the eventual attack "was a mere lucky accident." The corps commander did tell the three subordinates, however, that "when a lodgment is made in the enemy's position of sufficient extant, it will be intrenched." Three wagons loaded with intrenching tools will accompany the corps.[25]

Hancock stated that the offensive operation required a night march to a staging area on the farm of a Brown family, located beyond the lines of the Sixth Corps. Two staff officers would lead the columns, with Barlow in front, followed by Birney. Gibbon would leave his works later, and the artillery units would be led by aides of the corps's chief of artillery. The men could build fires before the march but not later, despite the cold, wet night. The march would be conducted "quietly" and the ranks "well closed up." Hancock expected them to start before ten o'clock.[26]

Before the three generals left to attend to the preparations, Hancock told them, "it was a movement of more than usual importance" and reminded them "of the gratitude which the country would feel for those officers who should contribute to the success of the enterprise." Barlow remained behind for some time, discussing details with Hancock. The brigadier proposed forming his division "in close column" and expected that his veterans "would take the burden of the principal attack."[27]

Orders for the march filtered down through the ranks. Many of the men had used the evening hours to sleep even in the "drenching rain." Earlier in the day they had received "a generous supply of rations," including one of whiskey. "I verily believe," remembered a lieutenant, "it had much to do with the daring charge and many of the reckless feats of the next." When they heard the instructions for the march, however, according to a 20th Massachusetts soldier, "many thought it was a sure fall back across the Rapidann [sic], and eventually to our old breastworks around Washington. We were mistaken."[28]

The guides, Hancock's chief of staff Charles H. Morgan and Captain George H. Mendell, an engineer officer, joined Barlow. Morgan, "who was what might be called a profane swearer," in the words of Barlow, could not hide his anger. The lieutenant colonel "loudly expressed indignation" at "being sent to conduct an important movement when they had no information whatever to the position or strength of the enemy." Barlow laughed and said to Morgan, "For Heaven's sake, at least, face us in the right direction, so that we shall not march away from the enemy, and have to go around the world and come up in their rear."[29]

About ten o'clock, with fires still burning in "a type of the meanest of Virginia weather," Barlow's troops started forth. Morgan and Mendell rode ahead, carrying dark lanterns to light "the tangled and tortuous path." Barlow led his column, accompanied by brigade commanders and colonels Nelson A. Miles and John R. Brooke. Barlow recalled that the colonels "were loud in their complaints of the madness of the undertaking." Soon, Barlow had to quiet Miles, "so emphatic" was he in his protestations.[30]

"Of all our many night marches," remembered a Yankee, "this one took the cake." "It was so dark that it could almost be felt," recalled another. Men stumbled into those in front of them as the column moved fitfully. "Every man followed his file leader," stated a captain, "not by sight or touch, but by hearing him growl and swear, as he slipped, splashed, and tried to pull his 'pontoons' out of the mud."[31]

"We dragged our weary way along," wrote a captain in Barlow's division. A private in the Irish Brigade stated later: "Sometimes we had to creep through the wet underbrush. We were a sorry looking lot of boys, judging by the way we felt. . . . It was the worst march we had to endure up to this time." Colonel James A. Beaver of the 148th Pennsylvania noted in his diary, "the storm was such that he shivered more than ever in his life."[32]

A brief panic ensued among Barlow's troops when several mules stampeded into a pair of New York regiments. The soldiers heard clanging noises as the mules' harnesses had chains on them. Believing that it was a Confederate cavalry attack in the darkness, many of the New Yorkers broke toward the rear. Officers restored order and, when they learned the cause, the men had "a good laugh."[33]

Barlow recounted that his division reached the Brown farm between midnight and 12:30 A.M. "I know that when we reached a certain point," he contended afterward, "I was simply told that there was the spot, and beyond that nothing." Birney's and Gibbon's troops arrived within the next hour or so. As each column halted, according to a staff officer, "the weary men, drenched to the skin, sunk down on the hillside, and were asleep as soon as they touched the ground."[34]

Gershom Mott had used the one-and-a-half story Brown farmhouse as his headquarters, posting a large national flag at the yard gate. John C. and Elizabeth Brown owned one of the largest farms in the area, comprising 1,772 acres. In 1860, the combined worth of their real and personal estates amounted to $54,000, which included seventeen female and five male slaves, whose ages ranged from seventy-seven years to four months old. When the Federals had arrived at the farmhouse, seven other family members lived with the elderly couple, including James, who had been discharged because of illness from the 9th Virginia Cavalry.[35]

Hancock joined his officers and men at the Brown farm. During his ride, he stopped at Sixth Corps headquarters, inquiring "for directions as to the way." When Hancock reached the farmhouse, he summoned his division commanders to a meeting. The Brown farm lay roughly three-fourths of a mile north of the apex of the "Mule Shoe."[36]

Before Hancock arrived, Barlow sought information about the ground Mott's troops had crossed in support of Emory Upton's attack on May 10. Barlow could not recall later whether he spoke to Mott, but he remembered that he did ask Lieutenant Colonel Waldo Merriam of the 16th Massachusetts if the officer could offer any information. Merriam provided "an impression" of the terrain and the enemy's fieldworks. Merriam "drew upon the wall a sketch of the position," recounted Barlow, "and this was the sole basis on which the dispositions of my division were made."[37]

At the council, Hancock used Merriam's drawing to orient the division commanders. With a compass, they ascertained the direction of the assault from the Brown residence toward "a large white house [McCoull's] known to be inside the enemy's works near the point we wished to attack," reported Hancock. Barlow's and Birney's command would comprise the front line, with Mott's behind and in support of Birney's, and Gibbon's in reserve.[38]

Barlow spoke up with his usual bluntness, telling his fellow officers that he would mass his four brigades into a compact formation along a narrow front, in a deployment similar to Upton's. "If I am to lead this assault," he declared, "I propose to have men enough when I reach the objective point to charge through hell itself and capture all the artillery they can mass on my front." The other generals objected to the plan, but Barlow could not be dissuaded.[39]

The council ended, and the commanders departed to make arrangements. "I never remember seeing General Barlow so depressed as he was leaving Hancock's headquarters that night," observed staff officer John D. Black. "He acted as if it was indeed a forlorn hope he was to lead." Barlow issued orders in a "subdued and tender" voice to his aides and said, as he often had in similar words: "Make your peace with God and mount, gentlemen; I have a hot place picked out for some of you today."[40]

The division commander's mood, as he related years afterward, reflected the fact that no one at Grant's and Meade's headquarters nor among Hancock's senior generals and staff officers possessed "information whatever to the position or strength of the enemy." Barlow went on, "at times a sense of the ludicrous, of the absurdity of the situation prevailed over the feeling of responsibility and indignation." Not since

Fredericksburg on December 13, 1862, when more than forty thousand officers and men assailed the heights outside of the town in a series of attacks, had so many of the army's infantryman been arrayed for a frontal assault as on this morning. And like that terrible December day, the price to be paid for commanders' decisions fell upon the army's rank and file.[41]

Barlow's regimental officers roused their men and began filing them into position about 3:00 A.M. The veteran troops moved "quietly and promptly" into ranks. The brigades of colonels Nelson A. Miles and John R. Brooke constituted the front of the division. Behind them aligned the brigades of colonels Thomas S. Smyth and Hiram L. Brown, twenty-two regiments in all.[42]

With open ground toward the Confederate salient, Barlow did as he had argued, deploying the units into a massed column. Each regiment formed a two-company front, or "double column on the center," with a depth of five companies. "Each regiment was folded in on itself like a fan," wrote Captain Alexander W. Acheson of the 140th Pennsylvania, "so as to have its men in the most compact form possible." Five paces separated each regiment, and ten paces each brigade. The 2nd Delaware covered the column's left flank, and the 66th New York acted as skirmishers.[43]

Birney shifted forward his two brigades, commanded by Brigadier General J. H. Hobart Ward and Colonel John S. Crocker, aligning them to the right of Barlow's front line. Behind Birney's ranks and to the right and slightly back of Barlow's rear brigades, Mott deployed his pair of brigades, under colonels Robert McAllister and William R. Brewster. Each division formed two battle lines, each two ranks deep. The 1st and 2nd United States Sharpshooters screened the front of the thirty-five regiments in the divisions as skirmishers.[44]

Hancock's final division, three brigades under Gibbon, acted as a reserve, posted several hundred yards primarily behind Barlow. Colonel Samuel S. Carroll and brigadiers Joshua T. Owen and Alexander S. Webb commanded the twenty-one regiments, a battalion of New Yorkers, and a company of Massachusetts sharpshooters. These veterans formed a battle line, two ranks deep.[45]

At 3:45 A.M. on May 12, Hancock informed army headquarters: "My troops are nearly formed. As it is misty I think I shall wait until it is a little more clear, by which time my troops will be formed." As the final ranks deployed, the Second Corps commander had approximately twenty thousand officers and men with him in seventy-eight regiments,

CHAPTER FIVE

one battalion, and one company. Many of them had been in the corps since its organization under George B. McClellan in 1862. They had come from their homes in Maine, Massachusetts, Connecticut, New York, New Jersey, Delaware, Pennsylvania, Ohio, West Virginia, Indiana, and Michigan.[46]

Likely to a man, they would have regaled anyone who would have listened with brags that they were the finest combat soldiers in the Army of the Potomac. The officers and men of Birney's and Mott's commands could boast of serving under Philip Kearny in the "Red Patch" division of the Third Corps. They had held the crossroads at Glendale during the Seven Days' Campaign: charged the "bloody lane" at Antietam and the stone wall at Fredericksburg; fought with tenacity at Chancellorsville; and defended the Peach Orchard, counterattacked into the Wheatfield, and repulsed Pickett's Charge at Gettysburg.

The historian of the 20th Massachusetts, the Harvard Regiment, wrote of the minutes while Hancock waited and a light drizzle fell. "The Second Corps had never before been massed into a solid body to move against the enemy, and never in such form as that in which it was now arrayed," he recounted. "Great events have a power of self-proclamation; and although nothing had been communicated to the troops as to what was expected of them, the feeling ran through the ranks that they were near to momentous happenings."[47]

One of those in the ranks remembered, however, that "every man in the corps had a presentment of what was coming." A Pennsylvania veteran confided, "A funeral like silence pervades the assembly, and like specters the men in blue await the order to attack." A staff officer remarked to some of the rank and file: "Gentlemen, today may be for some of us the last on earth. Whilst we are waiting here would not be well to say a prayer?" Men shook hands and bid farewell to one another.[48]

It was the waiting that veterans hated the worst, claimed Captain Alexander W. Acheson of the 140th Pennsylvania. Another captain described those moments before soldiers entered the fighting, arguing that what gnawed at them in quiet thoughts was "the instinctive dread of the unknown in battle, than the fear of death or combat. Something like the feeling which possesses one when in a dream he is falling from a great height." The waiting neared an end.[49]

Edward Johnson had been inspecting his division's lines in the Mule Shoe late on the evening of May 11 when he noticed the withdrawal of

Confederate batteries. Unaware of Robert E. Lee's decision about the movement, Johnson inquired as to the cause. He was informed that the movement was made in obedience to orders and "that a general move of troops was contemplated." To Johnson, the salient was "a point which with artillery was strong, but without it weak."[50]

Before long, Johnson received a message from one of his brigade commanders, George H. Steuart. "The enemy is moving and probably massing in our front," it read, "and we expect to be attacked at daylight. The artillery along our front has been withdrawn, by whose orders I know not, and I beg that it be sent back immediately." Reports from scouts and officers on picket duty seemed to confirm Steuart's intelligence about the Federals.[51]

The forty-eight-year-old Virginian had been a soldier for nearly three decades and had experienced difficult situations before. Johnson had graduated from West Point in 1838, fought Seminoles in Florida, earned two brevet ranks in Mexico, and served at frontier posts in California, Kansas, and Dakota Territory during the 1850s. When the Civil War began, he was appointed colonel of the 12th Georgia. On December 13, 1861, his regiment and other Confederate units repulsed an enemy attack at Camp Allegheny in the mountains of western Virginia. The victory brought him promotion to brigadier general and a nickname, "Allegheny" or "Old Allegheny."[52]

On May 8, 1862, in an engagement at McDowell, Virginia, Johnson suffered a serious wound from a bullet that struck him in an ankle. His recovery took months and, when he returned to duty, he walked with a "very perceptible" limp, using a staff "about as long as a rail almost as thick as the club of Giant Despair." Before long soldiers called him "Old Clubby," but not in his presence. Promoted to major general, Johnson acceded to command of Stonewall Jackson's former division before the outset of the Gettysburg Campaign.[53]

At Gettysburg, Johnson's veterans attacked Union defenses on Culp's Hill on the evening of July 2, making minor gains. Reinforced with three brigades and ordered to renew the offensive, Johnson sent the Rebels forward at daybreak. Protected by fieldworks, the Federals repulsed three distinct assaults. "We were into it hot and heavy," exclaimed an Alabamian. "I thought I had been in hot places before—I thought I heard Minnie balls, but that day capped the climax." The Confederates never had much of a chance. After six hours of unrelenting combat, they withdrew, having suffered a casualty rate that exceeded 25 percent.[54]

"The division suffered proportionally through the folly of our *hard fighting* Johnson," groused a member of the Stonewall Brigade in a letter to his sister. "He has none of the qualities of a general but expects to do everything by fighting." In Johnson's defense, he had his instructions, and the likelihood of success had never been favorable. He put it well in his report: "The enemy were too securely intrenched and in too great numbers to be dislodged by the force at my command."[55]

Johnson was an obstinate fighter and a capable division commander. He had the respect and confidence of his officers and men, not their soldierly affection. His rough-hewn personality and manners possessed a crustiness. He was ill-tempered, cursed at the troops, and knocked shirkers in battle with his walking club. One of his men described Johnson as a "brute." A staff officer claimed that the general made himself "agreeable or odious as the taste of one may determine."[56]

This surly, disagreeable soldier continued leading the division during the Bristoe and Mine Run campaigns. After undergoing a reorganization over the winter of 1864, the command began spring operations with brigadiers at the head of the four brigades and numbers of regiments with a full complement of field officers—majors, lieutenant colonels, and colonels. Six thousand officers and men stood in the division's ranks when the Federals crossed the Rapidan River.[57]

The division incurred grievous losses in the fighting along Orange Turnpike in the Wilderness on May 5 and 6. Brigadiers John M. Jones and Leroy A. Stafford were killed and mortally wounded, respectively. One-half of regimental field officers fell as did one-third of enlisted men. When Johnson's depleted ranks marched away from the Wilderness, Jedediah Hotchkiss described the command as "a mere remnant of the division that stormed Culp's Hill." By nightfall on May 11, Johnson had roughly 4,500 officers and men with him in the Mule Shoe.[58]

Stafford's mortal wound and the heavy casualties resulted in the consolidation of two Louisiana brigades under the command of Brigadier General Harry T. Hays. Although the army commander's orders stated that "each brigade will retain its present organization," the members of both brigades opposed the merger. "The troops of the old organizations feel that they have lost their identity," explained one of them, "and are without the chance of perpetuating the distinct and separate history of which they were once so proud. The loss of prestige must excite to some extent a feeling of discontent."[59]

Hays's leadership of the combined units lasted two days; he fell severely wounded on May 10, while overseeing the strengthening of the salient's earthworks. Apparently, the brigades' senior colonels, Zebulon York and William Peck, were absent from the command. Colonel William Monaghan of the 6th Louisiana temporarily replaced Hays. The Louisianans remained together in the salient's defenses until May 11, when Richard Ewell directed Monaghan to split the command and shift Hays's former brigade into the works vacated by George Doles's Georgians. Colonel Jesse Williams of the 2nd Louisiana assumed command of Stafford's former regiments.[60]

Monaghan's five regiments—5th, 6th, 7th, 8th, and 9th Louisiana—filed into the trenches on the right flank of Junius Daniel's North Carolina brigade of Robert Rodes's division. Like many of his troops, the forty-seven-year-old Monaghan had emigrated to America from his native Ireland, finding opportunity in Irish enclaves in New Orleans. When the war came, no Confederate state had more Irish in its regiments than Louisiana. In Monaghan's brigade, Irish immigrants or their descendants numbered from one-third to more than one-half in some of the regiments. In one company of the 7th Louisiana, more than 90 percent of the soldiers were of Irish lineage.[61]

Monaghan now commanded one of the army's most renowned units—famous for the members' valor on a battlefield and for their rowdiness, even lawlessness, in camp or on the march. The 1st Special Battalion, Louisiana Infantry, led by Major Chatham Roberdeau Wheat, had acquired the nickname of "Wheat's Tigers" for the battalion's fierce fighting at First Manassas. "Wharf rats," planters' sons, and even criminals served in the battalion, whose reputation for unruly behavior seemingly overshadowed its reputation for combat prowess. A former brigade commander, Richard Taylor, declared that the battalion was "so villainous . . . that every commander desired to be rid of it."[62]

Roberdeau Wheat fell rallying the Tigers at Gaines's Mill on June 27, 1862. Its losses that summer led to the battalion's disbandment in August, with its survivors transferred to other units. In time, Tigers applied to all Louisiana regiments in Lee's army, and their members wore the name proudly. Approximately eight hundred Tigers manned the works on the salient's western face on May 11.[63]

The Stonewall Brigade held the trenches from Monaghan's right flank to the earthworks' west angle. Brigadier General James A. Walker commanded the five Virginia regiments, which had earned their enduring name on Henry House Hill at First Manassas on July 21, 1861. As a cadet at the Virginia Military Institute, Walker had been sternly disciplined by Professor Thomas J. Jackson, resulting in Walker's expulsion weeks before graduation. He attempted to harm or to kill Jackson by throwing a brick at him from a dormitory window and later threatened to shoot him.[64]

Ironically, Walker's former professor, Stonewall Jackson, had urged Walker's promotion, a view endorsed by Lee, Ewell, and A. P. Hill. Walker received his brigadiership on May 16, 1863, and was assigned command of the Stonewall Brigade. He had been a captain in the 4th Virginia for a month in 1861, before securing the lieutenant colonelcy of the 13th Virginia in another brigade. When the brigade's five regimental commanders learned of Walker's appointment, however, they submitted their resignations, arguing that one of them or Jackson's chief of staff, Sandie Pendleton, should have been selected for the command. Lee rejected the resignations.[65]

By spring 1864, Walker had earned the rank and file's respect for his concern for their welfare and his leadership in combat. They bristled at times because of his strict discipline in camp, but his pugnacious and gruff demeanor endeared him to the enlisted men. A staff officer described the brigadier as "bold in battle and everywhere else." The Virginians accorded him high praise with the nickname, "Stonewall Jim."[66]

Like other brigades in Johnson's division, Walker's command lost perhaps one-third of its numbers in the Wilderness. By nightfall on May 11, roughly one thousand of them stood in the trenches. Their line ran from left to right: 2nd, 33rd, 27th, and 5th Virginia. On the right of the 5th Virginia, Major James Carrington's Charlottesville Artillery's four Napoleon cannon stood. The brigade's final regiment, the 4th Virginia, held the works next to the battery. A narrow farm lane to the McCoull house passed between 27th and 5th Virginia. Pine woods lay 200–300 yards in their front.[67]

The five Louisiana regiments of Stafford's brigade covered the salient's apex between the west and east angles. Thirty-one-year-old Colonel Jesse M. Williams commanded the brigade. He had led the Louisianans at Gettysburg. A member of the brigade argued years later that Williams "was as cool in battle and under fire as any man in Lee's army and should have been made a brigadier, but he was not a West Pointer."[68]

The deployment of Williams's regiments—1st, 2nd, 10th, 14th, and 15th Louisiana—remains uncertain. By holding the broad apex or nose of the salient, they could become trapped if an enemy assault broke through on either flank. To their front, extending 600–800 yards, lay an old, open field, dipping down into a swale or shallow ravine in front of their works. Fewer than six hundred Louisianans stood along the apex.[69]

On the Louisianans' right, defending a section of the salient's eastern face from the east angle southward, was the understrength brigade formerly commanded by John M. Jones. Six regiments, with many of the companies from southwestern Virginia, composed the brigade, now under the temporary leadership of Colonel William A. Witcher of the 21st Virginia. A staff officer, Lieutenant McHenry Howard, observed that "a part of the brigade . . . was said to be a good deal disheartened by the losses and for want of such a commander as Jones had been."[70]

The Virginians had incurred nearly six hundred casualties in the Wilderness fighting but had begun the campaign with roughly 1,850 officers and men in the ranks. On the night of May 11, three regiments—50th, 44th, and 25th Virginia—manned the works. The brigade's other three regiments—48th, 42nd, and 21st Virginia—were deployed as skirmishers outside of the salient. Probably fewer than five hundred of the Virginians remained within the salient.[71]

Brigadier General George H. Steuart's brigade of Virginia and North Carolina regiments completed Johnson's defenses, manning the trenches south from Witcher's right flank. A section of the works defended by Steuart's troops bent farther east, creating another angle in the works. Approximately 1,300 officers and men held the earthworks.[72]

Known in the army as "Maryland" Steuart to distinguish him from Virginian Jeb Stuart, the thirty-five-year-old West Pointer had commanded the brigade since the Gettysburg Campaign. His leadership had been capable, but not distinguished. On this night his line ran left to right: 3rd North Carolina, 1st North Carolina, 10th Virginia, 23rd Virginia, and 37th Virginia. These veterans came from the broad swaths of their respective states, from the coasts to the mountain chains. The 10th Virginia boasted the only remaining band in the Second Corps.[73]

On Steuart's right a section of unoccupied trenches stretched southwest about two hundred yards. As the defenses turned more southerly beyond the salient, Brigadier General James H. Lane's North Carolina regiments manned the earthworks, anchoring the left flank of Jubal Early's Third Corps lines. Early's divisions of Cadmus Wilcox and Henry Heth held three miles of works that extended beyond Fredericksburg Road. To their front lay Ambrose Burnside's Union Ninth Corps units.[74]

John Gordon's Confederate division of about 4,600 officers and men occupied the second line of works, which ran across the base of the salient. The command's orders were, Gordon noted in a postwar letter to Charles Venable, "generally to support any portion of the line around the long salient which might be attacked. This was Gen. Lee's general direction." Gordon continued, telling Lee's aide, "You remember there were constant rumors that the lines were to be attacked & at various places."[75]

As Gordon related, then, the Mule Shoe's defenders passed the waning hours of May 11, with mounting concerns, magnified perhaps by a chilling rain and pitch darkness. Orders had forbidden campfires. Not all of the Rebels believed, however, in an impending enemy attack. A Georgian noted, "Towards evening, rumors were freely circulated" that the Yankees were crossing the Rappahannock River. A North Carolinian, writing a letter to his wife at nine o'clock, stated, "just herd good nuse . . . old Grant is retreing."[76]

But persistent reports of "unusual movements" from scouts and skirmishers kept filtering back into the Mule Shoe. Skirmishers, likely from the 21st Virginia, sent a message that "there was a steady rumbling in front, indicating that a large force was being massed in front or passing around to our right." In reaction, Captain George Williamson and Lieutenant McHenry Howard of Steuart's staff stood on the earthworks for thirty minutes, listening, as Howard recounted, "to the subdued roar or noise, plainly audible in the still, heavy night air, like distant falling water or machinery."[77]

In the distance, on a night of sounds, Union bands played music for hours. A Confederate in the Mule Shoe thought the Federal bandsmen "played beautiful pieces," including "The Star-Spangled Banner." Major David W. Anderson of the 44th Virginia and officer of the day for Johnson's division believed the Yankees had massed one hundred bands. He distinctly remembered the drums and trumpets. He admitted that he was "unsure of their intentions."[78]

Like Anderson, Gordon professed, "it was impossible to obtain reliable information" of the enemy's plan. By midnight, however, Johnson had been convinced by the reports that the Federals had been concentrating for an assault on the salient. Johnson sent his adjutant, Major Robert W. Hunter, to Edgar Harrison's house to inform Ewell of the disturbing intelligence. The corps commander discounted the reports, telling Hunter, "General Lee had positive information that the enemy was moving to turn his right flank, and had been so informed by the most reliable scouts, and that it was necessary for the artillery to move accordingly."[79]

Hunter rode back to the McCoull house and relayed Ewell's words to Johnson, who said, "I will go at once." When Johnson and Hunter arrived at the Harrison house, they found Ewell "lying down, and apparently very uneasy." Johnson persuaded Ewell that the signs indicated an imminent assault. Johnson requested that the artillery be returned to their original positions in support of his infantry. Ewell agreed. It was one o'clock on the morning of Thursday, May 12.[80]

Ewell sent Major Henry Kyd Douglas, a staff officer, to the corps's artillery commander, Armistead Long, with orders to have the batteries returned to the salient by 2:00 A.M. Ewell informed army headquarters of his decision, which Lee approved, and instructed Gordon to be prepared to support Johnson in the event of any enemy attack. Complying, Gordon shifted the brigades of Clement Evans and John Hoffman into the reserve line of trenches that Rodes had just constructed behind Doles's Salient.[81]

Kyd Douglas, meanwhile, must have lost his way in the one-and-a-half-mile ride from the Harrison house to Spotsylvania Court House, where the artillery battalions had parked. The staff officer arrived at 3:30 A.M., having taken more than two hours to cover the distance. He delivered the orders to Long, who directed Major Richard C. M. Page to return to the salient with his three batteries "with all haste." Page's fourth battery had been detailed as escort for a wagon train.[82]

Long ordered Thomas Carter to oversee Page's return march to the salient, directing the colonel to have the fourteen cannon back by daylight, which was rapidly approaching. It took time, however, for the crews to be ready to leave. When they had arrived at the village that preceding night, "we were ordered to have the horses unhitched for rest and rubbing down, which was done," recalled Lieutenant S. H. Hawes. The battery of Carter's brother, Captain William Page Carter, led the march toward the salient.[83]

Upon Johnson's return to the Mule Shoe, he ordered his "command to be on the alert, some brigades to be awake all night, and all to be up and in the trenches an hour or so before daylight." He visited his ranks and the two batteries, instructing the officers and men to keep the "utmost vigilance." Johnson had officer of the day Anderson post sentries ten paces apart on top of the earthworks. In the Stonewall Brigade, company officers ordered that if the enemy attacked, the men were to hold each traverse "to the last extremity." In Williams's and Steuart's regiments, the infantrymen cleaned their rifles and drew more ammunition. At four

CHAPTER FIVE

o'clock, Anderson received orders to rouse sleeping regimental commanders and their troops.[84]

North of the Mule Shoe, lying along a farm lane to the Willis Landrum homestead, was posted the main Confederate skirmish line, comprising the 14th Louisiana, the 48th Virginia, and the 42nd Virginia. The 48th Virginia had been sent forward before daylight to relieve the 42nd Virginia, which still remained in position. Earlier, the Rebels had dug a line of dirt works on the lane's northern edge in front of the Louisianans and members of the 48th Virginia. The Confederates had stripped weatherboarding from the log Landrum house for the works. To the right of the 42nd Virginia, the 21st Virginia covered the eastern face of the salient, with the skirmish line running northwest to southeast.[85]

A blanket of fog had settled in as daybreak approached. About four o'clock Union bands ceased playing music. "The signs in front," wrote a Confederate, "began rapidly to take the definite form of attack." So, they waited.[86]

At the John Brown house, after Winfield Hancock sent his 3:45 A.M. message to army headquarters, he waited for fifteen minutes, until the hour designated for the assault. Hancock sought Francis Barlow's opinion about a further delay. Looking out a window, the division commander said: "It's too dark. I think it would be better to wait half an hour."[87]

Outside, the twenty thousand officers and men of the Second Corps finalized preparations. They placed fresh caps on their rifles and fixed bayonets. Pioneers moved within the regiments, ready to clear away the abatis in front of the enemy works. Groups gathered for prayers. Some of them would recall the hooting of owls and the chirping of birds. Officers delivered final instructions in whispers—no firing, rifles carried at right shoulder shift.[88]

Thirty more minutes passed until finally, at 4:35 A.M., Hancock ordered the advance. "The order to move to the attack wasn't half so disagreeable as one might think," admitted Private John W. Haley of the 17th Maine. Shortly before, Alexander Webb stepped in front of his ranks and spoke: "Men of the first Brigade, we are ordered to charge the enemy at this point. Keep together as well as you can. If you get broken up, follow the colors of the Nineteenth Massachusetts, I shall go with you. Forward!"[89]

What likely had been unspoken but understood mattered still. Even in this war's fourth spring, after three years of unimagined carnage, ideas kept these veterans in the ranks—duty, honor, the cause, and fulfilling the expectations of those at home. It could hardly be otherwise; for to ask them to step forth into the darkness, into the uncertainty, had to be for something more than themselves. Ahead loomed a testing unlike any before, nor again, in America's bloodiest of conflicts. Hell, measured in hours, abided.[90]

Union army advance upon Spotsylvania Court House. Sketch by Alfred Waud.
Courtesy of the Library of Congress.

The Spotsylvania Court House. Courtesy of the Library of Congress.

Spotswood Hotel. Courtesy of the Library of Congress.

Artist's print of battlefield at Spotsylvania Court House on
May 10, 1864. Courtesy of the Library of Congress.

Spotsylvania C.H.

McCoull house at Woodshaw farm. Headquarters of Edward Johnson. Courtesy of the Library of Congress.

Ruins of "LaVilla," home of Edgar and Ann Harrison and headquarters of Richard Ewell. Courtesy of the Library of Congress.

Confederate entrenchments at the Bloody Angle.
Courtesy of the Library of Congress.

Union Second Corps troops at the John Brown house, May 12.
Sketch by Alfred Waud. Courtesy of the Library of Congress.

Feby 12th 1864. The Brown House. A R Waud

Artist's print of the Mule Shoe struggle. Courtesy of the Library of Congress.

Union general Emory Upton's brigade at the Mule Shoe, May 12.
Sketch by Alfred Waud. Courtesy of the Library of Congress.

"The Toughest Fight Yet." Action at the Bloody Angle.
Sketch by Alfred Waud. Courtesy of the Library of Congress.

Artist's print, "Hancock's Corps Assaulting the Works at the 'Bloody Angle.'"
Courtesy of the Library of Congress.

Artillery shell in tree at the Bloody Angle. Courtesy of the Library of Congress.

Damaged trees in Mule Shoe after the fight. McCoull house reportedly in background. Courtesy of the Library of Congress.

Confederate dead at Harris farm after fight on May 19.
A similar scene would have been inside and outside Mule Shoe on May 13.
Courtesy of the Library of Congress.

{ 6 }

General, They Are Coming!

Twenty thousand officers and men of the Second Corps, Army of the Potomac, began moving forward at 4:35 A.M. on Thursday, May 12, 1864. In front, paces ahead in a long, single line, United States Sharpshooters and soldiers of the 66th New York acted as skirmishers, while veterans of the 2nd Delaware rimmed the Federals' left flank. In the heavy mist, they appeared indistinct, specters emerging from the early morning gloom.[1]

The Yankees came on at a "slow steady tramp," but within minutes they reached the enemy picket line along the Landrum farm lane. The Rebels were, recounted a New Englander, so "astonished at our appearance, marching on them out of the fog." The Federals captured many of the Louisianans and Virginians at the point of a bayonet. Those who eluded capture fled eastward. Some managed to trigger shots at the attackers, with one bullet killing Lieutenant Colonel David L. Stricker of the 2nd Delaware.[2]

Many of the blue-coated troops thought that they had overrun the main enemy works but, as a Pennsylvanian in the front rank stated, "the fire had been lighted." The Yankees started to advance at the double-quick and then to run, cheering loudly against orders. From the Mule Shoe, the Confederates peered through the fog until they saw their oncoming foes. Rifle fire flashed along the earthworks. A Southerner exclaimed: "Look out! boys! We will have blood for supper."[3]

Francis Barlow's division, with the regiments stacked in double columns and all officers on foot, crossed open ground in its advance. Once across the Landrum farm lane, Barlow's ranks followed a swale in the ground that funneled them to the left before approaching the salient's eastern face. Barlow said that they encountered only a "scattering and feeble fire" from the enemy. The "very thick abatis" slowed the attackers but, wrote Barlow, "this mass of men, coming so unexpectedly, was irresistible, and they surged over the works like a flood."[4]

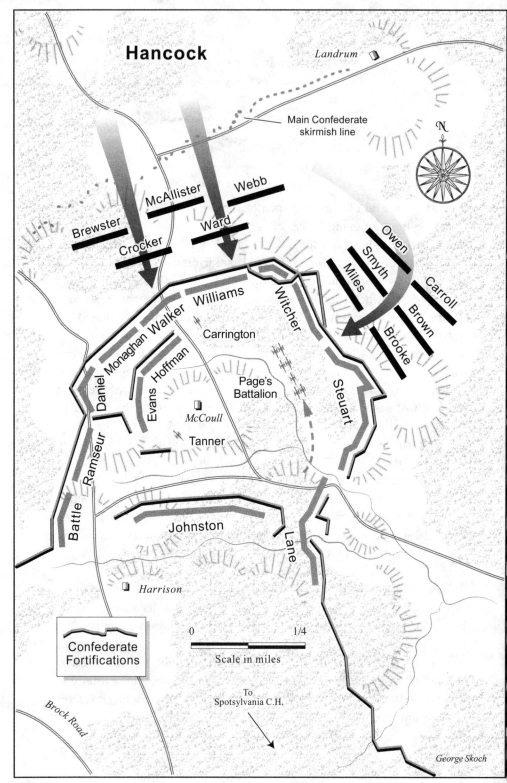

Hancock

Landrum

Main Confederate
skirmish line

N

McAllister   Webb

Brewster   Ward

Crocker

Owen

Smyth

Miles   Carroll

Brown

Brooke

Williams

Walker   Witcher

Monaghan   Carrington

Daniel   Hoffman

Evans   Page's
Battalion   Steuart

Ramseur   *McCoull*

Battle   Tanner

Johnston

Lane

Harrison

Confederate
Fortifications

0   1/4
Scale in miles

To
Spotsylvania C.H.

Brock Road

George Skoch

Union Second Corps Assault on Mule Shoe, 4:35 A.M.

Nelson Miles's brigade manned the right front of Barlow's columns and struck the Rebel earthworks held by William Witcher's three under-strength Virginia regiments—the 25th, 44th, and 50th. The color bearers of the 26th Michigan and 140th Pennsylvania each claimed the honor of placing the regimental flag on the works first. Behind both of them, how-ever, came their comrades "as if the devil had let loose," in the words of a gray-coated defender.[5]

Minutes later, nearly one thousand officers and men of Thomas Smyth's Irish Brigade climbed over the works. Private Henry J. Bell of the 116th Pennsylvania stopped on top of them and shouted amid the din, "Look out, throw down your arms, we run this machine now." No Con-federate likely heard him, but Bell's comrades and Miles's veterans did indeed "run this machine now." Against two enemy brigades, Witcher's five hundred or so Virginians seemingly disappeared under the onslaught.[6]

"Disorder and confusion," claimed a Yankee, characterized the struggle in the trenches and traverses. "Men became insane with the excitement of victory," admitted a Union officer, while another Federal declared, "Human life is held at a very cheap rate now." At such moments, individ-ual encounters defined the fury. A Virginian shot an enemy at close range, threw down his rifle, and said, "I surrender." Private Daniel Craw-ford of the 116th Pennsylvania saw his comrade fall and killed the Rebel. Close by, Private Billy Hager of Crawford's Company K met a handful of Southerners, leveled his rifle, and ordered them, "Throw down your arms, quick now or I'll stick my bayonet into you." They obeyed.[7]

A Virginian thrust his bayonet into the mouth of a soldier in the 140th Pennsylvania. The Federal seized the Rebel's rifle with his left hand and, with his right hand, plunged his bayonet into his foe's chest, killing him. Another Virginian, Private Ben Jones, thought of fighting until three Yankees confronted him and "had their guns leveled on me." Jones sur-rendered, arguing, "as Napoleon would done if he had been in my place."[8]

Like Jones, most of the Virginians gave up the struggle without much resistance. With words that applied to all of Witcher's regiments, the his-torian of the 50th Virginia related that it "was overwhelmed and the Union tide flowed over it." The 50th Virginia had 10 killed, 12 wounded, and 223 captured. The 44th Virginia suffered only one man slain and two wounded, while 16 officers and 158 enlisted men were captured. Dr. Abram Miller of the 25th Virginia claimed in a letter six days later that "the Reg were nearly all captured. We now have about 20 left." He added, "Our bri-gade will not be put in the fight unless it can't be avoided."[9]

Surgeon Miller confided to his wife what had become the talk in the army and the press in the struggle's aftermath: "I think our Brigade was to blame for the most of it. They have run on three occasions and no doubt they are to blame. The Brig. has never stood high and never will." A common view was expressed by a newspaper correspondent: "If Jones's [Witcher's] brigade had not given away it is possible, though not probable, that Johnson would have been able to maintain his ground."[10]

The Union assault had been "so terrific," stated a Confederate, that Witcher's troops had been simply overwhelmed by numbers. Barlow observed that enemy resistance "seems to have been very slight and ineffectual as if they were overpowered before they knew what was upon them." In the Virginians' defense, three of the brigade's regiments—the 21st, 42nd, and 48th—had been on picket duty, and their members had been either captured or trying to return to the salient when the Federals poured over the works, striking a badly weakened enemy command.[11]

Criticism of the Virginians' conduct awaited. For the present, their captors herded them into the trenches, where the Rebels sat down. An unarmed Captain Jonas A. Lipps of the 50th Virginia was still standing when a guard plunged his bayonet into Lipps's left arm above the elbow. A farm hand before the war, the strong Lipps pulled out the bayonet, seized the Yankee's rifle, and killed him. A Union captain witnessed the encounter and told Lipps, "Captain, you served him right."[12]

Among the Confederate prisoners was Edward Johnson. The division commander had ridden forward some three hundred yards from his headquarters at the McCoull house, arriving as the Federals closed on the salient's eastern face. "There was no surprise," he declared later. "My men were up and in the trenches prepared for the assault before the enemy made their appearance." Dismounting, Johnson endeavored to organize his fleeing troops. With him were his chief of staff Robert Hunter and officer of the day, David Anderson of the 44th Virginia.[13]

Johnson had his walking stick with him and used it, according to an account, "belaboring the men behind the works . . . to make them stand up." He shouted at the enemy troops, "Don't shoot into my men," before being taken prisoner. It was reported later by an eyewitness that Johnson "came near being killed by paying no heed to calls to surrender." Anderson was captured nearby, but Hunter, wearing a black coat without insignia, escaped.[14]

When Johnson had reached his troops, Major Richard Page's battalion of thirteen cannon was galloping into the salient. Page had been awakened at 3:40 A.M. with orders to move at once to the Mule Shoe. He roused his men and had them harness and hitch the horses and limber up the guns. Captain William Carter's King William (Virginia) Battery, consisting of a pair of ten-pounder Parrotts and a pair of twelve-pounder Napoleons, led the battalion's hurried return.[15]

The gun crews followed a narrow road through the woods, rolled through a marsh, and ascended the rise by the McCoull house. Carter's gunners unlimbered at the east angle behind Witcher's Virginians. The Confederates unlimbered one cannon, loaded it, and fired one round. Suddenly, they heard a shout—"Stop firing that gun"—and saw enemy infantrymen around the battery. The Federals seized the cannon and the artillerists.[16]

Captain Charles R. Montgomery's Morris (Virginia) Battery of three Napoleons halted behind and to the left of Carter's crews. While en route to the Mule Shoe, one of the gun crews had an accident and left the cannon behind. Montgomery's gunners managed to unlimber one piece as a crew member yelled to Lieutenant Charles Coleman, "Where shall I point the gun?" "At the Yankees," replied Coleman before a bullet struck the lieutenant, mortally wounding him. He never spoke again, and his remains were never recovered. The Federals bagged all three cannon and most of the artillerists.[17]

A section of two ten-pounder Parrotts from Captain Charles W. Fry's Orange (Virginia) Battery followed Montgomery's gun crews. "As we drove down into the marshy bottom and began to rise the hill to our positions," recounted Lieutenant S. Horace Hawes of the battery, "a sharp infantry fire met us, coming we couldn't tell from where, but seemed a cross fire." They arrived as Miles's and Smyth's Federals had shattered Witcher's ranks and seized Carter's and Montgomery's cannon. Hawes claimed later that one crew unlimbered a gun, loaded it, and fired a round of canister.[18]

"The smoke from the gun fell and obscured everything," asserted Hawes. "Before it fairly lifted they were upon us, and we were prisoners." Enemy gunfire wounded several of the Confederate artillerists, including the section's commander, Lieutenant William J. Deas, who was also captured. Hawes believed that had the artillery remained in the salient, it and Johnson's infantry would have repulsed the assault.[19]

Page's final battery, the Jeff Davis (Alabama) Artillery of four three-inch rifles, under Captain William J. Reese, entered the salient amid a worsening disaster along the trenches' eastern face. "After a hurried and difficult trip, over a rough and crooked road, crossed by boggy marshes," in the words of Private John Purifoy, the Alabama gun crews went into position near George Steuart's infantry brigade. When the battery arrived, however, Steuart's roughly 1,300 North Carolinians and Virginians were in a struggle for survival, assailed from the flank and the front.[20]

Steuart's men learned of the disaster to their north when fugitives from Witcher's regiments appeared out of the fog in a headlong rush. Behind them came a large disorderly throng of Miles's and Smyth's Federals, who were cheering as they closed in. "We could not believe our own ears," exclaimed a Confederate. A volley tore into the ranks of the 3rd and 1st North Carolina, posted along Steuart's left front. Some of the North Carolinians shouted, "The Yankees have flanked us."[21]

"For a short time the fighting was desperate," claimed Colonel Hamilton A. Brown of the 1st North Carolina. "The terrific onslaught of this vast multitude was irresistible." The pair of North Carolina regiments never had a chance, as the enemy assailed their ranks from the front, flank, and rear. The Federals captured nearly every member of the 3rd North Carolina and all except a reported thirty of the 1st North Carolina. Color bearer John Reams of Brown's regiment tore the flag from its staff, concealed it in his uniform, and secured it throughout his months in prison.[22]

The Yankees pouring over the earthworks belonged to the brigades of colonels John R. Brooke and Hiram L. Brown. Brooke's regiments were in front, and they and pioneers tore apart the heavy abatis, which Confederates called "tangle breeches." Brooke, said an officer, "is equaled by few officers in the army and should have been a brigadier-general long ago." Brown had commanded his troops only since May 10, when Colonel Paul Frank had been relieved for drunkenness.[23]

The Federals did not fire until they reached Steuart's line. Lieutenant Colonel George A. Fairlamb of the 148th Pennsylvania on Brooke's left stepped on to the works and, waving his sword, shouted, "Come on boys, the last day of the Rebellion is here." Fairlamb had barely spoken when a minié ball struck him, inflicting a severe wound.[24]

The 10th, 23rd, and 37th Virginia "fought desperately," with many of them resisting from the traverses. Earlier, their officers had had them draw old, damp loads from their rifles and ram in new, dry loads. The Confederates managed to fire volleys and wielded their bayonets against the Yankees. The struggle was, as Brooke reported, "a sharp, short fight." "Nothing but the formation of our attack," the Union colonel declared, "and the desperate valor of our troops could have carried the point."[25]

Almost completely surrounded, the Confederates were "compelled to surrender," as one of them admitted. Perhaps as many as two-thirds of the officers and men in the three Virginia regiments joined the North

Carolinians as prisoners. "We thought we had captured the whole Rebel Army," observed a Union staff officer. Colonel Brown of the 1st North Carolina professed later, "Every one who was present will ever remember the wreck and the anguish of that dark and direful day."[26]

Caught in the wreckage of Steuart's brigade were the four gun crews of the Jeff Davis Artillery. The Federals had closed on the Alabama gunners before they could unlimber the cannon. One crew, led by a sergeant, however, eluded the enemy infantrymen, saving a gun. Captain William Reese, a lieutenant, and thirty-three enlisted men were captured, while four gunners were killed. The battery would cease to exist as an organized unit. In a letter written to a newspaper three days later, a survivor blamed Steuart's troops for the battery's capture: "Some fought as become men and soldiers, whilst others have imprinted a stain upon their character that time cannot erase."[27]

George Steuart had joined his troops as a Union prisoner. The brigade commander had been captured at first by enlisted men, who then took him to Colonel James A. Beaver of the 148th Pennsylvania. "I would like to surrender to an officer of rank," Steuart stated.

"I will be very glad to receive your surrender, sir," responded Beaver. "Whom have I the honor to address."

"General Steuart."

"What! Jeb Stuart?" exclaimed Beaver.

"No, George H. Steuart of the infantry," answered the brigadier.

Beaver asked for his sword.

"Well, sah," drawled Steuart, "you all waked us up so early this mawnin that I didn't git it on."

Beaver ordered a private to escort Steuart to brigadier commander Brooke.[28]

The eastern face of the salient had been swept clear of its defenders. Barlow's Yankees had captured more than one thousand prisoners, a dozen cannon, and several enemy battle flags. "It will be one of the greatest charges in the history of the world," Lieutenant Morris Brown Jr. of the 126th New York bragged to his parents in a letter four days later. "It was grand but terrible." For the present, Brown and his comrades dealt with their prisoners and heard or witnessed the fury along the apex of the Mule Shoe.[29]

Captain William Seymour stood with fellow members of Colonel Jesse Williams's Louisiana brigade in the trenches along the Mule Shoe's blunt apex. They looked to the north through the fog as the morning's stillness had been shattered by gunfire and the cheers of thousands of men. "Never have I seen such an exciting spectacle as then met my gaze," remembered Seymour, the brigade's adjutant. "As far as the eye could reach, the field was covered with the serried ranks of the enemy." This May 12 marked Seymour's 32nd birthday and, as he noted later, "a stirring one it was."[30]

To the Louisianans' left, the five Virginia regiments of the Stonewall Brigade manned the breastworks. Minutes earlier, their commander, James Walker, had been awakened by a soldier, who exclaimed, "General, they are coming!" The brigadier stirred from his "dog" tent shelter and shouted, "Fall in!" The Virginians rushed into the trenches. The Yankees were that close, attested Walker, that "the heavy tramp of a large body of infantry and the sharp words of command could be distinctly heard."[31]

The Federals coming at the Confederate brigades—four lines, eight ranks deep—belonged to the divisions of David Birney and Gershom Mott, twenty-nine regiments from the disbanded Third Corps. Birney's brigades, under J. H. Hobart Ward and John S. Crocker, led the attack, followed by Mott's two brigades, under Robert McAllister and William Brewster. Before they had formed ranks and heard the orders at the Brown farm, "we little knew what our Corps was to do," the 17th Maine's color bearer, Edwin Emery, admitted to his sister in a subsequent letter.[32]

The two divisions had stepped forth when Francis Barlow's units advanced. Initially, Birney's and Ward's troops passed through woods and brush, with some of the men tripping and falling. When they cleared the trees, they overran the Rebel pickets along the Landrum lane, capturing most of them without firing a shot. A few of the enemy "skipped for dear life" and escaped. These Yankees also thought that they had captured the main Confederate line and started cheering. Officers ordered them forward double-quick across the three hundred yards of open ground.[33]

Ward's veterans struck the Mule Shoe just west of the east angle, charging into the Louisianans. Brigadier Ward had "seemed in a most gloomy mood" and had "fussed and fretted all day." He had drunk whiskey, which made him "on edge and full of fight." Before they advanced, Ward had told Lieutenant Colonel Charles H. Weygant of the 124th New York, "I expect you to take your regiment over the works this time or die in the attempt."[34]

Weygant's "Orange Blossoms," as they were known, joined fellow New Yorkers, Pennsylvanians, and Indianans in Ward's front line, swarming over the works and into the ranks of the Louisianans, who had fired one or two volleys at the oncoming Federals. The struggle was hand-to-hand for a few minutes. Private Stephen P. Chase of the 86th New York said of the Rebels, "they gave us quite a reception." The Louisianans' Colonel Williams was shot and killed at the outset. A fine officer, the thirty-three-year-old Williams had led the brigade at Gettysburg and periodically since then.[35]

"Great slaughter on both sides," a soldier in the 20th Indiana jotted in his diary afterward. Weygant remembered seeing a dead Confederate pinned to a tree by a fired ramrod. Allegedly, a handful of Southerners had surrendered and laid down their guns. When their captors passed on, the Southerners grabbed their rifles, shooting their foes in their backs. Indianans witnessed the treachery and bayoneted the Confederates to death.[36]

The fighting between Ward's Yankees and the Louisianans spilled over into the trenches held by the Stonewall Brigade. The Virginians manned the works along the apex from the Louisianans' left flank to the west angle and then along the salient's western face. Toward them directly came Crocker's Federals in two lines. Lieutenant Thomas Doyle of the 33rd Virginia recalled the enemy's approach: "The figures of the men seen dimly through the smoke and fog seemed almost gigantic."[37]

"We were ordered to reserve our fire until near enough to tell on them [the Yankees] with effect," offered Private James L. McCown of the 5th Virginia. When the Federals neared, the Confederates triggered their rifles, followed by the "pop! pop! pop! of exploding caps as the hammer fell upon them." The rain had dampened the powder in the paper cartridges, resulting in the misfires. Brigade commander Walker stated that a "muzzle loading musket with damp powder behind the ball is as useless to a soldier in an emergency like that as a walking cane."[38]

Crocker's blue-coated veterans surged over the earthworks and into the trenches. Union officers rode their horses up to the works and then stepped on top of them. The Virginians recoiled into the traverses, extracted the wet rounds, reloaded their rifles, and fought. "For a time, every soldier was a fiend," exclaimed Private John Haley of the 17th Maine. "The attack was fierce—the resistance fanatical." The 33rd Virginia's Lieutenant John P. Hite believed the struggle to be the "most desperate fight of the war."[39]

A Virginian, Private Andrew Long, remembered the fury: "No sooner would a flag fall than another carrier who picked it up would be shot or bayonetted. Men were so close their hands were at the end of gun muzzles as they shot each other. When ammunition ran out or got wet they crushed each other's skulls with gun butts." Private McCown wrote later:

"It was terrific beyond any description. Every twig seemed cut down." In the midst of the fighting, Captain George Washington Kurtz told McCown, "This is the hottest place I was ever in."[40]

"The din was tremendous and increasing every instant," related Lieutenant Doyle. "Men in crowds with bleeding limbs, and pale, pain-stricken faces, were hurrying to the rear, and, mingled with these could be seen many unwounded who had escaped from the wrecks of their comrades." He continued, "All that human courage and endurance would effect was done by these men on this frightful morning, but all was to no avail."[41]

On the Stonewall Brigade's right next to the Louisianans, Colonel William Terry swung the 4th Virginia perpendicular to the earthworks to confront Ward's Federals head-on. Like their comrades, Terry's veterans manned the traverses and "held with a steadiness worthy of their traditions." But, as Terry professed, "the overwhelming numbers of the enemy . . . made successful resistance impossible." He asserted later that his officers and men had been "sacrificed," with three out of four of them killed, wounded, or captured. Terry suffered a severe wound but escaped.[42]

Brigadier Walker had been standing with the 4th Virginia when the enemy attack struck. He stayed there as the Federals engaged the Virginians. "General Walker met them at the head of his men and fought like a tiger," stated a Confederate. A Yankee fired at him at close range, with the bullet shattering his left elbow joint. Some of the Virginians spared him from capture, carrying the unconscious general to a field hospital in the rear.[43]

Dr. Hunter McGuire, chief surgeon of the Second Corps, probed for the bullet, which awakened Walker. McGuire and another doctor discussed amputation of the arm. "I'd rather die than lose my arm," pleaded the general. A Dr. Galt, a skillful and experienced surgeon, did a resection of the elbow, sawing out the joint, suturing together the nerves and muscles of the upper and lower arm, and placing the injured limb between a pair of wooden splints.[44]

In the Mule Shoe, meanwhile, Gershom Mott's two Union brigades entered the fighting. Federal numbers prevailed, finally routing the Stonewall Brigade. The Yankees then swept down the salient's western face, attacking Colonel William Monaghan's Louisiana regiments.[45]

Monaghan withdrew the brigades about 150 yards to a rise and wheeled the ranks around to confront the charging Federals. The Tigers fired volleys, but their foes, "yelling like devils," closed in, igniting a frenzy of hand-to-hand combat. The Louisianans had been in such encounters before and, supported by Junius Daniel's North Carolinians of Robert Rodes's division, repulsed the Yankees. The stand by the Confederates limited the enemy's penetration along this section of the salient.[46]

The collapse of the apex line and the flight of its defenders exposed Captain James Carrington's four-gun Charlottesville (Virginia) Battery and Captain William Tanner's four-gun Richmond (Virginia) Battery. Initially, the gun crews were uncertain of the situation north of them as the "smoke and mist rendered all objects indistinct," in the words of an artillerist. A short time later, according to a member of Tanner's battery, "I never heard such yelling in my life, the whole earth seemed alive with Yankees."[47]

The fleeing Confederate infantrymen prevented the gun crews from opening fire until the infantrymen passed through and around the cannon. Carrington's and Tanner's artillerists managed to discharge rounds before being overrun by troops of Birney's and Mott's divisions. The Federals seized all eight of the Napoleons and dozens of the Virginians, including Carrington. The victorious troops began turning some of the guns around to fire on their retreating opponents.[48]

The Union Second Corps's final division, commanded by John Gibbon, had been assigned a reserve role in the assault. When the other three divisions advanced, Gibbon followed Francis Barlow's columns with two of his three brigades, under Brigadier General Joshua T. Owen and Colonel Samuel S. Carroll. These Federals came closely behind Barlow's troops against the salient's eastern face. As the Federals charged up the rise, "we broke into a run," stated Corporal William Haines of the 12th New Jersey, "and all line or formation was soon lost, as each man seemed trying to outrun his fellows, and we went up that slope for about two hundred yards just like a tornado."[49]

Confederate defenders still remained along this section of the salient and fired on Owen's and Carroll's attackers. The 1st Delaware's Color Sergeant David Riggs said to his comrades during the advance, "I'll plant this on the rebel breastworks or die in the attempt." He reached the slope and was killed. While urging his men forward, Captain Mitchell Smith, commanding the 71st Pennsylvania, died.[50]

Gibbon's troops joined Barlow's officers and men inside the works, where for a few minutes the struggle was "hand-to-hand and bloodthirsty in the extreme." Nearly every regimental commander in Carroll's brigade fell killed or wounded. Members of the brigade helped in seizing the cannon of Captain William Reese's Jeff Davis (Alabama) Battery.[51]

Gibbon's third brigade, led by Brigadier General Alexander Webb, joined in the assault, striking the Mule Shoe works near the east angle between Barlow's and David Birney's commands. Once in the trenches, Webb's veterans drove west against the Louisianans and then the Virginians of the Stonewall Brigade. One of Webb's officers claimed the combat to be the "fiercest hand-to-hand fighting of the war." Although seriously wounded, Major James W. Welch of the 19th Maine captured the flag of the 33rd Virginia.[52]

By now, the time neared 5:15 A.M., roughly forty minutes since the blue-coated attackers had started forth from the Brown farm. During those minutes the Mule Shoe had become engulfed in a frenzy of combat, marked by acrid, dense smoke; by the sounds of rifle and cannon fire, of men's screams, and of officers' shouts; and by utter confusion. The nature of a Civil War battle contained all of these characteristics to a degree, but in the early morning's darkness, fog, and drizzle amid the salient's trenches and traverses, the fury further disoriented the combatants. Their words afterward testified to the intensity of those moments that had enveloped them.[53]

The result of the fearful struggle had been a staggering reality within the Mule Shoe. In about half an hour, Edward Johnson's Confederate division had all but disappeared under an avalanche of Yankees. "What was left," in the words of one of them, amounted to fewer than 1,500 officers and men. The survivors appeared "played out—not worth a cent," but, to their credit, many of the Virginians, North Carolinians, and Louisianans had resisted in an untenable tactical situation. Left without artillery support and confronting nearly five times their numbers, Johnson's veterans had endeavored to make a defensive stand until overwhelmed.[54]

Nevertheless, soldiers, even tested fighters, cannot endure under such circumstances. They had been roused early from sleep, ordered into the trenches, heard rumors of an impending storm, and saw it appear through the fog in a flood tide of dark forms. Before long they were fighting Yankees in front and on the flanks. With the prospect of being wounded, killed, or sent to a prison camp, those who could fled. "The panic at one time was fearful," admitted staff officer Jedediah Hotchkiss.[55]

Rapidly overrun by fleeing Rebels and oncoming Yankees had been the batteries of James Carrington and William Tanner and the thirteen-gun battalion of Richard Page. A few of the artillerists managed to fire a round or more before being surrounded by bayoneted enemy rifles. Many of the artillerists must have felt helpless and angry, and some might have shared the bitterness of Thomas Carter, who declared that "the infantry behaved like curs" by abandoning the gun crews to their fate. Like many of their infantry comrades, scores of battery members were destined for a Northern prison.[56]

The reaction among the Confederates' foes, however, had been starkly different. While waiting at the Brown farm, they had felt apprehensive about another frontal assault; but in the aftermath of the fighting, the foreboding gave way to exhilaration over the stunning victory against a renowned enemy. Hundreds, if not thousands, of them "broke into a wild hurrah." Around them were the trophies from the assault—twenty cannon and a reported nearly thirty stands of colors. Seventeen officers and men who had seized the Confederate flags would be awarded the Medal of Honor.[57]

The greatest trophy was the droves of Rebel prisoners. At five o'clock, while the fighting continued, Winfield Hancock had wired army headquarters: "Our men have the works, with some hundred prisoners; impossible to say how many; the whole line moving up. This part of the line held by Ewell." Hancock's "hundred prisoners" amounted to an estimated three thousand or more. The 148th Pennsylvania's Colonel James Beaver scratched in his diary later that the captives "poured through the column by thousands." The Federals had started to herd them out of the salient into the open fields.[58]

Details from the Union regiments escorted the Confederate prisoners to the rear. One of the detachments, soldiers from the 53rd Pennsylvania, led several hundred captives and carried four enemy flags out of the salient. Lieutenant Harvey B. Wells of the 84th Pennsylvania asserted, "The prisoners were a ragged-looking delegation, and assumed a defiant air." Some of the captured Rebels helped wounded Yankees toward field hospitals.[59]

One prisoner, a Virginian in the Stonewall Brigade, related that "a heavy guard was placed over the captives as soon as taken, which was never for one instant relaxed." When they reached a "roadbed"—likely the Landrum farm lane—the Union escorts separated Confederate officers from the enlisted men. The guards marched the privates, corporals, and sergeants to a large field farther to the rear, where Federal provost marshals assumed responsibility for the prisoners.[60]

Among the Southern officers walked Edward Johnson and George Steuart. Guards took the two generals to Winfield Hancock, who was probably in the vicinity of the Landrum farm lane or homestead. Willis

Landrum, two adult women, and four children still remained in the one-and-a-half story, four-room house. They would not flee from their home until later in the afternoon.[61]

Lieutenant Wells saw Johnson and wrote later that the general "was sullen and morose as a man cheated out of a good dinner." Captain Winfield Scott of the 126th New York said that Johnson was "a large, well-built, red-faced man, dressed very plainly, and looked like a well-to-do Virginia farmer." Johnson thanked the guards for their kindness. "You are damned welcome," replied a sergeant.[62]

Hancock met Johnson and Steuart, greeting both men cordially. Hancock and Johnson had served together in the antebellum army, and Hancock, approaching his old friend and extending a hand, said, "I am glad to see you, Ned." "Under other circumstances I would be pleased to meet you," answered the Virginian. According to an account published in a Richmond newspaper three weeks later, Johnson "sat on a stump, covering his face, wept, alleging that he had rather been killed than taken prisoner."[63]

In turn, the Union corps commander held out his hand to the Confederate brigadier to shake, inquiring, "How are you, Steuart?" "Under the circumstances," answered the captive, "I decline to take your hand." Visibly displeased by the discourtesy, Hancock replied, "And under any other circumstances I should not have offered it." Hancock directed that Steuart be escorted on foot farther to the rear.[64]

Eventually, Steuart arrived at Sixth Corps headquarters, where Captain Edward Russell, a staff officer, described the captured general in a letter written three days later: "Stuart [sic] put on too many airs & when civilities were offered him acted so discourteously that he was permitted to march through the mud at the head of his command to the rear instead of riding as had at first been intended. A six mile tramp somewhat abated his haughtiness to the 'Yanks.'"[65]

Hancock saw to it, however, that after he and his old comrade shared a drink, the Union general had Johnson mounted on a horse as he was taken rearward. En route to Federal headquarters, Johnson met another fellow officer from their antebellum days together, Brigadier General Frank Wheaton, a Sixth Corps brigade commander. It was a cordial exchange, with the two men shaking hands and asking about each other. From there, the mounted escort took Johnson to the general-in-chief's headquarters, arriving by about 6:30 A.M.[66]

The Confederate general received a warm welcome from Ulysses Grant, George Meade, and their staff members. The mood at Union headquarters had been upbeat after receiving messages from Hancock. Meade stepped forth and shook hands with Johnson, asking, "Why, how do you do, general?" The pair of soldiers had been cadets together at West Point. Turning toward Grant, Meade said, "General Grant, this is General Johnson—Edward Johnson."

Grant shook his hand and remarked: "How do you do? It is a long time since we last met."

"Yes, it is a great many years," Johnson responded, "and I had not expected to meet you under such circumstances."

"It is one of the many sad fortunes of war," Grant reflected.[67]

The Northerner and the Southerner had been comrades in the conflict with Mexico. Grant offered Johnson a cigar and a camp stool to sit upon. Grant promised "to make you as comfortable as possible" as they reminisced. Theodore Lyman thought Johnson "was terribly mortified and kept coughing to hide his nervousness." The general-in-chief bid his fellow soldier farewell and left Johnson under the supervision of an adjutant, Brigadier General Seth Williams.[68]

Williams fed Johnson breakfast, and the two generals conversed. At one point, Johnson stated, "Doubtless you have gained an advantage, but you are much mistaken if you think we are beaten yet!" Finally, escorts led Johnson away as a prisoner. In time, he and Steuart were exchanged, with Johnson assigned to the western theater and Steuart returning to the Army of Northern Virginia.[69]

In the Mule Shoe, meanwhile, officers tried to restore order among upward of 19,000 Federals jammed together. "What ought to have been done was plain . . . ," Francis Barlow knew. "The occasion for 'charging,' for rush and confusion, was past, and the troops ought to have been soberly and deliberately put in position, and ordered to sweep down the rebel line." They had to press south farther into the salient. It was less than an hour since these veterans had advanced from the Brown farm and, as a Confederate admitted, "they were complete masters of the works within that limit."[70]

{ 7 }

The Situation Was Critical

General Robert E. Lee and the Army of Northern Virginia confronted a crisis of unknown magnitude minutes after five o'clock on the morning of Thursday, May 12, 1864. Officers and men of the Union Second Corps had overrun Edward Johnson's Confederate division and had scoured the Mule Shoe's trenches of its defenders. The Yankees had gouged a three-fourths mile gap in Lee's lines northwest of Spotsylvania Court House. In front of the nineteen thousand or more victorious troops now stood Brigadier General John B. Gordon and his three brigades of perhaps 4,600 veteran Rebels.[1]

Lee regarded Gordon as one of the most promising officers in the army. Without prior military training, the thirty-two-year-old Georgian had entered Confederate service as the unanimously elected major of the 6th Alabama. Seriously wounded at Antietam, he returned to active duty in March 1863, with the rank of brigadier. "Not to promote him," stated Porter Alexander, "would have been a scandal." When Jubal Early had replaced an unwell A. P. Hill at the head of the Third Corps after the battle at the Wilderness on May 8, Lee had selected Gordon as Early's successor.[2]

Six feet tall, thin, rail straight, and darkly handsome, Gordon possessed a personal magnetism on a battlefield. He could inspire with words or by example. One of his men told an artillery officer: "Did you ever see the Gin'ral in battle? He's most the prettiest thing you ever did see on a field of fight. It'ud put fight into a whipped chicken just to look at him."[3]

"Gordon always had something pleasant to say to his men," remembered Private John Worsham of the 21st Virginia, "and I will bear my testimony that he was the most gallant man I ever saw on a battlefield. He had a way of putting things to the men that was irresistible, and he showed them at all times that he shrank from nothing in battle." He had one of those rare memories for recalling his troops' names and faces. "He enjoyed the love and confidence of every man under him," declared an Alabamian.[4]

When Gordon's veterans saw his striking figure dressed "for a ball" before a fight, they hurriedly ate their rations, recalled one of them, "lest they should die before they had a chance to finish them." His tactics amid combat's fury often had a boldness, an originality to them. Artillery officer Thomas Carter said of the Georgian, "He is a giant on the field, not only by his personal courage but by that sort of instinct which teaches a leader to do the right thing at the right time & in the right manner."[5]

On this morning, Gordon had stirred his troops about three o'clock. Lee's instructions to Gordon from the day before had not changed, "generally to support any portion of the line around the long salient which might be attacked." In response to Richard Ewell's orders overnight, Gordon had posted the brigades of John S. Hoffman and Clement Evans in the rear of Johnson's left flank and Robert Rodes's division's right flank along the salient's western leg. Gordon's third brigade under Robert S. Johnston had bivouacked north of the Edgar Harrison residence.[6]

Before daylight, Gordon and his staff members heard "a roll of musketry" and then silence. Moments later, however, a soldier encountered Gordon and exclaimed, "General, I think there's something wrong down in the woods near where General Edward Johnson's men are." Gordon hesitated briefly to act, but the mounting clamor through the darkness and fog to the front convinced him, as he related years after the war: "I was at once impressed with apprehension that the enemy has carried our works." He sent his aides with instructions to Hoffman, Evans, and Johnston.[7]

Although Gordon judged the situation correctly, he could not have known the extent of the disaster that had enveloped Johnson's division. Gordon admitted afterward that he could see only a few rods ahead through the fog. He reacted instinctively, consolidating his scattered brigades and preparing for either a stand or a counterattack. He remained alone for minutes as his staff members failed to rejoin him.[8]

Within the Mule Shoe, the Union attackers struggled to reform the ranks. "A thoroughly mixed mass of soldiers never existed," wrote Captain Alexander W. Acheson of the 140th Pennsylvania. Francis Barlow observed as much, "Of course the troops which had made the assault were in the most complete confusion." Men huddled together; some rifled through the Confederate camps, gathering spoils. The soldiers did, however, manage to go forward into the woods by the McCoull house and south along the trenches on both sides of the salient.[9]

Barlow's and John Gibbon's troops pushed deeper in the trenches and across the traverses on the Mule Shoe's eastern leg, quickly encountering Brigadier General James Lane's five North Carolina regiments of Cadmus Wilcox's Third Corps division. Lane's veterans learned of the enemy's success in the salient when George Steuart's men came "flying in utter confusion in every direction." Behind them before long, the Yankees struck the 28th North Carolina and then the 18th North Carolina, capturing scores of Confederates.[10]

Lane, meanwhile, wheeled around his other three regiments—the 33rd, 37th, and 7th—to confront the Federals. Lieutenant Colonel William H. A. Speer of the 37th North Carolina stated that his troops rallied in an "arm" of the works on a hill, and "here took place one of the most desperate fights, for the times, of the war." The Yankees pressed ahead into frontal and flank musketry from the North Carolinians. The Rebels then counterattacked, bagging some prisoners and checking the enemy's penetration in this sector. Lane wrote that he did not see Lee or Gordon, "nor did I know anything of what was going on, on the left of the Army."[11]

Across the Mule Shoe on the western side, the Southerners had cobbled together a makeshift defensive line composed of Colonel William Monaghan's reformed ranks of Louisianans, three Georgia regiments—the 13th, 26th, and 38th—of Evans's brigade, and North Carolinians under Brigadier General Junius Daniel. The 45th North Carolina faced about in the works. Behind the infantry, four three-inch rifles of Captain Benjamin H. Smith Jr.'s 3rd Company Richmond (Virginia) Howitzers and four twelve-pounder Napoleons of Captain Asher W. Garber's Staunton (Virginia) Battery had deployed.[12]

The Louisianans, Georgians, and North Carolinians braced themselves as a massive, disorganized swarm of Yankees—members of the divisions of David Birney and Gershom Mott—emerged from the dense fog. Musketry flashed from the Confederate ranks and discharges spewed from cannon as the enemy, "yelling like devils," charged. The Rebels clung to a rise and traverses against repeated attacks. "We had to be low in our works to keep from being hit in the backs owing to the crooked works," wrote a North Carolinian in his diary. The defenders blunted the final Federal effort, limiting the breach in this section.[13]

Gordon, meanwhile, had met the 1,300 North Carolinians in Robert Johnston's four regiments. Lee had transferred the brigade into the division on May 8. During the preceding winter, evidently the entire rank and file had reenlisted for the duration of the conflict, earning praise for their patriotism and devotion to the cause in a resolution of the Confederate Congress. The 5th, 12th, 20th, and 23rd regiments composed the brigade.[14]

An antebellum lawyer, Johnston had entered Confederate service as a captain in the 23rd North Carolina. After distinguishing himself at the Battle of Williamsburg on May 5, 1862, he was elected colonel of the regiment in its reorganization. He fell severely wounded at Gettysburg, where the brigade, commanded by Alfred Iverson, suffered decimating losses in an attack on Oak Ridge on the afternoon of July 1, 1863. Promoted to brigadier general on September 2, 1863, Johnston was assigned to command of the brigade.[15]

When he received Gordon's orders to advance, Johnston filed the brigade into a column and went forward from its campsite near the Harrison house. Gordon joined Johnston at the head of the column between the second line of works along the salient's base and the McCoull house. Near the farmhouse, the North Carolinians encountered Richard Ewell, who was, according to Johnston, "under very great excitement, pulling his moustache with both hands." The corps commander shouted to Johnston, "Charge them Gen'l D[am]n em charge em."[16]

Johnston called back, "All right Gen'l but wait until my men get into position." The North Carolinians shifted into line. Gordon angled the brigade to the right front. "I moved with the utmost rapidity across an open field to the point of attack and entered the woods," recounted Johnston. Gordon rode with them, stating later, "You could not see a line of troops 100 yds. off."[17]

The North Carolinians collided suddenly with Federals from the divisions of Barlow and Gibbon. The two foes were only twenty paces apart at points when the Yankees triggered a volley. "A furious fight began at once," declared Johnston. Lieutenant Colonel John S. Brooks, commanding the 20th North Carolina, was killed as a bullet passed through his canteen into his side. Brooks had been a farmer before the war. A pair of Union officers shouted for the Confederates to surrender, and both were shot down where they stood.[18]

Johnston believed that the struggle in the woods near the McCoull house was "the most desperate situation I was in during the whole war." At one point, he thought that their opponents were wavering, so seizing the flag of his old regiment, the 23rd, he led his men forward. A spent minié ball struck him in the head, disabling him. Colonel Thomas M. Garrett of the 5th North Carolina assumed command of the brigade and was killed within minutes. The 20th North Carolina's Colonel Thomas F. Toon succeeded Garrett. Enemy numbers "overpowered," in Gordon's word, the Rebels, driving them back through the woods.[19]

A soldier in the 12th North Carolina described the woods as "one of the bloodiest scenes of the war." He added, "The ground was strewn with the dead and dying of the regiment and the brigade." More than two-thirds of his comrades in the 12th lay killed or wounded. In the 5th at the end of the day, only forty-two members answered roll call. "I do not remember any battle during the war that there was a closer and hotter fight," observed Johnston years later.[20]

Gordon wrote subsequently that the object of Johnston's charge "being by sheer audacity to confound the enemy until I could find out more of the situation and get my troops in line." He considered their fearful sacrifice as vital in buying critical time. With the North Carolinians' repulse, Gordon admitted, "I at once discovered that the situation was critical."[21]

Robert E. Lee rose early on Thursday, May 12, as he habitually did. Mounting Traveller, Lee rode from his headquarters in or near the village to the Edgar Harrison house. While en route, Lee might have encountered the artillery batteries on their return to the salient. Lee and his staff officers arrived at the Harrison residence, Richard Ewell's headquarters, almost assuredly before the Union assault went forth. The commanding general could not have been there long before those at the house heard "a sharp fire on Johnson's front."[22]

What happened next with Lee is subject to conflicting accounts. An aide, Charles Venable, claimed years later that Lee spurred Traveller into a gallop, evidently crossing the reserve line of works at the salient's base and halting near the woods around the McCoull farm. He found the field and woods "dotted with men coming to the rear" and "our army was at a great crisis," according to an eyewitness.[23]

"The occasion," wrote Venable of the army commander, "aroused all the combative energies of his soldier nature." Lee tried to rally the fleeing soldiers, doing so in his calm manner at such critical moments on a battlefield. Whether Ewell was with him at this time remains unclear. At some point, perhaps now, the two generals were together, endeavoring to stem the flow of the disorganized and defeated troops. Different versions agreed that the reactions of Lee and Ewell contrasted sharply.[24]

Lee remained, professed an artillery officer, "perfectly calm and self-possessed," while a staff officer related that the commander "quietly exhorted the men not to forget their manhood and their duty, but to return to the field." To others Lee allegedly said, "Boys, do not run away, go back, *go back*, your comrades need you in the trenches." Lee's manner and words halted those whom he met.[25]

Conversely, Ewell appeared to be "greatly excited and, in a towering passion." He "swore with all of his old-time vehemence and volubility," claimed a junior officer. To a group of fugitives, Ewell lashed out: "Yes, G[o]d d[am]n you run, run; the Yankees will catch you. That's right, go as fast as you can." Lieutenant Colonel William Allan, the corps's chief of ordnance, claimed Ewell "lost his head in the severity of the fight." When Lee witnessed Ewell's profane reaction, he apparently chided his subordinate: "You must restrain yourself; how can you expect to control these men when you have lost control of yourself? If you cannot repress your excitement, you had better retire." If accurate, it was the severest of rebukes from Lee.[26]

Lee's and Ewell's efforts at rallying Edward Johnson's shredded ranks could not withstand, however, the onrush of thousands of Union troops deeper into the Mule Shoe. Lee, Ewell, and their aides retired before the tide of Yankees. A blue-coated infantrymen recorded in his diary, "we went in 'pell mell,' 'helter skeler.'"[27]

"Another line beyond must be taken," as Captain Alexander Acheson of the 140th Pennsylvania described the advance toward the salient's base. "Another charge, over captured batteries, abandoned caissons, through deserted tents and camp equipment." The 12th New Jersey's Captain George Bowen wrote, "We followed up the enemy driving them before us through the woods and brush up to another interior line of entrenchments occupied by another line of troops."[28]

The dense fog blinded the Yankees to what lay beyond the fieldworks— roughly 2,300 Confederates in eight regiments. When the Federals struck the Mule Shoe, John Gordon ordered John S. Hoffman's Virginians and Clement Evans's Georgians to withdraw from their reserve position behind the salient's western leg. Three of Evans's six regiments had remained in place, fighting beside Louisianans and North Carolinians. Hoffman and Evans led their veterans south toward the Harrison house, halting past the reserve line of works that Gordon had had constructed along the salient's base.[29]

Hoffman brought his five regiments into line—the 58th, 13th, 52nd, 31st, and 49th Virginia. The brigade's senior colonel, Hoffman had succeeded Brigadier General John Pegram, who been wounded in a knee in the Wilderness on May 6. Captain Samuel Buck of the 13th Virginia regarded Hoffman "as brave as man could be, but no officer." Private William Smith of the 49th Virginia stated that the enlisted men thought Hoffman to be "a hard, brave fighter, but not a military man." A lawyer before the war, the forty-two-year-old Hoffman suffered from acute myopia and needed eyeglasses to see. Another Virginian described him as "a dull and slow man, unsuited to command . . . a brigade."[30]

On the Virginians' right flank, Evans deployed his three regiments—the 13th, 26th, and 38th Georgia. The thirty-one-year-old Evans had taken command of the brigade when Gordon assumed leadership of the division on May 8. An attorney and a judge before the conflict, Evans fought in most of the army's major battles as major and colonel of the 31st Georgia. He was, believed Private G. W. Nichols, "almost an idol in the brigade."[31]

A Georgian recalled, "The opening of the day was such as to inspire a longing for home and the comfortable fireside." But duty and other sentiments bound him and his comrades to the ranks as the fury approached. They had witnessed the "panic stricken" fellow soldiers of Johnson's division in their flight to the rear. "For veterans as we were," noted Private Smith, "we could see the seriousness of the disaster."[32]

Gordon had joined the Virginians and Georgians. While preparing to lead them forward in the charge, Lee appeared, reining in Traveller before the 49th Virginia on Hoffman's right, next to the Georgians. The commanding officer removed his hat and turned Traveller toward the front, planning, it seemed, to lead the men with Gordon. Unquestionably, Lee possessed a combative nature, his calm demeanor on a battlefield belying the fiery soul of a warrior. "In the writer's experience," observed Armistead Long in his memoirs, "General Lee never unnecessarily courted danger, though he never cautiously avoided it."[33]

At this time, as it had been on May 6 in the Wilderness, the army faced a crippling defeat, if not destruction. Lee believed, contended Long, that "his presence and action were necessary to stimulate the men to greater deeds of valor." The army's chief of ordnance, Lieutenant Colonel Briscoe G. Baldwin, agreed, maintaining that Lee's determination to be with the troops and to lead them resulted from "the critical state of things." "Gen Lee insisted on remaining under fire at the threatened point," explained Baldwin, "& that they [his aides] were all trembling but he should be struck."[34]

Gordon had reacted, meanwhile, to the commanding general's apparent inclination. Speaking in a loud voice so the officers and men could hear him, Gordon said, "General Lee this is no place for you." The brigadier then pointed to the troops and stated: "These men are Georgians and Virginians. They have never failed you and will not fail you here. You must go to the rear."[35]

Amid shouts of "General Lee to the rear. General Lee to the rear," Gordon took Traveller's bridle and turned the horse around. Reportedly, Sergeant William A. Compton of the 49th Virginia grabbed the reins and guided Lee through the ranks to the rear. Gordon seized the flag of a Georgia regiment, turned in the saddle, and shouted, "Forward, charge!" The Virginians and Georgians emitted yells and went forward.[36]

The scene might have been much like this description offered by the historian of the 63rd Pennsylvania years later: "When the Union men charged, it was with heads erect, shoulders squared and thrown back, and with a firm stride, but when the Johnnies charged, it was with a jog trot in a half-bent position, and though they might be met with heavy and blighting volleys, they came on with the pertinacity of bulldogs, filling up the gaps and trotting on with their never-ceasing 'ki-yi' until we found them face to face."[37]

On this morning, on this piece of war-torn Virginia soil, the "face to face" confrontation came at the reserve line of works at the salient's base. The Virginians and Georgians arrived almost simultaneously with a disorganized host of Yankees, who, "inspirited with success," had poured past the McCoull house, charging toward the Harrison home. On the way, some of them overran Asher Garber's Staunton Battery, capturing the four cannon. Men from all four Union divisions were among the attackers. "No attempt to keep a line," declared one of them.[38]

Private James Donnelly of the 20th Massachusetts related, "We came right plum up to an advancing line of battle before we were aware of it." Then with the opposing ranks twenty paces apart, both sides triggered volleys into their foes. Color bearers placed flags on the works and were gunned down. The 124th New York's commander, Charles Weygant, picked up the fallen banner of the 141st Pennsylvania, carried it to the works, and suffered a serious shoulder wound.[39]

Brigade commander Alexander Webb, whom Theodore Lyman called "the precise Webb," fell with a head wound thirty yards from the fieldworks. The 116th Pennsylvania's Lieutenant Colonel Richard C. Dale raised his sword and shouted to his men, "forward boys, forward boys." He scaled the works and disappeared amid the musketry and smoke. "Of course he was killed or captured," wrote Private Daniel Chisholm in a letter the next day, "as no one could live when the leaden hail was hissing like the continued buzzing of a swarm of bees."[40]

Like Dale, the commander of the 12th New Jersey, Lieutenant Colonel Thomas H. Davis, brandished his sword, urging his men forward, and was killed by a Confederate. The 14th Indiana's Colonel John Coons crossed the rifle pits on horseback and, as he fired his revolver at the enemy, the Rebels shot him dead. One gray-coated soldier shoved the muzzle of his musket nearly against Coons's chest. A Union staff officer described the Indianan as having "already attained an enviable reputation as an efficient officer and fearless leader."[41]

The Virginians and Georgians, however, had the momentum. "They charged with the greatest spirit," reported Gordon. In turn, the disorganized Union ranks had spent their power in the wild pursuit southward. Mainer Private John Haley called it "a feeble attempt to carry a second line. It was useless." Bay Stater Private Donnelly admitted, "It was our turn to fall back," adding that he and his comrades did so "on a dead run."[42]

The Confederates followed in what Gordon called a "headlong & resistless charge" that "carried everything before it." The Southerners bagged prisoners, including brigade commander Hiram Brown, and recaptured at least two guns of the Staunton Battery. Although accounts conflict as to when the incident occurred, it appears that during the Yankees' flight David Birney encountered a "grossly intoxicated" Hobart Ward. Birney had him removed from command and placed under arrest. Ward would be mustered out of service in July.[43]

As the Confederates approached the McCoull farm and adjoining woods, they swung to the right, charging toward the trenches and traverses along the salient's eastern leg. Among the trees, Col. J. Catlett Gibson of the 49th Virginia found brigade commander Hoffman "in a thicket of bushes." Hoffman was reaching toward his feet, prompting Gibson to ask where he had been shot. Hoffman replied that he had had his spectacles knocked off and "he could not see." Gibson told a soldier to help the myopic colonel find his eyeglasses and, if they could not be located in the fog and the day's dim early light, to lead him to the rear. Hoffman "could not see a yard without his specks," Gibson wrote later. Hoffman and the enlisted man found the spectacles, and the colonel continued on.[44]

The Virginians and Georgians pressed back Barlow's and Gibbon's Yankees into the "original works," as the soldiers came to designate them in their accounts. A Confederate stated that the advance "reminded me of a big bird hunt." Virginia Private William Smith claimed that their line "was disorganized, every man pressing forward himself." Colonel Gibson ordered a Union captain and about twenty men to surrender. A melee ensued as Gibson's troops bayoneted some of the Federals before he stopped the killing. When he asked the captain for his sword, the answer was, Gibson wrote, "in a language which I had never before heard spoken."[45]

As Gibson recounted, the fighting became close and personal in the trenches and traverses. "We all had some new experiences in that charge," asserted Captain Cyrus Coiner of the 52nd Virginia. "Officers fought with swords & pistols & the men their bayonets." Coiner's brother, Captain Joseph S. Coiner, fell mortally wounded, the bullet severing the main artery in his thigh. A fellow Virginian, Lieutenant M. S. Stringfellow, remembered, "I had a loaded revolver in my hand, and I emptied it, in many instances close enough to burn their clothing."[46]

Captain Coiner's superior officer, Colonel James H. Skinner, suffered a grievous wound. A minié ball struck his head below the left temple, passed through the left eye, and exited through his nose beneath the right eye. Blinded, Skinner was taken to the rear. He survived the wound and eventually regained sight in the right eye. Disabled from further field service, he was retired to the Invalid Corps. Twenty-four-year-old Lieutenant Colonel Thomas H. Watkins took command of the regiment as its members continued the struggle along the works.[47]

One of Skinner's men scribbled in his diary afterward, "That was the hardest fight we had fought since the war." Hoffman's Virginians regained the original earthworks but were repulsed by Nelson Miles's and Thomas Smyth's veteran Federals as the Virginians tried to push north in the trenches. The Confederates had seized three enemy colors, while the new flag of the 52nd Virginia had been "torn in shreds." Hoffman's troops now settled in behind the entrenchments and in nearby traverses, waging the struggle against the Yankees to the front and on their left flank.[48]

On the Virginians' right, Evans's final three regiments—the 61st, 60th, and 31st Georgia—had joined their comrades after crossing the salient, coming in on the brigade's right flank. The action at the works between the Georgians and Barlow's and Gibbon's Yankees became a hand-to-hand fight with clubbed muskets, bayonets, and rifles discharged within an arm's length. The 61st Georgia's color bearer, Francis Marion McDow, stuck the regimental flag on the works. The Federals grabbed the banner and McDow, who would die in a Union prison.[49]

"Evans' brigade was cut to pieces," claimed Private G. W. Nichols in his memoir. Nichols admitted, however, that he deserted his comrades, writing that he "ran back for dear life." Most of his comrades, however, clung to the breastworks and traverses and, like Hoffman's Virginians, incurred on this day a casualty rate that exceeded 33 percent. But their sacrifices had come at a critical time.[50]

There was some truth in a letter written eight days later by Georgian John J. Dillard when he bragged to a friend at home, "It has been the fortune of my Brig. To turn the tide of battle twice." In a span of thirty minutes or so, from 5:30 A.M. to 6:00 A.M., under John Gordon's aggressive and stellar leadership, Evans's and Hoffman's veterans had blunted the Federals' thrust into the heart of the Mule Shoe, sent their foes reeling, and recaptured a section of the original earthworks. Earlier, fellow Confederates had limited the enemy's penetration in the trenches on both sides of the salient. Nevertheless, thousands of Yankees still held long sections of the Mule Shoe's defenses.[51]

Richard Ewell's stepson and chief of staff, Major G. Campbell Brown, had been awakened with calls for the general's horse and "a sharp fire on Johnson's line." Mounting his horse, Brown followed Ewell into the salient, but in the fog and confusion the pair became separated. The staff officer rode toward the Mule Shoe's western leg and, along the way, issued instructions to different officers. Turning south, he located Joseph Kershaw, whose First Corps troops connected with Robert Rodes's Second Corps units. Brown asked Kershaw for reinforcements, but the division commander refused, arguing he had none to spare. Kershaw offered, however, to occupy a gap in the lines if any of Rodes's brigades were withdrawn to fight elsewhere.[52]

Brown headed north and found Brigadier General Cullen Battle, whose fine Alabama regiments held the works next to Kershaw's veterans. Brown instructed Battle to start retiring from the works. From there, the staff officer met Ewell again and explained what he had done. The corps commander directed Rodes to have Battle attack the enemy and Kershaw to replace the Alabamians in the defenses. Ewell then told his stepson to rally the "debris" of Edward Johnson's division.[53]

Cullen Battle had his regiments on the march when he received the orders to counterattack. The thirty-four-year-old general had been with the brigade since June 1862 and had led it since his promotion to brigadier in August 1863. On this morning he still suffered from a painful wound to his right foot, which he had received in the action at Laurel Hill on May 8.[54]

When Battle pulled his officers and men out of the trenches, he angled them to the northeast before swinging the column to the left and toward the salient's western face. To their right, John Hoffman's Virginians and Clement Evans's Georgians were charging toward the eastern fieldworks. The Alabamians shook out a battle line, consisting of the 61st, 6th, 12th, 3rd, and 5th regiments. When ready, they stepped forth.[55]

The Alabamians charged toward the reserve line of entrenchments located behind Doles's Salient. The Union troops of David Birney's and Gershom Mott's divisions held the works and were engaged with Junius Daniel's North Carolinians, William Monaghan's Louisianans, and the regiments of Georgians. Battle's veterans came in on their comrades' right, hitting the southern end of the works and pushing out the Yankees. "The brigade was a solid wedge driven into the very heart of the enemy," declared Battle. The Federals, however, maintained their grip on the original works along the salient's western side and a lengthy section of the reserve line.[56]

Robert Rodes, meanwhile, had assumed direction of the fight against Birney's and Mott's Federals. A native Virginian and graduate of the Virginia Military Institute, the thirty-five-year-old Rodes enjoyed seemingly universal respect and popularity within the army. "Astute, capable, brave, conscientious—he made a fine commander, respected and honored, unselfish and devoted," said a North Carolina private of Rodes. Another private remembered Rodes's "slow, genial smile," while a staff officer enthused: "I like him so much. He is very much admired by all and very popular."[57]

Artillerist Robert Stiles saw Rodes about six o'clock on this morning and left a graphic portrait of this Confederate warrior and fine division commander. "He was a man of very striking appearance, of erect, fine figure and martial bearing," recalled Stiles in his memoir. "He constantly passed and repassed in rear of our guns, riding a black horse. . . . Rodes' eyes were everywhere, and every now and then he would stop to attend to some detail of the arrangement of his line or his troops, and then ride on again, humming to himself and catching the ends of his long, tawny moustache between his lips."[58]

By the time Battle's Alabamians charged, Rodes had issued orders for Brigadier General Stephen Dodson Ramseur's North Carolina brigade to check the enemy's advance and to drive him back. An academy graduate, class of 1860, the twenty-six-year-old Ramseur had incurred a crippling wound in his right arm at Malvern Hill on July 1, 1862. He returned to duty in January 1863, with the rank of brigadier and command of this brigade. On a battlefield, he and Rodes were kindred spirits. "There were never, anywhere, two better fighters than Rodes and Ramseur, or two more attractive men," observed Porter Alexander.[59]

"I had my brigade under arms at early dawn," reported Ramseur. One of his men grumbled at the hour, writing, "We did not have time to fill our canteens, so we did not have a mouthful to eat or drink when we went into the fight." The North Carolinians filed out of the entrenchments, moving to the right and coming into line in front of the reserve line of works across the base of the salient. The 14th North Carolina formed two ranks on the left, then the 4th, 2nd, and 30th regiments. "This was a serious time with us," recalled J. W. Bone of the 30th North Carolina, "and would have been more so, if we could have really realized our position."[60]

Sunrise had been nearly an hour earlier, and the dense fog was dissipating. It had been a rainy, wet night, and the men were chilled. "Old veterans know how hard it is to fight before the blood gets warm," stated a North Carolinian. Their blood, however, warmed quickly as shellfire from distant Union batteries came shrieking in, exploding above the ranks. Ramseur described the artillery fire as "severe." Above the din, he cautioned the men to move slowly, keep alignment until ordered to charge, and not to fire.[61]

While Ewell and Rodes watched, the 1,400 veteran infantrymen advanced into the open ground west of the McCoull house. Ramseur rode in front, and, as one of his men recorded later in his diary, "our fellow soldiers were falling thick and fast around us until our ranks were very much depleted." The musketry, wrote an onlooker, "rose up rattling in one common roar."[62]

As they passed Junius Daniel's brigade on their left, their fellow North Carolinians watched. "For a moment it seemed to me our brigade . . . held its breath as these men went forward, apparently into the very jaws of death." Daniel stepped in front of his ranks and saluted Ramseur's troops. A minié ball then struck him in the bowels, and he collapsed with a mortal wound. Daniel lived until the next day, able to have a message of love sent to his wife. A private had written during the winter, "Daniel beat all the men he knew in taking care of his men." Colonel Bryan Grimes of the 4th North Carolina asserted that Daniel "was decidedly the best General from N.C."[63]

Ramseur signaled a charge, and his North Carolinians advanced at the double-quick toward the reserve or inner line of works. Ramseur still rode with his men until his "Yankee horse," as he called it, went down with a severe wound. A bullet hit him below the elbow in his disabled right arm, forcing him to the rear temporarily for treatment. The 4th North Carolina's Colonel Grimes assumed command of the brigade, leading them into the works and scattering the blue-coated defenders.[64]

Here the North Carolinians halted, lay down, and for the first time, opened fire on their foes. In their front, attested one of them, was "a living mass of Yankees, in full view of us." On Grimes's command, the North Carolinians rose "as one man w/bayonets & a yell advanced in concave lines," in the description of Captain Seaton Gales, Ramseur's chief of staff. As they charged, Private Disdale Stepp of Company F, 14th North Carolina began singing "Bonnie Blue Flag," his voice rising above the clamor of musketry and yells. About a dozen comrades joined in until Stepp, a native of Buncombe County, was killed.[65]

Ramseur's Confederates swarmed into the section of the main earthworks that had been manned by William Monaghan's Louisianans to the left of the Stonewall Brigade. The Confederates drove the defenders out of the trenches and over the parapets in a melee of hand-to-hand combat. The officers and men of the 14th and 4th regiments had become "all mixed up together," their flags barely five paces apart. "Then the fight commenced in earnest," declared one of them. Grimes believed that he had lost already one-third of his men.[66]

In a precursor of the hell that came to mark this day, the opponents stood feet apart on the opposite sides of the entrenchments. A Union soldier grabbed the hair of the 30th North Carolina's adjutant and pulled him across the works. Another Yankee seized an enemy's regimental flag. The Federals had the advantage of holding the defenses and nearby traverses on the ridge, pouring their fire down into the Rebels. "Men were killed while squatting just as low and as close to the breastworks as it was possible for them to get," recounted Thomas Watkins of the 14th North Carolina.[67]

With the Confederates caught in the plummeting musketry, Colonel Risden Tyler Bennett of the 14th North Carolina proposed to Grimes to shift his regiment to the right and to charge the Yankees. "This bold and hazardous offer was accepted as a forlorn hope," observed Ramseur. Grimes ordered the attack. The North Carolinians clawed ahead from traverse to traverse. Birney's and Mott's Union veterans then met them in a fearful reckoning for this small patch of Virginia soil. "Charge after charge came rushing on us," stated a member of the 2nd North Carolina. "We fought fearful odds, and it was here for the first time that I ever knew the enemy to run upon our bayonets, but they came down with such fury we pitched many of them with the bayonet right over the ditch."[68]

The North Carolinians bagged prisoners and pressed ahead, repulsing their foes "with great slaughter." They reached to where a lane from the McCoull farm passed over the earthworks close to the west angle in the salient defenses. Union Colonel Robert McAllister said of the enemy, "Encouraged by their success so far and with traverses in their recaptured works behind which their sharpshooters could take deadly aim and be protected, our position was critical."[69]

The Confederates had wrested a crucial section of occupied works from the enemy, regaining possession of the salient's western defenses and reducing farther the extent of their foes' hold on the Mule Shoe's entrenchments. Ewell called their achievement "a charge of unsurpassed gallantry." The 2nd North Carolina's Captain Matt Manly described it as "the crowning glory of the career of Ramseur's Brigade." In a letter to his wife, Ramseur exclaimed proudly: "In the great fight of the 12th my Brigade, more than any other, saved the day. We made the most daring effective charge I ever saw."[70]

Afterward, Lee, Ewell, and Rodes personally thanked Ramseur. According to Bryan Grimes, Lee stated that the brigade "deserved the thanks of the country; we had saved the army." For the present, however, the North Carolinians held the ground, enduring, in Ramseur's words, "terrific direct enfilade & reverse fire." He had rejoined the troops with his right arm in a sling. Although he remained unscathed, he informed his wife afterward that his overcoat had four bullet holes in it. While their casualties mounted, Ramseur's veterans awaited help.[71]

By 6:00 A.M., Union General-in-Chief Ulysses S. Grant's massive offensive strike had ground down to a temporary halt. The Second Corps's assault had been a stunning success, wrecking an entire Confederate division and bagging thousands of prisoners and a long row of cannon. The victors stormed deeper into the salient toward a second line of fieldworks. Ahead beckoned Spotsylvania Court House and the possible crushing defeat of the vaunted Army of Northern Virginia. The Federals' stalwart foes rallied, however, limited the penetration along the salient's faces, and shoved the Yankees back with spirited counterattacks. "The momentum of the assault had been so broken," argued William Swinton, a *New York Times* correspondent and early historian of the Union army.[72]

Ninety minutes after the Federals had charged, the reality within and without the Mule Shoe was a bloody stalemate. Union infantrymen and artillerists were busy removing captured enemy cannon, caissons, lim-

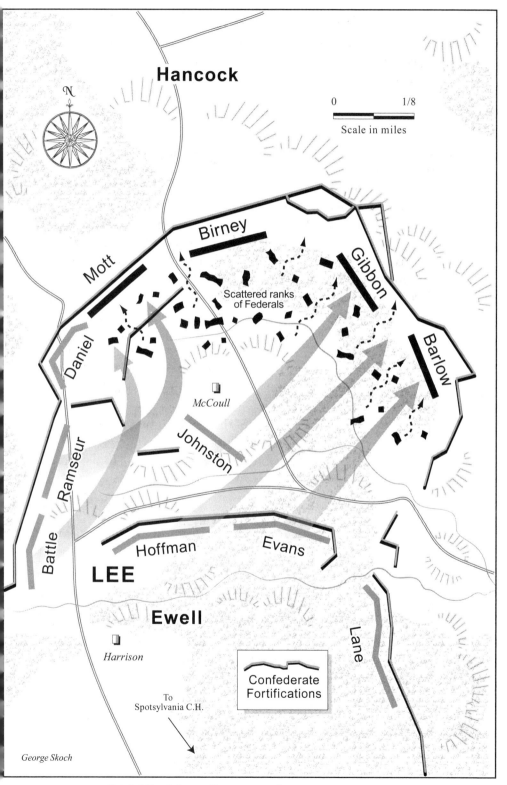

Hancock

N

0   1/8
Scale in miles

Birney

Mott

Gibbon

Daniel

Scattered ranks
of Federals

Barlow

McCoull

Ramseur

Johnston

Battle

Hoffman

Evans

LEE

Ewell

Lane

Harrison

To
Spotsylvania C.H.

Confederate
Fortifications

George Skoch

Initial Confederate Counterattacks, 5:00 A.M.–6:00 A.M.

bers, and horses. A few guns had been turned, and crews were working them on the Rebels. Second Corps infantrymen held the broad apex and along part of the eastern trenches and traverses. Outside the salient's faces, however, the Federals were "jammed on each other." Francis Barlow thought they were forty deep.[73]

Second Corps commander Winfield Hancock had telegraphed headquarters at 5:55 A.M., requesting reinforcements from the Sixth Corps. "It is necessary that General Wright should attack at once," the message read. "All of my troops are engaged." George Meade replied at once: "Your good news is most welcome. Burnside attacked at the appointed hour. Wright is ordered in at once on your right. Hold all you get and press on."[74]

Grant's offensive had been predicated on the use of the Fifth, Sixth, and Ninth corps. So at 6:00 A.M., Meade wired Fifth Corps commander Gouverneur Warren: "Keep up as threatening an attitude as possible to keep the enemy in your front. Wright must attack and you may have to. Be ready and do the best you can." At the same time, Grant's chief of staff, Brigadier General John A. Rawlins, telegraphed Ambrose Burnside, commander of the Ninth Corps: "General Hancock is pushing forward vigorously. He has captured 3 [sic] generals. Push on with all possible vigor." Units of Burnside's corps had charged at the designated time against the Rebels' eastern works south of the salient but, after a brief, limited success, their attack had also stalled.[75]

Grant's and Meade's assessment of the tactical situation at the front relied on Hancock's telegrams. "We all stood around Grant's Headq'rs in the woods on the opposite side of the road," wrote Theodore Lyman, "anxiously awaiting for news, 5:15 A.M." When Hancock's message arrived informing them of the capture of prisoners and works, "Gen. Rawlins, with his hard hollow voice," related Lyman, "broke out into loud, coarse exultation 'By G[od]! They are done. Hancock will just drive them to H[ell]!'"[76]

When Grant learned of the assault's initial success, he remarked: "That's kind of news I like to hear. I had hoped that a bold dash at daylight would secure a large number of prisoners." According to staff member Horace Porter, the general-in-chief "seemed in excellent spirits" even before they heard from Hancock. Grant "counted upon important results from the movements," recounted Porter, "although he appreciated fully the difficulties to be encountered."[77]

From headquarters, however, neither Grant nor Meade knew that the offensive had stalled, even receded. They almost certainly expected the entry of Sixth Corps units and the renewal of attacks by Burnside's troops to be decisive blows. Hancock's officers and men might have offered counterarguments. For them, the exuberance of their initial victory had given way to a stark reality, even a portending nightmare.[78]

Robert E. Lee and his veteran command had confronted an imminent disaster for the second time in seven days. An infantry division had been overwhelmed, its ranks decimated, with many of its survivors in headlong flight to the rear. Aggressive leadership and the fighting prowess of its officers and men, however, had blunted the Union offensive and had shoved it back. This initial success "can only be accounted for, I think, by that wonderful morale of the Army of Northern Virginia," wrote artillerist Porter Alexander.[79]

Although a temporary, bloody impasse had been reached, the daunting numerical advantage of its foes still threatened the Confederate army with a crippling defeat, if not possible destruction. Lee understood the continuing danger. When he had been turned back as the brigades of John Hoffman and Clement Evans charged, he met Thomas Carter. Lee instructed the artillery officer to assemble all the cannon he could to cover the army's right flank from the salient south past the courthouse village.[80]

Lee started riding away, halted, and returned, reportedly saying, "Colonel Carter, I wish to impress upon you the necessity of holding this line."

"I assure you, General," replied the artillery colonel, "the line will be held or every man will die in his tracks."[81]

Carter and other officers immediately began patching together a row of cannon. They amassed three batteries each from the battalions of Carter M. Braxton and William Nelson and "a portion" of Robert Hardaway's battalion, about thirty guns in all. The line of batteries ran north from outside the village, while the remaining gun crews with Hardaway unlimbered in the rear of the salient. As these latter artillerists deployed their cannon, Hardaway was wounded, and Captain Willis J. Dance took command of the battalion.[82]

The Confederate commander, meanwhile, met Major Robert W. Hunter, John Gordon's chief of staff, and directed him to "collect together the men of Johnson's division and report to General Gordon." In about thirty minutes, Hunter and others had gathered between three hundred and four hundred survivors from the infantry command. Lee also directed engineers to begin construction of a new defensive line several hundred yards south of the Edgar Harrison farm. But as the *New York Times* correspondent William Swinton correctly noted later, "Lee seemed to be determined to retake, at any cost, the line wrested from him."[83]

{ 8 }

The Very Air Smelled of a Fight

Ambrose Burnside's return to the conflict's eastern theater had begun inauspiciously. The former commander of the Army of the Potomac had floundered amid the Wilderness's thickets and trees. His Ninth Corps troops had been ordered to solidify the gap in the army's lines between Orange Turnpike and Orange Plank Road on the morning of May 6. They arrived hours behind schedule, however, incurred casualties, and contributed little to the Union effort. "Burnside somehow is never up to the mark when the tug comes," complained an officer.[1]

When the Federals marched toward Spotsylvania Court House, Burnside's divisions had trailed the other corps, swinging north, then south, filing into position east of Fredericksburg Road. The corps operated as an independent command since Burnside outranked George Meade by seniority, receiving its orders directly from Ulysses S. Grant. The lieutenant general's instructions to Burnside for the offensive on May 12 read, "You will move against the enemy with your entire force promptly and with all possible vigor at precisely 4 o'clock tomorrow morning." Grant had detailed his aides, Cyrus Comstock and Orville Babcock, to Burnside's headquarters "to impress upon him the importance of pushing forward vigorously," as Grant put it in his memoirs.[2]

Burnside had available slightly more than thirteen thousand officers and men in three infantry divisions for the attack. A fourth division, composed of United States Colored Troops (USCT), had been detached, guarding the army's ponderous wagon train. Numbering seven thousand officers and men in two brigades, the USCT division was the first unit of freedmen and former slaves to be associated with the army. On May 7, staff officer Theodore Lyman had come upon these troops "massed in a hollow" in the Wilderness. Reflecting the prejudice against African Americans in the army, Lyman wrote later in his journal: "It made me sad to see them—Can we not fight our own battles." Grant, Meade, and other senior officers, though not Burnside, doubted the fighting capabilities of the USCT rank and file.[3]

Burnside had conferred with Comstock and Babcock and decided the assault should be on the right toward the Second Corps and nearer the salient. He assigned the Second Division, under Brigadier General Robert B. Potter, to lead the attack, supported by the First Division, commanded by Major General Thomas L. Crittenden.[4]

Crittenden had joined the Ninth Corps on the evening of May 11. A Kentuckian, the forty-four-year-old general had served in the west until fall 1863. In the aftermath of the Union defeat at Chickamauga, army commander Major General William S. Rosecrans preferred charges against Crittenden and two other generals. An investigation acquitted the three officers, and Crittenden was transferred to the east. When Lyman met the Kentuckian, the staff officer described him as the "queerest-looking party you ever saw, with a thin, staring face, and hair hanging down to his coat collar—a very wild appearing major-general, but quite a kindly man in conversation, despite his terrible looks."[5]

Burnside had requested Crittenden as a successor to Brigadier General Thomas G. Stevenson, who had been mortally wounded. On the morning of May 10, a Confederate sharpshooter shot Stevenson in the head as the general ate breakfast with his staff members. They believed, wrote chief of staff Charles Mills, that they were "entirely out of fire." Stevenson died hours later. "It is a terrible blow to us," wrote Mills. "His loss is irreparable," professed the adjutant. Stevenson was a "kind-hearted, considerate, generous-spirited man."[6]

Robert Potter's division began its advance at the appointed hour of 4:00 A.M. on May 12. According to Lyman: "Potter is tall, with a full, phlegmatic black eye. He is particular about his dress, of few words, and reputed an excellent division commander." On this morning, Colonel Simon G. Griffin's six regiments of Maine, New Hampshire, and Vermont soldiers manned the division's right front. On their left, six regiments of troops from Massachusetts, Rhode Island, New York, and Pennsylvania, under the temporary command of Colonel John I. Curtin of the 45th Pennsylvania, extended the column south. Curtin had replaced the brigade's veteran commander, Colonel Zenas R. Bliss, after Bliss's horse fell on him, severely injuring his ankle. As his troops went forward, Bliss lay in a bed in the rear.[7]

Potter advanced "column of Brigades," angling north and then turning west. On Potter's left, Crittenden's two brigades, nine regiments in all, trailed, moving in support. Farther to the left and rear, Brigadier General Orlando B. Willcox's pair of brigades, with eleven regiments, deployed as a reserve. Skirmishers rimmed Griffin's front of three regiments across. The Federals crossed a creek and stumbled through thickets and a marshy swamp but continued on for nearly a mile, encountering no "serious opposition," in adjutant Mills's words.[8]

Up ahead, the roar of cannon fire and musketry from the Second Corps's assault on the Mule Shoe rolled toward the Union soldiers through the fog. Fortune favored Griffin's New Englanders on this morning as they struck the gap in the enemy fieldworks between the right flank of Edward Johnson's division in the salient and the left flank of Cadmus Wilcox's Third Corps division. Griffin's Yankees arrived when James Lane's North Carolinians were under a fierce assault from Francis Barlow's and John Gibbon's Federals, who had routed George Steuart's Rebels.[9]

Griffin's men scaled the works and plunged into the ranks of the 28th and 18th North Carolina. Yankees from the Second and Ninth corps engulfed the two Confederate regiments, capturing prisoners and the flag of the 18th North Carolina and driving the survivors rearward. Lane tried to rally them, shouting: "You must hold your ground. The honor and safety of the army demand it." One account claimed that a North Carolina private killed a Federal infantryman, who had leveled his rifle to shoot the Confederate brigadier at a distance of ten feet.[10]

The New Englanders kept going, seizing a pair of cannon posted on a rise behind the North Carolinians. On their left, Curtin's blue-coated infantrymen entered the struggle. "The fighting was terrific," remembered a soldier in the 11th New Hampshire. Lane asserted later that his veterans fought from the traverses, triggering "death dealing volleys." At points the opponents were so close that a North Carolinian, who "had got rattled and lost his bearings," stumbled into the ranks of the 45th Pennsylvania. When one of the Pennsylvanians invited him to join them, the prisoner "was the happiest man on the job when he found that nobody was going to hurt him."[11]

Confederate division commander Cadmus Wilcox, meanwhile, ordered the brigades of generals Alfred Scales and Edward Thomas from their reserve position northeast of the village to Lane's support. Wilcox directed his chief of staff, Major Joseph A. Engelhard, to conduct the brigades forward. The 2,600 Confederates formed ranks—Scales's North Carolinians on the left, Thomas's Georgians on the right—and charged, coming in on Lane's right flank. Their arrival intensified the fighting and proved to be decisive.[12]

The three Confederate brigades counterattacked, reclaimed the earthworks, and drove Potter's Federals down the ridge and across the swamp. The Yankees rallied on a hill and fought. The 45th Pennsylvania's Sergeant Eugene Beauge looked at the dead and wounded on the ground they had crossed and recalled years later that "being a farmer's boy the scene reminded me right away of a harvest field on the old farm in Tioga County and forsooth it was a harvest field we were on—the harvest field of Death with human forms as the ghastly sheaves."[13]

The North Carolinians and Georgians pursued. Seizing the flag of the 33rd North Carolina, Lieutenant Colonel Robert V. Cowan led Lane's brigade toward the enemy's reformed ranks. A Georgian with Thomas described the pursuit in his diary afterward: "We crossed our breastworks and advanced several hundred yards under a terrible fire of grape canister shells and minie balls, we had a steep bluff to go down and a wide ditch to cross in a field in full view of the enemy."[14]

The opposing lines raked each other with musketry at places only a hundred yards apart. Union and Confederate batteries shelled enemy ranks. Some of the Rebels lay on the ground, firing and reloading their rifles. Casualties mounted. One of the fallen was Private Charles H. Farmer of the 35th Georgia, fatally wounded by a bullet in the bowels. He had a premonition of his death the day before and gave his pocket book to a lieutenant for safekeeping. He died on this May 12, his twentieth birthday.[15]

Potter had requested support from Crittenden, but that division had been slow in coming up on Potter's left. Crittenden had not assumed official command of his two brigades until 4:00 A.M., the hour designated for the advance. The Kentuckian possessed "no knowledge of the troops" in his new command, according to one of them. When Potter's message arrived, Crittenden instructed brigade commander Colonel Daniel Leasure to send three regiments to Potter. When Crittenden asked for a fourth one, he "seemed astonished when informed that Colonel Leasure had no more regiments under his control."[16]

Crittenden's other brigade commander, Lieutenant Colonel Stephen M. Weld Jr., recorded later in his diary that the rank and file "had no idea that we were going right into a fight." As the two brigades advanced, they came under heavy artillery fire from batteries in three Confederate battalions commanded by lieutenant colonels William Nelson, William Pegram, and William T. Poague. Weld shifted one regiment to Potter and another one to Leasure, but Crittenden's effort stalled before the enemy cannon and infantry.[17]

In a string of telegrams, Grant and Winfield Hancock urged Burnside to press the attack and to connect with Hancock's Second Corps troops in the salient. In turn, Burnside ordered Potter and Crittenden to renew the offensive, but their men faltered before the Confederate musketry and cannon fire. Poague claimed later, "Burnside was easily repulsed with heavy loss." A stalemate ensued as the Southern infantry withdrew into their original works. Potter's troops consolidated their position, while later in the morning six regiments from Crittenden's division attacked Rebel entrenchments farther south in a futile charge.[18]

Unlike Hancock, Burnside remained at his headquarters in the rear. As more messages arrived from Grant and Hancock, he became irritable. His assault had been piecemeal and costly. Potter's two brigades had seized the enemy's works in a gap in their lines, but no timely reinforcements appeared to exploit the capture. The corps's third division under Orlando Willcox never entered the action. The "tug" had come once again for Burnside, and once again he had not been "up to the mark."[19]

Bugles and the sound of gunfire awakened many officers and men of the Union Sixth Corps on the morning of May 12. They belonged to the smallest infantry corps in the army, numbering perhaps 18,500 present for duty on this day. During the previous night they had been shifted behind and in support of their comrades in the Second Corps, whose attack had broken the predawn silence. Nearly two hours later, couriers brought orders, and for these Yankees—men mostly from New England, New York, and Pennsylvania—their time had come on this foggy Thursday.[20]

At 6:00 A.M., army headquarters ordered Sixth Corps commander Horatio Wright "to attack at once vigorously" on the right of the Second Corps. Wright had been in command of the corps since the death of John Sedgwick on May 9. Wright had been with the corps since the Gettysburg Campaign. "Wright was another engineer officer, well educated, of good, solid intellect, with capacity for command, but no special predilection for fighting," observed Assistant Secretary of War Charles Dana, who accompanied the army and kept the War Department informed. Staff officer Charles Whittier noted, however, that Wright was a "well-mannered, temperate man—not at all deficient in physical courage, but when responsibilities came on him he took to drink."[21]

Brigadier General Thomas H. Neill's division initiated the Sixth Corps offensive. The thirty-eight-year-old Pennsylvanian and academy graduate had led the command since May 6, when one of the army's finest division commanders, George W. Getty, fell wounded during the Wilderness fighting. On May 9, before Laurel Hill, Neill had begun withdrawing his troops without orders. When staff officer Whittier found him, Neill had "entirely lost his nerve," in the aide's judgment. The brigadier was, believed Whittier, a "wreck from no fault of his, simply tension too great for him to bear."[22]

Wright had selected Neill's division for the attack as it was posted closest to Hancock's right flank and the salient, lying on part of the John Brown farm. The corps's other two divisions, commanded by brigadiers David A. Russell and James B. Ricketts, had bivouacked farther to the west on the farm of an Alsop family. In turn, Colonel Oliver Edwards's three regiments of Massachusetts and Rhode Island veterans—a fourth regiment had been detached on picket duty—were closest to the Mule Shoe and went in first from Neill's division. An experienced and capable officer, Edwards had recently taken command of the brigade as its senior colonel.[23]

The roughly nine hundred New Englanders stepped forth, marching toward the Mule Shoe's west angle. They crossed the Landrum farm lane, where Colonel John C. Tidball, Hancock's artillery chief, had posted nearly thirty cannon in five batteries. The Union gun crews had turned the enemy's fieldworks along the lane and unlimbered their pieces behind them, a scant four hundred yards from the salient. The artillerists were working their guns as Edwards's men passed.[24]

The infantry column cleared woods into the open fields opposite the salient's western face and apex. A shelf of ground extended forty yards north from the apex before dropping into an east-west ravine. The low ground offered the Federals a sheltered approach to the salient. Edwards likely wheeled the regiments into line in the ravine under artillery fire from Confederate batteries arrayed in front of the Edgar Harrison house. It was around seven o'clock and, up ahead, the Mule Shoe was engulfed in a boiling cauldron of killing and maiming. "The contest was life and death," as a Union officer put it.[25]

The New Englanders struck the salient's log and dirt defenses on both sides of the west angle, connecting on their left with the Excelsior Brigade of Gershom Mott's Second Corps division. Edwards's right regiment, the 10th Massachusetts, came in south of the angle along the western face's entrenchments, directly opposite the section and traverses manned by Dodson Ramseur's North Carolinians. Here the struggle escalated rapidly. "Our men fought the Rebels close to the other side of the breast works," recounted a member of the Union regiment, "and knocked their guns aside, and jumped on the works and shot them down." Ramseur's veterans, however, raked the Yankees' ranks with enfilading and frontal fire. Edwards later confirmed that the 10th Massachusetts suffered heavy losses.[26]

Before long, Brigadier General Frank Wheaton's five regiments of Pennsylvanians and New Yorkers advanced toward the enemy's works on the right of the 10th Massachusetts. Confederate batteries pummeled their lines, and Ramseur's and Cullen Battle's gray-coated infantry lashed them with musketry. A Pennsylvanian asserted that the Rebels were "waiting for the attack, and in full force in the works." Wheaton claimed his men charged to within fifty yards of the entrenchments. "Here we were exposed to a terrible musketry fire," reported the brigadier, "losing heavily, including many valuable officers." Wheaton withdrew the regiments into a swale for protection.[27]

Under orders to support Edwards's New Englanders, Neill's third brigade, five regiments from Maine, New York, and Pennsylvania under Colonel Daniel D. Bidwell, arrived. A forty-four-year-old New Yorker, Bidwell halted the brigade in the woods opposite the west angle. He decided to send forward only the 49th and 77th New York as reinforcements for Edwards. The pair of regiments cleared the tree line.[28]

Ahead, minié balls churned the ground and filled the air. The "spurts of dirt were as constant as the pattering drops of a summer shower," thought an officer. "Overhead the swish and hum of the passing bullets was like a swarm of bees." The New Yorkers wheeled to the left and approached the enemy's parapet to the right of the 10th Massachusetts. Ramseur's North Carolinians and Battle's Alabamians met the oncoming Federals with sheets of rifle fire. Bidwell's veterans reached the earthworks and engaged their foes.[29]

Sixth Corps commander Wright and staff had trailed Neill's brigades, halting in a slight ravine. At Hancock's request, one of his aides, Major William Mitchell, had conducted Wright to the front to observe the situation with the Second Corps. As Mitchell described the corps's position, an enemy shell burst above the group. A piece of it struck Wright in the thigh, "knocking him several feet and injuring him severely, but fortunately not disabling him."[30]

Theodore Lyman joined the wounded general and staff officers. He had been sent by George Meade to "ascertain progress in Wright's front." Lyman noticed nearby "a dead infantryman, on his back, with knees drawn up" and "a frowsy red beard." Soon David Birney arrived, complained about the Confederate artillery fire, and rode away. Wright remained in the hollow, sipped whiskey for the painful contusion, and endeavored to direct the corps's operations.[31]

Meade, meanwhile, had intervened directly in Wright's command, dispatching Neill's final unit, Colonel Lewis A. Grant's Vermont Brigade, to support of the Second Corps on the salient's eastern face. The army commander had reacted to a request from Hancock. Francis Barlow's and John Gibbon's men were piled up, dozens deep, against the outside of the entrenchments, held tenaciously by John Hoffman's Virginians and Clement Evans's Georgians. Barlow had expressed concern for the safety of his left flank with the failure of Burnside's units to connect with his division. Barlow had withdrawn John Brooke's brigade, sending it back to the Landrum farm to reorganize and to replenish its ammunition. Barlow then asked Hancock for reinforcements to secure his left flank, which resulted in Meade redirecting Grant's brigade.[32]

Hancock had not instructed Grant that his regiments were to fill the gap between the Second and Ninth corps. When the Vermonters appeared, they crowded into the rear of Barlow's and Gibbon's jumbled mass of troops. "There was no organized line in our front," reported Grant. The Vermonters' presence added to the confusion and angered Barlow, who had been trying to restore order. He rode to Hancock's headquarters at the Landrum house, exclaiming to the corps commander, "For God's sake, Hancock, do not send any more troops in here."[33]

Since 4:34 A.M., roughly twenty-four thousand Union infantrymen in five divisions of ninety-six regiments in fifteen brigades had assaulted the Mule Shoe defenses manned by Edward Johnson's Confederate division. The Federals had routed Johnson's command but, less than three hours later, the general-in-chief's grand offensive had been stalemated by counterattacks from about 7,500 Rebel infantrymen in twenty-five regiments in five brigades. Months earlier, before a congressional committee, a former commander of the Union army, Joseph Hooker, had testified that Lee's "army has, by discipline alone, acquired a character for steadiness and efficiency unsurpassed, in my judgment, in ancient or modern times." More of such men were coming into the Mule Shoe.[34]

Private David Holt and his comrades in the 16th Mississippi had spent a rainy, miserable night in their camps west of the Po River. Awakened by distant gunfire before 5:00 A.M., May 12, Holt stirred from his mud puddle bed and ate "morsels of wet corn pone and a small piece of [uncooked]

bacon." "I had noticed what looked like a bundle of dirty rags lying a little ways off in the pasture," recalled Holt. A mounted courier arrived before long and halted by the "bundle," which proved to be the Mississippian's brigade commander, Brigadier General Nathaniel H. Harris.[35]

Harris's regiments and those of brigadiers Abner Perrin and Ambrose R. Wright had been guarding the army's left flank west of the river by Block House Bridge. The message brought by the courier came from division commander William Mahone, ordering Harris and Perrin to march rapidly to Spotsylvania Court House. Robert E. Lee had requested two brigades from Mahone when he recognized at once the magnitude of the crisis that confronted his army.[36]

When Harris read the order, he shouted: "Attention Brigade! Fall in. March by the right flank and follow the courier!" The Mississippians scrambled into a column on the road to the village. Harris mounted his horse and turned to them: "Come on boys, double quick!" Ahead, Perrin's Alabamians filed into the roadbed and led the march. As the Confederates accelerated the pace, Harris urged: "Keep the ranks closed up! Push forward boys! Hell's to pay! Pass the word down the line!"[37]

"We floundered along in the mud at double-quick," wrote Holt. They struck the road west of the village before seven o'clock and heard of the rout of Edward Johnson's division. Lee's aide, Charles Venable, met the two brigades, instructing them to move by the left flank toward the salient. Holt recounted that as they crested a hill the battle's roar was deafening. Cannon fire burst over their heads, and they halted and lay down. Perrin's Alabamians kept moving deeper into the Mule Shoe.[38]

Perrin rode at the head of his Alabamians, leading them to the McCoull farmstead, where he found Lee, Richard Ewell, Robert Rodes, and John Gordon "engaged in an earnest and animated discussion." The scene was, according to one of Perrin's veterans, "appalling. The field was covered with fugitives, some of the artillery was rushing headlong to the rear, and it looked as if some dreadful catastrophe had happened or was about to happen to the army." While the generals conversed, the Alabamians lay on the ground to avoid bullets.[39]

"Perrin was looking from one to the other as if at a loss for his orders," noted an observer. The immediate concern was for Dodson Ramseur's position in the works south of the west angle. Earlier, Georgia troops from Brigadier General William Wofford's First Corps brigade had advanced to the support of Junius Daniel's North Carolinians and Cullen Battle's Alabamians to the left of Ramseur. One of the Georgians stated that they drove the Yankees "beyond our rifle pits."[40]

Gordon settled the matter, saying to Perrin, "I will take responsibility and order you to charge." Perrin shouted, "Attention" and, up and down the line of five regiments, about 1,300 officers and men, rose from the ground. One of the Alabamians remembered that as he stood in McCoull's yards "bits of leaves" from a cherry tree near the gate were falling. "The enemy must have been overshooting us wonderfully," he wrote later, "for, if the bullets had been sweeping close to the ground as thick as they were through that tree, I don't see how any of us could have gotten through."[41]

Perrin spurred his horse to the left front of his brigade, drew his sword, and said loudly, "Forward, my brave Alabamians." Enemy musketry from the salient's apex and west angle lashed the Confederate ranks as they ascended the ridge toward Ramseur's right flank. The 9th Alabama lost three color bearers in succession while crossing the ground. "With the accustomed yell, our brigade drove at the enemy at a rushing step," exclaimed an Alabamian.[42]

When the attackers reached the inner line of works, Perrin leaped his mount over them into a curtain of musketry. Several bullets struck the general, with one of them severing his femoral artery. While on the march from the Wilderness days earlier, the thirty-seven-year-old native South Carolinian allegedly had predicted, "I shall come out of this fight a live major general or dead brigadier." Now he lay mortally wounded, saying to a few of his men, "Carry me back, boys." He died soon afterward. "A nobler spirit or braver man has not been offered as a sacrifice to this war," declared a Richmond newspaper correspondent.[43]

Colonel John C. C. Saunders of the 11th Alabama succeeded Perrin. The general's fall, however, caused confusion, with the ranks splitting apart. On the brigade's left, the 8th and 9th Alabama wrested a fifty-foot section of the secondary works from the enemy and then, "without regard to organization, but every man for himself," they reached the main parapet. On the right, the 10th, 11th, and 14th regiments, led by Saunders, clawed their way through a blistering fire of musketry and artillery discharges until they joined Ramseur's North Carolinians.[44]

From outside the original entrenchments and from the high ground on the right, the Yankees raked the Rebel-held trenches and traverses. The musketry "exceeded anything I ever heard in its rapidity and volume," professed a soldier. Another Confederate compared the waves of minié balls to a "very river of death." An Alabama officer directed his troops, "Now you stand here, and as you see them come I will run a bayonet through them and pitch them over to you and you catch them." An Alabama private confessed, "I regard this day as the most dismal one I ever passed through."[45]

Harris's Mississippians, meanwhile, had halted on the road west of the courthouse village, awaiting further orders. Harris believed that they had been there for thirty minutes when Lee and staff members rode up. The Confederate commander reportedly inquired to whose brigade the troops belonged and then started them toward the Mule Shoe. Lee and his aides rode at the head of the column. A rumor passed swiftly along the ranks that he planned to lead them in an attack. Harris, who had been near the end of the column when informed of Lee's presence, hurried forward and joined the commanding general.[46]

As the Mississippians proceeded, they came under a galling fire from Union batteries posted along the Landrum farm lane. A solid shot from a cannon struck near the front of the column and ricocheted in front of Traveller, causing Lee's favorite mount to rear. At once, Harris implored Lee, "for God's sake," to "go back." The men shouted for him to retire, and he agreed if they promised "to recapture the lost works." Private William C. Compton of the 16th Mississippi reportedly took Traveller's reins and turned the horse's head rearward. In a postwar account, Thomas T. Roche of the same regiment claimed that he and his comrades had concluded that Lee "did not intend to lead them."[47]

Before Lee rode away, he instructed Venable to guide the brigade to the McCoull house and have Harris report to Rodes for orders. Entering the Mule Shoe, the Mississippians passed Ewell, who was leaning on a crutch and alone, except for a courier. Venable located Rodes, who had just received a plea for immediate help from Ramseur. In Harris's words, Rodes "informed me that my command was expected to form on the right of Ramseur's brigade . . . and recapture the works." Rodes assigned a staff officer to lead the Mississippians forward.[48]

Harris had commanded the brigade for less than three months, but the thirty-nine-year-old, who before the war was an attorney in Vicksburg, Mississippi, was popular with the rank and file. He had been colonel of the 19th Mississippi until promoted to brigadier in February. On this morning he was evidently "mounted upon a shaggy, captured horse, which he named 'Yankee,'" wrote one of his men, "and which he always rode in action, inclining somewhat to the belief that on 'Yankee' he would escape the storm of missiles, and which he did, he was a conspicuous figure."[49]

Harris's four regiments, the 16th, 12th, 19th, and 48th, comprising 1,350 officers and men, marched west of the McCoull farmstead, descended the hill, crossed the spring branch, and followed the family's wagon road up the rise. A survivor of the Stonewall Brigade, lying on the ground with comrades, saw them and yelled, "Boys, you are going to catch hell today." Union shellfire began exploding above the column. Rodes's staff officer fled, in Harris's words, "in the most shameful and disgraceful manner, and I was thus left in total ignorance of our lines as well as those of the enemy." Fortunately, he soon encountered a private from the 10th Alabama, who informed him of the location of Ramseur's right flank.[50]

The 16th Mississippi led the column on the wagon road. Colonel Samuel E. Baker rode at the head of the regiment. "A heavy fog and the smoke from guns, screened our advance," wrote Private Buxton Conerly of Company E. When Union infantrymen in the captured works saw the approaching Mississippians, they lashed the enemy column with fearful musketry. A dozen members of Company C were killed or wounded in the initial blast of gunfire. Baker reeled in the saddle and fell dead on the ground. More bullets hit him, riddling his body. A bookkeeper in Natchez before the war, Baker had possessed "a commanding presence."[51]

"The enemy seemed to have concentrated their whole enginery of war at this point," the 16th Mississippi's Sergeant James Kirkpatrick scribbled later in his diary. Harris admitted in his report, "I should have advanced by the line of battle." Under "a most terrific fire of musketry and artillery," according to Harris, he filed the regiments to the right by the flank, fronted them, and, with their left on the farm road, ordered a charge. A Georgian called these Mississippians "the grandest body of men that I ever saw (taking the whole war through)."[52]

The Mississippians charged, "pell-mell, every man for himself." Their foes punished them with rifle fire. "I never saw bullets fly thicker," proclaimed a private in the 48th Mississippi, "and do not see how any us escaped being shot to pieces." A sergeant declared, "Our men fell dead fast and thick." A Federal wrote, "The enemy were so thick that every shot from a Union rifle carried its victim with it." But the Confederates kept going, reaching the main entrenchments to the right of Ramseur's brigade. Some of the Mississippians overlapped the mingled ranks of North Carolinians and Alabamians.[53]

The Confederates' hold on the earthworks needed to extend farther up the ridge toward the west angle. Harris stood on the parapet amid the musketry from the Yankees along the salient's apex and from within traverses. He directed his right regiments, the 12th and 16th, to wheel right and charge. "Apprehending the desperate and bloody character of the prospective charge, the men at first hesitated," recounted Thomas Roche. To their front, however, they saw the flag of the 16th Mississippi, carried by Sergeant Alexander Mixon, advancing up the slope. Turning to his comrades, Mixon urged them to follow, his "clarion-like voice" resounding along the ranks.[54]

Yard by bloody yard, traverse by deadly traverse, the Mississippians ascended the ridge. "The battle at this point became a hand to hand conflict," stated Harris, "the bayonet and butt of the musket being freely used; the Union troops contesting the possession of each traverse stubbornly." A Union soldier hurled his bayoneted rifle like a spear toward a Mississippian who had killed a Federal officer. "The force which he threw it drove the bayonet entirely through his chest," related a fellow Southerner. The Confederate "uttered the most unearthly yell I ever heard from human lips, as he fell over backward with the gun sticking in him." At the forefront was Mixon, who planted his flag on the parapet and died with a bullet to his head. The Rebels made it nearly to the west angle but had seized traverses along the way and perhaps nearly three hundred prisoners.[55]

"Our brigade, with others," a member of the 16th Mississippi informed a hometown newspaper, "was called upon to retake the works, and it proved one of the hardest tasks that human beings ever undertook." Even more severe than the difficulty was the cost. Harris estimated his losses at one-third in the valiant effort. Among the slain were Lieutenant Colonel Abram M. Feltus of the 16th and Colonel Thomas J. Hardin of the 19th. Their deaths and Baker's were "regarded by all as a heavy and irreparable calamity," asserted one of the men. "No officers were more beloved, or the recipients of more unbounded confidence."[56]

The Mississippians' charge elicited deserved praise. "Never did a brigade go into fiercer battle under greater trials," Charles Venable wrote Harris in a postwar letter, "and never did a brigade do its duty more." Robert Rodes attested, "It was the bravest deed I have ever seen performed!" Months later, Richard Ewell offered his view to Harris: "The manner in which your brigade charged over the hill to recapture our works was witnessed by me with intense admiration, for men who could advance so calmly to what seemed and proved almost instant death. I have never seen troops under a hotter fire than was endured on this day by your brigade and some other."[57]

Skilled leadership and the valor of officers and men had brought them to within yards of the west angle. But thousands of Yankees, piled rows deep, held the salient's broad apex. Harris knew that he had not enough men to retake the apex and, according to a Mississippian, "the contest assumed truly desperate character." It was about nine o'clock, rain kept falling, and another Confederate brigade approached the entry way to hell.[58]

Like Harris's and Perrin's commands, Brigadier General Samuel McGowan's South Carolina brigade had received marching orders about daylight. Since May 9, these Southerners had been at the far end of Jubal Early's Third Corps line, guarding Fredericksburg Road. During the night of May 11–12, they had moved into position about a half mile north of the courthouse village and about two miles from the salient's apex. On this morning they started forth in "a torrent of rain" around six o'clock. From the north, the familiar sound of musketry and cannon fire rolled toward them as they slogged through muddy fields.[59]

The South Carolinians composed one of the army's proudest units; they were veterans who had learned soldiering under a redoubtable fighter, Maxcy Gregg, in 1861 and 1862. They had earned a distinctive record at Gaines's Mill, Antietam, and Fredericksburg, where Gregg fell mortally wounded. They boasted of being the first Confederates in Gettysburg's town square on July 1, 1863. At the Wilderness, however, Union Second Corps troops had routed the South Carolinians on May 6. "This disaster to their prestige was mortifying in the extreme to our brave soldiers," argued Joseph N. Brown of the 14th South Carolina, "and their minds were well prepared to retrieve it at the next opportunity." They had been on so many bloody fields, added Brown, that they appeared "lost to all sense of fear."[60]

At the column's front, mounted on a "handsome" gray horse, rode the "portly form" of McGowan. A college graduate, Mexican War veteran, militia general, and up-country lawyer and politician, the forty-four-year-old native had been a notable figure in antebellum South Carolina. He had survived a serious wound to an ear in a duel with a fellow attorney, fought with rifles at twenty paces. He commanded militiamen in the firing on Fort Sumter and, in the spring of 1862, was elected colonel of the 14th South Carolina. A year later he received promotion to brigadier over two senior colonels in the brigade. Wounded in the leg at Chancellorsville, the 260-pound general now needed a cane when on foot.[61]

McGowan possessed "great personal magnetism," which endeared him to his troops. Sergeant B. F. Brown of the 1st South Carolina described McGowan as "a rousing stump speaker and a capital anecdote teller." The officers and men enjoyed gathering for one of his speeches, particularly when he had been away from them for a period of time. Before this campaign began, he told them, "Boys, you remember what I said to you some time ago, that I wanted you to drive the Yankees from Dan to Beersheba."[62]

The route of the march brought the South Carolinians toward the salient's base. McGowan halted them at "a sharp angle in the works near a brick-kiln." The approximately 1,750 South Carolinians waited in the heavy rain and gooey soil for perhaps an hour or more. Lee joined them sometime after eight o'clock, informing McGowan that the line had been broken, "but we will have it all right very soon." Lee directed McGowan to march north and to report to Ewell for orders.[63]

McGowan closed up the ranks and led them forward deeper into the Mule Shoe. "The very air smelled of a fight—as old soldiers called it," according to a Confederate veteran. Union artillery shells exploded overhead and plowed into the ground, "bespattering us with dirt," recounted a South Carolinian, "crashing down the limbs about us and the Minnie balls whistled around us at a terrific rate." Near the McCoull house, McGowan met Ewell, who directed McGowan to Rodes for orders. The division commander soon rode up, asking the identity of the troops. "McGowan's South Carolina brigade," came the reply. "There are no better soldiers in the world than these," declared Rodes.[64]

"You South Carolinians will do," Rodes added. "Boys, go right in." He ordered them to fill the gap on the right of Harris's Mississippians. Colonel Brown thought, "A feeling of unrest among officers of high rank indicated disaster." McGowan brought the five regiments into line by "a little old house [McCoull's] and its surrounding naked garden." The general instructed regimental commanders to keep aligned on the wagon road. Color bearers stepped in front of the regiments and unfurled the flags. Major William S. Dunlop's battalion of sharpshooters rimmed the line as skirmishers. When all was ready, McGowan shouted, "Forward! My brave boys."[65]

With cheers and at the double-quick, "now we entered the battle," in the words of one of them. From the beginning, however, McGowan's veterans had difficulty keeping alignment on the crooked farm lane. They were also uncertain where Harris's right flank lay. Enemy musketry "was so desperate that staff officers would not go near enough to point out where we must enter," recounted Brown. "Therefore we went where the firing was heaviest."[66]

They leaned into "a whirlwind of rifle balls," pushing ahead to the inner or reserve line of "low temporary breastworks," as a South Carolinian described them. McGowan halted the advance, but Lieutenant Colonel

Thomas F. Clyburn—it was his twenty-first birthday—waved the 12th South Carolina forward on the right of the farm lane in a reckless charge. "They entered the point of greatest danger," described a Rebel, "and received a concentrated fire of artillery that crashed through the works, and the fusillade of infantry from the front and across the traverses on the right flank."[67]

When the brigade reached the reserve line, McGowan reportedly dismounted and stood on the works to locate the enemy line. Almost immediately, a bullet struck him in the right arm but fortunately did not hit a bone. McGowan relinquished command to his senior colonel, Benjamin T. Brockman of the 13th South Carolina. Brockman had barely time to issue orders before he fell with wounds to the head and left arm. The limb required amputation, and Brockman died in Richmond on June 8.[68]

McGowan headed rearward, seeking medical attention. While enroute, he met Lee, saying to the army commander, "General, I am wounded am now seeking a surgeon." Lee allegedly smiled and remarked: "Only wounded! I am agreeably surprised that you were not killed. You are the largest officer in the army, General McGowan, and you ride the largest horse."[69]

By the time this encounter occurred, the South Carolinians had scrambled over the inner works and, in the words of one of them, "it was plainly a question of bravery and endurance now." With the loss of McGowan and Brockman, command responsibility fell to Colonel Joseph Brown. His 14th South Carolina was on the left end of the brigade line. It appears that Brown and Lieutenant Colonel Isaac Hunt of the 13th South Carolina in the center issued orders for a charge. It also appears that their veteran troops had decided the matter already and had followed their comrades in the 12th South Carolina.[70]

"With a terrific yell," the Confederates swept toward the west angle and entrenchments along the apex. "The sight we encountered was not calculated to encourage us," wrote South Carolinian James F. J. Caldwell. "The trenches, dug on the inner side, were almost filled with water. Dead men lay on the surface of the ground and in the pools of water. The wounded bled and groaned, stretched or huddled in every attitude of pain. The water was crimsoned with blood."[71]

The attackers veered to the left or west as if driven by a terrible wind of musketry from their front and right flank. Many, if not most, of the South Carolinians became entangled with Harris's Mississippians, who shouted at the South Carolinians, "Go to the right." Amid the fury, they wheeled by the right flank, facing east. "The men realized the perilous position in which they are placed," recounted Captain James Armstrong of the 1st South Carolina. Armstrong's regiment and the 12th led the bloody, plodding advance along the trench and from traverse to traverse. With each step in the trench, with each captured traverse, South Carolinians fell.[72]

Armstrong's commander, Colonel Camillus W. McCreary had been wounded during the charge from the inner works. Now his successor, twenty-six-year-old Lieutenant Colonel Washington P. Shooter, collapsed into a traverse, mortally wounded with a bullet in the chest. "He was a most gallant and efficient officer," stated Caldwell, and men rushed to his aid. Shooter said to them, "I know that I am a dead man; but I die with my eyes fixed on victory." A soldier in the regiment retrieved his "watch, pocket book and other personal effects." A few feet away his brother, Lieutenant Evander C. Shooter, lay dead on the ground. A third brother, Sergeant Van Shooter, had been slain in the Wilderness a week earlier.[73]

The South Carolinians and some Mississippians kept driving toward the west angle and the entrenchments along the apex. At the forefront of the surge, Private Charles E. Whilden carried the flag of the 1st South Carolina. The forty-year-old soldier suffered from epilepsy and could have been exempted from military service. Instead, he tried time and again to enlist until he was finally accepted in January 1864. Ordered to Virginia, the volunteer joined the regiment.[74]

On this morning, Whilden led the charge up the slope toward a grim place. When enemy gunfire tore at the colors, he ripped the flag from the staff and wrapped it around his body. Wounded in the left shoulder, Whilden reached the original works, where his fellow Rebels wrested the angle and about a hundred yards of works to the east from their blue-coated foes in a frenzy of hand-to-hand combat. Few, if any, of Whilden's comrades likely had expected that the "old" recruit would seize a critical moment and act with valor. Four decades later, the eighty-year-old veteran still retained the regimental banner.[75]

The charge of the South Carolinians to the Mule Shoe's apex brought them, in the judgment of an officer, into "one of the fiercest and most bloody struggles of the war." "The musketry then roared, we became mixed up with other troops, every man fighting for himself," as a member of the 1st South Carolina described fighting later. "The place was too hot for orders. You could scarcely get your head above the works unless you would get a bullet into it."[76]

Another South Carolinian wrote a letter to his wife on May 15: "One traverse would be filled with our men and another with the enemy side by side with in a few feet of each other, and the fire so heavy that neither would raise their heads the outside of the works was lined by the enemy." A comrade called it "the forlorn attempt to hold its assailants at arm's length." In the estimation of James Caldwell, there had come to be an acceptance of the reality that engulfed them: "The question became, pretty plainly, whether one was willing to meet death, not merely to run the chances of it."[77]

Soldiers in David A. Russell's Union Sixth Corps division awoke well before daylight on this rainy Thursday. They boiled coffee and fried pork over "smoky pine fires" before filing into marching ranks. Like their comrades in Thomas Neill's division who had entered the struggle at the salient, Russell's veterans had been directed to be "in readiness to move wherever needed." For reasons unexplained, Russell's four brigades marched initially toward the army's right flank, farther away from the fighting at the Mule Shoe. Around seven o'clock, however, they received orders to move to the left, behind the corps's lines, and to support the Second Corps.[78]

Emory Upton's brigade led the division's march northward past the Shelton house toward the Brown farm. The column proceeded "to within 400 yards of the Brown house," recounted Upton, "when we turned to the right [south], and came out about the same distance to the right [west] of the Landrum house." A staff officer appeared, exclaiming, "We are gone to lose the day." Russell joined Upton and ordered the colonel to advance in support of the beleaguered right flank of the Second Corps, located near where Upton had attacked on May 10. Upton rode ahead on a reconnaissance while his regimental commanders hurried the troops forward at the double-quick. It was about 9:30 A.M.[79]

Upton came upon a tactical stalemate. Five hours of unrelenting combat had seen the ground won by the attackers regained almost completely by the defenders in fierce counterattacks, the final ones by Nathaniel Harris's Mississippians and Samuel McGowan's South Carolinians. The foes bloodied each other across the salient's main earthworks and among the traverses. Direction of the offensive had been reduced seemingly to funneling reinforcements into the ill wind that still swept across the Mule Shoe. The Yankees' hold on the west face, however, appeared to be wavering.[80]

The Excelsior Brigade of Gershom Mott's Second Corps division had been withdrawn, exposing the Federals' left flank along the west face.

Upton's instructions had been to relieve Mott's units but, when he viewed the action from a wooded knoll opposite the west angle, he decided to advance toward it. He termed it in his report as the point "of vital importance to hold." As his regiments joined him in the woods, Upton ordered his leading unit, the 95th Pennsylvania, to advance.[81]

The Pennsylvanians cleared the tree line and pushed forward into "a furious storm of bullets." When they reached a hollow about a hundred yards from the west angle, Upton had them lie down as Confederate musketry tore up the ground in front of them. In the swale was the 10th Massachusetts, a Sixth Corps regiment in Neill's division. These Massachusetts veterans had returned from the salient's works when the Excelsior Brigade withdrew and sought shelter in the depression.[82]

Upton had gone forward with the Pennsylvanians and confronted the 10th Massachusetts's Colonel Joseph B. Parsons: "This is no position for this regiment. Swing this regiment over this slope and up against the works." Parsons refused. Upton demanded to speak with Parsons's brigade commander, Colonel Oliver Edwards. When Edwards appeared, he instructed Parsons to obey the order, as Upton outranked both of them. Parsons declined once more. By now Upton's other regiments—the 5th Maine, 121st New York, and 96th Pennsylvania—had arrived. Frustrated and angry, Upton ordered them to charge.[83]

The 5th Maine led the attack. As they emerged from the hollow, the Mainers "received a tremendous fire," recounted Parsons. "No troops could stand such a fire and they were driven back in confusion, leaving the ground strewn with their dead and wounded." The 121st New York and 96th Pennsylvania followed and were met by "a heavy volley at close range." A private in the 96th Pennsylvania jotted in his diary afterward that they "Broke and run" but "rallied [and] reformed" in the swale, where they lay down.[84]

Upton's ranks connected with Second Corps troops on their left while extending to the right "behind crest oblique to the works." "I can not imagine how any of us survived the sharp fire that swept over us at this point," attested a Pennsylvanian, "a fire so keen that it split the blades of grass all about us, the minnies moaning as they picked out victims by the score." One of Upton's aides recounted, "Our troops got gunpowder crazy, and standing up in the most exposed position, would fire with deliberate aim."[85]

Russell's other three brigades commanded by Henry Eustis, Nelson Cross, and Henry W. Brown entered the struggle, coming in on Upton's right flank. Eustis's four regiments met a stream of wounded as it ascended the ridge, charging directly toward the west angle and the Mississippi-ans and South Carolinians. The 5th Wisconsin's left companies reached the works, while the brigade's ranks extended to the northwest, almost perpendicular to Upton's line in the shallow ravine. The foes, wrote a Wisconsin soldier, "shot and stabbed each other until the rebel breastworks were filled with dead in gray, and outside, on the glacis in front, the corpses in blue were piled on each other in heaps."[86]

Colonel Nelson Cross's veterans from New York and Pennsylvania followed Eustis's men, filling gaps in the line. Behind them came the New Jersey brigade, temporarily led by Colonel Henry W. Brown. These six regiments passed through "a thicket of scraggy pines with dead limbs," before emerging unto clear ground on the Federals' right flank opposite North Carolinians. When the Confederates saw them, they blasted the enemy's ranks with musketry. In the 15th New Jersey, wrote Lieutenant Edmund Halsey, "the right wing was almost entirely swept away in an instant."

The Federals charged, with men "falling everywhere." The 15th New Jersey reached the Confederate entrenchments, capturing a flag and scores of Rebels. The cost was fearful. Captain James Walker was killed, shot in the head. "He fell back dead, with both arms outstretched," wrote one of his men. Captain Cornelius C. Shimer fell dead, also with a bullet in the head. Lieutenant George C. Justice, stood on the works, waving his sword, until shot down by "one of the skulking prisoners." Justice's men bayoneted the Confederate to death.[87]

"For one-half hour the battle raged with savage fury," wrote a New Jerseyman. "Officers stood upon the works to stimulate courage of their men and were shot down with muskets resting against their persons." A comrade affirmed, "No experience during the whole time the Fifteenth was in the service was more destructive than the half hour, from ten o'clock to half-past ten, of the morning of May 12th." The Rebels repulsed the attack, driving their foes back into the woods. More than two hundred Yankees lay dead or wounded on the open ground and at the works.[88]

Winfield Hancock, meanwhile, had dispatched John Brooke's Second Corps brigade and Lewis Grant's Sixth Corps Vermont regiments from the salient's east leg to support their comrades engaged along the west face and around the west angle. Entry of the reinforcements into this furious action added to the disorganization in the densely packed ranks. The Vermonters joined Upton's men in the hollow, while Brooke's troops pushed forward where Frank Wheaton's and Daniel Bidwell's Sixth Corps brigades opposed Mississippians and North Carolinians. "Never during

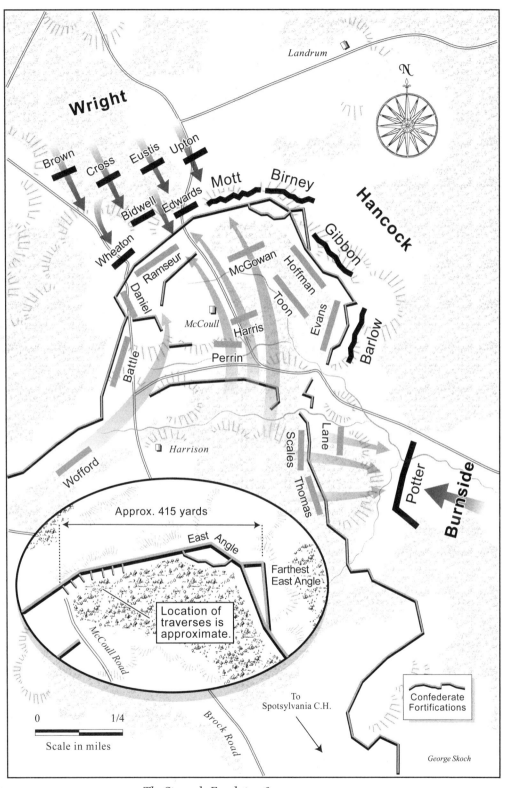

Landrum

Wright

Brown   Cross   Eustis   Upton

Mott   Birney

Hancock

Bidwell   Edwards

Wheaton

Ramseur   McGowan   Hoffman   Gibbon

Daniel   Toon   Evans

McCoull   Harris   Barlow

Battle   Perrin

Wofford   Harrison

Scales   Lane

Thomas   Potter

Burnside

East Angle

Approx. 415 yards

Farthest
East Angle

Location of
traverses is
approximate.

McCoull Road

To
Spotsylvania C.H.

Confederate
Fortifications

0   1/4

Scale in miles

Brock Road

George Skoch

The Struggle Escalates, 6:30 A.M.–10:00 A.M.

the war have I seen such desperate fighting," declared a staff officer in Brooke's brigade.[89]

Above the unbroken roar of musketry, artillery shells burst, raining down shards of iron on infantrymen on both sides. In a broad arc from the Landrum lane to the west beyond the Shelton house, at least a dozen Union batteries fired hundreds of rounds of ordnance. From within the salient and farther south to past the Harrison residence, Confederate gun crews rammed in charges and pulled lanyards. Some Federals worked captured enemy cannon.[90]

A section of Batteries C and I, 5th United States Artillery, commanded by Lieutenant Richard Metcalf, rolled up to the right of Upton's men and opened fire with canister. Gray-coated defenders responded, abandoning the works and charging toward the pair of cannon. The Rebels gunned down horses and crew members, getting to within a hundred feet of the guns before Union infantry and loads of double canister repulsed the attackers. Upton's chief of staff, Captain J. D. Fish, was killed as he helped carry forward more rounds of canister. Metcalf lost more than half of his men, either killed or wounded, and all of his horses. Infantrymen volunteered to work the guns.[91]

The western bend or angle in miles of Confederate entrenchments had become, as Upton described, the point "of vital importance to hold" for both opponents. Thousands of men, thrust into a cauldron, stood at places only feet apart and had the sole purpose of slaying and injuring those opposite them. Frontal and enfilading fire ran down the works on each side of the angle. The fighting had become a death struggle, personal and up close. At this time, admitted a New Yorker, "it was hard to tell who were the masters."[92]

{ 9 }

The Death-Grapple of the War

By Thursday, May 12, Major General Gouverneur K. Warren, commander of the Union Fifth Corps, had managed to test the patience of General-in-Chief Ulysses S. Grant. Warren's assaults on May 5 in the Wilderness and on May 8 at Laurel Hill had lacked alacrity, coordination, and aggressiveness, characteristics the commanding general expected from a ranking officer. Late on the afternoon of May 5, Warren had even refused to renew a frontal attack on the Confederate defenses along Orange Turnpike.[1]

Warren's intellect and soldierly aptitude were unquestioned. Second in the class of 1850 at West Point, the thirty-four-year-old New Yorker had commanded an infantry regiment and then a brigade before being appointed the army's chief engineer with the rank of brigadier general. While Winfield Scott Hancock recovered from his serious wound at Gettysburg, Warren earned promotion to major general and temporary command of the Second Corps during operations in the late summer and fall of 1863. With the army's reorganization in March 1864, Warren replaced George Sykes in command of the Fifth Corps.[2]

Staff officer Theodore Lyman said of Warren, "He was a man of sleepless energy, activity and study—his mind never still; a master of his art, and of a daring spirit; but promotion was too rapid and in the wrong direction." Warren "did not exactly take the direction of command of troops." As a corps commander, he possessed little faith in the abilities of subordinates and tended "to make severe criticisms on others." He could be both a difficult superior officer and a recalcitrant subordinate officer.[3]

Warren had an apparent predisposition to question orders with which he disagreed. His refusal to renew attacks on May 5 had not been the first time that he had canceled an assault. During the Mine Run Campaign, while in command of the Second Corps, Warren had been ordered to undertake an offensive strike on the morning of November 30, 1863. When

Warren viewed the formidable enemy works behind Mine Run, he informed army headquarters that he had called off the attack. George Meade called the news "astounding intelligence." Evidently controlling his volcanic temper at his subordinate's decision, Meade joined Warren, examined the Confederate defenses, and agreed that a charge would result in a bloody repulse. One of Warren's staff officers admitted that the general's worst failing was that he was "always ready to set up his judgment against that of his superior officers."[4]

The Fifth Corps's failed assaults at Laurel Hill on May 8 and 10 likely had reaffirmed Warren's view of the needless sacrifice of lives with frontal attacks. On May 8, however, with superior numbers, Warren had conducted hurried, piecemeal charges, which resulted in fearful casualties. Captain Amos M. Judson of the 83rd Pennsylvania recounted the impact of the abortive offensives, "This day was a disastrous one for the Eighty-Third and did a great deal towards impairing, for the time, the *morale* of the men; for they all knew that they were rushed into the fight without any display of skill or foresight on the part of their commanding generals."[5]

For a week, then, Warren had witnessed the fruitlessness and price of frontal assaults against a skilled and prepared opponent behind fieldworks. By daylight on May 12, Warren had his troops "in readiness," posted in entrenchments west of Brock Road and opposite earthworks manned by Rebel veterans of Charles Field's First Corps division. At 6:00 A.M., Meade wired Warren: "Keep up as threatening an attitude as possible to keep the enemy in your front. Wright must attack and you may have to. Be ready and do the best you can." Thirty minutes later, Warren issued a circular to his three division commanders, alerting them to expect an advance "at any moment." Before long, Sixth Corps commander Wright sent a message to Warren—"we are hard pressed"—and urged him "to support my right and extend it."[6]

Meade followed Wright's request with a telegram to Warren at eight o'clock: "Attack immediately with all the force you can, and be prepared to follow up any success with the rest of your force." The corps commander evidently was dumbfounded by Meade's orders. Laurel Hill had been a killing ground, with some of the army's best veteran troops refusing to advance farther up the slope. Warren responded, noting that the directive "leaves me no time to attack the key points first." He added: "Your orders have been issued and reiterated. It does not take many men from the enemy to hold the intrenchments in my front."[7]

Warren complied initially with a probe of enemy defenses by three regiments from Colonel Jacob B. Sweitzer's brigade. The 9th and 32nd Massachusetts and 62nd Pennsylvania, led by Colonel George L. Prescott, went forward. "I knew what the result would be when I started," argued Prescott. The Federals passed the ruins of the Spindle house and ascended the rise. When they were fifty yards from the fieldworks defended by Brigadier General John Bratton's South Carolina brigade, the entrenchments blazed with rifle and artillery fire. "A line of their dead was laid down across the entire front of my brigade," reported Bratton, as his men's volleys tore into the Union ranks. It was more than the Yankees could withstand, and they scattered in "fleeing hordes."[8]

In the aftermath of the repulse of Sweitzer's regiments—the 32nd Massachusetts lost more than half its men—Warren hesitated to undertake the ordered offensive. His veteran officers and men remained in place behind their fieldworks. Confederate batteries had kept firing for several minutes as if reminding their foes what awaited. But the Federals knew from recent experience that death walked the ground before Laurel Hill. Warren canceled the attack and informed army headquarters: "My left cannot advance without a most destructive enfilade fire until the Sixth Corps has cleared its front. My right is close up to the enemy's works, and ordered to assault. The enemy's line here appears to be strongly held."[9]

Meade was furious when he received Warren's message. The army commander had been under increasing pressure from Grant, who wanted the Confederate lines assailed along their entire length regardless of the casualties. Like no one before him, Grant had a killer's mindset, a relentless determination to inflict harm on his foes until they were no more, an understanding of war's arithmetic against a numerically inferior opponent. The achievement of that end, and the burden, lay with those in the Mule Shoe and in front of Laurel Hill.[10]

Grant, Meade, and others at headquarters dismissed the impregnability of Confederate defenses on Laurel Hill. Warren had an old, close friend at headquarters, Meade's chief of staff Andrew Humphreys. The aide explained the sentiment at headquarters on that morning: "The manner in which the contest there [Mule Shoe] was carried on and the reinforcements the enemy received together with the fact that Burnside was attacking on the east side of the salient, led to the conclusion that the enemy could not be very strong in Warren's front." Humphreys noted, however, that headquarters had no reliable information that the Confederates had withdrawn units from Laurel Hill. Sixth Corps staff officer

Oliver Wendell Holmes Jr. echoed Humphreys's assessment, stating that Warren "represented himself harder pressed than he was."[11]

At 9:15 A.M., Meade had Humphreys send a message to Warren: "The order of the major-general commanding is preemptory that you attack at once at all hazards with your whole force, if necessary." Fifteen minutes later the chief of staff advised his friend, "Don't hesitate to attack with the bayonet. Meade has assumed the responsibility and will take the consequences."[12]

In the ranks of the Fifth Corps, meanwhile, the men lay quietly on the muddy ground as the rain intensified. "We had no hint of what was developing elsewhere," remembered Major Abner R. Small of the 16th Maine. "Nine o'clock came, and passed. Then out of the watery haze on our right came an aide, who made his way quietly along the line, dropping a word to this and that commander, only a ripple, and all was still again." More minutes elapsed until "we heard the command to go forward."[13]

Major Small's regiment served in the division of Brigadier General Lysander Cutler. Before Cutler's troops had crossed the works and formed two lines of battle, however, off to their left Brigadier General Charles Griffin's division had initiated the Fifth Corps's assault. As they had done four days earlier, Warren's units advanced in uncoordinated, piecemeal attacks. Griffin sent in regiments from two brigades, directing them across the fields of the Spindle farm and into "a perfect hailstorm of balls."[14]

"At every moment I could hear the dull peculiar thud sound of a ball as it entered some poor fellow," Sergeant Charles T. Bowen of the 12th U.S. Infantry recorded later in his diary. "The yells of the wounded I can hear yet." Confederate brigadier Bratton described the scene from Laurel Hill's crest as his South Carolinians "routed and put the whole [enemy] mass to flight, most precipitate and headlong." Bratton continued, "In their haste and panic a multitude of them ran across a portion of open field and gave our battery and my line on the right a shot at them." Captain Porter Farley of the 140th New York had it right: "It proved an utter failure."[15]

Warren's third division, Brigadier General Samuel Crawford's Pennsylvania Reserves, followed Griffin's regiments. When they had cleared a woodline and started up the slope, they met a wall of musketry and shellfire from Colonel William F. Perry's five Alabama regiments and supporting batteries. The Federals' ranks staggered under the fusillade from the Rebel earthworks and refused to go farther. Crawford ordered a withdrawal, and the Fifth Corps's assaults ended as Crawford's and Cutler's veterans returned to their fieldworks. Speaking for most, if not all, of his comrades in the corps, a Pennsylvanian believed that Laurel Hill possessed an "evil genius."[16]

Cutler's veterans came next. One of the division's, if not the army's, finest field officers, Lieutenant Colonel Rufus Dawes of the 6th Wisconsin, argued that their attack was "manifestly hopeless at the outset." The first line of Federals reached a ravine and halted. Behind them came the second of two brigades, joining their comrades in the depression. Confederate batteries and musketry from Colonel Dudley M. Dubose's Georgia regiments poured into the blue-coated ranks. "In less than fifteen minutes after we became engaged the ravine lay full of dead men, while hundreds of wounded were on their way to the hospital," related Sergeant Edward B. Fowler of the 150th Pennsylvania.[17]

Either instinct or experience, likely both, kept many Federals behind an invisible line; veterans knew that to cross it meant death or maiming. "Officers stormed back and forth in a useless effort to make the troops advance further," wrote Sergeant Fowler. Some of the bravest scrambled out of the ravine into blasts of canister and "terrible sheets of flame" from Georgians' rifles. Those who dared seemed to vanish under the killing gale from the crest. In the ravine, according to Fowler, "the ranks were fast disappearing, and to hold men to such an unequal contest was only a useless sacrifice of life."[18]

When Cutler learned from officers sent to him of the attack's failure and the grim situation in the ravine, he sought permission for a withdrawal from Warren. Although he had predicted and had forewarned headquarters of such an outcome, the corps commander understood the likely reaction of Grant and Meade to the abandonment of the offensive. Warren instructed Cutler, "Report to me in writing if you think your troops cannot carry the position in their front." Cutler complied: "My brigade commanders report that they cannot carry the works. They are losing badly, and I cannot get them up the hill."[19]

Confederate division commander Charles Field summarized the action, writing that the Yankees "made a determined effort to break through, but they were repulsed with great slaughter." Chief of artillery William N. Pendleton noted the artillery's contribution to the enemy's repulse, declaring that the Federal assault "was shivered by the tremendous destructiveness of missiles hurled upon them at close range from our guns." Field's troops had sustained minimal casualties.[20]

Humphreys had joined his friend Warren at Fifth Corps headquarters. When the pair of generals received confirmation of the assault's repulse, Humphreys canceled further attacks. "I also again assailed the enemy's intrenchments, suffering heavy loss, but failing to get in," as Warren described the operation in his report. One of his staff officers, Washington Roebling, offered his judgment, asserting that the attacks were "quickly repulsed as was anticipated." Roebling said of the officers and men in the charges, "it is not a matter of surprise that they had lost all spirit for that kind of work." The undertaking had ended, the aide conceded, "with the predictable slaughter."[21]

Meade and Grant, meanwhile, had learned few details of the progress of Warren's offensive. Around ten o'clock, as eddies of men flowed rearward out of the ravine, Meade informed the general-in-chief: "Warren seems reluctant to assault. I have ordered him at all hazards to do so, and if his attack should be repulsed to draw in the right and send his troops as fast as possible to Wright and Hancock." Grant replied thirty minutes or so later, "If Warren fails to attack promptly, send Humphreys to command his corps, and relieve him."[22]

Before long headquarters learned of the offensive's outcome. Warren had attacked as ordered, Humphreys surely told Meade, so the army commander did not relieve him. Early in the afternoon, however, Meade acted upon his words to Grant, directing Warren to send Griffin's division to support the Second Corps and Cutler's division to support the Sixth Corps in the salient struggle. Crawford's regiments and two brigades of Marylanders and heavy artillerists manned the abandoned fieldworks in a single rank.[23]

Warren's performance brought inevitable criticism, even questions about his fitness for corps command. Assistant Secretary of War Charles Dana telegraphed his boss, Edwin Stanton, that night at seven o'clock. "Warren alone has gained nothing," Dana stated. "His attacks were made in the forenoon, with so much delay that both Grant and Meade were greatly dissatisfied, but when they were made they were unsuccessful, though attended with considerable loss."[24]

Grant's willingness to have Warren relieved of command indicated his mounting frustration with and lack of confidence in the corps commander. Grant explained his thinking to his staff: "I feel sorry to be obliged to send such an order in regard to Warren. He is an officer for whom I had conceived a very high regard. His quickness of perception, personal gallantry, and soldierly bearing please me, and a few days ago I should have been inclined to place him in command of the Army of the Potomac in case Meade had been killed. But I began to feel, after his want of vigor in assaulting on the eighth, that he was not as efficient as I had believed, and his delay in attacking and the feeble character of his assaults today confirm me in my apprehensions."[25]

Meade shared the general-in-chief's concerns about Warren's conduct, expressing his views to Grant's chief of staff, John Rawlins, in a letter written weeks later. Meade understood that Warren could object to making an assault on Laurel Hill as he was on the ground, where "his opportunities were much better than mine" for judging the success or failure of an attack. Meade respected Warren's judgment in such matters and might have deferred to him. Instead, Warren indicated he would obey orders and attack vigorously when he did not. This Meade could not accept, for his subordinate had "no right to delay executing his orders under any circumstances." Warren should have informed Meade of his reluctance and then proceeded with the assault unless instructed otherwise.[26]

Meade's criticisms of Warren had more merit than Grant's, but neither commander knew the tactical situation on the ground. Warren's reluctance to assail Laurel Hill had justification. Contrary to the opinion at headquarters, Confederate defenses still bristled with enemy infantry and artillery. When Humphreys joined Warren, the army's chief of staff, agreeing with his friend that further attacks would only result in the senseless effusion of blood, canceled the offensive. Neither Grant nor Meade witnessed the continued "evil genius" of Laurel Hill.[27]

For more than six hours the Mule Shoe had acted as a billowing whirlpool, pulling in more than thirty-two thousand Union attackers and upward of 13,500 Confederate counterattackers. At 11:00 A.M., Horatio Wright's last Sixth Corps division, a pair of brigades under Brigadier General James B. Ricketts, were ordered into the struggle. The eleven regiments—officers and men from a half dozen states—numbered more than three thousand in the ranks.[28]

Wright had remained in the hollow beyond the salient and there he met Ricketts, whom Theodore Lyman described as "the little sturdy, Puritan looking man." A West Pointer, the forty-six-year-old Ricketts had been in the army for twenty-five years, receiving command of the division in March 1864. A few of his regiments had served under Robert Milroy in the Shenandoah Valley, where they and Milroy's other units were routed by Confederates in June 1863. Merited or not, "'Milroy's weary boys' had a woeful reputation."[29]

Wright had concerns about the command and, when he conferred with Ricketts, inquired, "Do you think the men will go up?"

"I think they will," replied Ricketts. "I have been talking to the officers and I think they will."

"Very well, then," directed the corps commander. "Move in by the left flank and attack."[30]

Ricketts brought forward his two brigades, commanded by colonels Benjamin Smith and John W. Schall. As he noted in his diary, the brigadier advanced only "part" of the brigades. The 126th Ohio of Smith's brigade went in first. The regiment "was made of plain American boys from the farms and shops of Northeastern Ohio," in the words of a speaker at the dedication of its monument. The Ohioans charged to within a hundred yards of the salient's earthworks and lay down.[31]

"They loaded lying," recalled one of the Ohioans, "then rising to their knees, took deliberate aim at the heads of the rebels above the parapet and fired." No man cheered as they worked their rifles. Some of them stood up to fire and were soon shot down. Their commander, Lieutenant Colonel Aaron W. Ebright, was struck a glancing blow by a bullet to his head, knocking him down and forcing him to relinquish command. The Ohioans clung to the position for two hours, firing fifty rounds for each man and suffering losses of 25 percent. "This I consider the most severe engagement in which my regiment participated during the present campaign," declared Ebright in his report.[32]

The gunfire was "incessant," in the word of a staff officer. When troops in Schall's brigade advanced, they became "almost instantly engaged." The officers and men of the 10th Vermont in the brigade reached the Mule Shoe and found themselves fighting Rebels on the opposite side of the works. The Federals pulled out wounded comrades in the Sixth Corps from beneath dead bodies and captured some enemy prisoners, who claimed "they were ordered to hold those works or die in the attempt."[33]

It was minutes past noon when the Ohioans and Vermonters, charging in support of their fellow soldiers in the Sixth Corps, had entered "the death-struggle" within and without the Mule Shoe. Along the entrenchments Union flags stood opposite Confederate flags. "The contest had become beyond all comparison the closest and fiercest of the war," asserted a member of Winfield Hancock's staff. A Louisianan staff officer contended, "Never before during the war had so many men fought within so contracted a space."[34]

"All around that salient was a seething, bubbling, roaring hell of hate and murder," recalled a Mainer. To a fellow New Englander, it appeared as if "the heavens and earth seemed convulsed." Incessant musketry blended with the roar of cannon into the thunderous sound. Amid the roar, the reality could be heard of the "grating sound" of a bullet on bone or the "heavy thud" of a bullet on flesh.[35]

By this stage in the conflict, veteran troops in both armies had reconciled themselves to the necessity of killing fellow human beings. A member of the Union Iron Brigade had confided earlier to his parents, "It is strange what a predilection we have for injuring our brother man, but we learn the art of killing far easier than we do a hard problem in arithmetic." A fellow Yankee disagreed, arguing that killing demanded "the hard courage," for the deliberate act went against their view of themselves as human beings and conflicted with the Christian beliefs of most of them.[36]

The carnage the men had witnessed, and the loss of comrades, friends, and kin, had changed them. As the war progressed and the casualties mounted, there was, in the estimation of historian Drew Gilpin Faust, an "emerging delight in killing," motivated in part by a need for vengeance. A Vermont soldier stated with irony, "The more we get used to being killed, the better we like it." Still, the act of killing an enemy required work, whether it was duty, self-defense, or retribution that assuaged conscience. Soldiers preferred doing so from a distance, not seeing the result up close. But on this day the Mule Shoe offered no such deliverance.[37]

On both sides of the parapet the veterans also understood that the killing and maiming possessed a democratic commonality. "War is a leveler, like death," believed the 17th Maine's Private John Haley, "the best and the meanest blood here mingled." While much of the combat was up close and personal along the works and among the traverses, a minié-ball or a shard from an artillery shell could find anyone, unseen and at random. "The safe or unsafe place on the fighting line is about as difficult to pick out before hand as it is to tell where and when the next bolt of lightning will strike," observed a Union veteran. "One of the incalculable and surprising things connected with battles is the irregular, uncertain, disproportionate, and eccentric way that losses occur in action."[38]

By midday the struggle had been ongoing without cessation for more than seven hours. "At noon," remembered a North Carolinian, "the water so bloody in the ditches, that one inexperienced would have taken it for blood entire." He believed it was a foot deep. Likely speaking for many of his comrades, a South Carolinian told his wife, "all the bitterness and hate of the enemy seems concentrated in this desperate crusade against us." James Caldwell of the 1st South Carolina declared, "It was plainly a question of bravery and endurance now."[39]

The worst of the fury engulfed the foes along the Mule Shoe's western face and around the west angle, where officers and men mainly of the Union Sixth Corps battled Louisianans, North Carolinians, Mississippians, and South Carolinians. "At some points," wrote a Southern newspaperman, "the two armies fought on opposite sides of the entrenchments the distance between them not being more than the length of their muskets." But the bloodletting enveloped the Federals who filled the low ground in front of the salient and the Confederates who manned the traverses. It was as if a dark spirit wrapped all within its folds.[40]

"The grimmest figure it is possible to conceive of the soldier in action was presented by the soldier fighting here," related a Union veteran. "The men stood in red mud up to their ankles; their clothing was dripping moisture; their shoulders, arms and faces were smeared with the plastic red soil which attached itself to the musket butt every time the gun was loaded. Their lips were blackened and parched from biting cartridges to release the powder. They fought without food or drink or any thought of it."[41]

The closeness of their opponents and intensity and duration of the fighting left searing memories of the struggle with those who survived. The long hours of combat belonged not to the armies' senior leadership but to the captains, lieutenants, sergeants, and privates trapped within a seemingly godforsaken place. As a South Carolinian professed years later, any man who was there "will remember [the Mule Shoe] as the most terrible that was encountered during that four years of death and destruction."[42]

Whether days later or years ahead, the men wrote of the incidents, of the scenes, and of what they had endured. "I never expect to be fully believed when I tell what I saw of the horrors of Spotsylvania," declared a Union officer in the Sixth Corps, "Because I should be loath to believe it myself, were the case reversed." A Louisiana captain, writing to his wife three days later, stated, "I have been in a good many hard fights, but I never saw anything like the contest of the 12th."[43]

"This was the place to test individual courage," argued James Caldwell of the 1st South Carolina. "Some ordinarily good soldiers did next to nothing, others excelled themselves." He remembered a tall soldier in the 14th South Carolina, who stood above the parapet, took careful aim at a Yankee, and fired. He then knelt and reloaded his rifle before rising and shooting. "The balls flew around him like hail, from front and flank," wrote Caldwell, who thought the man fired at least a hundred times from noon to dark. Finally, while aiming one more time at an enemy soldier, he staggered from a bullet in the chest and fell dead.[44]

A fellow South Carolinian informed his hometown newspaper, "It was almost certain death for a man to put his head above the works." But like the soldier in the 14th South Carolina, Private W. W. Davenport in Caldwell's regiment stood up "and shot all day" as comrades handed him loaded rifles. "He was not afraid of all the guns in Grant's army" and went through it unscathed. Not far away, Sergeant Philip H. Force of the same unit mounted the works and shot at the Federals. He seemed, said an eyewitness, "as calm and collected as if he were drilling in camp." His friends pleaded with him to step into the trench. "By and by," he replied, before bullets struck him in the throat and forehead, killing him instantly.[45]

"The Yankees pushed their men up to our Breast Works and our men were cutting them down as fast as flies," a Southerner told his parents. Union soldiers mounted the entrenchments and shot at the Confederate defenders. "Where we would stab over with our bayonets," wrote a Vermonter, "men would jump up on the works and his comrades would hand him our muskets and he would stand there and fire until shot down when another would take his place and so continue."[46]

One of those daring Yankees was the 2nd Vermont's Private Wallace W. Noyes, who had entered the army as a substitute for a conscripted man. Noyes mounted the parapet and, like others, fired at his foes while comrades passed loaded rifles to him. He shot at least fifteen times before stepping down. After the war, a newspaper said of Noyes, "he stood on the wall of the fort at Spotsylvania in the bloody angle, and was the only man that lived in that spot." Noyes was awarded the Medal of Honor for his bravery.[47]

Union regiments rotated in and out of the fighting along the entrenchments. A soldier in the 5th Maine of Emory Upton's brigade wrote, "We were up to the works several times during the day, but when the rebs would concentrate fire on us we would gradually lose ground till we would be, perhaps three or four rods from the works, then we would press forward and gain them again." During one advance a Confederate captain and a dozen men crossed over the works and surrendered. The prisoners were covered in mud and blood, with the captain telling his captors, "the Devil couldn't stand it in there."[48]

While urging his men to pass over the salient's fieldworks, Major William Ellis of the 49th New York was shot through his arm and body by a ramrod and mortally wounded. "A young man of great promise," Captain Orrin P. Rugg was shot in the breast and died while being carried to the rear. He was survived by his wife of a few months in Elmira, New York.

Major Henry P. Truefitt Jr., commanding the 119th Pennsylvania, was killed, and his successor, Captain Charles P. Warner, fell dead soon afterward. Upton cited Ellis and Truefitt in his report, "who by their gallant conduct excited the admiration of all."[49]

A Yankee soldier told his wife in a letter that "the enemy fight like tigers, and so do our boys. It is a life struggle on each side." Upton reported, "Neither [side] would give ground." Thomas Watkins of the 14th North Carolina in Stephen Dodson Ramseur's veteran brigade claimed that this fight was the only battle he had been in which the foes were "near enough to club and bayonet each."[50]

Watkins recounted that during a heated exchange of musketry, he went to Colonel R. Tyler Bennett and asked what should be done with five Union prisoners who had surrendered earlier to Watkins and were lying in a traverse. Bennett answered that Watkins should tell them to go to the rear. When the North Carolinian informed them of his orders, one of the Yankees responded that "I had as well shoot them where they were, as it would be certain death to go out in the fusillade of shot and shell." The prisoners stood up and proceeded to the rear, but all of them were shot and killed within ten paces from the traverse. "I never regretted any incident of the whole war more than this one," professed Watkins.[51]

Nathaniel Harris's Mississippians held the works along the western face on Ramseur's right, their line extending north toward the west angle. A Union Sixth Corps staff officer described the fighting along this section of the entrenchments, "The men were reaching over the breast-works and firing into the confederates on the other side, as well as trying to punch them with bayonets, and the confederates were doing the same thing." Rifles became so hot and foul that they were discarded while comrades in the rear passed other ones forward.[52]

"A tall, brawny" Mississippian threw down his musket during the action and seized a hatchet. He killed one Yankee with it, and his comrades grabbed theirs and wielded them against their foes. The Mississippians had gathered up hatchets from battlefields "so that we were well supplied," attested one of them. About a dozen of Harris's men, however, crossed the works and fled toward the Yankees, but they were killed by their fellow soldiers. "I did not see any of them reach the enemy's lines," stated a Mississippian.[53]

The counterattack of McGowan's South Carolinians had brought them in on the right of the Mississippians and on both sides of the west angle. The right wing of the brigade had seized roughly one hundred yards of the apex and the string of traverses in the rear of the entrenchments. On the South Carolinians' right, Union soldiers, primarily from David Birney's and Gershom Mott's divisions, held the rest of the apex to the east angle and the traverses opposite the Confederates. "At this point," argued a South Carolinian, "occurred the hardest fighting of the day."[54]

Stephen P. Chase of the 86th New York recalled, "Neither side dare show their heads" above the parapet. He continued, "We would reach our gun over the work, depress it as much as we could and fire, and they did the same." Francis Asbury Wayne Jr. of the 1st South Carolina, described the fighting in a letter to his mother: "We fought behind breastworks, & nearly every man that was killed or wounded on our side was shot through the head. Men were killed before behind & on either side of me. I met with several very narrow escapes a ball having struck the rim of my hat & one grazed my shoulder. I fought almost ankle deep in the blood & brains of our killed & wounded."[55]

"The slaughter was terable," Union brigade commander Robert McAllister told his wife. "It was the assailant point when the enemy retook the earthworks, and to give up would be destruction for our army." A member of the 1st Massachusetts in McAllister's brigade observed: "Every thing that ingenuity could invent or daring accomplish, was attempted on both sides to gain even the slightest advantage. It seemed to be the death-grapple of the war."[56]

The Yankees put their caps on bayonets and lifted them above the works to draw Rebel fire. Men, said one of them, "did not dare poke up a finger for fear of having it shot off." Rifles fouled; volunteers dared bringing forward ammunition, and flags were shredded by the gunfire. A drunken Union artillery officer rode along the line, waving his hat and shouting for the men to charge. He miraculously escaped unharmed.[57]

The 84th Pennsylvania's Lieutenant Harvey B. Wells related that men in his company tired of lying down on the ground and wanted to fill their canteens and stretch their legs after hours of fighting. "Although knowing it was almost instant death," asserted Wells, "they would rise up and run for the rear." The lieutenant added, "I never during over four years of active service in the army witnessed so many individual acts of daring and foolhardiness on the part of soldiers as on this day." Wells had thirty-one men in his company, of whom nineteen were killed or wounded. He believed half of them had been shot while taking chances.[58]

A South Carolina "lad" suffered a wound and started walking to the rear. A captain stopped him and asked, "Where are you going?"

"To the field hospital," came the answer.

"For what purpose?" stated the officer.

The soldier opened his coat and revealed a bloody breast. The officer begged his pardon and told him to hurry to a surgeon.[59]

Major William Lester of the 13th South Carolina remembered witnessing a young soldier fall dead into the bloody water in the trench. His father, who served in the regiment, saw his son slump down, ceased fighting, and lifted the body on to the banks of the trench. As he stooped over his son, the man was shot and killed, his lifeless body lying on top of his son's.[60]

Critical to the Confederates' defensive struggle in the Mule Shoe was maintaining their hold on the series of traverses, which a Union sergeant described as "the central part of the hornets nest." The traverses extended perpendicularly from the main works, generally twelve to fifteen feet in length, with "great pits" between them from the removal of dirt for the parapets. Nathaniel Harris stated in his report that "had it not been for some traverses in the works" their position would have been "wholly untenable."[61]

The Federals tried to seize them from their foes, but the Rebels clung to the traverses, protecting the flanks of their comrades behind the entrenchments. "The traverses served a double purpose," wrote a Yankee afterward, "they prevented us from enfilading those interior faces, and each traverse formed with the front line from which it projected a little fortress, behind which the enemy gathered in groups and poured a deadly fire into our ranks. Echoing Harris's view, a Georgian attested: "The traverses were invaluable to our line, suffering from flank fire. Without them the line would have been untenable."[62]

The Georgians served in Clement Evans's brigade, whose ranks and those of John Hoffman's Virginia regiments had fought the Federals in the divisions of Francis Barlow and John Gibbon to a standstill along the Mule Shoe's eastern face. Although the fighting around the east angle and down the salient's leg seemed to lack the ferocity of the action to the west, "it was a ghastly and horrible example of the organized brutality that we call war," in the judgment of a Pennsylvania staff officer.[63]

The opponents, likewise, fired over the parapet, plunged bayonets through crevices between the logs in the works, and swung muskets as clubs. A Massachusetts soldier declared that "it was so bloody, and had such an aspect of savagery about it, that it is well to leave the details to be filled in by the imagination of those who wish for the completed picture." One of Barlow's soldiers thought the salient to be a "hissing cauldron of death."[64]

A New Yorker said the combat "was bruising and it was being bruised." Seven color bearers in the 106th Pennsylvania of the Philadelphia Brigade had been shot when Corporal William Wagner took the flag. Wounded three times, Wagner kept planting it on the works until he grew too weak from the loss of blood. Captain Thomas Kelly, commander of another regiment in the brigade, the 69th Pennsylvania, was mortally wounded and died in a hospital in Fredericksburg six days later. A letter from Governor Andrew Gregg Curtin had arrived at brigade headquarters during the day, promoting Kelly to lieutenant colonel.[65]

The Pennsylvanians fought mainly Hoffman's Virginians. Their foes, wrote a member of the 71st Pennsylvania, "lay in heaps, across and on top of each other. The writhing of the wounded and dying who lay beneath the dead bodies, moved the whole mass." A Federal remembered that their own dead, lying on the earthworks, were riddled by the musketry.[66]

Like the Pennsylvania regiments of the Philadelphia Brigade, the 19th Massachusetts served in Gibbon's division. A Massachusetts soldier recalled that some of his comrades had become so exhausted by the rapid loading and firing of their rifles that they could no longer stand up, sat down, and passed loaded muskets up to others. Their faces had become "so begrimed with powder to be almost unrecognizable."[67]

The Massachusetts veteran claimed later that some Confederates held up white flags as if to surrender and then fired on their foes. One Rebel waved a white flag in front of Company C. Private William Edward Fletcher, and an orderly sergeant mounted the parapet. The sergeant asked if they wanted to "come in." A Confederate said yes, and the sergeant told them, "then drop your guns and come over." The enemy soldier raised his rifle and shot the sergeant in the head. Fletcher killed the gray-coated rifleman and jumped off the works.[68]

Sergeant John B. G. Adams in the Bay State regiment began singing "The Battle Cry of Freedom." His comrades soon joined in, followed by officers and men in other units. A fellow sergeant, Charles B. Brown, had his legs mangled and nearly severed by an artillery shell. Before being carried to the rear, Brown handed his commission as a lieutenant and a photograph of his fiancée to a comrade, requesting that the items be sent home. Brown died early on the morning of May 13.[69]

"At one time," wrote Lieutenant Thomas F. Galwey of the 8th Ohio, another regiment in Gibbon's division, "the shower of musket-balls, shrapnel, and every sort of projectile falling in the midst of us was trying to the nerves of our coolest." Amid the roar, however, Galwey heard a comrade shout, "Annie, come this way." He saw a woman, who "was about twenty-five years of age, square-featured and sun-burnt, and dressed in Zouave uniform in the Vivandiere style." She was laughing and, thought Galwey, searching for the 114th Pennsylvania, which she likely served with, selling them personal provisions.[70]

Some of Barlow's and Gibbon's men, like others, never forgot certain moments. Barlow sent one of his aides, John D. Black, to Hancock with a request for reinforcements. While enroute, Black met an officer "who seemed about to speak with him when a shell surgically took off the man's head directly above the jaw." The man fell backward, and Black saw "the tongue moving as if speaking."[71]

The 26th Michigan's Newton T. Kirk came upon a captain who was lying wounded on the ground. "He was a noble looking man," remembered Kirk. "*His face was very calm but it was the calmness of death.*" The officer asked Kirk to remove letters from a haversack and to tell the captain's friends at home of his fate if Kirk survived. "Among his papers was the picture of a beautiful woman," stated Kirk. He gave the captain a drink of water, shook his hand, and left him. Kirk survived the Andersonville prison camp and the war. Returning home, he located the dead man's friends, fulfilling the request.[72]

Adjutant Joseph W. Muffly of the 148th Pennsylvania described Corporal William S. Van Dyke of Company G as "bright, vivacious, loved by all with whom he become acquainted." In summer 1862, the eighteen-year-old Van Dyke had volunteered instead of entering a college as he had planned. On this spring afternoon as he fought beside his comrades, an artillery solid shot decapitated him.[73]

Gibbon's and Barlow's troops' foes, the Virginians and the Georgians mainly, held most of the entrenchments along the eastern face, except for a two-hundred-yard section immediately south of the east angle. The Confederates manned the traverses behind the works and pushed forward several times to dislodge the Federals' hold on the outer side. The Yankees described the enemy efforts as charges, while the Rebels claimed that the enemy also tried time and again to retake the original fieldworks.[74]

Despite the numbers against them, Hoffman's and Evans's veteran brigades held on tenaciously to the earthworks and traverses, which a Yankee called "horse-stalls." Volunteers in the 13th Virginia worked a pair of captured cannon that the Federals had been unable to withdraw from the salient. Private William W. Smith of the 49th Virginia wrote: "My little gun became so foul that I could not press the breech lock into place. I had to stop in the midst of the battle and with my gun-screw take it to pieces and clean it." With the constant musketry, he was undoubtedly not alone in having to do so.[75]

Colonel J. Catlett Gibson of Smith's regiment related that during the combat Lieutenant Everett Early approached him and said that he and his two friends "must have a pop at the enemy." The three young men had been detailed to attend the University of Virginia but had not left for the school. Gibson demurred, arguing he did not want a college student killed. Early, however, picked up a dead man's rifle and cartridges, firing several shots at the enemy. Soon Early came running to Gibson, exclaiming: "I have been shot in the arm and I would not take a thousand dollars for it. I have got what I wanted, come on boys."[76]

A soldier in the 21st Virginia told his comrades that he needed a change of underclothing. He opened a captured enemy knapsack, found the articles of clothing, and undressed, even removing his socks. He then calmly put on the new undergarment and socks and his muddy uniform. Picking up his rifle, he resumed firing at the Yankees. Private John Worsham, who had witnessed much as a veteran, thought it "about the coolest thing I saw during the war."[77]

"Infantrymen, from opposite sides of the works, climbed up and fired into the faces of their opponents," as Clement Evans described the struggle between his Georgians and the Yankees. "They grappled one another and attempted to drag each other across the breastworks; bayonet thrusts were made through crevices; . . . the dead and dying had to be flung to the rear to give room for the living, fighting ones, in the trenches." Evans believed that no "human ear ever listened to a more steady and continuous roar of musketry and artillery than that which arose from that field of fierce contention."[78]

It was the ceaselessness of the roar, the deafening thunder of fire from tens of thousands of rifles and from scores of cannon. Artillery crews rammed in charges of solid shot, shell, and canister and pulled lanyards. The row of Union guns along the Landrum farm lane and the batteries farther to the north and west pounded the defenders in the Mule Shoe. Confederate chief of artillery William Pendleton reported, "That fire from the enemy was at times most furious." Two-gun sections and four-gun batteries rolled forward toward the salient, belching canister or "canned hell fire" into enemy ranks. "This was, I believe," asserted a Federal, "the first if not the only instance in the history of the war, where artillery charged on breastworks."[79]

Batteries from seven Confederate battalions in the three infantry corps engaged enemy artillery and blasted Union attackers. Gun crews were posted within the salient in front of and behind the Harrison house, and on a hill north of the courthouse village. Cannon from the Third Corps covered the ground along Fredericksburg Road, opposite the Union Ninth Corps. First Corps artillery chief Porter Alexander entered in his diary: "Gen Action on whole line."[80]

An artillery ordnance officer stated that the men "had a hard time in getting wagons up to the batteries so severe was the fire." A staff officer said, "It was a wild day's work." He observed, however, that "the artillery itself seemed to become tired, for I noticed that in the morning, the reports of the guns were sharp, quick and vicious and that toward evening they roared more sullenly and, though as loud, were lazier in their utterances."[81]

The thunderous clamor abated around two o'clock in the afternoon, when the fighting ceased briefly along the apex and in the traverses as men on both sides believed that their opponent had surrendered. Accounts conflict as to whether either the Yankees or the Rebels initially raised white handkerchiefs. It was a confused situation, with Union and Confederate officers conferring for a few minutes. To a Mississippian, it was "the sort of a parley in which everybody talked and nobody listened. Men are not like women, who can talk and listen at the same time."[82]

"To those who reflected a moment," observed South Carolinian James Caldwell, "it should have been plain that we were deceiving ourselves. . . . But a general infatuation prevailed—a silly infatuation, if it had not involved so much. So the two lines stood, bawling, gesticulating, and what not." When the discussions ended and a young Confederate soldier fired at a Union officer as he returned to his lines, the combat resumed, ending the infatuation.[83]

During the momentary lull, a Mississippian had stood and looked to the north from where the Yankees had come and to the east and west along the main earthworks and in the traverses. "The field presented one vast Golgotha in immensity of the number of the dead . . . ," he recalled years later. "The ground [to the north] was almost covered with the dead and wounded, while between the lines they were literally piled. . . . The writer counted fifteen stands of colors lying between the lines, some of them having fallen against our breastworks—the brave hands which had borne them so gallantly now lying cold in death."[84]

General Robert E. Lee had witnessed the rout of Edward Johnson's division and the possible destruction of the Army of Northern Virginia. He and key subordinates had fashioned counterattacks that had blunted the massive Union offensive, repelled it, and fought it to a standstill. In the crisis, Lee had ignored his personal safety, seemingly intent on leading a counterstrike until his veteran troops forced him back. He had ordered the construction of a new defensive line in the rear, while he sought offensive opportunities on the sprawling battlefield.[85]

As the combat abated in sections of the Mule Shoe, Lee rode to the extensive fieldworks of the army's Third Corps, which zigzagged south from the salient's eastern leg to across Fredericksburg Road. The Confederate commander halted about 2:00 P.M. at a bulge in the defenses, dubbed Heth's Salient for division commander Henry Heth. From there, thought Lee, he might strike the left flank of Ambrose Burnside's Union Ninth Corps.[86]

Lee quickly met with brigade commander James Lane and inquired for Captain William T. Nicholson of the 37th North Carolina. A member of the regiment claimed in a postwar memoir that Lee personally knew Nicholson, who commanded the brigade's sharpshooter battalion. Lee pointed to an enemy battery and directed the captain to ascertain whether Union infantry supported the guns. Earlier, a shell from a Ninth Corps cannon had mortally wounded Lieutenant Oscar Lane, aide and brother of the brigadier.[87]

Nicholson took five soldiers with him on the reconnaissance. They crossed the works and came to their pickets, who warned the captain not to pass beyond the skirmish line. Nicholson and one man crept forward, viewed the battery, and drew fire from Union skirmishers. A shot hit the soldier, breaking his leg. Nicholson carried the crippled man over his shoulder, but the musketry brought artillery shell fire from the Union gun crews. A shell fragment struck and killed the soldier, but Nicholson escaped unscathed, reporting to Lee that the enemy flank lay unprotected.[88]

Lee instructed Lane and Colonel David A. Weisiger, who was temporarily commanding William Mahone's Virginia brigade, to advance and to assail the enemy's left flank, to rout the blue-coated infantry, and to seize the enemy's cannon. "Main object of this movement" was, as explained to Lane, "to relieve Ewell's front" in the salient, which "at that time was heavily pressed by the enemy." It was an audacious undertaking for two brigades, whose ranks numbered perhaps 2,400 officers and men, against Burnside's infantry corps of roughly 13,000 officers and men and fourteen artillery batteries.[89]

Lane sent forward the 7th and 33rd North Carolina, under the command of the 33rd's Lieutenant Colonel Robert Van Buren Cowan. The two regiments angled southeast, crossing the entrenchments between Heth's Salient and a brick kiln, before turning north and entering an oak woods. Cowan deployed a line of skirmishers, a pair of companies from each regiment, and had them advance. The North Carolinians scattered enemy pickets, while Cowan prepared to charge. Lane arrived, however, with the brigade's other three regiments, brought all units into a battle line, and posted the four companies of skirmishers on the right flank. Weisiger's five Virginia regiments formed ranks about one hundred yards to the rear and covered Lane's left flank. A courier rode up shortly with orders from acting corps commander Jubal Early to advance "at once, and rapidly."[90]

Beyond the woods, meanwhile, the Ninth Corps divisions of Thomas Crittenden and Orlando Willcox had started forward in an assault on Heth's Salient. Since the repulse of the corps's earlier attack on the Confederate works, General-in-Chief Ulysses S. Grant had prodded Burnside to renew the offensive. "Move one division of your troops to the right to the assistance of Hancock, and push the attack with the balance as vigorously as possible," Grant had directed in a 10:20 A.M. telegram. "Wright and Warren have been attacking vigorously all day. See that your orders are executed."[91]

The tone of Grant's messages infuriated Burnside, who did not comply immediately. He accused the general-in-chief's staff officer, Cyrus Comstock, of denouncing Burnside's leadership secretly to Grant. Comstock later denied the allegation. Finally, about midday, after some conflicting decisions, Burnside ordered a renewal of the offensive. He assigned Willcox's division to lead the effort, supported by Crittenden's brigades.[92]

When Willcox received his instructions, he informed Burnside that the enemy would likely try to turn his left flank. According to staff officer Charles Mills, officers in the Ninth Corps had expressed concern for the vulnerability of that flank throughout the morning. "We were on the extreme left of the army during Thursday's fight," Mills wrote home three days later, "and woefully afraid of our flank we were, for it was very weak." But despite Willcox's misgivings about the tactical arrangement, Burnside reiterated his orders "to advance as soon as possible with his whole force."[93]

Willcox shook out a battle line with Colonel John F. Hartranft's brigade on the left and Colonel Benjamin C. Christ's regiments, commanded temporarily by Colonel William Humphrey, on the right. The division commander brought forward two artillery units—Battery G, 7th Maine Light Artillery and 34th New York Light Artillery—to join the 19th New

York Battery, the target of the Confederate attack. The 2nd Michigan, two hundred officers and men, deployed in support of the cannon. Willcox's troops advanced about two o'clock.[94]

The collision between the opposing forces came rather swiftly. The Confederates cleared the woods of enemy skirmishers and, as Willcox had predicted, slammed into the left flank of Hartranft's brigade, held by the 17th Michigan. Colonel Constant Luce of the regiment reported that a Pennsylvania private touched his arm and said, "The enemy was on my left advancing." Luce could not see well in the thick woods. "I stooped over to see them [the Rebels] when he [the private] was knocked across my back, killed by a piece of shell," wrote Luce. "I fell on my face, the man across my back."[95]

Lane's North Carolinians came swarming through the woods, surrounding the Michiganders. A wild, confusing melee ensued. Luce regained his feet and, with forty-eight of his men, escaped. They managed somehow to herd nearly sixty Rebels as prisoners toward the rear. The Union regiment, however, lost 104 killed, wounded, and captured along with a stand of colors.[96]

The North Carolinians kept going, attacking the 51st Pennsylvania. With their numbers reduced with six companies detached as skirmishers, the Pennsylvanians never had much of a chance. The Confederates grabbed prisoners and the regiment's national and state flags. "The loss of the colors chagrined the men tenfold more than the loss of their comrades," declared a Pennsylvanian, "for by some it was looked upon as a most damning disgrace, by others as a high mark of credit" for engaging the enemy at close quarters. More than a hundred Pennsylvanians were casualties.[97]

Lane's veterans and Weisiger's Virginians now charged toward the six-gun 19th New York Battery. The 37th North Carolina spearheaded the attack, with Lieutenant Charles T. Haigh waving his sword in one hand and his hat in the other, yelling to his comrades: "Charge, boys, charge! The battery is ours!" Lane exclaimed, "I have never seen a regiment advance more beautifully than it did in the face of such a murderous fire." The New Yorkers raked the ground with canister. Haigh collapsed mortally wounded.[98]

The Confederates pushed up the ridge into the artillery blasts and musketry from the 2nd Michigan and other Union troops. Willcox described the enemy onslaught as a "furious assault." The Rebels shot down the New York artillerists and the battery's horses. Men from the 2nd Michigan ran forward and began working the cannon with the unscathed gunners and battery drivers. They rammed in more charges of canister and pulled lanyards.[99]

Private Augustus Floyd of the 18th North Carolina wrote, "Being foolhearted I followed our Colonel with others." Floyd and his comrades reached the battery, and swirling hand-to-hand struggle for the cannon ensued. "Much confusion prevailed here," reported Willcox, "the captors of one moment being prisoners the next." Lane and his field officers had gone in on foot and, during the fighting, a Yankee took aim at the Confederate general. Sixteen-year-old Private Peter A. Parker shot and killed the enemy soldier before he could fire. "I am indebted for my own life," Lane allegedly told Parker.[100]

Weisiger's brigade, meanwhile, entered the fighting on the North Carolinians' left. Lane claimed in his report that the Virginians accidentally fired into his ranks before striking a Union battle line. Weisiger's Confederates engaged three regiments from Christ's brigade, now under Humphrey's temporary command. For the first time in their history, the Virginia regiments found themselves, according to one of them, in "a most spirited hand to hand contest with a brigade of the enemy."[101]

Humphrey's regiments—the 50th Pennsylvania, 20th Michigan, and 1st Michigan Sharpshooters—had been advancing toward Heth's Salient when the Virginians plowed into their left flank, igniting a swirling struggle. "No words can describe the scene that ensued," asserted a soldier in the 20th Michigan. Sergeant John F. Sale of the 12th Virginia jotted afterward in his diary, "This was the hottest place I have been in since [Second] Manassas." Color bearer Benjamin May of the Virginia regiment fell mortally wounded, shot by a Yankee only ten feet away.[102]

"The first I knew of our being surrounded was when I heard some one say, 'Surrender you Yank, its all up with you,'" stated Sergeant James Levan of the 50th Pennsylvania. "I looked up and saw a terrible big officer swinging his sword over my head." Levan and others fled rearward, but more than one hundred Pennsylvanians were captured. A member of the 12th Virginia's ambulance corps bagged ten of them, using a musket he picked up from the ground that would not fire.[103]

The Pennsylvanians and Michiganders, however, fought stubbornly. Lieutenant Charles E. Denoon of the 41st Virginia put it simply, "We had a rough roll and a terrible fight." The 12th Virginia's Lieutenant James E. Phillips remembered: "Here I lost my brother, Sgt. R. O. Phillips. After my brother was killed, I did not care about anything." Lieutenant Colonel William F. Niemeyer of the 61st Virginia had confided earlier to a fellow officer that he expected to be killed this afternoon. He survived the action but, just before sunset, he died almost instantly from a shard of an artillery round.[104]

The 1st Michigan Sharpshooters reached Heth's Salient and crossed over the works but were forced to withdraw. By now, the Confederate offensive had crested and was receding. Lane claimed the capture of three flags and about four hundred prisoners. His brigade and Weisiger's suffered losses likely exceeding 600. Union general Willcox reported his casualties as 768 killed and wounded but only 292 missing. His men had captured eighty Rebels, including Colonel William M. Barbour, commander of the 37th North Carolina.[105]

The Confederates retreated to outside of the courthouse village, where division commander William Mahone met officers in Lane's brigade. According to a postwar account, Mahone demanded that Colonel Cowan of the 33rd North Carolina and Lieutenant William H. McLaurin of the 18th North Carolina hand over to him two of the captured Union flags. The officers refused, and Mahone upbraided them for their "cowardly disorder" during the withdrawal.[106]

With his hat in one hand and a cocked revolver in the other, Cowan stepped toward the mounted general. "Among other severe epithets he called Mahone a cowardly son of a b[itc]h," recounted McLaurin, who also had drawn his revolver, "and told him he would have to apologize for his language toward us or he would kill him on the spot." Mahone "made a most profound apology," turned his horse, and rode away. Cowan expected to be court-martialed for threatening a senior officer but, according to McLaurin, Mahone always saluted both men when he encountered them after the incident.[107]

Mahone, however, did not let the matter of who captured the flags rest, gathering testimony from officers and enlisted men in Weisiger's brigade. The Confederates had seized three flags from the two Federal infantry regiments and a guidon from the 19th New York Battery. Lane rebutted, arguing that the Virginians never left the woods, although the evidence clearly contradicted his assertion. "I had better opportunities of witnessing the performance of Mahone's [Weisiger's] Brigade than did General Mahone himself," declared Lane. Mahone appealed to Cadmus Wilcox, but, in the end, the North Carolinians received credit for the capture of the four colors. Lee personally commended Lane for his brigade's performance.[108]

The afternoon struggle on this section of the battlefield had one final spasm, as two of Crittenden's brigades advanced toward Heth's Salient.

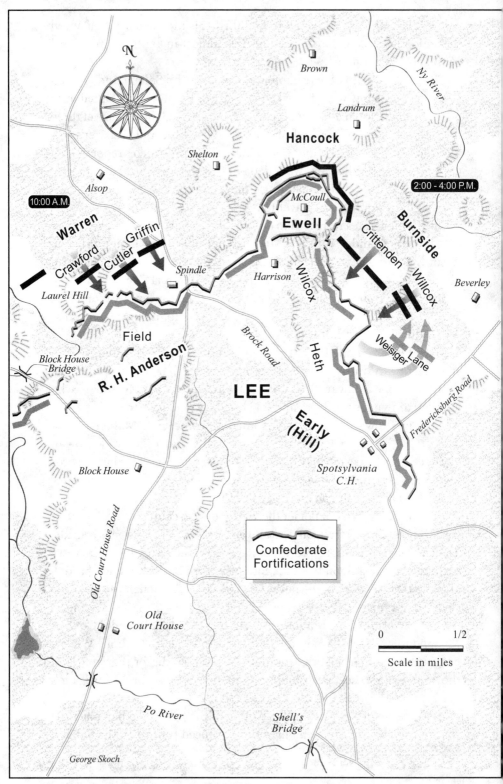

Assaults by Warren and Burnside, 10:00 A.M. and 2:00 P.M.–3:00 P.M.

Colonel Daniel Leasure's three regiments led the charge, followed by Lieutenant Colonel Stephen Weld Jr.'s brigade. Confederate infantry and artillery repulsed the Union effort. "If there was ever a hell on earth it was then," wrote a 56th Massachusetts soldier in Weld's command. Crittenden's aide Charles Mills admitted in a letter, "There was almost a skedaddle at the end of it, but we managed to keep men up."[109]

Both commanders, Lee and Grant, had seen their offensives fail to achieve any decisive results. Lee's attack with two brigades lacked the numbers to roll up the ranks of the Union Ninth Corps. For Grant, the assaults by Warren's Fifth Corps and Burnside's units had been lethargic and uncoordinated. "[Burnside] is a damned Humbug—Warren who is a ditto did about the same," grumbled a Sixth Corps staff officer. Both leaders must have known that the outcome of the hours-long, fearful struggle lay not along the fringes of the extensive fieldworks but with the officers and men at their core, inside and outside the Mule Shoe.[110]

{ 10 }

Carnage Infernal

It had been a dozen or more hours since the Union offensive had turned the Confederate salient at Spotsylvania Court House into a slaughter-house. The fighting had been relentless, merciless. The foes killed and maimed each other at "the length of their muskets." Like a whirlwind, the combat had drawn in roughly 55,000 fellow Americans. And still it raged.[1]

With each passing hour, with more comrades falling dead or wounded, many, if not all, of them must have believed that they had become ensnared in an unending nightmare. As noted, most men in both armies had long ago come to accept, even to affirm, the reality of combat, the killing at times of their enemy. Patriotism and belief in their respective causes provided the necessity for and the meaning to the butchery on battlefields. A soldier's duty and a shared bond with comrades also contributed to a willingness to inflict harm or death upon one's opponent.[2]

Many officers and men believed in God's will—that their fate in combat had been prescribed and that they would be ultimately rewarded if they fell. Although his words address the Union army, Henry Blake of the 11th Massachusetts spoke for Yankees and Rebels alike when he wrote: "The religious belief of the army was simple, and consisted of two articles of faith: first, that 'man will die when his time comes'; and secondly, that 'a soldier who is slain in the service of his country is sure to enter the gates of heaven.'" Blake argued that his fellow soldiers remained steadfast in these beliefs.[3]

Thursday, May 12, 1864, in and around the Mule Shoe, the struggle must have tested the combatants to the very core of their beliefs. For those who stood there it might have been as a Southern newspaperman wrote the next day. Among the Confederates, he observed, "each man knew that he was fighting the battle for the possession of Richmond—the battle, indeed, for the independence of the Confederate states and the thought of yielding to the foe never once entered his mind." In turn, their opponents "exhibited a courage and resolution worthy of a better cause."[4]

The carnage, however, smothered the ground. The Mule Shoe's voracious appetite for souls remained unappeased. "I don't expect to go to hell," asserted Private David Holt of the 16th Mississippi, "but if I do, I am sure that Hell can't beat that terrible scene. Indeed I am sure that the hell on earth is a pledge for the hell after death."[5]

A soldier in the 1st South Carolina penned a graphic description of the actuality of it for readers of a Charleston newspaper:

> The ground in front was carpeted with Yankee dead, and our trenches filled with our own dead—very few wounded. I was splashed over with brains and blood. In stooping down or squatting to load, the mud, blood and brains mingled, would reach up to my waist, and my head and face were covered or spotted with the horrid paint. The Yankees would charge up against our lines, made up from a ditch about two feet deep, stick their guns over and fire. We, in turn, rose up and fired as they retreated, and generally with good effect. Officers and men say that such fighting was never seen before.[6]

As the afternoon darkened into the evening then, the charnel house that was the Mule Shoe gathered more dead. About six o'clock, Confederate general Richard Ewell sent a dispatch to Mississippi brigade commander Nathaniel Harris, stating that if the salient's defenders could hold on until sundown, "all would be well." Similar instructions likely went to the other senior officers with the brigades. Sunset was an hour away at 6:59 P.M.[7]

Ewell had remained close to the fighting, with his headquarters still at the Edgar Harrison farmhouse. He apparently stayed outside of the residence, working in the front yard. At one point, Colonel J. Catlett Gibson of the 49th Virginia sought out the corps commander to acquire ammunition for his regiment. "Ewell was standing before a portable field table with writing material on it," recounted Gibson years later, "and his staff a short distance in his front, and shells falling fast and furious all around." The danger to the general and his aides was ever present and, when a shell exploded nearby, the one-legged general would hop on his good limb and would "curse with the vehemence of an old trooper and the unction of a new church member."[8]

At the time of Ewell's instructions to subordinates, a planned Union attack on the salient's defenders had been canceled. George Meade had ordered Gouverneur Warren to shift two Fifth Corps divisions to the support of the Second and Sixth corps. Lysander Cutler's four brigades led the Fifth Corps movement, arriving opposite the Mule Shoe shortly after three o'clock. Charles Griffin's division trailed Cutler's command, not coming up until more than an hour later.[9]

The redeployment of Cutler's and Griffin's troops was at the direction of Ulysses S. Grant. The general-in-chief desired a renewal of assaults on the salient. In his postwar memoir, Grant wrote that he had spent much of the morning continuously passing along the army's lines from "wing to wing." By early afternoon, he joined Meade at the residence of Benjamin and Ann Armstrong, located beside Fredericksburg Road about a mile north of and across the Ny River from the John Brown farm. Wounded Union soldiers had been carried to the "humble-looking farmhouse." The Armstrong place served Grant's purpose, as he put it, of "a central position most convenient for receiving information from all points."[10]

When Grant arrived at the Armstrong homestead, he sat on the front porch and spoke with Ann Armstrong and her daughter. The Armstrongs were pro-Union and Benjamin had fled to the north for his safety. During their conversation, she said to Grant that with Federals' presence in the area, "the gates have been opened for my escape from this hell." She and her daughter provided some food for their guests, with Meade "highly tickled at the fresh butter."[11]

By three o'clock, Grant and Meade had settled on an assault with the officers and men of the Fifth and Sixth corps. Meade assigned Horatio Wright, commander of the Sixth Corps, to "organize a heavy column of assault from both corps." By now, Wright had moved his headquarters from the hollow behind his troops to the Willis Landrum farm, where he joined Winfield Hancock, Francis Barlow, and David Birney. One of Wright's aides, Oliver Wendell Holmes Jr., noted that bullets kept whistling around the headquarters.[12]

When Cutler's division appeared, Wright parceled out the four brigades instead of preparing them for an attack. Wright explained to army headquarters, "Cutler's division has been put in the first line to relieve exhausted troops who have been firing all day, and can't be used for this purpose [of an assault]." Wright directed three of the brigades toward the salient's western face and west angle and the fourth unit to the left. Cutler's veterans soon marched into what one of them described as the "warmest fight we have yet been called upon to enter." Here they remained, "silencing the enemy," through the night and into the next morning.[13]

Wright, meanwhile, informed the army's chief of staff Andrew Humphreys that he doubted if he had enough troops for an attack. "I shall,

CHAPTER TEN

however," he stated, "make all the preparations and assault, or not, according to my discretion and that of General Hancock, unless positively ordered." At 5:10 P.M., he notified headquarters that he had canceled the offensive because, in part, he could not "insure a reasonable prospect of success." Hancock "fully concurs in the views I have expressed," Wright added.[14]

Wright's and Hancock's judgment was probably sound. Cutler's entry into the struggle only added more troops to the masses of Federals piled up outside of the salient. Cutler's brigades came under heavy enemy musketry and bogged down almost immediately. The Confederates had fought more than twice their numbers to a standstill. It is difficult to conclude that a few more thousand Yankees would have broken the impasse. An hour or so after Wright acted, Grant telegraphed the War Department, "The enemy are obstinate and seem to have found the last ditch."[15]

The Confederates' "last ditch" centered upon the west angle and its adjacent entrenchments. This section of works extended roughly five hundred feet from the McCoull farm lane on the left to about one hundred yards along the apex on the right. Mississippians and South Carolinians, their ranks mingled, manned the "last ditch," opposing Yankees primarily from the Second and Sixth corps. "All the efforts of the enemy seeming to be directed against the position held by my command," reported Nathaniel Harris. In turn, a Union officer asserted in a letter the next day: "The Rebels fight like very devils! We have to fairly *club* them out of their rifle pits."[16]

Nothing in the foes' collective experiences compared in ferocity and duration to the struggle for this five-hundred-foot section of works and traverses. A Northerner described the combat as "savage," while a Southern lieutenant thought that "perhaps the hardest fighting in that section occurred during this war." Ewell believed that "the fighting was of the most desperate character."[17]

Harris maintained that his Mississippians repulsed "desperate and repeated efforts of the enemy to dislodge them." Union musketry and canister charges shredded the log breastworks until they "resembled hickory brooms." A New Englander watched artillery rounds fly over him and his comrades, thinking, "they looked just like a bird darting through the air." The rifle and cannon fire continued to sound as "one common roar."[18]

The unrelenting contest "was perfectly fearful," stated a Confederate surgeon. The Yankees fought "with the greatest determination, and it strained us to the utmost to hold our own." The Mississippians and South Carolinians, however, held on. "The heroism of this foe is awfully sublime," contended Sergeant F. M. Thrasher of the 108th New York years later. "No men on this broad earth ever battled more bravely or showed more loyalty to their cause than did these erring Americans."[19]

In the midst of the "carnage infernal," as the 17th Maine's Private John Haley called it, incidents or encounters occurred that survivors never seemed to forget: Union brigade commander Colonel John Crocker walking on top of the works urging his men to lay low; a captain in the 5th Maine, whose mangled body had been pierced by more than twenty bullets; John Calvin Work of the 61st Pennsylvania, the third of five brothers killed in the war; and the 7th Indiana's Captain Alexander B. Pattison remembering the prayer he put in his diary: "Father spare me from more sorrows. For our griefs are more than we can bear. My best men are falling around me and I am untouched. I am not better than they."[20]

Inside the Mule Shoe there was John Patterson of the 16th Mississippi. At one point Union infantrymen stormed over the parapet, driving Patterson's comrades toward traverses. He straddled the trench, however, wielding his musket as a club and knocking down four Yankees. "Then he crumpled up like a bundle of bloody rags," recounted a fellow Mississippian, "and sank down into the ditch." Nearby, John Berryman Crawford also lay dead. In March, he had written to his wife, "wee ant half whip hear." He added, "I want to see you and home mity bad once more in life my Dear." It was not to be.[21]

Lieutenant Colonel Horace Porter of Grant's staff contended, "The battle near the 'angle' was probably the most desperate engagement in the history of modern warfare, and presented features which were absolutely appalling." A New Yorker stated, "The dead were piled in swaths and winnows, both outside and inside the works." Charles Weygant, commander of the 124th New York, thought that there were enough dead bodies to erect a three-foot high wall of them on the top of the fieldworks. A South Carolinian later told Samuel McGowan that the trenches "ran with blood."[22]

Nowhere did the carnage appear grislier than in and around the west angle. There was a "mass of torn and mutilated corpses," in Porter's words. "If a man wants to see hell upon earth," exclaimed Confederate Berry Benson, "let him come and look into this black, bloody hole." The Federals had their name for it, "Hell's Hole." But by the time the struggle had ended, Confederates knew that stretch of works with its slight curve as the "Bloody Angle."[23]

The hours-long engagement had become a physically exhausting and mind-numbing ordeal for both Yankees and Rebels. The closeness of the fighting had shaped the nightmarish reality. "All the long day the soldiers could not expose themselves," explained Lieutenant Harvey S. Wells of the 84th Pennsylvania. "They could not rise up from a reclining position to stretch their tired limbs, or go back for water, as a rebel bullet would surely be sent after them." Berry Benson wrote, "Everybody seemed fagged out, and I don't think there is one but will say with me that he hopes never to have such a fight again."[24]

In Stephen Dodson Ramseur's brigade, the 4th North Carolina's Walter Raleigh Battle, writing to his mother, echoed Benson's words: "There is not a man in this brigade who will ever forget the sad requiem which those minie balls sang over the dead and dying for twenty-two hours. They put me in mind of some musical instrument; some sounded like wounded men crying; some like humming of bees, some like cats in the depth of night; while others cut through the air with only a 'Zip' like noise. I know it to be the hottest and hardest fought battle that has ever been on this continent."[25]

"I had never before imagined such a struggle to be possible—though I saw Gaines' Mill and Gettysburg," attested Campbell Brown. "Our suffering was terrific, not a mouthful of food, nor a drop of water had we had since early in the morning," swore a Mississippian. "In fact, no one thought of food." Unable to fight on, enervated men simply sank down in the mud at the risk of being shot.[26]

The 5th Virginia's Private Andrew Long in the Stonewall Brigade had been wounded in the left shoulder and lost consciousness during the Union Second Corps assault on the Mule Shoe. He lay for hours and, when he awakened, he craved a drink. "When I came to I crawled to a puddle of water through which men had been walking and fighting all day—and drank," recalled Long. "All I wanted was water regardless of how dirty. There was mud, blood, and brains in this puddle."[27]

Long's experience was not uncommon. A Union officer witnessed many wounded men drag themselves to pools of water, while those who could not move lay on their backs or sides and opened their mouths to the falling rain. Around a sinkhole outside of the salient, its water tinged red by blood, "were a hundred wounded men drinking and groaning."[28]

Many of the wounded faced a different horror. "A long, ghastly procession of the wounded went limping or crawling to the rear," wrote an officer in the Union Second Corps. Those who could make it to field hospitals, marked by a red flag in the rear, were among the fortunate. "Some of the wounded were almost entirely buried by the dead bodies of their companions that had fallen upon them," testified a captain in the 2nd Vermont.[29]

It was arguably worse for wounded Confederates, who fell in several inches of muddy and bloody water in the trenches and the traverses. "I did not see it," related Captain J. W. Williams of the 5th Alabama, "but was told that in a great many instances one would fall wounded, and be pinned to the earth by one that was killed falling across his body. Our men would go over and roll the dead men off the wounded, and in that way saved the lives of many that would have been crushed to death."[30]

Among the fallen, Union and Confederate, were volunteers who risked their lives to carry ammunition from the rear to their comrades on the firing lines. The endless gunfire depleted the supplies of rifle cartridges in both armies. "The ripple and sputter and crack of the musketry fire never abated," professed a Massachusetts soldier. Some Federals claimed that they shot more than 400 rounds of ammunition. Thousands surely expended more than 100 rounds.[31]

The Yankees used pack mules primarily and some volunteers to haul the wooden cartridge boxes. Sergeant Major Charles McClenahan of the 49th Pennsylvania was one of the volunteers. He made three trips to the rear despite being told he could not return to the regiment because of the Rebel gunfire. "The boys have shot all their ammunition," McClenahan told an officer, "and they must have it."[32]

The Confederates relied solely on volunteers, who emerged from the trenches or traverses and braved the enemy fire as they hurried to the rear. "Great difficulty was experienced in procuring supplies of ammunition, man after man being shot down while bringing it in," reported Nathaniel Harris. The 9th Alabama "lost" three or four men who had been sent back. In Harris's Mississippi brigade, courier Asbury W. Hancock and privates F. Dolan and Holden Pearce secured cartridges time and again, placing the boxes on tied pieces of tent cloth and having them dragged down the ranks for distribution.[33]

Rain had fallen sporadically during the afternoon but, in the evening, thunderstorms rolled in, bringing downpours and adding to the misery. The Mule Shoe's defenders remained trapped. A withdrawal would have been doomed from the outset with the enemy just across the entrenchments. When sundown came, Ewell's promise, "all will be well," must have seemed like a mockery.[34]

Increasingly, more Confederates reached their limits and raised flags of truce in order to surrender. Across the breastworks, Yankees lowered their rifles said, "Come over!" "Come over!" Often, when white handkerchiefs or shelter tent halves were lifted up, shouts of "Shoot them fellows! Shoots them fellows!" were heard. On one occasion twenty or thirty men jumped on the parapet only to be cut down by a volley from their comrades.[35]

Nightfall provided cover for the ammunition carriers but not an end to the fighting. "Dark came, but no relief," wrote James Caldwell. "The water became a deeper crimson, the corpses grew more numerous. Every tree about us, for thirty feet from the ground, was marked by balls." Caldwell's acting brigade commander, Joseph Brown, offered a description: "Darkness was only broken by the flashing of the guns to light up the horrid scene. . . . Every flash of the guns lights up the ghostly faces of the death, with whom the ground is thickly strewn."[36]

In an 8:20 P.M. telegram, chief of staff Andrew Humphreys informed Winfield Hancock that the army would not resume offensive actions the next day and to "rest, as far as practicable." With their lines outside of the salient seven to ten deep, the Union commanders had been withdrawing units from the struggle since late afternoon. More regiments and brigades filed rearward after dusk and nightfall. Most of the officers and men likely appeared like those in the 108th New York in the Second Corps. "The 108th looked like so many demons," according to Sergeant F. M. Thrasher, "dark eyes piercing out of their sockets, smutty faces, clothes tattered and torn, stomachs lean and gaunt."[37]

A collection of units from the Second, Fifth, and Sixth corps remained behind, primarily from Colonel Oliver Edwards's four New England regiments. Edwards had tried to withdraw three of his regiments, but division commander Thomas Neill ordered him back. The colonel protested, arguing that his men were "too exhausted to stand, load, and fire much longer." Neill explained that he had been directed by corps commander Horatio Wright to pull out the brigades of Emory Upton and Daniel Bidwell and have Edwards's Massachusetts and Rhode Island veterans cover their section of the works. Neill placed Edwards "in command of its angle all night." Edwards recalled, "I left him feeling that the load imposed upon my brigade was heavier than they should have been expected to carry."[38]

Division commander David Russell joined the disgruntled colonel, acknowledging, "it is bad Edwards but cannot be helped now." Russell promised to send Edwards an infantry regiment and, if he were not relieved by three o'clock the next morning, to bring forward Russell's entire division as replacements. When the heavy artillery unit, the thousand-man 10th New Jersey, arrived at the front, Upton's and Bidwell's regiments hurried rearward under rifle fire from the Confederates. Edwards had his men gather cartridges from the dead and wounded.[39]

Gunfire between the foes slackened at times and then flared up again. Thunder still rumbled, lightning streaked the night sky, and rain poured down. "It was the most miserable night of the war—mud, bullets, rain, no supper, no breakfast," complained a Georgian. Exhaustion felled many on both sides. "Numbers of the troops sank, overpowered, into the muddy trenches and slept soundly," recounted South Carolinian Caldwell. A Confederate courier was killed while asleep.[40]

A group of Fifth Corps soldiers fashioned beds from cedar boughs. "So tired were we that I slept first rate although the rain poured down all night," one of them wrote afterward. "Every hour or two some fellow would get hit & cry out but the remainder would merely look up to see who it was & say poor fellow poor something like it & then go to sleep again."[41]

About midnight a red oak tree crashed to the ground, falling on and injuring some South Carolinians. The tree stood behind the trenches to the east of the Bloody Angle. The nearly twenty hours of musketry had sawed it off about five feet above the ground. "The foliage of the tree was trimmed away effectually as though an army of locusts had swarmed in its branches," chronicled a newspaperman. Dr. Charles Macgill later measured the stump, noting its 22-inch diameter and 61-inch circumference.[42]

Not long afterward, a Confederate band offered, as if it were, a requiem for the fallen, playing George Frideric Handel's "Dead March." In the distance, amid the rainy darkness, Union musicians responded with "Nearer My God to Thee." Then the Federal band finished with "Home Sweet Home."[43]

On a ridge nearly three-fourths of a mile south of the Mule Shoe's apex, Confederate pioneer troops and members of Edward Johnson's shattered division had been laboring throughout the day and into the night on a new defensive line. Construction had begun on these fieldworks on May 11 so the salient could be abandoned. While the men built the fortifications, bullets from the struggle to the north came whistling around them.[44]

Robert E. Lee likely visited the site a number of times. Richard Ewell rode back from his headquarters at the Harrison house to view the construction. Private John Casler of the Stonewall Brigade helped build the works and recounted that Lee and Ewell encouraged the men, saying, "the fate of the army depended on having that line done by daylight" the next

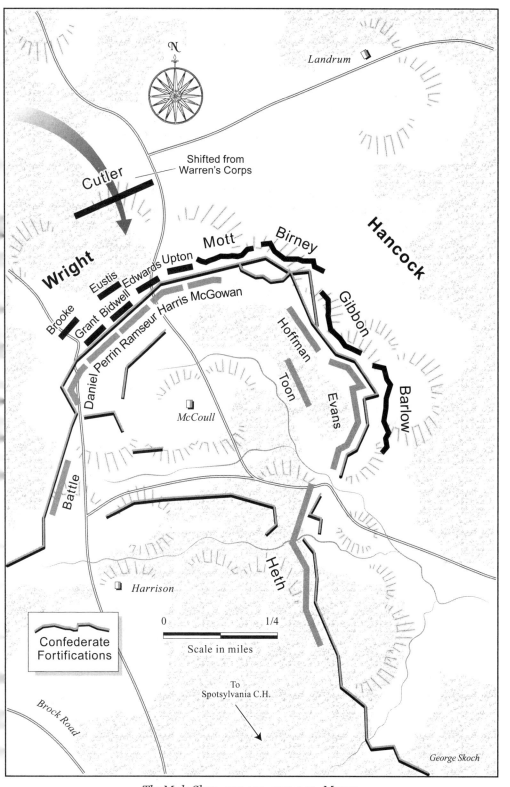

The Mule Shoe, 4:00 A.M.–5:00 A.M., May 13

morning. "I knew by the way they acted," wrote Casler, "that it was a critical time."[45]

The officers and men completed the new line of earthworks around 2:00 A.M. on May 13. Union staff officer Theodore Lyman visited the defensive line two years later, describing it as "a curiosity of field fortifications." The works had a high parapet, and "the line was divided into a series of square pens, with banks of earth heavily riveted with oak logs." It had elevated posts for sharpshooters that reminded Lyman of "a wooden camp chimney." Seventy years later in a survey filed for the National Park Service, it was noted that the Confederate defenses remained strong, well-preserved works. But, the author added, "this is the most unusual line of works I have ever seen."[46]

News of the line's completion reached the Mule Shoe's defenders by three o'clock, accompanied by orders for a withdrawal. Officers whispered instructions along the ranks as a regiment at a time abandoned the trenches and traverses. Rifles still flashed occasionally in the rainy darkness, but "slowly and noiselessly," the Confederates retired. "We conducted it so well," noted Caldwell, "that the enemy were not aware of the movement, or else, (as I think most likely,) they had become so dispirited by our stubborn resistance . . . that they had left only a skirmish line to keep up appearances. At all events, they did not attempt to parsue us."[47]

"We looked like a lot of painted devils," thought a Mississippian. "We could hardly tell one another apart," asserted fellow Mississippian David Holt. "No Mardi Gras Carnival ever devised such a diabolical looking set of devils as we were. It was no imitation of red paint and burnt cork, but genuine human gore and gun powder smoke." A North Carolinian stated, "Everyone looks as if he had passed through a hard spell of sickness, black and muddy as hogs."[48]

Nathaniel Harris's Mississippians halted in a grove of trees and built fires. "Our men stood around in groups, inquiring of each other about their missing comrades—some in tears at the loss of a brother or near relative," recalled Private Buxton Reives Conerly. The South Carolinians, meanwhile, stopped their withdrawal and had hardtack, cornbread, and bacon for breakfast. "We were thankful to receive that," confessed Wallace I. Delph of the 1st South Carolina.[49]

When John Hoffman's brigade halted in the rear, a private approached Captain J. W. Baker of the 13th Virginia. "One of my company with his head and neck all bloody," recounted Baker, "came to me after the fight and explained to me what a d[am]n fool he had been risking his life for

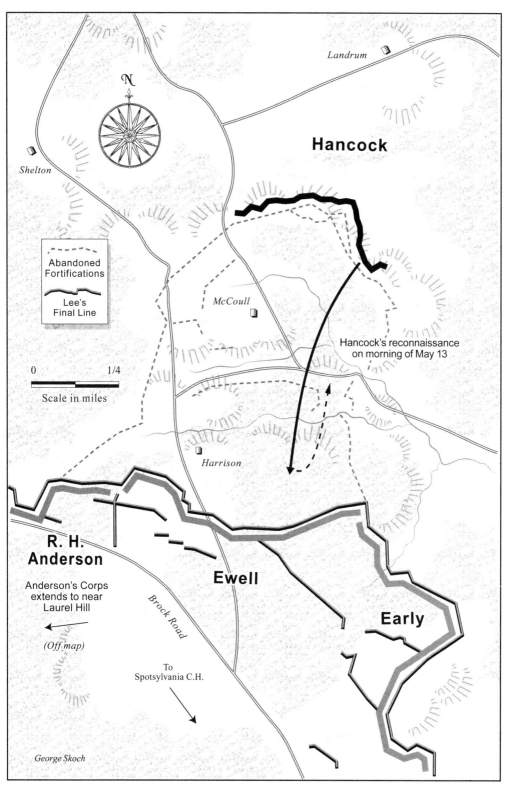

Lee's Line on May 13

Jef Davis or any other Davis, assuring me confidentially that that was the last time."[50]

The sun rose several minutes past five o'clock on Friday, May 13. Union officers and men cautiously approached the Mule Shoe, finding that their foes had withdrawn during the night. At 5:30 A.M., Sixth Corps commander Horatio Wright wired army headquarters at the Armstrong house: "My troops are in possession of the angle of the rebel works, and so far as can be discovered the enemy has abandoned his position. I have sent out a small reconnaissance to ascertain the condition of things in the front."[51]

When Wright's message arrived, George Meade directed that commanders "push forward from all parts of the line to feel for the enemy." "The first news which passed through the ranks the morning after the battle of Spotsylvania was that Lee had abandoned his position during the night," Charles Dana related. "Though our army was greatly fatigued from the enormous efforts of the day before, the news of Lee's departure inspired the men with fresh energy, and everybody was eager to be in pursuit."[52]

Federal skirmishers from the Second Corps probed forward in the morning's early light south through the salient. Passing the McCoull farm, the Yankees advanced toward the Edgar Harrison farmstead, where they encountered a Rebel picket line. A clash occurred, with the Confederates driving back their foes. Second Corps commander Winfield Scott Hancock reported the information to army headquarters, which instructed him "to send forward a force to ascertain where the enemy is and his position."[53]

Colonel Samuel Carroll's brigade of John Gibbon's division drew the assignment. Angling across the salient, Carroll's veterans soon received gunfire from Confederate skirmishers. Carroll had been wounded in the right arm at the Wilderness and had the arm in a sling. Riding in front of his men on this morning, he was struck in the left arm, the minié ball fracturing a bone. He relinquished command and sought medical aid. Later at a hospital in Fredericksburg, it was reported that he "was suffering terribly from an ex-section of the arm." The wound disabled the highly capable officer for weeks.[54]

Carroll's officers and men scattered the Rebels, capturing prisoners and a battle flag. They pushed on, finally locating the enemy's new defensive line on the ridge roughly 370 yards south of the Harrison farm. When

Hancock was informed of the discovery, he notified headquarters. His reports and those of Fifth Corps commander Gouverneur Warren confirmed that Lee's army remained on the battlefield and behind earthworks. In fact, the Confederate line of entrenchments stretched unbroken from those of Richard Anderson's First Corps in the west through the newly constructed works of Richard Ewell's Second Corps in the center to those of Jubal Early's Third Corps in the east across Fredericksburg Road.[55]

The intelligence from the front ended any hope or idea of a defeated Confederate army in retreat. If the reconnaissance had found that Robert E. Lee had begun a withdrawal, Ulysses S. Grant had wanted a vigorous pursuit undertaken at once. Instead, Meade ordered his three corps commanders "to feel the enemy's position" with one of their divisions. The movement, however, accomplished little, and the day would pass "without serious fighting" in Hancock's words.[56]

At the Mule Shoe, meanwhile, the gruesome work of gathering the wounded and burying the dead had begun. The destruction had been staggering. "The bodies of the fallen lay all over the field," described Captain Mason Tyler of the 37th Massachusetts. "Horses and men chopped into hash by the bullets, and appearing more like piles of jelly than the distinguishable forms of human life, were scattered all over the plain. Caissons and artillery carriages were cut into slivers. Trees large and small were cut down. . . . The ground was soaked with blood and water, with here and there pools deeply dyed with the same ingredients."[57]

Universally, to a man, the nature and extent of the carnage stunned, even sickened, the veteran soldiers who saw it on this day. A *New York Times* correspondent called it "a perfect Golgotha" that "presents a spectacle of horror that curdles the blood of the boldest." A member of the 2nd Vermont stated, "I have seen horrid scenes since this war commenced, I never saw anything half so bad as that." Similarly, Captain George Bowen of the 12th New Jersey asserted, "I thought I had seen slaughter before, but this beats them all." An eyewitness claimed the dead lay three deep on both sides of the apex's length.[58]

Francis Barlow and Lewis Grant compared the "mass of dead and wounded" to the numbers in the sunken road or "Bloody Lane" at Antietam on September 17, 1862, the conflict's bloodiest single day. "Men were piled up one on another like sacks of grain at a depot," staff officer Peter Vredenburgh informed his father in a letter. A New Yorker thought that he "could have walked upon the slain stepping from body to body" among the fallen Yankees for a quarter of a mile. A Massachusetts officer noted,

"It was bad enough on our side of the breast work but on theirs it was awful."[59]

The 10th Vermont's Captain Lemuel A. Abbott recorded in his diary that the earthworks were "filled with dead and wounded where they fell, several deep, nearly to the top in front, extending for 40 feet back, sloping to one deep." Abbott's regimental commander, Lieutenant Colonel William White, confided to his wife, "I have been through some *awful* scenes, and have seen sights that were *terrible* to behold." Surgeon A. T. Hamilton of the 148th Pennsylvania contended, "Such heaps of rebel dead who fell behind their own deep trenches I think never were seen elsewhere to exceed those of Spotsylvania."[60]

Colonel William Penrose of the 15th New Jersey walked into the Mule Shoe and counted 150 corpses in a space of twelve feet by fifteen feet. A staff officer claimed that 450 slain Rebels covered less than an acre of ground. A Pennsylvanian, Lieutenant Harvey B. Wells, saw within traverses, or "compartments," as he described them, "two, three and four deep, tangled-up with each other, bodies and limbs interwind, actual heaps of dead." Sitting in a corner of a traverse was a dead Confederate "in a position of apparent ease, with the head entirely gone, and the flesh burned from the bones of the neck and shoulders." A Union officer who went among the traverses confessed, "Those that saw say they never wish to see such a sight again."[61]

The burial details discovered uncounted numbers of wounded men, Union and Confederate, underneath the stacks of dead bodies. "Below the mass of fast decaying corpses," recalled a Yankee, "the convulsive twitching of limbs and the writhing of bodies showed that there were wounded men still alive and struggling to extricate themselves from their horrid entombment." A Pennsylvanian noted in his journal that four or five Rebels lay on top of each other throughout the trenches and "sometimes the lowest on the bottom are wounded and alive, yet were covered with mud and smothered."[62]

Crews endeavored to identify the Union slain, but so many were, admitted a survivor, "shot to pieces so as to be totally unrecognizable." Staff officer John Black and an officer in the 26th Michigan located the body of a friend after his comrades told them where he had fallen. "There was no semblance of humanity about the mass that was lying before us," recalled Black. "The only thing I could liken it was a sponge." The details gathered many such corpses into blankets before interring them. When they did identify the dead Federal, they wrote his name, company and regiment on "a board of a cracker box," which they stuck in the ground at the head of the grave.[63]

The Federals concluded their work at the salient the next morning, May 14, and moved away. Evidently, hundreds of the fallen remained unburied. Confederate burial details and soldiers entered the abandoned Mule Shoe and, like their foes, they were stunned by the scene. Mississippian Thomas Roche went to the Bloody Angle. "On entering this pit," professed Roche, "a spectacle utterly horrible met my gaze. It surpassed description. In it the men lay four deep, their bodies and limbs interlaced and entertwined."[64]

The crews covered the bodies that had been left half buried in the trenches. In many cases they could distinguish comrades from enemies only by the color of the uniforms. They identified the remains of Brigadier General Abner Perrin and interred them near the angle, marking the grave with a cedar post. By the time the Southerners had finished the work, the burial parties from both armies had turned the McCoull farm into a cemetery with hundreds of graves. Willis Landrum claimed later that five hundred bodies had been buried on his 170-acre farm. Wounded men remained untended and corpses remained unburied for days, however, along the earthworks outside of Spotsylvania Court House.[65]

"May God in his mercy never again permit us to behold such a field of carnage and death," pleaded a Rebel afterward. Vermont Captain Lemuel Abbott asked in his diary, "Could anything in Hades be any worse?" In words shared by countless men in both armies, Private Samuel Brooks of the 37th Massachusetts confessed to his wife, "This is a wickit war."[66]

"Fredericksburg is one vast hospital," a Union officer wrote to his sister on May 15. "The 'red flag' & wounded men appear everywhere." Patients from the Wilderness and the fighting at Spotsylvania Court House filled churches, warehouses, abandoned stores, and residences in the river town. Walking wounded could be seen on streets, while ambulances and wagons hauled hundreds daily to Aquia Landing on the Potomac River for transport to hospitals in the capital.[67]

The fighting at the Mule Shoe had flooded anew the makeshift hospitals in Fredericksburg on May 12 and 13. The Second Corps established an advance ambulance depot of 240 vehicles on the Landrum farm. The ambulances hauled 3,560 wounded on May 12 and 3,193 the next day. According to nurse Jane Stuart Woolsey, the ride from the battlefield to

Fredericksburg was a harrowing ordeal for the wounded men as they jolted about in the wagons. "I would rather a thousand times have a friend killed on the field than suffer in this way. . . . Many die on the way." One injured Union sergeant, Sergeant Nathaniel Bunker of the 56th Massachusetts, wrote later that the trip in an ambulance took nearly eighteen hours, with men crying in pain, others pleading to be put out of their misery, and a few silently praying.[68]

Bunker's ordeal was undoubtedly similar to thousands of other wounded soldiers. "The proportion of severe wounds was unusually large," reported Dr. Thomas A. McParlin, the army's medical director, "not over one-fourth of the number being able to walk back to the hospitals." McParlin noted, "The amount of shock and depression of vital power" was "much greater" than in the campaign's earlier actions.[69]

While nurse Woolsey complained that "no words can express the horrible confusion" in Fredericksburg, a wounded Captain David Lewis of the 8th Ohio wrote to a newspaper, "we have as good a care as we could expect." Surgeons could not save all of them, with one doctor noting that 131 patients died over two days more than a week after the Mule Shoe struggle. He also recorded that 8,000 patients were hauled to Aquia Landing in one day for transport north.[70]

The standard figure for Union casualties on May 12 is nine thousand killed, wounded, and missing or captured. Published medical reports totaled losses for the campaign from May 8 to 21, not for individual days. Furthermore, official and unofficial numbers conflict, but it seems that the casualties might have exceeded the accepted figure. No definitive number will likely be determined, but more Federals fell on May 12 than on any other day during the campaign outside of Spotsylvania Court House.[71]

Confederate casualties on May 12 have been calculated at 8,000 killed, wounded, and captured. Official records, newspaper articles, regimental histories, and a modern numerical study indicate that the losses might have been higher, perhaps around 8,500. The figure given often for Rebel prisoners is, for instance, 3,000. According to the diary of the Union army's provost marshal, he received 3,427 officers and men as captives. Not only for Edward Johnson's division but also for those of Robert Rodes, John Gordon, Cadmus Wilcox, and William Mahone, the struggle for the Mule Shoe marked their bloodiest day in the campaign. Casualties for the Army of Northern Virginia at the two-day battle in the Wilderness were slightly more than 11,000, and for the entire Spotsylvania Campaign nearly

12,700. The two Union assaults on the salient on May 10 and 12 inflicted 10,000 of those losses.[72]

A soldier in the 4th North Carolina, Jacob Nathaniel Raymer, speaking for many, portrayed the reality of Mule Shoe in a May 13 letter when he exclaimed: "Blood! blood! It seems about everything we can lay our hands on is clothed with blood! Two-thirds of our wounded are struck in the head, neck, and face—this is the result of fighting behind breastworks."[73]

{ 11 }

Such a Place

One day after the Union offensive against the Confederate salient at Spotsylvania Court House, Ulysses S. Grant wrote to his wife, Julia. "The world has never seen so bloody or so protracted a battle as the one being fought and I hope never will again," stated her husband. "The enemy were really whipped yesterday but their situation is desperate beyond anything heretofore known. They lose this battle they lose their cause. As bad as it is they fought for it with gallantry worthy of a better."[1]

Grant's May 13 letter contained elements of truth. The assault by Winfield Scott Hancock's Second Corps shattered the ranks of Edward Johnson's Confederate division, corralled thousands of prisoners, captured a score of cannon, and tore open a gap of nearly three-fourths of a mile in the center of the Army of Northern Virginia's lines. The breakthrough knifed deeper into the salient, threatening the destruction of the Rebel army. But then the enemy's desperation and gallantry limited the penetration, drove back the disorganized Federal troops, and regained sections of the original earthworks. Before long the fighting descended into a fearfully bloody, hellish ordeal.[2]

The lieutenant general's grand offensive had been characterized, however, by random or cobbled-together planning and preparations. Responsibility rested with Grant. Staff officers had endeavored to gather intelligence on the enemy's salient but, as the officers and men of the Second Corps stood in ranks to attack, neither Hancock nor his division commanders possessed reliable information. In fact, they did not know the exact location of the Mule Shoe, the nature of the surrounding terrain, the shape and extent of its defenses, or the number of Confederate infantry and artillery within its confines.[3]

The generals had depended upon a sketch on the wall of the John Brown house that had been drawn by a regimental commander in Gershom Mott's division. He had gone forward in the command's advance on the evening of May 10, cautioning that the sketch was only "an impression" of the ground and the enemy's earthworks. The sketch was, recounted Francis Barlow, "the sole basis on which the dispositions of my division were made." Barlow contended further that the attack "was a mere lucky accident" when it struck the salient.[4]

Once Hancock's twenty thousand officers and men routed Johnson's brigades and plunged south through the salient as a disorganized swarm, the attack had reached a critical juncture. The victorious and enthused Yankees needed reinforcements in organized ranks to extend the assault and to widen the gap. Although Grant's grand offensive had entailed all four of the infantry corps, the nearest unit, the Sixth Corps, was too far away to enter the action at that time.[5]

Grant had proposed a massive assault after learning of Emory Upton's initial success on the evening of May 10. Upton's ultimate repulse resulted from a lack of support and enemy resistance. Evidently, little forethought had been given to following up Hancock's attack in a timely fashion with additional units. "Grant's failure to position fresh troops to exploit the breakthrough proved fatal to his plan," in the judgment of Gordon Rhea, author of a multivolume study of the Overland Campaign.[6]

Francis Barlow addressed this issue in a postwar account. "Except in the first assault the operations of this day were a failure," declared the Second Corps division commander. "At the close we had made no substantial advance beyond the ground won by the first attack. A great opportunity had been lost. The reason for this, in my opinion, was that no one had foreseen the magnitude of the success which was coming, and hence no one was prepared for it."[7]

Once Robert E. Lee's stalwart veterans had forged a tactical stalemate on the battlefield with counterattacks, the Union army's senior leadership crowded more troops into the fury, adding to the slaughter and gaining no advantage. Maneuver did not matter by then, as the combat had been reduced to a slugfest at close quarters. "The great historical fight of this day," staff officer Theodore Lyman entered into a notebook on May 12, "extended over a front of only 1,000 to 1,500 yards along the faces of the salient." "Indeed we had *too many* troops, as the generals justly said," Lyman added. "The lines got mixed and jammed together and were hard to handle."[8]

An astute observer, Confederate artillerist E. Porter Alexander, offered an "obvious conclusion" from the struggle on May 12. "It is that there is a maximum limit to the force which can be judiciously employed in an attack," Alexander noted in a postwar account. "An excessive force may paralyze its own efforts, and this was the practical outcome of this day's battle."[9]

Hancock contended years later that Grant or Meade should have assumed command of the fighting at the front, conjecturing that "a great deal more might have been done." In Hancock's view, the "great obstruction lay in the fact that there was no corps commander [at the front] who was invested with the general command." Hancock argued further that Grant or Meade might have found a weakness in the Confederate defenses and had the authority to coordinate the units from different corps to exploit it.[10]

Neither the general-in-chief nor the army commander rode to the battlefield during the action. After midday, Meade shifted headquarters to the Armstrong farmstead, a couple of miles north of the Mule Shoe. Grant and his staff soon joined Meade and his aides. They communicated with the corps commanders by telegraph, seeking timely information, prodding them to act, and issuing orders. The burden of command with the troops belonged to Hancock, Gouverneur Warren, Horatio Wright, and Ambrose Burnside, not Grant and Meade.[11]

Grant had failed to plan carefully, to foresee "the magnitude of the success," in Barlow's words. Once the fighting began, however, the haphazard preparations were compounded by the lackluster performances of the corps commanders. Grant expected aggressiveness from them, but the army's legacy consisted of cautiousness, of not taking risks, of seeking not a decisive victory but an avoidance of defeat. The ghosts of the army's past hovered over the battlefield as certainly as the failures of its senior leadership.[12]

The selection of Hancock and the Second Corps to lead the offensive with the main attack had merit. Although the effects of his serious Gettysburg wound required daily medical attention and sapped his once vigorous physical stamina, Hancock remained one of the army's finest corps commanders. But by midmorning, when the Confederates had brought the offensive to a standstill, Hancock and senior officers seemingly relinquished control of the fighting. They gathered at the Landrum farm, leaving decisions at the Mule Shoe to brigade and regimental commanders. Hancock requested reinforcements and kept army headquarters informed but stayed on the farm.[13]

An opportunity for a second breakthrough existed, however, on the salient's thinly held eastern face, where Barlow's and John Gibbon's veterans opposed a pair of enemy brigades. Accounts indicate that the level of combat in this section of the Mule Shoe paled in comparison to the struggle that engulfed the Bloody Angle and adjoining works. Throughout the afternoon and evening, Barlow's and Gibbon's troops did not press any sustained thrust on the Virginians and Georgians. Barlow admitted later that his division accomplished little after the opening assault. Responsibility for the failure to locate and to exploit a weakness in the Rebels' defenses belonged ultimately to Hancock, who was on the battlefield.[14]

While Hancock's performance lacked its usual fire and imposing presence amid the strife, the conduct of his fellow corps commanders adversely impacted the Union offensive. Horatio Wright had been in command of the Sixth Corps since John Sedgwick's death on May 9. Ordered by Meade to attack the salient's defenders on May 12, Wright parceled units into the action, relieving other commands. In the afternoon he joined Hancock at the Landrum farm. Wright possessed "no special predilection for fighting," according to Charles Dana. Like others at his rank, Wright seemed incapable of taking risks.[15]

In Grant's thinking, the Fifth and Ninth corps had crucial roles in the offensive. Meade ordered Gouverneur Warren that the Fifth Corps was to attack "at all hazards." Opposed to the general-in-chief's tactics of frontal assaults, however, Warren balked in implementing Meade's instructions. When the corps's units advanced, they did so piecemeal. Warren's obstinacy and lack of aggressiveness nearly resulted in his removal from command by Grant. Days later, to John Rawlins, Meade confided that he regarded Warren as a "serious embarrassment" but hoped that he might "overcome the difficulty."[16]

The failings of the army's former commander, Ambrose Burnside, had become increasingly evident not only to Grant but also to many in the army. Burnside had been directed to attack "with your entire force promptly and with all possible vigor" at the same time as Hancock. Instead, Burnside's uncoordinated and understrength advance did not go forth until more than two hours later. In the afternoon, the enemy nearly rolled up his left flank. Burnside appeared immovable and incapable of leading even a corps.[17]

At the divisional level, Barlow, Gibbon, and David Birney performed very capably during the main assault, further enhancing their reputations as generals. But in their troops' exuberance with the rout of Johnson's Rebels, the officers began losing tactical control of the badly disorganized and mixed-up units. As the hours-long combat continued through the afternoon and into the night, the generals' leadership waned. Conversely,

Gershom Mott's mediocre performances on May 10 and 12 resulted in his temporary demotion to brigade command. His division, with ranks reduced from casualties and the mustering out of regiments, was consolidated into Birney's command. David Russell proved to be a promising replacement for Wright at the head of his Sixth Corps division.[18]

More than a dozen colonels at the head of brigades distinguished themselves in the fighting. In the Second Corps, John Brooke, Samuel Carroll, and Nelson Miles were promoted to brigadier to rank from May 12, while Thomas Smyth earned his generalship as of October 1, 1864. Five colonels in the Sixth Corps—Daniel Bidwell, Edward Bragg, Oliver Edwards, Lewis Grant, and Emory Upton—received their brigadierships at various times. Upton's promotion was dated May 12, or as a soldier in the 121st New York put it to his mother on May 17, "our Col is promoted to General for saveing the Battle on the 12th." Although none of them ended the war as a brigadier general, Robert McAllister, William Robinson, Benjamin Christ, and Stephen Weld Jr. merited commendation at the head of their brigades.[19]

For the Union general-in-chief, the Mule Shoe struggle provided further evidence of the need for his imprint upon the Army of the Potomac. Grant was coming to recognize that he had to rid the army's senior leadership of its defensive thinking. Regardless of setbacks or cost in blood, under Grant there would be no turning back. For the first time a warrior oversaw the army's operations.[20]

As Grant assumed greater control over the army, Meade's role was reduced. On May 13, the general-in-chief recommended Meade and William T. Sherman for promotion to major general in the Regular Army, telling Secretary of War Edwin Stanton that the two men "are the fittest for large commands I have come in contact with." In time, Meade received the permanent rank but, a few days after Grant's dispatch to the War Department, Meade told a pair of visiting senators "that gradually, and from the very nature of things, Grant had taken control, and that it would be injurious to the army to have two heads." Meade confessed to his wife, "If there was any honorable way of retiring from my present false position I should undoubtedly adopt it." His role had become that of an executive officer or chief of staff.[21]

In the end, at the Mule Shoe outside of Spotsylvania Court House, May 12 had demonstrated once again that the bedrock of the Army of the Potomac was the valor and resilience of its rank and file. Although one of them admitted afterward, "I never want to see another charge," he and his comrades were, like Grant, determined to keep going until war's end.

To be sure, the army remained a sputtering machine, its leaders made costly decisions, and its common soldiery paid the price in blood. The roads that led away from the Mule Shoe, however, brought these steadfast Yankees ultimately to Appomattox.[22]

On May 16, with the fighting still ongoing around the courthouse village, General Robert E. Lee issued a congratulatory address to the officers and men of the Army of Northern Virginia. It read in part:

> The heroic valor of this army, with the blessing of Almighty God, has thus far checked the advance of the principal army of the enemy, and inflicted upon it heavy loss. The eyes and hearts of your countrymen are turned to you with confidence, and their prayers attend you in your gallant struggle. Encouraged by the success that has been vouchsafed to us; and stimulated by the great interest that depends upon the issue, let every man resolve to endure all and brave all, until by the assistance of a just and merciful God, the enemy shall be driven back and peace secured to our country.[23]

Four days earlier, before sunrise, Lee and the army had confronted perhaps the greatest crisis in its existence. Within an hour, the enemy had routed a Confederate division and had cleaved open a dangerous gap in the center of Lee's army. The Confederate commander rode into the shattered ranks, rallying the fugitives and beginning to rescue the army from the grave situation. As in the past, at such times Lee relied upon the fighting prowess of his veteran officers and men.[24]

Critical to the initial success of the Union assault had been the removal of Confederate artillery batteries from the salient during the previous night. By the afternoon of May 11, based upon intelligence reports, Lee had convinced himself that Grant was withdrawing toward Fredericksburg, arguably Lee's worst miscalculation of an opponent's intentions during the war. Lee told Ewell later, according to an eyewitness, that "he had been misled in regard to the enemy in our front, by his scouts, and that the fatal mistake was in removing the artillery on the line." In turn, Ewell asserted subsequently, "if the artillery had been in position we would have destroyed [the Federal] army."[25]

As the Yankees surged deeper into the Mule Shoe and the crisis worsened, Confederate reserves counterattacked. Lee had grasped quickly that perhaps the fate of the army and the cause loomed. He "made more than one narrow escape," chronicled a Southern newspaperman, "his clothing covered with mud thrown upon him by bursting shells." He summoned more brigades and ordered them in. "Lee seemed determined to retake that angle," stated a Georgian.[26]

"The onus of the fight fell on us to retake the position," wrote a South Carolinian. Brigade after Rebel brigade charged into the salient, recapturing sections of the original entrenchments and pushing the Federals out of most of the defenses. "In no previous operations did the Army of Northern Virginia display higher soldierly qualities," declared Second Corps artillery chief Armistead Long. "Regardless of numbers, every breach was filled, and with unparalleled stubbornness the lines were maintained."[27]

A Virginian asked years later, "Was there ever another army that would not have been demoralized and forced to retire from such a situation," as the rout of Edward Johnson's division? The Rebels praised their foes for "obstinacy and courage." But brigade commander Robert Johnston put it well in a letter to a former comrade: "It was just a day of plain hard fighting where the safety of the army depended upon every man doing his full duty and never letting the enemy gain an inch with blood letting. It was surely a weak line to hold back a powerful enemy but then every confederate there had to fight about four of the enemy and they did it."[28]

In a series of counterattacks, nine Confederate brigades had charged into the heart of the salient by the McCoull farm. John Gordon's three brigades—Robert Johnston's North Carolinians, John Hoffman's Virginians, and Clement Evans's Georgians—had slowed the Federal thrust into the Mule Shoe, repulsed it at the reserve line of works at its base, and drove the Yankees back to the original entrenchments and traverses. At different times during the morning, Abner Perrin's and Cullen Battle's Alabama brigades, along with William Wofford's Georgians, had joined the struggle. But it was the brigades of Stephen Dodson Ramseur's North Carolinians, Nathaniel Harris's Mississippians, and Samuel McGowan's South Carolinians that had stepped into the worst of the fighting at the Bloody Angle and adjoining earthworks.[29]

Lee's aide, Charles Venable, said of the Mississippians, "Never did a brigade go into fierce battle, under greater trials and never did a brigade do its duty more nobly." Months later, Richard Ewell praised Harris's veterans in a letter to its commander. "Your brigade and two others . . . confronted successfully this immense host [of Union troops]," asserted Ewell, "and not only won from them nearly all the ground they had gained, but so shattered their army that they were unable again to make a serious attack until they received fresh troops." Another Confederate wrote after the war, "Mississippi under Harris holds the place of honor on this day."[30]

McGowan's South Carolinians manned the works on the right of the Mississippians. A fellow Rebel praised both brigades, describing them as "an insurmountable barrier between the army and ruin." Colonel Joseph Brown, who had succeeded a wounded McGowan, declared that he "never saw anything to equal in desperate character that of the Bloody Angle." Two years after the conflict, McGowan told a newspaperman, "if ever troops 'held their own' under the most difficult circumstances and immortalized themselves, my brigade in 'the bloody angle' on the 12th of May, I think it may be said, with perfect modesty and entire truth, that nothing in the history of the world surpasses it."[31]

Ramseur's North Carolinians had gone in ahead of the Mississippians and South Carolinians, seizing a section of works along the western face. Ramseur boasted in a letter, "On the 12th my Brigade did some of the best fighting of the war." He noted, "Gen'l Ewell called me the hero of the day & Gen'l Lee sent for me to thank me." According to Bryan Grimes, Lee rode to the brigade, praised it for its gallantry, "saying that we deserved the thanks of the country—that we had saved his army." In a postwar account, staff officer Venable thought the Confederates' counterattacks and defensive stand in the Mule Shoe "a wonderful feat of arms, in which all the troops engaged deserve the greatest credit for endurance, constancy, and unflinching courage; but without unjust discrimination, we may say Gordon, Rodes, and Ramseur were the heroes of this bloody day."[32]

Venable's view of the day's heroes had justification. Arguably the army's finest division commander, Robert Rodes had rallied units along the western face and had limited the enemy's penetration along that section during the Federals' breakthrough. Rodes then ordered in Ramseur and Battle and, according to eyewitnesses, seemed to be everywhere on the battlefield. In a September 1864 letter, Rodes asked Ewell to give him "my share of the glory" for the Wilderness and the Mule Shoe.[33]

Gordon was the army's rising star, and his brigades' counterattacks sealed the breach and bought crucial time for other units to enter the struggle. Lee rewarded him with promotion to major general, recommending that the Georgian rank from May 12. The commission was, however, dated May 14, which caused Lee to complain, according to Gordon, "of the lack of consideration at Richmond when he handed me the commission." By month's end, Ramseur was assigned to command of a division, with promotion to major general on June 1.[34]

Other brigade commanders, such as Johnston, Harris, McGowan, Evans, Perrin, and Battle, distinguished themselves. McGowan's successor, Joseph Brown, and Perrin's, William Saunders, proved capable. Bryan Grimes deservedly earned promotion to replace Junius Daniel, who had been mortally wounded on May 12 while in command of his North Carolina brigade. The Mule Shoe struggle, however, exacerbated the attrition in the army's field grade officers: majors, lieutenant colonels, and colonels. Sixty-nine field grade officers were killed or mortally wounded, wounded, or captured during the Spotsylvania Campaign, most of them on May 12. Combined with the approximately 150 who had fallen at Gettysburg and the dozens in the Wilderness, leadership at that command level had reached a crisis, which only deepened.[35]

For Lee, however, the Mule Shoe fight further demonstrated the mounting liabilities of Richard Ewell as commander of the Second Corps. It was Lee, not Ewell, who bore responsibility for the removal of artillery, which critically weakened the salient's defenses. To Ewell's credit, he rode into the shattered ranks of Johnson's division, trying to stem the rearward flood of officers and men. But the one-legged general lost his composure during the crisis, an unforgivable act to many in this redoubtable army. Lee had admonished Ewell at the time for losing "control of yourself." The former army commander told an interviewer after the war that he had "found Ewell perfectly prostrated by the misfortune of the morning, and too much overwhelmed to be efficient."[36]

Finally, on May 19, Ewell's Second Corps advanced in a reconnaissance-in-force toward the Federal right flank near a Harris family farm near Fredericksburg Road northeast of the courthouse village. While trying to extricate Rodes's troops from the fighting, Ewell had his horse killed under him, and he fell hard on the ground. William Allan of the general's staff wrote in a memoir that Ewell "at one time lost his head in the severity of the fight." Lee arrived on the field and according to Allan's notes of his postwar interview with Lee, Ewell "lost all presence of mind, and Lee found him prostrate on the ground, and declaring he cd not get Rodes div. out." The army commander then instructed Ewell to order Rodes to withdraw and, if he could not do so, Lee could.[37]

Whether Lee discovered Ewell literally on the ground or overcome by the pressures of commands remains debatable. Nevertheless, Lee had witnessed enough. He had given his senior generals discretion in the execution of orders but, as a staff officer noted, provided "only it be a success." On May 25, Ewell reported that he was physically unfit for duty from a severe case of diarrhea. Lee assigned Jubal Early to temporary command of the Second Corps two days later. When Ewell informed Lee that he could return to duty, the army commander suggested that he take more time to recover fully.[38]

Ewell responded to Lee by providing a certificate from Dr. Hunter H. McGuire, who stated that the general was fit for duty. On May 31, Ewell reported for duty, informing army headquarters that "I am unwilling to be idle in this crisis and, with the permission of the commanding general, I would prefer to remain with this army until circumstances may admit of my being replaced in command of my corps." Two weeks later, however, Ewell was assigned to command of the Richmond's defenses. Lee offered subsequently that he had been "very reluctant to displace him, but felt compelled to do so." Allan recalled that members of Ewell's staff "all felt that his removal was inevitable & indeed was proper."[39]

Early had led the Third Corps during the campaign in place of A. P. Hill, whose unspecified illness lingered. Hill stayed with the army, riding in an ambulance. On May 15, Hill watched as Brigadier General Ambrose Wright mismanaged an attempt by his Georgia brigade to seize a hill along the Po River. When Lee arrived, a furious Hill threatened to bring Wright before a court of inquiry. "These men are not an army; they are citizens defending their country," Lee admonished Hill. "General Wright is not a soldier; he is a lawyer; I cannot do many things I could do with a trained army. The soldiers know their duties better than general officers do, and they have fought magnificently." A still ailing Hill requested and received command of his corps six days later.[40]

In their own words, the army's rank and file echoed Lee's words to Hill that they had "fought magnificently." A soldier in the 21st Virginia wrote home, "The valor of our army by the grace of God has repulsed one of the grandest and most desperate efforts that was ever made at a peoples subjugation." Colonel R. Tyler Bennett of the 14th North Carolina declared after the war that the battle for the Mule Shoe transformed its defenders from "ordinary mortals, to the supreme beatitudes in life." To Bennett, May 12 was "the memorable day of the war."[41]

A pair of Richmond newspapers offered their views on the struggle before the end of May. "I question whether in the annals of modern history so frightful a slaughter has ever been inflicted by an army acting on the defensive upon its assailants," opined one of them. The Richmond *Examiner* editorialized on May 28, "On that day [May 12] the question whether they [Yankees] could beat Lee in the field and put him into a disastrous retreat, was forever settled."[42]

Lee's chief of staff, Walter Taylor, however, gave a divergent assessment of the day in a letter on May 15. "The 12th was an unfortunate day for us—we recovered most of the ground lost but cd not regain our *guns*," he observed. "This hurts our pride—but we are determined to make our next success all the greater to make amends for this disaster. Our men are in good heart & condition—our confidence, certainly mine, unimpaired. Grant is beating his head against a wall."[43]

The Army of the Potomac and the Army of Northern Virginia remained in the area around Spotsylvania Court House for eight days after the Mule Shoe struggle. Most of the movement and action transpired on both sides of Fredericksburg Road as the Federals pushed farther south in an effort by Grant to maneuver Lee's army out of its entrenchments. On the night of May 13–14, under orders from Grant, the Fifth Corps withdrew from its earthworks, swung north and east across the Ny River and, angling south, passed behind the lines of the Ninth Corps east of Fredericksburg Road. The strung-out column of infantry and artillery units arrived fitfully at their designated position on the left flank of the Ninth Corps hours past sunrise on May 14.[44]

The Sixth Corps trailed the Fifth Corps, extending the line farther southeast of Fredericksburg Road. Late in the afternoon, Emory Upton's brigade advanced to Myer's Hill, opposite the fieldworks of the Confederate Third Corps. A clash ensued, with Upton's regiments driven from the rise. With Upton's repulse the armies settled in for the night.[45]

For the next three days, exchanges of gunfire between opposing skirmish lines marked the action. Rain continued to fall periodically, deepening the mud. During this time, Grant awaited the arrival of thousands of reinforcements from the Washington defenses and the drying of roads. On May 18, he ordered assaults on the enemy's lines by the Second and Ninth Corps. The frontal attacks ended in bloody repulses despite the gallantry of the Union officers and men. Winfield Hancock stated that his Second Corps troops lost "quite heavily," while Ambrose Burnside reported that his units suffered "consider loss," adding that "it was concluded that [the enemy's works] could not be carried by assault." Afterward, Grant issued orders for a movement toward the North Anna River to begin at midnight on May 19.[46]

Believing that his opponent might be endeavoring once again to turn the Confederate right flank, Lee instructed Richard Ewell to undertake a reconnaissance-in-force to ascertain whether the reports were accurate.

The march consumed most of the day, as Ewell's six-thousand-man force had to detour in a wide arc before advancing toward the Federals' right flank near "Bloomsbury," the home of Clement and Mary Harris, located about two and a half miles northeast of Spotsylvania Court House.[47]

Ewell's command appeared in the fields west of Bloomsbury about 5:00 P.M., encountering an eight-thousand-man division of heavy artillery under Brigadier Robert O. Tyler, whose troops had arrived from the capital defenses two days earlier. When the fighting commenced, the Harris family sought shelter in the cellar. In their first real combat, fighting as infantrymen, Tyler's officers and men held their ground. Hancock rushed David Birney's division into the engagement, while units from the Fifth Corps came in on Tyler's left. The struggle lasted until ten o'clock, when the Confederates withdrew. Ewell reported his losses at about 900 killed, wounded, and missing, while the Federals incurred 1,500 casualties.[48]

The Harris engagement delayed the Union movement for a day but, on May 21, the army resumed the march toward Richmond. To the west in parallel columns marched Lee's veterans. The two-week campaign in the farmers' fields and woods encircling Spotsylvania Court House cost the Federals nearly 19,000 casualties, while the Confederates suffered losses of more than 12,600 killed, wounded, and captured or missing. Slightly more than 55 percent of the combined casualties, or about 17,500, occurred in the hellish ordeal at the Mule Shoe. But, as a *New York Times* correspondent maintained, "the most terrible collision breaks neither one of these armies; a swift succeeding series of shocks has not yet broken either of them."[49]

When the armies marched away from Spotsylvania Court House, eleven months of conflict lay ahead; eleven months of being in daily contact; eleven months of being filthy in trenches; eleven months of random death from unseen killers; eleven months of frontal attacks and bloody repulses; eleven months of the changing face of warfare, foretelling a terrible future of unimagined slaughter.

What lay behind was the Mule Shoe, the blood-soaked ordeal that defined the campaign and marked a passage into a darker struggle. Wherever the roads led—North Anna, Cold Harbor, and Petersburg—the troops erected fieldworks that became more refined, more complex, and more formidable. Behind these fortifications, the soldiers slaughtered their foes who dared to attack across a killing ground in front. It had begun in the darkness on a slight rise two miles northwest of Spotsylvania Court House, where bone-weary Confederates felled trees and dug dirt.[50]

But the Mule Shoe meant more, much more, to the Yankees and Rebels who fought in and outside the entrenchments and among the traverses. Those long hours left an indelible imprint reflected in words that echo through history and speak for uncounted thousands of comrades. A Union officer, Lieutenant Robert Robertsons, described the carnage simply: "The ground drank its fill of blood." Corporal DeWitt Clinton Beckwith of the 121st New York declared, "This was the worse day's experience I ever had, and it thoroughly disgusted me with war." The 8th Ohio's Lieutenant Thomas Galwey expressed a common sentiment: "Bloody Angle at Spotsylvania exceeded all the rest in stubbornness, ferocity, and in courage." Chaplain Alanson A. Haines of the 15th New Jersey agreed with Galwey: "The Twelfth of May, 1864. Terrible day awful, murderous conflict! Combine the horrors of many battle-fields, bring them into a single day and night of twenty-four hours, and the one of May 12th includes them all."[51]

"Our fellows say that men were just like devils that day—didn't care for life, their own or anybody else's," recounted a civilian, who had heard stories of the Mule Shoe fight from Confederate veterans. The mapmaker and staff officer Jedediah Hotchkiss believed the salient battle was "the hardest of the war." An officer in the 9th Alabama proclaimed, "I regard this day as the most dismal one I ever passed through."[52]

Stating a view held by many, a private in the 14th North Carolina affirmed, "I don't suppose there is any man that can express the relief he felt after getting out of such a place." A fellow North Carolinian told his folks, in a letter of May 14, "last Thursday though is the day that will be remembered by both armies as long as one man is left to tell the tale." In another letter written weeks later, a Georgian averred to his sister, "the 12th day of May 1864 will be even memorable & even remembered as the most bloody & obstinate struggles, which have ever marked the annals of war, or added fresh horrors to this most bloody & cruel drama that is now being acted."[53]

In his reminiscences, Confederate general John Gordon called the Mule Shoe struggle a "wrestle of the giants on the same breastworks," with "no parallel in the annals of war." He went on, portraying the fury, "an unexampled muzzle-to-muzzle fire; the longest roll of incessant unbroken musketry; the most splendid exhibition of individual heroism and personal daring by large numbers, who, standing in the freshly spilt blood of their fellows, faced for so long a period and, at so short a range the flaming rifles as they heralded the decrees of death." Fellow division commander Cadmus Wilcox, writing decades later, was blunt: "There is no parallel to this fight in the history of this war—not any I know of since the introduction of fire-arms."[54]

Thirty years after the battle, a Mississippian wrote to a former comrade in Nathaniel Harris's brigade about May 12, stating with pride, "[I] can hardly believe that I was one of the boys that helped make history on that day." Union staff officer and future Supreme Court jurist Oliver Wendell Holmes Jr. observed: "War, when you are at it, is horrible and dull. It is only when time has passed that you see that its message was divine." If it were as Holmes believed, then the Mule Shoe had been steeped in the divine on Thursday, May 12, 1864.[55]

Brigadier General Nelson Miles returned to Spotsylvania Court House, Virginia, on May 5, 1865. As a colonel, the Massachusetts native led a Second Corps brigade in the attack on the Mule Shoe nearly a year earlier. Miles now commanded a division, and with the war ended, he and his troops were on the march north, to Washington, D.C. He had halted his command and camped on the Willis Landrum farm near the former Confederate salient.[56]

Miles's corps commander, Winfield Hancock, had used the Landrum farmhouse as his headquarters during the fighting for the salient. At the time, sixty-six-year-old Willis Landrum and his second wife, forty-eight-year-old Lucy, owned the four-room house and the 170-acre farm. When the battle began on May 12, the couple and their four children—Bettie, Cornelius, Edward, and Lucy—fled from their home. They did not return to the house until after the armies headed south toward the North Anna River.[57]

Upon the Landrums' return, the scene must have staggered them. Countless freshly dug graves seemed everywhere, while abandoned artillery lunettes lined the family's farm lane. Inside their home, blood-stained floors marked its use as a field hospital. Twelve-year-old Edward Landrum remembered, "Our house was shot all to pieces, and the furniture destroyed and the fragments taken to build breastworks." The family discovered that the Federals had carried off their seven feather beds as material for the works. "What the Yankees put them in for I can't imagine," wrote Edward.[58]

To the south, within the confines of the Mule Shoe, the McCoull farmhouse bore the scars of the fighting. The three McCoull sisters had remained in their home, sheltering in the cellar as the fighting raged outside on their doorstep. The house had all of its roof shingles shot off.

Years later the dwelling's wartime damage could be seen. A visitor noted in 1881, "Tall oaks surround the house, which is a weather-beaten, rickety structure that clearly has been through the mills." At some point in the postwar years, new owners replaced the clapboards and, in the process, retrieved sixty pounds of bullets from the old lumber.[59]

Miles, meanwhile, witnessed the considerable damage done to the two farmhouses. He and his staff members visited the Mule Shoe, searching for the stump of the red oak whose trunk had been severed by rifle and artillery fire near the Bloody Angle. Unable to locate it, the general and aides rode into the village for a dinner at the Spotswood Hotel. Nearly every building in the crossroads town had been struck by rifle and/or artillery fire during the two-week campaign. The hotel, which had been established as an ordinary or tavern in 1799, had its walls and four pillars pockmarked by bullets and pieces of artillery shells. Across the road, the courthouse had a "huge piece" of the building torn from its lower story.[60]

The Union officers inquired of the owner, Joseph Sanford, who denied any knowledge of the stump's whereabouts. A waiter, however, betrayed its location in the hotel's smokehouse. It had been taken there by local folks as a historic treasure. When Sanford refused to unlock the door to the building, the Federals used an axe to break in and retrieve it. Upon the division's arrival in the capital, Miles had the stump placed in the War Department.[61]

Later that autumn, a Union veteran visited the War Department and saw a stump from the Mule Shoe on each side of the edifice's entrance. In 1876, the War Department displayed the famous stump for six months at the Centennial International Exhibition in Philadelphia, Pennsylvania. Eventually, the federal government paid Sanford's son $1,000.00 for the relic. Today, the Bloody Angle's stump is among the collections of the Smithsonian's National Museum of American History.[62]

At roughly the same time Miles and his division passed through the area, Joseph Sanford, contacted the War Department, "promising to bury the bodies of all Union soldiers killed near this place, and remaining unburied." Sanford requested three barrels of flour and two barrels of pork for the work. He evidently received the barrels from the government but whether he fulfilled his promise remains uncertain. Congress established the Fredericksburg National Cemetery in 1865, but internments of Union dead from the Wilderness and Spotsylvania did not begin until the next year.[63]

When the reburial work began in 1866, the laborers disinterred 1,450 Federals and an unknown number of Confederates from Woodshaw, the Neil McCoull farm. The Northern dead went to Fredericksburg; the Southern dead, to the Confederate Cemetery in Spotsylvania Court House. The latter graveyard had been established by the Spotsylvania Ladies' Memorial Association, whose "object . . . will be to rescue from neglect and devastation the remains of those who offered up their lives in behalf of the 'Lost Cause.'" Brigadier General Abner Perrin's remains would not be removed until 1903, when they were placed in City Cemetery in Fredericksburg.[64]

The battlefield drew other visitors after the war had ended. A journalist, John Townsend Trowbridge, had come south to tour the battlefields in the region. He stopped at Chancellorsville and the Wilderness before heading to Spotsylvania. While on the way, he met a local man, who surmised that Trowbridge was a northerner. When the newspaperman inquired how the fellow knew Trowbridge was from the North, the man answered, "Because no South'n man ever goes to the battlefields; we've seen enough of 'em."[65]

It appears that most of the early visitors to the battlefield were from the North. The Mule Shoe, in particular, drew the curious. Former staff officer Theodore Lyman returned in 1866 with a group of men. The reburials had begun, but Lyman stated that graves were everywhere. Another former Union soldier came back that year and left a description, "Full one-half of the trees in the wood, at a point where the fiercest struggle ensued within the salient of the confederate works, were dead, and nearly all the others were scarred from the effect of musket balls."[66]

Over time, visitors stopped regularly at the McCoull and Landrum farms. LaVilla, the Edgar and Ann Harrison home, had been destroyed by fire, with only ruins left behind. The McCoull Woodshaw farm was sold at auction for $1,500.00 in May 1889, purchased by a John W. Harper of Fauquier County, Virginia. A visitor to the battlefield and the farm wrote, "This house is just as it was 30 years ago, the weather boarding perforated on all sides by balls." A sign on the house read, "Relics for sale here." Harper sold the property, which contained five hundred acres at the time, "to Northern parties" for $2,100.00 in 1902. The house burned to the ground in March 1921.[67]

On the night of Sunday, February 14, 1897, fire destroyed the Landrum farmhouse; the ruins were marked by a pair of blackened chimneys that stood at each end of the homestead. Either before or after the fire, the

Landrums had built a house near the apex of the salient. Described as a "yellowish, clay-plastered house," it stood for an indeterminate number of years. The family continued to own the Bloody Angle and adjoining works into the twentieth century. Edward Landrum told visitors to the Mule Shoe that "our fellows called it the bloody bend."[68]

In 1930, Edward T. Stuart of the Girard Trust Company of Philadelphia bought the thirty-five-acre property from the Landrums at a court sale. A Civil War buff, Stuart donated four acres, including the Bloody Angle, to the Federal government two years later. Stuart had placed a granite marker over the site where the red oak stump had stood.[69]

Man and nature altered the Mule Shoe battlefield over time. For years, visitors or relic hunters could find pieces of canteens and knapsacks "in abundance." Someone discovered a rifle with an inscription on the leather strap: L. Dugal, Company F, 146th New York. The Union veteran was located in Denver, Colorado, and the rifle was sent to him. Edward Landrum recalled that during the first few years he plowed the fields, he uncovered six skeletons. He claimed, "Visitors from the north took them away as relics."[70]

A Pennsylvanian, who journeyed to the salient in 1881, wrote that young pines and persimmon trees covered sections of it. "Ditches . . . are now partly filled with leaves . . . while briars, wild vines, the ox eye daisy and blue-flowered nettles now set traps to trip the footman in his rambles." Flowers still covered the ground twenty-five years later when a visitor from Ohio arrived in the spring. He thought, however, "It is a strange and dreary battleground, so unlike many I have seen." He added, "At night the dismalness is increased." By the time the Philadelphian Stuart purchased the land, encroaching thickets blanketed "that scene of frightful strife."[71]

Through the years Civil War veterans returned, both from the North and the South. In 1909, former members of the 15th New Jersey and of Clement Evans's Georgia brigade held "an informal reunion." The New Jersey veterans had come to dedicate their monument and to return captured flags, which had belonged to the Georgians. Five years later, on May 15, 1914, eight veterans of the 126th Ohio unveiled their monument, which marked the regiment's farthest advance on May 12, fifty years earlier.[72]

When Ohioan T. C. Harbaugh traveled to the battlefield, he had a Confederate veteran act as a guide. Stopping at the Bloody Angle, Harbaugh said, "It is a dark spot." The former member of the Army of Northern Virginia replied, "It is the heart of hell."[73]

Acknowledgments

My book has benefited from the advice and assistance of talented folks whose expertise, generosity, and encouragement have improved the quality of this work. All errors of omission and commission are, however, entirely mine.

I wish to thank the librarians and archivists at the institutions cited in the bibliography for their cooperation and for permission to publish from their manuscript collections. The following individuals merit my particular recognition and gratitude:

Lisa Shaffer, bibliographic services assistant and interlibrary loan coordinator, Centre County Library, for her diligent efforts in securing rare books and publications during my research.

John Cummings, local historian of Spotsylvania County, for sharing material on the families who lived in the area in May 1864.

John J. Hennessy, chief historian/chief of interpretation, Fredericksburg and Spotsylvania National Military Park, and fellow historian, for his exceptional efforts before, during, and after my research trip to the park's library.

Nicholas Picerno, noted preservationist and Civil War collector and a dear family friend, for his constant encouragement and willingness to listen to my arguments.

Robert K. Krick, the modern authority on the Army of Northern Virginia and a friend, for guiding my early research endeavors and for sharing copies of rare accounts with me.

David Ward, a fellow historian and a friend of many years, for reading the entire manuscript and offering insightful critiques and welcome corrections.

Daniel Laney, Civil War preservationist, historian, and deeply valued family friend, for reading the entire manuscript and offering perceptive analysis and cogent arguments.

Dr. Carolyn Janney, John L. Nau III Professor in the History of the American Civil War and director, John L. Nau III Center for Civil War History, University of Virginia, for generous assistance and discerning comments on each chapter of the manuscript.

Dr. Peter S. Carmichael, Robert C. Fluhrer Professor of Civil War Studies and director of the Civil War Institute at Gettysburg College, for his endorsement of my manuscript to UNC Press.

Mark Simpson-Vos, Wyndham Robertson editorial director at UNC Press, for his belief in my book and constant support.

Maria Garcia, assistant editor, for her gracious and persistent help on a myriad of details.

Erin Davis, senior production editor at Westchester Publishing Services, for overseeing the excellent work of the copyediting staff.

Don Fehr, my agent at Trident Media Group, for his patience, advice, and diligent efforts on my behalf.

Our son, Jason Wert; our daughter-in-law, Kathy Wert; our grandchildren, Rachel and Gabriel Wert; our daughter, Natalie Wert Corman; and our son-in-law, Grant Corman, for their ceaseless love and support, for all that they are and do, and for all that they mean to Gloria and me.

My wife, Gloria, my cherished love and best friend, for being by my side over these many years of research and writing, of typing every word, of careful editing, of stoic patience and boundless encouragement. Without her none of my work is possible or of meaning.

Jeffry D. Wert

Notes

Abbreviations

Works cited by the author and short titles will be in full in the bibliography. These abbreviations are used in the endnotes:

ADAH	Alabama Department of Archives and History
AHEC	United States Army Heritage Education Center
AHS	Atlanta Historical Society
ALPLM	Abraham Lincoln Presidential Library and Museum
AU	Auburn University
BG	*Blue & Gray Magazine*
BHS	Bethel Historical Society
B&L	*Battles and Leaders of the Civil War*
BPL	Boston Public Library
BOWC	Bowdoin College
BU	Boston University
CU	Cornell University
CV	*Confederate Veteran*
CWT	*Civil War Times*
DU	Duke University
EU	Emory University
FSNMP	Fredericksburg-Spotsylvania National Military Park
HANDL	Handley Library
HC	Hamilton College
HSMC	Historical Society of Montgomery County
IU	Indiana University
LC	Library of Congress
LSU	Louisiana State University
LVA	Library of Virginia
MCHA	Monmouth County Historical Association
MDAH	Mississippi Department of Archives and History
MHS	Massachusetts Historical Society
MNBP	Manassas National Battlefield Park
MSU	Michigan State University
NA	National Archives
OR	*U.S. War Department, War of the Rebellion: A Compilation of the Official Records of the Union and Confederate Armies*
PMHSM	*Papers of the Military Historical Society of Massachusetts*

PSU	Pennsylvania State University
RNBP	Richmond National Battlefield Park
SANC	State Archives of North Carolina
SCHS	South Carolina Historical Society
SHSP	*Southern Historical Society Papers*
SHSW	State Historical Society of Wisconsin
SOR	*Supplement to the Official Records of the Union and Confederate Armies*
SPPL	South Portland Public Library
TSLA	Tennessee State Library and Archives
TU	Tulane University
UGA	University of Georgia
UM	University of Michigan
UNC	University of North Carolina
USC	University of South Carolina
USM	University of Southern Mississippi
UT	University of Texas
UU	University of Utah
UVA	University of Virginia
VHS	Virginia Historical Society
VMI	Virginia Military Institute
VTHS	Vermont Historical Society
WLU	Washington and Lee University
WRHS	Western Reserve Historical Society
WVU	West Virginia University

Chapter 1

1. Ruffner, *44th Virginia Infantry*, 49, 51; Krick, *Lee's Colonels*, 31, 409; *PMHSM*, vol. 4, 112.

2. Howard, *Recollections*, 294; Mackowski and White, "Battle," 13, 21; *CV*, vol. 31, 297; *Meridian Daily Clarion*, June 11, 1864; Ruffner, *44th Virginia Infantry*, 51.

3. Freeman, *Lee's Lieutenants*, vol. 3, 392–96; Ruffner, *44th Virginia Infantry*, 51; Howard, *Recollections*, 294.

4. Seymour, *Civil War Memoirs*, 123; *SHSP*, vol. 21, 245.

5. Sears, *Lincoln's Lieutenants*, 624; Gallagher and Janney, *Cold Harbor*, 5; Page, *Letters*, 43–44.

6. Gallagher and Janney, *Cold Harbor*, 5; A. Ted Barclay–Sister, May 2, 1864, Barclay Correspondence, WLU; William D. Rutherford–My own darling, April 26, 1864, Rutherford Papers, USC.

7. Wert, *Glorious Army*, 284.

8. Wert, *Glorious Army*, 284.

9. *SHSP*, vol. 4, 153; Wert, *Cavalryman*, 325.

10. Ivy W. Duggan–Editor, April 25, 1864, Duggan Papers, UGA; John Garibaldi–Wife, April 5, 1864, Garibaldi Correspondence, VMI; *Washington Evening Star*, September 25, 1921; *Staunton Spectator and Vindicator*, March 1, 1864.

11. *PMHSM*, vol. 4, 87, 88; Long, *Memoirs*, 323; Gallagher, *Wilderness Campaign*, 42, 43, 44; *Savannah Morning News*, July 20, 1864.

12. Gallagher, *Wilderness Campaign*, 44; Sheehan–Dean, *Why*, 153; Carmichael, *War*, 78; Isaac Lefever–Mrs. Catherine Lefever, May 20, 1864, Lefever Letters, SANC.

13. Gallagher, *Wilderness Campaign*, 36, 44, 49, 50, 51; R. E. Dunn–My Dear Bro., April 22, 1864, VHS; Stephens, *Intrepid Warrior*, 342–43.

14. Dowdey and Manarin, *Wartime Papers*, 695–96; Dozier, *Gunner*, 188; Wert, *Glorious Army*, 182.

15. Bond and Coward, *South Carolinians*, 133.

16. *PMHSM*, vol. 4, 36; *B&L*, vol. 4, 119; Lowe, *Meade's Army*, 172; Krick, *Staff Officers*, 214, 283, 293.

17. Dowdey and Manarin, *Wartime Papers*, 667.

18. Wert, *Glorious Army*, 7, 8.

19. Wert, *Glorious Army*, 9; Rafuse, *Robert E. Lee*, 255.

20. Wert, *Glorious Army*, 9; Harsh, *Confederate Tide Rising*, 56, 68; Carmichael, *Audacity*, 2.

21. Smith, *Freeman on Leadership*, 153–57; Weigley, *Great Civil War*, 256; Carmichael, *Audacity*, 11; Harsh, *Confederate Tide Rising*, 68.

22. Wert, *Glorious Army*, chaps. 2–9.

23. Wert, *Glorious Army*, 277, 278; Wise, *Long Arm*, 694.

24. Sword, *Southern Invincibility*, 169.

25. Carmichael, *Audacity*, 11, 12, 60; Dowdey and Manarin, *Wartime Papers*, 667; *SHSP*, vol. 4, 153.

26. Wert, *Sword*, 320–21.

27. Carmichael, *Audacity*, 11, 12; Weigley, *Great Civil War*, 256.

28. Carmichael, *Audacity*, 11; Weigley, *Great Civil War*, 256; Harsh, *Confederate Tide Rising*, 70; Wert, *Glorious Army*, 9, 285.

29. Weigley, *Great Civil War*, 256; Tower, *Lee's Adjutant*, 148

30. Lowe, *Meade's Army*, 119; Meade, *Life and Letters*, vol. 2, 177, 183; Clarke B. Hall–author, August 30, 2019, electronic message.

31. Meade, *Life and Letters*, vol. 2, 177; Grant, *Personal Memoirs*, vol. 2, 117; Wert, *Sword*, 326.

32. Grant, *Personal Memoirs*, vol. 2, 117; Meade, *Life and Letters*, vol. 2, 162.

33. Scott, *Fallen Leaves*, 241; Wert, *General James Longstreet*, 50.

34. Lowe, *Meade's Army*, 107, 121; Williams, *Diary*, 344; Grimsley, *And Keep Moving On*, xiii.

35. Wert, *Sword*, 327; Lowe, *Meade's Army*, 126; Williams, *Diary*, 344.

36. Wert, *Sword*, 327; Lowe, *Meade's Army*, 107; Sears, *Lincoln's Lieutenants*, 619.

37. Meade, *Life and Letters*, vol. 2, 176, 177, 178; Grant, *Personal Memoirs*, vol. 2, 117.

38. Meade, *Life and Letters*, vol. 2, 178; Grant, *Personal Memoirs*, vol. 2, 116.

39. *OR*, 36, pt. 1, 18; Grant, *Personal Memoirs*, vol. 2, 117.

40. Meade, *Life and Letters*, vol. 2, 178, 181, 182.

41. Meade, *Life and Letters*, 177; Sears, *Lincoln's Lieutenants*, 612–15; Wert, *Sword*, 325–26, 328.

42. Meade, *Life and Letters*, vol. 2, 173–88; Sears, *Lincoln's Lieutenants*, 612–15; Wert, *Sword*, 325–26.

43. Wert, *Sword*, 307–8.

44. Wert, *Sword*, 308, 309; *OR*, 27, pt. 1, 93, 94

45. Wert, *Sword*, 310–22.

46. Wert, *Sword*, 308, 22.

47. Wert, *Sword*, 114, 266–67.

48. Wert, *Sword*, 268; Scott, *Fallen Leaves*, 189; Lowe, *Meade's Army*, 118; Dana, *Recollections*, 189.

49. Wert, *Sword*, 323; A. Spafford–Wife, February 14, 1864, Spafford Papers, NC.

50. Wert, *Sword*, 323, 324.

51. Wert, *Sword*, 329; Sears, *Lincoln's Lieutenants*, 615; Meade, *Life and Letters*, vol. 2, 164, 165.

52. Meade, *Life and Letters*, vol. 2, 165; Wert, *Sword*, 329.

53. Meade, *Life and Letters*, vol. 2, 165; Wert, *Sword*, 329; Sears, *Lincoln's Lieutenants*, 616–17; Rhea, *Battle of the Wilderness*, 41.

54. William Orr–Father, March 28, 1864, Orr Papers, IU: Wert, *Sword*, 329; Humphreys, *Virginia Campaign*, 3.

55. Meade, *Life and Letters*, vol. 2, 183; John L. Barnes–father & mother, March 25, 1864, Barnes Letter, AHEC; Lowe, *Meade's Army*, 117.

56. Lowe, *Meade's Army*, 124–25; Dame, *From the Rapidan*, 64; Samito, *"Fear,"* 180; Wert, *Sword*, 330, 331.

57. Wert, *Sword*, 331.

58. Gallagher, *Wilderness Campaign*, 6, 7; *OR*, 36, pt. 1, 15; *B&L*, vol. 4, 110, 112.

59. Chesson, *Journal*, 145.

60. Mackowski and White, *Season*, 5.

61. Gallagher, *Fighting For*, 345, 346.

62. Gallagher, *Fighting For*, 345, 346: Wert, *General James Longstreet*, 376.

63. Wert, *General James Longstreet*, 376; Gallagher, *Fighting For*, 346.

64. Gallagher, *Fighting For*, 346; A. B. Simms–Sister, May 4, 1864, Simms Family Papers, AHS.

65. Tower, *Lee's Adjutant*, 155; *CV*, vol. 26, 354; Dawson, *Reminiscences*, 129; Wert, *General James Longstreet*, 200.

66. Wert, *General James Longstreet*, chap. 14, quote on 296; *Washington Post*, June 11, 1893.

67. Gallagher, *Wilderness Campaign*, 143; Rhea, *Battle of the Wilderness*, 41; Robertson, *General A. Hill*, 225; Freeman, *Lee's Lieutenants*, vol. 3, xxix; Dozier, *Gunner*, 206.

68. Rhea, *Battle of the Wilderness*, 41; Freeman, *Lee's Lieutenants*, vol. 3, xxix; Robertson, *General A. Hill*, 225.

69. *OR*, 36, pt. 1, 1070; *SOR*, vol. 6, 270; William N. Pendleton–My Darling Love, May 3, 1864, Pendleton Papers, UNC.

70. Ivy W. Duggan–Editor, April 25, 1864, Duggan Papers, UGA; Evans, *16th Mississippi*, 243; Power, *Lee's Miserables*, 2; H. D. Brown–Friend, April 24, 1864, Bolton Family Papers, VHS; Alexander McNeill–My Dear Wife, April 30, 1864, McNeill Letters, FSNMP.

71. Henry Clay Albright–Brother, April 16, 1864, Albright Papers, SANC; John G. LaRoque–Nannie, May 1, 1864, LaRoque Letters, UGA; Samuel S. Brooke–My dear Sister, March 17, 1864, Brooke Papers, VMI: Hugh Dickson–Pa, May 4, 1864, Dickson Civil War Letters, USM; John Garibaldi–Wife, April 22, 1864, Garibaldi Papers, VMI; Stephens, *Intrepid Warrior*, 378.

72. Young, *Lee's Army*, 12, 229, 230; Albert W. Blair–father and mother, April 27, 1864, Blair Letters, SANC; John Berryman Crawford–Wife, March 18, 1864, Crawford Letters, MDAH; Francis M. Howard–Brother, April 19, 1864, Howard Letter, AHEC; Raymer, *Confederate Correspondent*, 124.

73. Bean, *Stonewall's Man*, 199.

Chapter 2

1. Power, *Lee's Miserables*, 18; Schaff, *Battle*, 58, 59.

2. Neese, *Three Years*, 237.

3. Memoirs, George Papers, LC; Gallagher, *Fighting For*, 350; Power, *Lee's Miserables*, 21.

4. McCown, Memoirs, HANDL; *PMHSM*, vol. 4, 23; Wert, *Sword*, 334.

5. Scott, *History of Orange County*, 114; Agassiz, *Meade's Headquarters*, 87; *PMHSM*, vol. 4, 23; Wert, *Sword*, 334.

6. Trudeau, *Bloody Roads*, 35; Rhea, *Battle of the Wilderness*, 78; Wert, *Sword*, 334.

7. Gallagher, *Wilderness Campaign*, 146; Wert, *General James Longstreet*, 379–80.

8. Dame, *From the Rapidan*, 71; Savannah *Morning News*, July 20, 1864.

9. Walter, Diary, 12, FSNMP; Freeman, *Lee's Dispatches*, 170–71; W. H. Taylor–Genl, May 4, 1864, Polk-Brown-Ewell Papers, UNC; W. H. Medill–Sister, March 15, 1863, Hanna–McCormick Family Papers, LC.

10. Walter, Diary, 12, FSNMP; Gallagher, *Wilderness Campaign*, 147; Rhea, *Battle of the Wilderness*, 102, 126, 127; Young, *Lee's Army*, 232; Wert, *Sword*, 335; *SHSP*, vol. 14, 523; Cozzens, *B&L*, vol. 5, 483.

11. Wert, *Sword*, 335; Cozzens, *B&L*, vol. 5, 483; Brown, *Colonel*, 239; Winik, *April 1865*, 91.

12. Rhea, *Battle of the Wilderness*, 145–70; Powell, *Fifth Army Corps*, 610; Wert, *Sword*, 336, 337.

13. Small, *Road*, 194.

14. Azariah Bostwick–Sister, June 5, 1864, Bostwick Letters, FSNMP; Wert, *Brotherhood*, 291, 292; Rhea, *Battle of the Wilderness*, 132, 172–79.

15. Rhea, *Battle of the Wilderness*, 179–84, 252; *OR*, 36, pt. 1, 1070–71; *PMHSM*, vol. 4, 29; Williams, *Stonewall's Prussian Mapmaker*, 122; Freeman, *Lee's Lieutenants*, vol. 3, xxix.

16. Rhea, *Battle of the Wilderness*, 126, 127, 132–34; Wert, *Cavalryman*, 339; Walter, Diary, 12, FSNMP.

17. Rhea, *Battle of the Wilderness*, 192; Wert, *Sword*, 337, 338; Louis Gourdin Young–Uncle, May 7, 1864, Gourdin Papers, EU; James W. Wright–Father, Mother, and Fanny, May 9, 1864, Wright Collection, SANC.

18. Wert, *Sword*, 338; Rhea, *Battle of the Wilderness*, 195–99, 200–204, 222–29; Long, *Memoirs*, 333; Hess, *Lee's Tar Heels*, 211, 212; Walker, *History*, 415.

19. Rhea, *Battle of the Wilderness*, 241, 242; *SHSP*, vol. 14, 523.

20. Rhea, *Battle of the Wilderness*, 241, 242; Gallagher and Janney, *Cold Harbor*, 5; Sorrel, Diary, VHS; Charles Venable–James Longstreet, July 25, 1879, Longstreet Papers, DU; C. C. Taliaferro–John W. Daniel, January 1, 1907, Daniel Papers, UVA.

21. *SOR*, vol. 6, 718, 719, 777; Morrison, *Memoirs*, 184, 185; Walter, Diary, 12, 13, FSNMP; Robertson, *General A. P. Hill*, 261.

22. Grant, *Personal Memoirs*, vol. 2, 193, 196; Trudeau, *Bloody Roads*, 78, 79; Rhea, *Battle of the Wilderness*, 264–67.

23. Wert, *Sword*, 338; Diary, Halsey Papers, AHEC; Samuel Moore–My Dearest Ellen, March 6, 1864, Moore Papers, UNC; Kepner, Diary, FSNMP; Baquet, *History*, 116.

24. Robson, *How*, 134; Wilkeson, *Recollections*, 67.

25. Wert, *General James Longstreet*, 381, 383; Charles Venable–James Longstreet, July 25, 1879, Longstreet Papers, DU; Rhea, *Battle of the Wilderness*, 283–85.

26. Wert, *General James Longstreet*, 383; Charles Venable–James Longstreet, July 25, 1879, Longstreet Papers, DU; Gallagher, *Wilderness Campaign*, 153.

27. Charles Venable–James Longstreet, July 25, 1879, Longstreet Papers, DU; Wert, *General James Longstreet*, 383, 384; John Fairfax–Joseph Bryan, August 1, 1902, Fairfax Papers, VHS.

28. Moxley Sorrel–James Longstreet, July 21, 1879, Longstreet Papers, DU.

29. Ural, "Little Body," 69, 70; Gallagher, *Wilderness Campaign*, 177; Stocker, *From Huntsville*, 160; Royall, *Some Reminiscences*, 32; Dula, "Civil War Incidents," 3, DU; Jedediah Hotchkiss–My Dear Sara, May 7, 1864, Hotchkiss Papers, LC; Tate, *Col. Frank Huger*, 95; *SOR*, vol. 6, 717.

30. Gallagher, *Fighting For*, 346; Wert, *Sword*, 340; Charles Venable–James Longstreet, July 25, 1879, Longstreet Papers, DU.

31. Wyckoff, *History*, 245; Cutrer, *Longstreet's Aide*, 124; Wert, *Sword*, 341.

32. Wert, *General James Longstreet*, 386, 387; Taylor, "War Reminiscences," VHS; Styple, *Writing*, 212; *OR*, vol. 51, pt. 2, 893.

33. Wert, *Sword*, 341; Rhea, *Battle of the Wilderness*, 321–23; Richard Ewell's preliminary report on the Battle of the Wilderness, n.d., Polk-Brown-Ewell Papers, UNC.

34. Wert, *Sword*, 342; Rhea, *Battle of the Wilderness*, 406, 416–25; Samuel Bradbury–Family, May 19, 1864, Bradbury Collection, DU.

35. Rhea, *Battle of the Wilderness*, 389–92; Wert, *Sword*, 342.

36. Menge and Shimrak, *Civil War Notebook*, 13; Walker, *History*, 432–33; Wert, *Sword*, 342; Rhea, *Battle of the Wilderness*, 390–98.

37. Brown, *Colonel*, 239; Gwynne, *Hymns*, 55.

38. Soule, Diary, AHEC; Rhea, *Battle of the Wilderness*, 435, 436.

39. Young, *Lee's Army*, 235; Krick, *Lee's Colonels*, passim; Williams, *Stonewall's Prussian Mapmaker*, 122; Davis, *Confederate General*, vol. 3, 162, 167; vol. 5, 21.

40. Wert, *Sword*, 343; Rhea, *Battle of the Wilderness*, 431–33, 443–44; Rosenblatt and Rosenblatt, *Hard Marching*, 215.

41. Gallagher, *Fighting For*, 354; Gallagher, *Wilderness Campaign*, 153; Robertson, *General A. Hill*, 260, 261; Gallagher, *Lee: The Soldier*, 11, 29; Rhea, *Battle of the Wilderness*, 442–45

42. Wert, *Glorious Army*, 278; Gallagher, *Lee: The Soldier*, 29, 174.

43. Gallagher, *Wilderness Campaign*, 14; Grimsley, *And Keep Moving On*, 27; Rhea, *Battle of the Wilderness*, 431.

44. Rhea, *Battle of the Wilderness*, 432–33; Wert, *Sword*, 343; Gwynne, *Hymns*, 59.

45. Glatthaar, *General Lee's Army*, 371; Corbin, Diary, 34, AHEC.

Chapter 3

1. Mackowski and White, *Season*, 149; *Yorkville Enquirer*, October 8, 1881; Bloomsburg, *Star of the North*, May 18, 1864; *Staunton News Leader*, September 21, 1931; *Beckley Post-Herald*, July 16, 1974.

2. Bloomsburg, *Star of the North*, May 18, 1864; a Richmond, Virginia, newspaper article printed in *Dublin Irish People*, July 30, 1864; Rhea, *Battles*, 46; Diary, Wyman Papers, AHEC.

3. Porter, *Campaigning with Grant*, 76; *OR*, 36, pt. 2, 481; Tower, *Lee's Adjutant*, 162.

4. *OR*, 36, pt. 2, 481.

5. Rhea, *Battles*, 19–23, 24; Richard H. Anderson–Edmund B. Robins, May 14, 1879, Anderson Papers, BU; Smith, *History Corn Exchange*, 405.

6. Gallagher, *Wilderness Campaign*, 126, 127, 129; Rhea, *Battles*, 27, 32–36; *Richmond Sentinel*, May 21, 1864; Garnett, *Riding with Stuart*, 53, 54, 57.

7. *PMHSM*, vol. 4, 171; Lowe, *Meade's Army*, 143.

8. Grant, *Personal Memoirs*, vol. 2, 211; Rhea, *Battles*, 15, 37–38, 42–43.

9. Rhea, *Battles*, 37, 38; Wert, *Sword*, 345; Wilkeson, *Recollections*, 77.

10. Rhea, *Battles*, 38; Wert, *Sword*, 345; Harris, Reminiscences, AHEC.

11. Wert, *Sword*, 345; Nevins, *Diary*, 355; Wilkeson, *Recollections*, 77; Small, *Road*, 134; Rhea, *Battles*, 39; Porter, *Campaigning with Grant*, 78, 79.

12. Wert, *Sword*, 345; Rhea, *Battles*, 39; Thompson, "My Journal," LC.

13. Rhea, *Battles*, 39–41; *Richmond Sentinel*, May 21, 1864; Lee, "Report," VHS; Graham, "Report," FSNMP; *Chicago Tribune*, May 19, 1864.

14. Rhea, *Battles*, 40–41; *OR*, 36, pt. 2, 551, 552.

15. Rhea, *Battles*, 45–47; Lee, "Report," VHS; *Richmond Sentinel*, May 21, 1864; J. W. Watts–General, September 1, 1897, Munford-Ellis Family Papers, DU.

16. Carmichael, *Audacity*, 66; Tower, *Lee's Adjutant*, 162; Rhea, *Battles*, 17, 19, 22.

17. Carmichael, *Audacity*, 66; Rhea, *Battles*, 22, 23, 46; *New York Daily News*, May 10, 1936.

18. Rhea, *Battles*, 43, 46; Freeman, *Lee's Lieutenants*, vol. 3, 374; Sorrel, *Recollections*, 238.

19. Sorrel, *Recollections*, 238.

20. Sorrel, *Recollections*, 238, 239.

21. Carmichael, *Audacity*, 66; Freeman, *Lee's Lieutenants*, vol. 3, 375; Davis, *Confederate General*, vol. 1, 28–29; Gallagher, *Fighting For*, 365.

22. Richard H. Anderson–Edward B. Robins, May 14, 1879, Anderson Papers, BU; *OR*, 36, pt. 2, 1056; Carmichael, *Audacity*, 66, 67; Rhea, *Battles*, 46, 50.

23. Richard H. Anderson–Edward B. Robins, May 14, 1879, Anderson Papers, BU; *OR*, 36, pt. 1, 1056; "A History of the Sunflower Guards," 24, Claiborne Papers, UNC.

24. Garnett, *Riding with Stuart*, 57, 58; *OR*, 36, pt. 1, 1056; Richard H. Anderson–Edward B. Robins, May 14, 1879, Anderson Papers, BU; "History of the Sunflower Guards," 24, Claiborne Papers, UNC; Rhea, *Battles*, 51–52.

25. *OR*, 36, vol. 1, 1056; "History of the Sunflower Guards," Claiborne Papers, UNC; *SHSP*, vol. 7, 129; *CV*, vol. 38, 59; Rhea, *Battles*, 52, 53.

26. Wycoff, *History*, 253; St. Georges Parish, Spotsylvania County, Va., 1860 Census, 106, 107; Slave Schedules, St. Georges Parish, 1860 Census, 71; Nonpopulation Schedules, 1850–1880, Schedule 4, St. Georges Parish, 31; John Cummings–author, May 18, 2021, Wert, Personal Collection, electronic message.

27. Wyckoff, *History*, 253; "History of the Sunflower Guards," 24, Claiborne Papers, UNC; *OR*, 36, pt. 1, 1056; Rhea, *Battles*, 53–54; Wert, *Cavalryman*, 344.

28. "History of the Sunflower Guards," 24, Clairborne Papers, UNC; Wyckoff, *History*, 253; Wert, *Cavalryman*, 344, 345; Rhea, *Battles*, 52–57.

29. Wyckoff, *History*, 253; Richard W. Anderson–Edward B. Robins, May 14, 1879, Anderson Papers, BU; Rhea, *Battles*, 60–65.

30. *SHSP*, vol. 7, 129; Wert, *Cavalryman*, 344, 345; Rhea, *Battles*, 65, 66.

31. Carmichael, *Audacity*, 67; Rhea, *Battles*, 77; *OR*, vol. 51, pt. 2, 902.

32. Robertson, *General A. Hill*, 268; *SHSP*, vol. 14, 532; Bernard, *Civil War Talks*, 217; *OR*, 36, pt. 2, 974, and 51, pt. 2, 902, 903; Jones, *Lee's Tigers*, 201; Freeman, *Lee's Lieutenants*, vol. 3, 390, 391.

33. *OR*, 36, pt. 1, 1071; Rhea, *Battles*, 77, 85.

34. "Harrison Gazeteer, vol. 1," Hotchkiss Papers, LC; Jones, *Campbell Brown's Civil War*, 255; *Yorkville Enquirer*, October 6, 1881; *Dayton Herald*, June 8, 1906; St. Georges Parish, Spotsylvania County, Va., 1860 Census, 106; Slave Schedules, St. Georges Parish, 1860 Census, 71.

35. "Harrison Gazeteer, vol. 1," Hotchkiss Papers, LC; *Carlisle Valley Sentinel*, September 2, 1881; *Yorkville Enquirer*, October 6, 1881; Mackowski and White, "Battle," 63, 64; *Boston Globe*, July 2, 1899; *Fredericksburg Free Lance*, July 9, 1904; Cross, "Historic People," FSNMP.

36. Mackowski and White, "Battle," 63; "Harrison Gazeteer, vol. 1," Hotchkiss Papers, LC; St. Georges Parish, Spotsylvania County, Va., 1860 Census, 106.

37. *PMHSM*, vol. 4, 106, 234; Gallagher, *Spotsylvania Campaign*, 81; *SOR*, vol. 6, 677; *SHSP*, vol. 14, 150; *Montgomery Daily Advertiser*, May 28, 1864.

38. *PMHSM*, vol. 4, 106; Rankin, *23rd Virginia Infantry*, 79; *SHSP*, vol. 33, 20, 21; Hess, *Trench Warfare*, 49; Gallagher, *Spotsylvania Campaign*, 81, 82; Toney, *Privations*, 79–81.

39. Mackowski and White, "Battle," 10–11; Gallagher, *Spotsylvania Campaign*, 81; *SOR*, vol. 6, 677; Hess, *Trench Warfare*, 47; *PMHSM*, vol. 4, 234.

40. *Richmond Dispatch*, August 27, 1905; Rhea, *Battles*, 90–91; Cozzens, *B&L*, vol. 5, 488.

41. Stephens, *Intrepid Warrior*, 389; Walker, *History*, 465; *Edgefield Advertiser*, June 1, 1864; *Southern Watchman*, June 1, 1864; Brown, *Colonel*, 94; *Pickens Keowee Courier*, August 31, 1910; Mackowski and White, "Battle," 12–13; Gallagher, *Spotsylvania Campaign*, 82.

42. Gallagher and Janney, *Cold Harbor*, 113; *OR*, 6, 842; Jedediah Hotchkiss–My Own Dear One, April 21, 1864, Hotchkiss Papers, LC; Davis, *Confederate General*, vol. 5, 179.

43. *Southern Watchman*, June 1, 1864; *Edgefield Advertiser*, June 1, 1864; *Richmond Daily Dispatch*, May 13, 1864; Howard, *Recollections*, 293; Mackowski and White, "Battle," 12.

44. *Edgefield Advertiser*, June 1, 1864; *PMHSM*, vol. 4, 59; *Richmond Times-Dispatch*, March 19, 1905; Koonce, *Doctor*, 128.

45. *PMHSM*, vol. 4, 59; *SHSP*, vol. 14, 529; Thomas T. Munford–My dear Sir, May 9, 1864, Munford Letter, LVA.

46. *PMHSM*, vol. 4, 59, 60; Pfanz, *Richard S. Ewell*, 378; *SHSP*, vol. 14, 529.

47. *SHSP*, vol. 14, 150; Gallagher, *Fighting For*, 381; Rankin, *23rd Virginia Infantry*, 79; Gallagher and Janney, *Cold Harbor*, 110.

48. *CV*, vol. 28, 384, and vol. 34, 8; *SHSP*, vol. 21, 233; Fry, *2nd Virginia Infantry*, 62.

49. Gallagher, *Spotsylvania Campaign*, 83; *SHSP*, vol. 21, 233; *Columbia Democrat*, July 2, 1864; *Boston Globe*, May 12, 1914; Pfanz, *Richard S. Ewell*, 378.

50. Worsham, *Foot Cavalry*, 132; Brown, *Colonel*, 135; *Glimpses*, vol. 4, 372; *Pickens Keowee Courier*, August 31, 1910; *Laurens Advertiser*, August 6, 1895; Watkins, Memoir, FSNMP; *Philadelphia Weekly Times*, February 20, 1886; Hess, *Trench Warfare*, 62; Waitt, *History*, 311; *New York Daily News*, May 10, 1936.

51. *Galveston News*, July 15, 1893; Brown, *Colonel*, 94, 248; Rhea, *Carrying the Flag*, 199; Rhea, *Battles*, 234.

52. Rhea, *Battles*, 90; Gallagher, *Spotsylvania Campaign*, 82; Ward, *96th Pennsylvania*, 251; *Philadelphia Weekly Times*, February 20, 1886; "Harrison Gazeteer, vol. 1," Hotchkiss Papers, LC; Mackowski and White, *Season*, 147; Slave Schedules, St. Georges Parish, 1860 Census, 63.

53. Mackowski and White, *Season*, 147; "Harrison Gazeteer, vol. 1," Hotchkiss Papers, LC; *Wilmington Journal*, June 2, 1864; *OR*, 36, pt. 1, 1072.

54. *SHSP*, vol. 21, 239; Gallagher, *Spotsylvania Campaign*, 115, n. 2; *PMHSM*, vol. 4, 107, *OR*, 36, pt. 1, 1024; Davis, Memoir, 90, FSNMP.

55. Doyle, *Memoir*, LC; Worsham, *Foot Cavalry*, 133; Hess, *Trench Warfare*, 47; Phillips, Civil War Diary, VMI.

56. *PMHSM*, vol. 4, 234; Rhea, *Battles*, 90, 112; Gallagher, *Spotsylvania Campaign*, 82; Hess, *Trench Warfare*, 47.

57. *OR*, 36, pt. 2, 529.

58. Rhea, *Battles*, 91, 100–103.

59. McCown, Memoirs, May 9, 1894, HANDL.

60. Rhea, *Battles*, 92, 93; *OR*, 36, pt. 1, 684.

61. Stevens, *Three Years*, 328; Whittier, "Reminiscences," 11, BPL; Rhea, *Battles*, 93; Edward Russell–My dear sisters, May 15, 1894, Russell Letters, FSNMP; *PMHSM*, vol. 4, 178; Best, "Through the Wilderness," UM.

62. Ward, *96th Pennsylvania*, 221; Chadwick, *Brother*, 225; *OR*, 36, pt. 1, 228; Whittier, "Reminiscences," 11, BPL; Holmes, *Touched With Fire*, 109; Rhea, *Battles*, 94.

63. *New Orleans Republican*, November 14, 1868; Holmes, *Touched With Fire*, 109, 110; Edward Russell–My dear sisters, May 15, 1894, Russell Letters, FSNMP; Whittier, "Reminiscences," 11, BPL; James S. Anderson–Parents, May 19, 1864, Anderson Papers, SHSW.

64. Mackowski and White, *Season*, 41; Rhea, *Battles*, 95; Porter, *Campaigning with Grant*, 90; Graham, "Report," FSNMP; Ward, *96th Pennsylvania*, 221; Thomas and Sauers, *Civil War Letters*, 180.

65. Rhea, *Battles*, 104–14, 124.

66. Rhea, *Battles*, 97–99; Wert, *Sword*, 354.

67. Wert, *Sword*, 355; Rhea, *Battles*, 114.

68. Mackowski and White, *Season*, 99, 115, 149; *Yorkville Enquirer*, October 6, 1881; *Boston Globe*, July 2, 1899; *Dayton Herald*, June 8, 1906; *Staunton News Leader*, September 21, 1931; *PMHSM*, vol. 4, 63, 236.

Chapter 4

1. *OR*, 36, pt. 1, 3.

2. Diary, May 11, 1864, Crockett Papers, UT.

3. Eugene Blackford–My Dear Sister, May 14, 1864, Blackford Letters, AHEC; Tower, *Lee's Adjutant*, 162.

4. *OR*, 36, pt. 2, 600; Rhea, *Battles*, 130–31.

5. *OR*, 36, pt. 2, 596; Rhea, *Battles*, 131, 133.

6. *OR*, 36, pt. 1, 356–57; Muffly, *Story*, 120; Burr, *Life*, 99; Rhea, *Battles*, 132–34, 135.

7. *OR*, 36, pt. 1, 356–57; Walker, *History*, 451–55; Rhea, *Battles*, 135–40; Walker, *General Hancock*, 187, 188.

8. Muffly, *Story*, 120; Burr, *Life*, 99, 100, 102; Chesson, *Journal*, 150.

9. *OR*, 36, pt. 2, 600; Rhea, *Battles*, 142–43.

10. Hess, *Union Soldier*, 6.

11. Hess, *Trench Warfare*, 52; Rhea, *Battles*, 144–149.

12. Rhea, *Battles*, 146; Page, *History*, 244.

13. Rhea, *Battles*, 145, 149; Walker, *General Hancock*, 191.

14. Rhea, *Battles*, 149, 177; *PMHSM*, vol. 4, 223; Chamberlin, *History*, 233, 234; Carmichael, *War*, 65.

15. Rhea, *Battles*, 177–81; *PMHSM*, vol. 4, 223; Walker, *General Hancock*, 191.

16. Ward, *96th Pennsylvania*, 199; Best, *History*, 29, 31.

17. Ward, *96th Pennsylvania*, 199; Best, *History*, 29, 31; Michie, *Life*, xi–xii, xv–xvi, xxvi–xxviii.

18. Ward, *96th Pennsylvania*, 222, 223; Rhea, *Battles*, 163; Mackowski and White, *Season*, 46.

19. Ward, *96th Pennsylvania*, 223; Hess, *Trench Warfare*, 55; *OR*, 36, pt. 1, 667.

20. Agassiz, *Meade's Headquarters*, 139; Page, *Letters*, 66.

21. Ward, *96th Pennsylvania*, 223; Rhea, *Battles*, 163; *OR*, 36, pt. 1, 661.

22. *OR*, 36, pt. 2, 608; Rhea, *Battles*, 165; Emory Upton–My dear Colonel, April 18, 1879, Upton Papers, BU.

23. Emory Upton–My dear Colonel, April 18,1879, Upton Papers, BU.

24. Ward, *96th Pennsylvania*, 223; Best, *History*, 135–36; Rhea, *Battles*, 163.

25. The standard number of troops under Upton is 5,000, but recent research by David Ward places that figure at or below 4,500. See Ward, *96th Pennsylvania*, 233; Hess, *Trench Warfare*, 55; Rhea, *Battles*, 164.

26. *OR*, 36, pt. 1, 661, 667; Rhea, *Battles*, 164; Ward, *96th Pennsylvania*, 225, 240; Keiser, Diary, FSNMP; Irby G. Scott–Loved ones at Home, June 8, 1864, Scott Papers, DU.

27. *Portland Transcript*, June 11, 1864; Best, *History*, 125; Emory Upton–My dear Colonel, April 26, 1879, Upton Papers, BU; *OR*, 36, pt. 1, 661; Cross, "Historic People," FSNMP; Rhea, *Battles*, 166.

28. Emory Upton–My dear Colonel, April 26, 1879, Upton Papers, BU; Ward, *96th Pennsylvania*, 231, 235; Hess, *Trench Warfare*, 56; Keiser, Diary, FSNMP; Best, *History*, 129.

29. Rhea, *Battles*, 169; Irby G. Scott–Loved ones at Home, June 8, 1864, Scott Papers, DU; Keiser, Diary, FSNMP; *OR*, 36, pt. 1, 668.

30. *OR*, 36, pt. 1, 668; Rhea, *Battles*, 169; Ward, *96th Pennsylvania*, 237, 239, 240; Keiser, Diary, FSNMP; Irby G. Scott–Loved ones at Home, June 8, 1864, DU; Asbury Jackson–Mother, May 11, 1864, Harden Papers, DU.

31. *OR*, 36, pt. 1, 1072; Irby G. Scott–Loved ones at Home, June 8, 1864, Scott Papers, DU; Barton, Recollections, 51, HANDL; Doyle, Memoir, LC; Gales, Diary, FSNMP.

32. *OR*, 36, pt. 1, 1072; Ward, *96th Pennsylvania*, 240; Rhea, *Battles*, 170–73; Gales, Diary, FSNMP; Doyle, Memoir, LC; *Greensboro Record*, July 30, 1903.

33. "Bobbie"–Aunt, May 11, 1864, "Bobbie" Letter, AHEC; Charles M. Miller, My dear Sir, February 23, 1905, Daniel Papers, UVA; Robert D. Johnston–John W. Daniel, August 6, 1895, Daniel Papers, DU.

34. Robert D. Johnston–John W. Daniel, August 6, 1895; Jedediah Hotchkiss–My Dear Wife, May 11, 1864, Hotchkiss Papers, LC; Charles M. Miller–My Dear Sir, February 23, 1905, Daniel Papers, UVA; "Bobbie"–Aunt, May 11, 1864, "Bobbie" Letter, AHEC.

35. Robert D. Johnston–John W. Daniel, August 6, 1895, Daniel Papers, DU; Barton, Recollections, 52, HANDL; *PMHSM*, 4. 4, 107.

36. Ward, *96th Pennsylvania*, 240; Rhea, *Battles*, 171–74; G. C. Brown, My Dear Mother, May 11, 1865, Polk-Brown-Ewell Papers, UNC; Emory Upton–My dear Colonel, April 26, 1879, Upton Papers, BU.

37. *Greensboro Record*, July 30, 1903; Green, Diary, UNC; *OR*, 36, pt. 1, 668.

38. *OR*, 36, pt. 1, 490; Walker, *History*, 467; Holmes, *Touched with Fire*, 111; Gallagher, *Fighting For*, 376; Ward, *96th Pennsylvania*, 234.

39. *OR*, 36, pt. 1, 668; Keiser, Diary, FSNMP; Rhea, *Battles*, 174.

40. *OR*, 36, pt. 1, 668–69; Morse, *Personal Experiences*, 87; Ward, *96th Pennsylvania*, 245, 246.

41. Rhea, *Battles*, 175; Emory Upton–My dear Colonel, April 18, 1879, Upton Papers, BU; Lowe, *Meade's Army*, 150; Holmes, *Touched with Fire*, 113; Mackowski and White, "Battle," 8.

42. Walker, *History*, 191; *PMHSM*, vol. 4, 223; Rhea, *Battles*, 181, 184, 185.

43. Rhea, *Battles*, 187; *Or*, 36, pt. 2, 983; *Confederate Union*, May 31, 1864; Asbury Jackson–Mother, May 11, 1864, Harden Papers, DU.

44. "Bobbie"–Aunt, May 11, 1864, "Bobbie" Letter, AHEC.

45. Rhea, *Battles*, 187; Robert D. Johnston, Gen. Lee's Story, Daniel Papers, DU; Ashbury Jackson–Mother, May 11, 1864, Harden Papers, DU; Davis, *Confederate General*, vol. 2, 73.

46. *OR*, 36, pt. 2, 983; R. E. Lee–Lt. Gen Ewell, May 10, 1864, Lee–Jackson Collection, WLU.

47. Ward, *96th Pennsylvania*, 244; Rhea, *Battles*, 188; Asbury Jackson–Mother, May 11, 1864, Harden Papers, DU.

48. Walker, *General Hancock*, 194; McAllister, *Civil War Letters*, 417.

49. *OR*, 36, pt. 1, 4; Lowe, *Meade's Army*, 156.

50. Porter, *Campaigning with Grant*, 97–98.

51. *OR*, 36, pt. 1, 4.

52. *OR*, 36, pt. 1, 4.

53. Rhea, *Battles*, 213; Unidentified Artilleryman–Home Circle, May 16, 1864, Ames Papers, FSNMP; *Wisconsin State Journal*, May 19, 1864.

54. Rhea, *Battles*, 215–16; Porter, *Campaigning with Grant*, 99; Mackowski and White, *Season*, 148.

55. Rhea, *Battles*, 215–16; Porter, *Campaigning with Grant*, 99; Doyle, Memoir, LC.

56. Porter, *Campaigning with Grant*, 99; Grant, *Personal Memoirs*, vol. 2, 228; Walker, *General Hancock*, 196; *PMHSM*, vol. 4, 245–46.

57. *OR*, 36, pt. 2, 629.

58. *OR*, 36, pt. 1, 191, 192; pt. 2, 629, 635, 637, 638, 641, 642; Gallagher, *Spotsylvania Campaign*, 48.

59. *OR*, 36, pt. 2, 629, 635, 643; Rhea, *Battles*, 86, 108, 317.

60. Porter, *Campaigning with Grant*, 100; *OR*, 36, pt. 1, 358; Walker, *General Hancock*, 195, 196.

61. Rhea, *Battles*, 217; *OR*, 36, pt. 1, 358; Porter, *Campaigning with Grant*, 100; Walker, *General Hancock*, 196.

62. Asbury Jackson–Mother, May 11, 1864, Harden Papers, DU.

63. Howard, *Recollections*, 290; *PMHSM*, vol. 4, 109; Gallagher and Janney, *Cold Harbor*, 113.

64. *SHSP*, vol. 21, 233; Doyle, Memoir, LC; *Glimpses*, vol. 4, 305; *Muncie Star Press*, September 3, 1911; Howard, *Recollections*, 290; Hess, *Trench Warfare*, 59; *SOR*, 6, 678.

65. Davis, *Three Years*, 339; *Muncie Star Press*, September 3, 1911; Green, Diary, UNC; Doyle, Memoir, LC; Colt, *Defend the Valley*, 312; John G. Webb–Father, May 11, 1864, Webb Letters, AHEC.

66. Jones, *Campbell Brown's Civil War*, 253; Carmichael, *Audacity*, 69; Buckner M. Randolph Diary, Randolph Family Papers, VHS; Pfanz, *Richard S. Ewell*, 382; *PMHSM*, vol. 4, 63; *OR*, 51, pt. 2, 916–17.

67. Pfanz, *Richard S. Ewell*, 382; Carmichael, *Audacity*, 69; Rhea, *Battles*, 220; Robert D. Johnston, Gen. Lee's Story, Daniel Papers, DU.

68. Rhea, *Battles*, 216; William N. Pendleton–My Dear Daughter, May 13, 1864, Pendleton Papers, UNC; Gallagher, *Spotsylvania Campaign*, 115, 117; Jones, *Campbell Brown's Civil War*, 253.

69. *OR*, 36, pt. 1, 1086; Long, *Memoirs*, 339; Jones, *Campbell Brown's Civil War*, 255; *PMHSM*, vol. 4, 63; Gallagher, *Spotsylvania Campaign*, 15; Purifoy, Memoir, 230, ADAH; *SHSP*, vol. 21, 240.

70. *OR*, 36, pt. 1, 1024, 1037, 1044; *SHSP*, vol. 21, 240; Roche, "Bloody Angle."

71. *OR*, 36, pt. 1, 1024, 1037; *SHSP*, vol. 21, 240; Cannan, *Bloody Angle*, 49; Letter fragment from Frank [?], n.d., and William Maupin–My dear Major, May 5, 1905, Daniel Papers, UVA.

72. William Maupin–My dear Major, May 5, 1905, Daniel Papers, UVA.

73. *OR*, 36, pt. 1, 1024n; Dozier, *Gunner*, 244; Gallagher and Janney, *Cold Harbor*, 114.

74. Robert A. Hardaway–N. B. Johnston, June 25, 1894, Hardaway Letter, RNBP.

75. Robert A. Hardaway–N. B. Johnston, June 25, 1894, Hardaway Letter, RNBP; Pfanz, *Richard S. Ewell*, 382, 383.

76. Cozzens, *B&L*, vol. 5, 490; William N. Pendleton–My Dear Daughter, May 13, 1864, Pendleton Papers, UNC; Carmichael, *Audacity*, 70.

77. McCown, Memoirs, HANDL; Morrison, *Memoirs*, 186.

78. Morrison, *Memoirs*, 187.

Chapter 5

1. Wert, *Sword*, 78, 167, 200; Bandy and Freeland, *Gettysburg Papers*, vol. 2, 353.

2. Wert, *Sword*, 200, 245, 292; Favill, *Diary*, 234–35; Bingham, "Memoirs."

3. Wert, *Sword*, 50, 77, 245, 292; Dana, *Recollections*, 190; Joseph H. Law–Mary, May 7, 1863, Law Family Papers, AHEC; Smith, *History Nineteenth Regiment*, 77.

4. Chesson, *Journal*, 169, 182; John W. Geary–Henry J. Hunt, July 17, 1879, Hunt Papers, LC.

5. Wert, *Sword*, 77, 200; Chesson, *Journal*, 145.

6. Wert, *Sword*, 300, 324, 357, 392; Lowe, *Meade's Army*, 118.

7. *PMHSM*, vol. 4, 245; Gallagher, *Spotsylvania Campaign*, 48.

8. Theodore Lyman–Mimi, May 20, 1864, Lyman Papers, MHS.

9. Warner, *Generals in Blue*, 34; Davis, *Life*, 25, 26, 40, 41.

10. Warner, *Generals in Blue*, 34; Wert, *Sword*, 325–26, 329.

11. Agassiz, *Meade's Headquarters*, 266; Silliker, *Rebel Yell*, 39.

12. Lowe, *Meade's Army*, 118; Agassiz, *Meade's Headquarters*, 266.

13. Warner, *Generals in Blue*, 18–19; Welch, *Boy General*, 19, 21, 24; Samito, *"Fear,"* xvii, xix.

14. Warner, *Generals in Blue*, 19; Wert, *Sword*, 88; Samuel S. Parmelee–[?], April 9, 1864, Parmelee and Parmelee Papers, FSNMP.

15. Warner, *Generals in Blue*, 19; Samito, *"Fear,"* 163, 164.

16. Samito, *"Fear,"* 163, 164.

17. Samito, *"Fear,"* 163, 164; Frederick, *Story*, 235; Chesson, *Journal*, 78, 146; Samuel S. Parmelee–[?], April 9, 1864, Parmelee and Parmelee Papers, FSNMP.

18. Lowe, *Meade's Army*, 9, 111, 147; Scott, *Fallen Leaves*, 243, 244; Samuel S. Parmelee–[?], April 9, 1864, Parmelee and Parmelee Papers, FSNMP.

19. Warner, *Generals in Blue*, 171, Wert, *Brotherhood*, 98.

20. Wert, *Brotherhood*, 98–101; Gaff, *On Many a Bloody Field*, 95.

21. Wert, *Brotherhood*, chaps. 8–9.

22. Warner, *Generals in Blue*, 171; Lowe, *Meade's Army*, 119; Wert, *Brotherhood*, 299.

23. Scott, *Fallen Leaves*, 189, 244n; Wert, *Sword*, 196; Lowe, *Meade's Army*, 118; Chesson, *Journal*, 72.

24. *OR*, 36, pt. 1, 635; *PMHSM*, vol. 4, 245, 246, 257, 275, 276.

25. *PMHSM*, vol. 4, 257, 276; *OR*, 36, pt. 1, 635.

26. *PMHSM*, vol. 4, 246, 257, 276; *OR*, 36, pt. 1, 635.

27. *PMHSM*, vol. 4, 276.

28. Green, "From the Wilderness," 97; *Philadelphia Weekly Times*, February 20, 1886; Miller, *Harvard's Civil War*, 356.

29. *OR*, 36, pt. 1, 334; Walker, *History*, 468; *PMHSM*, vol. 4, 246, 247.

30. Mulholland, *Story*, 206; Bloodgood, *Personal Reminiscences*, 249; Stewart, *History*, 192; Burr, *Life*, 106; Muffly, *Story*, 257, 855, 856; *PHMSM*, vol. 4, 247.

31. Longacre, *To Gettysburg*, 200, 201; Muffly, *Story*, 257; *Philadelphia Weekly Press*, October 27, 1886.

32. *Philadelphia Weekly Press*, October 27, 1886; Menge and Shimrak, *Civil War Notebook*, 15; Muffly, *Story*, 257.

33. Simons, *Regimental History*, 205, 206; *Montpelier Examiner*, June 27, 1896; Walker, *History*, 468.

34. *PMHSM*, vol. 4, 247, 257; *OR*, 36, pt. 1, 321, 440; Lash, *"Duty Well Done,"* 392; Galwey, *Valiant Hours*, 208, 209; Bruce, *Twentieth Regiment*, 370; Muffly, *Story*, 258; Burr, *Life*, 107.

35. St. Georges Parish, Spotsylvania County, Va., 1860 Census, 79, 80; Slave Schedules, St. Georges Parish, 1860 Census, 59, 60; Mackowski and White, *Season*, 148.

36. Howe, *Touched with Fire*, 113; Samito, *"Fear,"* 191; Mackowski and White, *Season*, 148; *Anderson Intelligencer*, August 23, 1905; Lash, *"Duty Well Done,"* 391.

37. *PHSHM*, vol. 4, 249.

38. *OR*, 36, pt. 1, 335; Rhea, *Carrying the Flag*, 188.

39. Samito, *"Fear,"* 191, 192; *OR*, 36, pt. 1, 335; Rhea, *Battles*, 224; Walker, *History*, 459.

40. Samito, *"Fear,",* 192.

41. *PMHSM*, vol. 5, 247.

42. *PMHSM*, vol. 5, 249; *OR*, 36, pt. 1, 107, 137n, 409; *Boston Globe*, May 12, 1914; *Philadelphia Weekly Times*, February 20, 1886; Favill, *Diary*, 296, 297.

43. Walker, *General Hancock*, 196, 197; Nosworthy, *Bloody Crucible*, 402; *Philadelphia Weekly Press*, October 27, 1886; *OR*, 36, pt. 1, 335, 409.

44. *OR*, 36, pt. 1, 108, 335; Nosworthy, *Bloody Crucible*, 402; Mackowski and White, "Battle," 13; *PMHSM*, vol. 4, 250; *Boston Globe*, May 12, 1914.

45. *OR*, 36, pt. 1, 107–8, 335; Nosworthy, *Bloody Crucible*, 402; Mackowski and White, "Battle," 12, 13; Bruce, *Twentieth Regiment*, 371.

46. *OR*, 36, pt. 1, 107–8; pt. 2, 656; Bruce, *Twentieth Regiment*, 371; Nosworthy, *Bloody Crucible*, 402.

47. Bruce, *Twentieth Regiment*, 374.

48. *Philadelphia Weekly Times*, February 20, 1886; Lash, *"Duty Well Done,"* 392.

49. *Philadelphia Weekly Press*, October 27, 1886; Livermore, *Days and Events*, 190.

50. *OR*, 36, pt. 1, 1079.

51. *OR*, 36, pt. 1, 1080; *PMHSM*, vol. 4, 113; Visit to Bloody Angle, c. 1900, Daniel Papers, UVA.

52. Davis, *Confederate General*, vol. 3, 186–87; Freeman, *Lee's Lieutenants*, vol. 3, xlvi.

53. Stiles, *Four Years*, 218; Davis, *Confederate General*, vol. 3, 187.

54. Wert, *Gettysburg*, chaps. 3 and 4; *Mobile Evening News*, July 24, 1863.

55. Ted Barclay–Sister, July 8, 1863, Barclay Papers, WLU; *OR*, 27, pt. 2, 504.

56. Stiles, *Four Years*, 218; Davis, *Confederate General*, vol. 3, 187; Brown, Memoirs, TSLA.

57. *Richmond Times*, February 4, 1893; *OR*, 36, pt. 1, 1023.

58. *Richmond Times*, February 4, 1893; *OR*, 36, pt. 1, 1023; *Greensboro Record*, June 29, 1903; Howard, *Recollections*, 292; Evans, *Confederate Military History*, vol. 3, 451; Wert, *Sword*, 351.

59. *OR*, 36, pt. 1, 1023; pt. 2, 974; 43, pt. 1, 610; Jones, *Lee's Tigers*, 201–2.

60. Jones, *Lee's Tigers*, 203, 204; Gannon, *Irish Rebels*, 237, 238, 239; Krick, *Lee's Colonels*, 276–77, 403.

61. Gannon, *Irish Rebels*, xiii; Jones, *Lee's Tigers*, 6.

62. Krick, *Lee's Colonels*, 396; Gannon, *Irish Rebels*, xiii; Jones, *Lee's Tigers*, 34, 35, 249.

63. Krick, *Lee's Colonels*, 396; Jones, *Lee's Tigers*, 104, 111, 249; *Richmond Times*, February 4, 1893.

64. Mackowski and White, "Battle," 12; Davis, *Confederate General*, vol. 6, 86, 87; Wert, *Brotherhood*, 235.

65. Davis, *Confederate General*, vol. 6, 86, 87; Wert, *Brotherhood*, 235.

66. Davis, *Confederate General*, vol. 6, 87; Colt, *Defend the Valley*, 284; CV, vol. 10, 36; Biography of Walker by a doctor, 4, Walker Papers, UNC.

67. Fry, *2nd Virginia Infantry*, 64; Walker, *5th Virginia Infantry*, 59; *SHSP*, vol. 21, 233; Carrington, Recollection; Wilfred Cutshaw Account, 1904–1907 Spotsylvania Folder, Daniel Papers, UVA; Mackowski and White, "Battle," 12.

68. Krick, *Lee's Colonels*, 403; Mackowski and White, "Battle," 12; *Bellevue Bossier Banner*, August 7, 1913.

69. *OR*, 36, pt. 1, 1023; *Bellevue Bossier Banner*, August 7, 1913; *SHSP*, vol. 21, 234; Howard, *Recollections*, 292; Young, *Lee's Army*, 88, 274.

70. Chapla, *48th Virginia Infantry*, 2; Armstrong, *25th Virginia Infantry*, 6, 76; *Richmond Times-Dispatch*, October 29, 1906; Krick, *Lee's Colonels*, 409; Howard, *Recollections*, 292.

71. Young, *Lee's Army*, 84, 270; Armstrong, *25th Virginia Infantry*, 78; *Richmond Times*, April 2, 1893; *Mobile Advertiser and Register*, June 1, 1864; Mackowski and White, "Battle," 13.

72. *PMHSM*, vol. 4, 92; Rankin, *23rd Virginia Infantry*, 76; Young, *Lee's Army*, 86, 87, 272.

73. Davis, vol. 6, *Confederate General*, 2–3; Mackowski and White, "Battle," 12; *PMHSM*, vol. 4, 84, 93.

74. *PMHSM*, vol. 4, 111; *Fayetteville Semi-Weekly Observer*, June 16, 1864; Mackowski and White, "Battle," 13.

75. Young, *Lee's Army*, 94, 97, 115, 276, 278, 286; Nichols, *Soldier's Story*, 150; John B. Gordon–My Dear Col., November 24, 1878, Venable Papers, VHS.

76. Cannan, *Bloody Angle*, 50; Azariah Bostwick–Sister, June 5, 1864, Bostwick Letters, FSNMP; George W. Pearsall–[wife], May 11, 1864, Pearsall Letters, SANC.

77. Gordon, *Reminiscences*, 274; Howard, *Recollections*, 294.

78. *SHSP*, vol. 21, 251, 252; *Richmond Times*, April 2, 1893; Letter fragment from Frank [?], n.d., Daniel Papers, UVA; Ruffner, *44th Virginia Infantry*, 49, 51.

79. *OR*, 36, pt. 1, 1080; *SHSP*, vol. 33, 336, 337; *Raleigh Daily Conservative*, May 21, 1864; Pfanz, *Richard S. Ewell*, 383.

80. *OR*, 36, pt. 1, 1080; *SHSP*, vol. 33, 337; *Raleigh Daily Conservative*, May 21, 1864; Pfanz, *Richard S. Ewell*, 383.

81. Pfanz, *Richard S. Ewell*, 384; Hess, *Trench Warfare*, 62; *OR*, 36, pt. 1, 1078.

82. *OR*, 36, pt. 1, 1044, 1072, 1086; *SHSP*, vol. 21, 240; S. H. Hawes–Colonel, October 7, 1905, Daniel Papers, UVA.

83. *OR*, 36, pt. 1, 1044; S. H. Hawes–Colonel, October 7, 1905, Daniel Papers, UVA; *SHSP*, vol. 21, 240.

84. *OR*, 36, pt. 1, 1080; *SHSP*, vol. 21, 251; vol. 33, 337, 338; Carrington Recollection, Daniel Papers, UVA; Doyle, Memoir, LC; *PMHSM*, vol. 4, 113; Richmond *Times*, April 2, 1893.

85. *Richmond Times*, April 2, 1893; Chapla, *48th Virginia Infantry*, 72; Mackowski and White, "Battle," 13, 21, 52; "Harrison Gazetteer," vol. 1, Hotchkiss Papers, LC; Cross, "Historic People," FSNMP.

86. Chapla, *48th Virginia Infantry*, 72; *Meridian Daily Clarion*, June 11, 1864.

87. *OR*, 36, pt. 2, 654; Rhea, *Battles*, 229.

88. Washburn, *Complete Military History*, 70; *OR*, 36, pt. 1, 409; Silliker, *Rebel Yell*, 155; Mackowski and White, *Season*, 70; Muffly, *Story*, 856.

89. Silliker, *Rebel Yell*, 155; Waitt, *History*, 308.

90. Carmichael, *War*, 6, 7.

Chapter 6

1. *OR*, 36, pt. 1, 122, 198, 335.

2. *OR*, 36, pt. 1, 358; Washburn, *Complete Military History*, 70; Miller, *Harvard's Civil War*, 358; *Glimpses*, vol. 4, 303; *SHSP*, vol. 21, 243; Muffly, *Story*, 857.

3. Muffly, *Story*, 259, 857; *OR*, 36, pt. 1, 358; Grant, *Personal Memoirs*, vol. 2, 230; *Washington National Tribune*, June 16, 1904; Walker, *History*, 470; Mackowski and White, "Battle," 22.

4. Mackowski and White, "Battle," 54; *OR*, 36, pt. 1, 335; *PMHSM*, vol. 4, 250, 252, 253; Priest, *One Surgeon's Civil War*, 102.

5. *OR*, 36, pt. 1, 373, 379, 384, 409; Stewart, *History*, 197; *Philadelphia Weekly Times*, October 27, 1886; Wert, *Sword*, 351.

6. *Mobile Advertiser and Register*, June 1, 1864; *Richmond Daily Dispatch*, May 16, 1864; Powell Reynolds–Sir, May 19, 1864, Reynolds Letters, WVU; King, *My Experience*, 24; Washburn, *Complete Military History*, 73; Mulholland, *Story*, 210.

7. Newton T. Kirk Account, Kirk Papers, MSU; Mulholland, *Story*, 209, 210.

8. *Philadelphia Weekly Press*, October 27, 1886; Gallagher, *Spotsylvania Campaign*, 86.

9. Wheelan, *Bloody Spring*, 201; Ruffner, *44th Virginia Infantry*, 51; Chapla, *50th Virginia Infantry*, 91, 93; Abram S. Miller–Julia, May 18, 1864, Miller Papers, HANDL.

10. Abram S. Miller–Julia, May 18, 1864, Miller Papers, HANDL; Driver, *52nd Virginia Infantry*, 56; *Richmond Daily Dispatch*, May 18, 1864.

11. Robert D. Trieves–Lizzie Brewer, May 14, 1864, Dinwiddie Papers, VHS; *Richmond Times-Dispatch*, October 29, 1906; *PMHSM*, vol. 4, 250.

12. *Richmond Times*, April 2, 1893; Chapla, *50th Virginia Infantry*, 93, 168.

13. *OR*, 36, pt. 1, 1080; *Richmond Dispatch*, May 16, 1864; *SHSP*, vol. 21, 252; vol. 33, 338.

14. *OR*, 36, pt. 1, 1080; *Edgefield Advertiser*, June 1, 1864; *SHSP*, vol. 21, 252; vol. 33, 338, 339; *Southern Bivouac*, vol. 3, no. 8, 272, 273; Howard, *Recollections*, 301; Memoir, vol. 9, Allan Papers, UNC.

15. *OR*, 36, pt. 1, 1044, 1080; Wise, *Long Arm*, 739; Newman, Recollections, FSNMP; *SHSP*, vol. 7, 535, and vol. 21, 240; *New Orleans Times-Picayune*, February 10, 1873.

16. *SHSP*, vol. 7, 536; vol. 21, 240; S. H. Hawes–Colonel, October 7, 1905, Daniel Papers, UVA; Freeman, *Lee's Lieutenants*, vol. 3, 402; Newman, Recollections, FSNMP.

17. Wise, *Long Arm*, 739, 791; *SHSP*, vol. 7, 535, 536; Freeman, *Lee's Lieutenants*, vol. 3, 402; Laboda, *From Selma*, 209.

18. S. H. Hawes–Colonel, October 7, 1905; Wilfred Cutshaw–My dear Major Carrington, October 7, 1905, Daniel Papers, UVA; Wise, *Long Arm*, 739; *OR*, 27, pt. 2, 458; *SHSP*, vol. 7, 536; Gallagher, *Spotsylvania Campaign*, 86.

19. S. H. Hawes–Colonel, October 7, 1905, Daniel Papers, UVA; Gallagher, *Spotsylvania Campaign*, 86; *SHSP*, vol. 7, 535, 536.

20. Purifoy, Memoir, 230, ADAH; *Montgomery Advertiser*, December 14, 1914; *CV*, vol. 24, 223; *OR*, 27, pt. 2, 458; *SHSP*, vol. 7, 536.

21. *CV*, vol. 31, 297; *Wilmington Semi-Weekly Advertiser*, August 13, 1896; Rhea, *Battles*, 237; Map, Lyman Papers, MHS.

22. *Wilmington Semi-Weekly Advertiser*, August 13, 1896; *Richmond Daily Enquirer*, June 6, 1864; Clark, *Histories*, vol. 1, 152, 153, 204; Krick, *Lee's Colonels*, 377; Rhea, *Battles*, 237.

23. *OR*, 36, pt. 1, 410; Hess, *Trench Warfare*, 67; *CV*, vol. 31, 297; Favill, *Diary*, 284, 286; Mahood, "*Written in Blood*," 247.

24. *OR*, 36, pt. 1, 410; Muffly, *Story*, 154, 768.

25. *OR*, 36, pt. 1, 410; Howard, *Recollections*, 295; *Montpelier Examiner*, June 27, 1896; Rankin, *37th Virginia Infantry*, 82.

26. *SHSP*, vol. 14, 151; Rankin, *37th Virginia Infantry*, 82; *Wilmington Semi-Weekly Advertiser*, August 13, 1896; Muffly, *Story*, 750; Clark, *Histories*, vol. 1, 153.

27. *SHSP*, vol. 7, 535, 536; *CV*, vol. 24, 224; Purifoy, Memoir, 230, ADAH; Laboda, *From Selma*, 217, 223; *Montgomery Advertiser*, December 14, 1914; *Selma Daily Reporter*, May 30, 1864.

28. *PMHSM*, vol. 4, 114; Muffly, *Story*, 123.

29. *OR*, 36, pt. 1, 416, 1044; *Boston Globe*, May 12, 1914; Morris Brown Jr.–My Dear Parents, May 16, 1864, Brown Collection, HC.

30. Seymour, *Civil War Memoirs*, 4, 123, 124.

31. Seymour, *Civil War Memoirs*, 124; *SOR*, vol. 6, 680; Barton, Recollections, 53, 54, HANDL; *Richmond Times*, February 4, 1893.

32. Weygant, *History*, 319; *OR*, 36, pt. 1, 108, 470, 491; Mackowski and White, "Battle," 13; Edwin Emery–[Sister], n.d., Emery, Diaries, BOWC.

33. *OR*, 36, pt. 1, 470; Grant, *Personal Memoirs*, vol. 2, 230; Weygant, *History*, 322; Green, "From the Wilderness," 99; Chase, Memoirs, 104, FSNMP.

34. Dunn, *Harvestfields*, 236; Weygant, *History*, 320.

35. Weygant, *History*, 319, 322; R. G. Cobb–A. J. Bachelor, June 14, 1864, Bachelor Papers, LSU; Chase, Memoirs, 104, FSNMP; Krick, *Lee's Colonels*, 403; Jones, *Lee's Tigers*, 205.

36. Rhea, *Battles*, 239; Weygant, *History*, 323; Dunn, *Harvestfields*, 237.

37. Rhea, *Battles*, 240; *SHSP*, vol. 21, 235; McCown, Memoirs, HANDL; Doyle, Memoir, LC.

38. McCown, Memoirs, HANDL; Bean, *Liberty Hall Volunteers*, 189; *SHSP*, vol. 21, 235; *SOR*, vol. 6, 681; *Richmond Times*, February 4, 1893.

39. *SOR*, vol. 6, 681; *Richmond Times*, February 4, 1893; Silliker, *Rebel Yell*, 155; Hite, Diary, HANDL.

40. Wallace, *5th Virginia Infantry*, 59; McCown, Memoirs, HANDL.

41. Doyle, Memoir, LC.

42. *SHSP*, vol. 21, 236; McMurran, Memorandum Book, LVA; *Richmond Enquirer*, June 7, 1864; *Staunton Spectator and Vindicator*, May 17, 1884; *Jackson Clarion-Ledger*, June 11, 1864; *SOR*, vol. 6, 683.

43. Phillips, Civil War Diary, VMI; *Mobile Advertiser and Register*, June 1, 1864; Biography of Walker by a doctor, typescript, 4, 143, Walker Papers, UNC; Caldwell, *Stonewall Jim*, 109.

44. Biography of Walker by a doctor, typescript, 143, 144, Walker Papers, UNC; Caldwell, *Stonewall Jim*, 109, 110.

45. *OR*, 36, pt. 1, 491; McAllister, *Civil War Letters*, 418, 418n; Gannon, *Irish Rebels*, 241, 243; Jones, *Lee's Tigers*, 205, 206.

46. Jones, *Lee's Tigers*, 206; Gannon, *Irish Rebels*, 243, 244.

47. *OR*, 27, pt. 2, 458; Wise, *Long Arm*, 739; William Maupin–My dear Major, August 5, 1905, and Letter fragment from Frank [?], n. d.; Davis, Memoir, Daniel Papers, UVA.

48. *OR*, 36, pt. 1, 481, 485, 491; 1904–1907 Spotsylvania folder; Letter fragment from Frank [?], n.d.; Davis, Memoir; Carrington, Memoir, Daniel Papers, UVA.

49. *OR*, 36, pt. 1, 338, 431; Bruce, *Twentieth Regiment*, 376; Lash, *"Duty Well Done,"* 392, 393; Longacre, *To Gettysburg*, 201–2.

50. Seville, *History*, 110; Lash, *"Duty Well Done,"* 394.

51. Rhea, *Battles*, 243; *OR*, 36, pt. 1, 339, 448; Galwey, *Valiant Hours*, 210, 212; *Indianapolis Journal*, April 23, 1893.

52. *OR*, 36, pt. 1, 440, 441, 443; Rhea, *Battles*, 243; Waitt, *History*, 308; Bruce, *Twentieth Regiment*, 377; Miller, *Harvard's Civil War*, 358.

53. Carmichael, *War*, 156, 158; Smith, *Smell*, 47.

54. Powell Reynolds–Sir, May 19, 1864, Reynolds Letters, WVA; John J. Dillard–[Friend], May 20, 1864, Dillard Papers, DU; George Ring–My Own Darling, May 15, 1864, Ring Papers, TU; *Richmond Enquirer*, May 24, 1864.

55. McDonald, *Make Me a Map*, 204.

56. Dozier, *Gunner*, 244.

57. Hays, *Under*, 240; King et al., *History*, 299, 300; Laboda, *From Selma*, 222; *Jackson Clarion-Ledger*, June 11, 1864; *OR*, 36, pt. 1, 1020, 1021.

58. *OR*, 36, pt. 1, 335, and pt. 2, 656; *Glimpses*, vol. 4, 373; Muffly, *Story*, 122.

59. Myers, *We Might*, 174; Chesson, *Journal*, 152; Weeks, "152nd N.Y.," SPPL; Galwey, *Valiant Hours*, 209; *Philadelphia Weekly Times*, February 2, 1886.

60. Account of a soldier in the 33rd Virginia, Hotchkiss Papers, LC; Howard, *Recollections*, 300.

61. *Montpelier Examiner*, June 17, 1896; Myers, *We Might*, 174; "Harrison Gazeteer," vol. 1, Hotchkiss Papers, LC; Cross, "Historic People," FSNMP; Mackowski and White, *Season*, 148.

62. *Philadelphia Weekly Times*, January 7, 1882, February 20, 1886; *Montpelier Examiner*, June 27, 1896.

63. *OR*, 36, pt. 1, 359; Mackowski and White, *Season*, 62; *Philadelphia Weekly Times*, January 7, 1882; Sauers and Tomasak, *Ricketts' Battery*, 164; *Richmond Examiner*, June 2, 1864.

64. *OR*, 36, pt. 1, 359; *Montpelier Examiner*, June 27, 1896.

65. Edward "Ned" Russell–My dear sisters, May 15, 1864, Russell Letters, FSNMP.

66. *Philadelphia Weekly Times*, January 7, 1882; Rhodes, *All for the Union*, 151; Lowe, *Meade's Army*, 153.

67. Lowe, *Meade's Army*, 153; Dana, *Recollections*, 195; Porter, *Campaigning with Grant*, 104.

68. Dana, *Recollections*, 196; Porter, *Campaigning with Grant*, 104, 105; Lowe, *Meade's Army*, 153; *PMHSM*, vol. 4, 105n.

69. *PMHSM*, vol. 4, 105n; Lowe, *Meade's Army*, 153; Porter, *Campaigning with Grant*, 105; Davis, *Confederate General*, vol. 3, 187; vol. 6, 3.

70. *PMHSM*, vol. 4, 253; Roche, "Bloody Angle."

Chapter 7

1. *OR*, 36, pt. 1, 1078; Rhea, *Battles*, 242, 246; Young, *Lee's Army*, 94, 97, 115, 276, 278, 286.

2. *OR*, 36, pt. 2, 974; Davis, *Confederate General*, vol. 3, 8, 9.

3. Tankersley, *John B. Gordon*, 2, 3; Stiles, *Four Years*, 188, 212.

4. Worsham, *One*, 146–47; Tankersley, *John B. Gordon*, 7; *CV*, vol. 22, 506.

5. *CV*, vol. 12, 193; Freeman, *Lee's Lieutenants*, vol. 3, xxxiv; Dozier, *Gunner*, 259.

6. *OR*, 36, pt. 1, 1078; John B. Gordon–My Dear Col., November 24, 1878, Venable Papers, VHS; Nichols, *Soldier's Story*, 150.

7. *OR*, 36, pt. 1, 1078; Rhea, *Battles*, 247, 248; John B. Gordon–My Dear Col., November 24, 1878, Venable Papers, VHS; *Fayetteville Semi-Weekly Observer*, June 16, 1865.

8. *OR*, 36, pt. 1, 1078; John B. Gordon–My Dear Col., November 24, 1878, Venable Papers, VHS; Gordon, *Reminiscences*, 275.

9. *OR*, 36, pt. 1, 336, 410; *Boston Globe*, May 12, 1914; *Philadelphia Weekly Press*, October 27, 1886; *PMHSM*, vol. 4, 253–54; Silliker, *Rebel Yell*, 156; Welch, *Boy General*, 118.

10. *SOR*, vol. 6, 720–21, 755, 768; *SHSP*, vol. 9, 146.

11. Lane, Memoir, FSNMP; *SHSP*, vol. 9, 146; *SOR*, vol. 6, 721, 756, 762, 768; Pfanz, *Richard S. Ewell*, 385; James H. Lane–Sir, October 6, 1900, Carrington Manuscript, DU.

12. Clark, *Histories*, vol. 3, 50; Swisher, *Warrior*, 178; *OR*, 27, pt. 2, 458; Wise, *Long Arm*, 738, 739; *Richmond Times-Dispatch*, October 29, 1905.

13. *OR*, 36, pt. 1, 370, 505; Clark, *Histories*, vol. 3, 51; Seymour, *Civil War Memoirs*, 124; Gannon, *Irish Rebels*, 243; Stephens, *Intrepid Warrior*, 393; Hess, *Trench Warfare*, 67; John J. Dillard–[Friend], May 20, 1864, Dillard Papers, DU; Green, Diary, UNC.

14. *OR*, 36, pt. 1, 1078; Young, *Lee's Army*, 115, 286; *Raleigh Daily Confederate*, February 3, 1864.

15. Davis, *Confederate General*, vol. 3, 198–99; Carr, *History*, 19.

16. Clark, *Histories*, vol. 2, 243; John B. Gordon–My Dear Col., November 24, 1878, Venable Papers, VHS; Robert D. Johnston–Senator Daniel, June 30, 1905, notes of Daniel, Daniel Papers, DU; Gallagher, *Spotsylvania Campaign*, 90; Pfanz, *Richard S. Ewell*, 385.

17. Robert D. Johnston–Senator Daniel, June 30, 1905, notes of Daniel, and Robert D. Johnston–John W. Daniel, August 6, 1895, Daniel Papers, DU; *SHSP*, vol. 4, 529; Gordon, *Reminiscences*, 277; John B. Gordon–My Dear Col., November 24, 1878, Venable Papers, VHS; Mackowski and White, "Battle," 12.

18. *OR*, 36, pt. 1, 1078; Robert D. Johnston–John W. Daniel, August 6, 1895, Daniel Papers, DU; "A Foot-race for a Flag," Daniel Papers, UVA; Krick, *Lee's Colonels*, 66; Clark, *Histories*, vol. 2, 121; *Raleigh News and Observer*, April 11, 1897; *Wilmington Morning Star*, October 6, 1895.

19. Robert D. Johnston–John W. Daniel, August 6, 1895, Daniel Papers, DU; Clark, *Histories*, vol. 1, 289; vol. 2, 244; G. Alston–My Dear Sir, September 6, 1922, Alston Letter, FSNMP; *Daily Confederate*, May 25, 1864; *OR*, 36, pt. 1, 1078; *Jackson Clarion-Ledger*, June 11, 1864.

20. Clark, *Histories*, vol. 1, 289, 642; Robert D. Johnston–John W. Daniel, August 6, 1895, Daniel Papers, DU.

21. John B. Gordon–My Dear Col., November 24, 1878, Venable Papers, VHS; *OR*, 36, pt. 1, 1078.

22. *SHSP*, vol. 14, 529; Pfanz, *Richard S. Ewell*, 385; Jones, *Campbell Brown's Civil War*, 253.

23. *SHSP*, vol. 14, 529; *Buffalo Sunday Morning News*, May 19, 1912; Gallagher, *Spotsylvania Campaign*, 89, 90; Koonce, *Doctor*, 129; Mackowski and White, *Season*, 85.

24. *Buffalo Sunday Morning News*, May 19, 1912; *SHSP*, vol. 14, 529; Koonce, *Doctor*, 130; Gallagher, *Spotsylvania Campaign*, 89, 90; Seymour, *Civil War Memoirs*, 125.

25. Gallagher, *Spotsylvania Campaign*, 89, 90; Seymour, *Civil War Memoirs*, 125; Koonce, *Doctor*, 130; *New Orleans Times-Picayune*, December 6, 1895.

26. Seymour, *Civil War Memoirs*, 125; Gallagher, *Spotsylvania Campaign*, 16, 90; Memoir, Allan Papers, UNC; *New Orleans Times-Picayune*, December 6, 1865.

27. *Philadelphia Weekly Press*, October 27, 1886; Swinton, *Campaigns*, 452; "Battlefield near Spotsylvania C. H., Thursday, May 12, 1864," Emery, Diaries, BOWC.

28. *Philadelphia Weekly Press*, October 27, 1886; Mackowski and White, "Battle," 25.

29. *OR*, 36, pt. 1, 1078; Young, *Lee's Army*, 94, 97, 276, 278; "Lee to the Rear at Spotsylvania," undated newspaper article, Daniel Papers, UVA; Randolph, Memoir, VHS; Riggs, *13th Virginia Infantry*, 48; *Richmond Daily Dispatch*, June 2, 1864; *SHSP*, vol. 33, 18.

30. Snider, Diary, FSNMP; Mackowski and White, "Battle," 14; *Edgefield Advertiser*, May 11, 1864; Buck, *With*, 104; William W. Smith–My dear Major, October 26, 1904, Daniel Papers, UVA; Krick, *Lee's Colonels*, 194.

31. Davis, *Confederate General*, vol. 2, 104–5; Mackowski and White, "Battle," 14; Stephens, *Intrepid Warrior*, 389; Nichols, *Soldier's Story*, 146.

32. *National Tribune Scrapbook*, 70; Snider, Diary, FSNMP; *Richmond Times-Dispatch*, January 8, 1905.

33. John B. Gordon–My Dear Col., November 24, 1878, Venable Papers, VHS; *Richmond Sentinel*, May 25, 1864; *Richmond Times-Dispatch*, January 8, 1905; Azariah Bostwick–Sister, June 5, 1864, Bostwick Papers, FSNMP; Long, *Memoirs*, 341.

34. Long, *Memoirs*, 341; Memoir, Allan Papers, UNC; *Edgefield Advertiser*, June 1, 1864.

35. John B. Gordon–My Dear Col., November 24, 1878, Venable Papers, VHS; Gordon has a different version of his words to Lee in his *Reminiscences*,

278–79; *SHSP*, vol. 14, 529; *Richmond Sentinel*, May 25, 1864; *Lancaster Ledger*, June 7, 1864.

36. John B. Gordon–My Dear Col., November 24, 1878, Venable Papers, VHS; *Richmond Sentinel*, May 25, 1864; *The Confederate*, May 28, 1864; Azariah Bostwick–Sister, June 5, 1864, Bostwick Papers, FSNMP; *Lancaster Ledger*, June 7, 1864; *Savannah Morning News*, July 20, 1864.

37. Hays, *Under*, 240–41.

38. *OR*, 36, pt. 1, 470; *New York Times*, May 18, 1864; *Philadelphia Weekly Times*, February 20, 1886; Miller, *Harvard's Civil War*, 359, 360; Wise, *Long Arm*,791; Cannan, *Bloody Angle*, 88.

39. Miller, *Harvard's Civil War*, 360; *Pittsburgh Post-Gazette*, May 12, 1914; *SHSP*, vol. 21, 247; *OR*, 36, pt. 1, 474; Waitt, *History*, 308; Dunn, *Harvestfields*, 238; Weygant, *History*, 324, 326.

40. Lowe, *Meade's Army*, 124; Chesson, *Journal*, 152; Miller, *Harvard's Civil War*, 360; Longacre, *To Gettysburg*, 204; Menge and Shimrak, *Civil War Notebook*, 112.

41. Longacre, *To Gettysburg*, 203, 204; Galwey, *Valiant Hours*, 210; *Indianapolis Journal*, April 23, 1893.

42. *OR*, 36, pt. 1, 1079; Snider, Diary, FSNMP; Bowan, Diary, AHEC; *Muncie Star Press*, September 3, 1911; *Boston Globe*, May 12, 1914; Silliker, *Rebel Yell*, 156; Miller, *Harvard's Civil War*, 360.

43. John B. Gordon–My Dear Col., November 24, 1878, Venable Papers, VHS; Pfanz, *Richard S. Ewell*, 385; Wise, *Long Arm*, 791; *OR*, 36, pt. 1, 471; Rhea, *Battles*, 244; Warner, *Generals in Blue*, 538; Cannan, *Bloody Angle*, 89.

44. Snider, Diary, FSNMP; Mackowski and White, "Battle," 14; *Richmond Times-Dispatch*, December 11, 1904; *SHSP*, vol. 32, 204; Rhea, *Battles*, 252.

45. Snider, Diary, FSNMP; *SHSP*, vol. 32, 205, 213; *Richmond Sentinel*, May 25, 1864.

46. Driver, *52nd Virginia Infantry*, 56; *SHSP*, vol. 21, 248.

47. Driver, *52nd Virginia Infantry*, 150, 160; Adam Wise Kersh–Brother, May 12, 1864, Kersh Letters, FSNMP; Krick, *Lee's Colonels*, 350.

48. John B. Gordon–My Dear Col., November 24, 1878, Venable Papers, VHS; Rhea, *Battles*, 252; Ashcraft, *31st Virginia Infantry*, 68; *Richmond Sentinel*, May 25, 1864; *Richmond Times-Dispatch*, December 11, 1904; Driver, *52nd Virginia Infantry*, 56; Snider, Diary, FSNMP.

49. Stephens, *Intrepid Warrior*, 393, 395; Mackowski and White, "Battle," 14; Rhea, *Battles*, 252; Nichols, *Soldier's Story*, 152.

50. Nichols, *Soldier's Story*, 152, 153; Young, *Lee's Army*, 276, 278.

51. John J. Dillard–[Friend], May 20, 1864, Dillard Papers, DU; *OR*, 36, pt. 1, 359, 1079; Rhea, *Battles*, 255, 259.

52. Jones, *Campbell Brown's Civil War*, 253, 254.

53. Jones, *Campbell Brown's Civil War*, 254, 255.

54. Jones, *Campbell Brown's Civil War*, 254; Davis, *Confederate General*, vol. 1, 74–75; *OR*, 36, pt. 1, 1084.

55. Rhea, *Battles*, 256; *Jackson Clarion-Ledger*, June 11, 1864; Mackowski and White, "Battle," 14, 16.

56. Rhea, *Battles*, 256; *Jackson Clarion-Ledger*, June 11, 1864; Mackowski and White, "Battle," 16.

57. Davis, *Confederate General*, vol. 5, 107–8; Smith, *Anson Guards*, 279.

58. Stiles, *Four Years*, 261.

59. *OR*, 36, pt. 1, 1082; Bryan Grimes–My Dearest Wife, May 14, 1864, Grimes Papers, UNC; Davis, *Confederate General*, vol. 5, 74–75, 108.

60. *OR*, 36, pt. 1, 1082; Johnston, *Civil War Letters*, 29; Bone, "My War Story," 31, SANC.

61. *OR*, 36, pt. 1, 1082; Stikeleather, Reminiscences, 65, SANC; Kundahl, *Bravest*, 225; Rhea, *Battles*, 256.

62. Young, *Lee's Army*, 105, 281; *Salisbury Watchman*, June 6, 1864; Pfanz, *Richard S. Ewell*, 385; J. Francis Shaffner–My Dear Carrie, May 18, 1864, Shaffner Papers, UNC; Diary, Ardrey Papers, DU; Clark, *Histories*, vol. 1, 256.

63. Gallagher, *Stephen Dodson Ramseur*, 108; Watkins, Reminiscences, FSNMP; Bryan Grimes–My Dearest Wife, May 14, 1864, Grimes Papers, UNC; *Raleigh Daily Confederate*, August 16, 1864; *Raleigh News and Observer*, May 11, 1888.

64. Johnston, *Civil War Letters*, 29; Gallagher, *Stephen Dodson Ramseur*, 108; *Salisbury Watchman*, June 6, 1864; *New Bern Our Living and Our Dead*, November 5, 1873; Pfanz, *Richard S. Ewell*, 386; Richard L. Apple–My Dear Wife and Family, May 17, 1864, Apple Letters, FSNMP.

65. *OR*, 36, pt. 1, 1082; *Daily Confederate*, May 25, 1864; Craig and Baker, *As You May Never See*, 75; Gales, Diary, FSNMP; Stikeleather, Reminiscences, 67, 68, SANC.

66. *OR*, 36, pt. 1, 1082; Diary, Ardrey Papers, DU; Gales, Diary, FSNMP; Johnston, *Civil War Letters*, 28; Bryan Grimes–My Dearest Wife, May 14, 1864, Grimes Papers, UNC.

67. Hess, *Trench Warfare*, 68; Bryan Grimes–My Dearest Wife, May 14, 1864, Grimes Papers, UNC; Watkins, Memoir, FSNMP; Clark, *Histories*, vol. 1, 723.

68. *OR*, 36, pt. 1, 1082; Bryan Grimes–My Dearest Wife, May 14, 1864, Grimes Papers, UNC; Diary, Ardrey Papers, DU; Watkins, Memoir, FSNMP; Gallagher, *Stephen Dodson Ramseur*, 110; Lane, "Some Recollections," SANC.

69. Bryan Grimes–My Dearest Wife, May 14, 1864, Grimes Papers, UNC; Diary, Ardrey Papers, DU; Rhea, *Battles*, 258; McAllister, *Civil War Letters*, 418–19.

70. *OR*, 36, pt. 1, 1072; Clark, *Histories*, vol. 1, 172; Stephen D. Ramseur–My Dearest Nellie, June 4, 1864, Ramseur Papers, UNC.

71. Stephen D. Ramseur–My Dearest Nellie, May 19, 30, June 4, 1864, Ramseur Papers; J. Francis Shaffner–My Dear Carrie, May 18, 1864, Shaffner Papers, UNC; Grimes, *Extracts*, 52; *OR*, 36, pt. 1, 1082; Clark, *Histories*, vol. 1, 257.

72. *OR*, 36, pt. 1, 336; Rhea, *Battles*, 259; Gallagher, *Fighting For*, 377; *Chicago Tribune*, May 15, 1864; Swinton, *Campaigns*, 452.

73. *OR*, 36, pt. 1, 336; John C. Tidball Letter, n.d., Record Group 94, NA; Unidentified Artilleryman–Home Circle, May 16, 1864, Ames Papers, FSNMP; Walker, *General Hancock*, 199; *PMHSM*, vol. 4, 254.

74. *OR*, 36, pt. 2, 656.

75. *OR*, 36, pt. 2, 661, 677; Rhea, *Battles*, 252–55.

76. Lowe, *Meade's Army*, 153.

77. Porter, *Campaigning with Grant*, 101, 103.

78. Swinton, *Campaigns*, 452; Gallagher, *Fighting For*, 377; *Chicago Tribune*, May 15, 1864; Pfanz, *Richard S. Ewell*, 386.

79. Gallagher, *Fighting For*, 377.

80. *CV*, vol. 31, 371.

81. *CV*, vol. 31, 371.

82. *OR*, 36, pt. 1, 1037, 1044, 1045; Wise, *Long Arm*, 792.

83. *SHSP*, vol. 33, 339, 340; Mackowski and White, "Battle," 26; Swinton, *Campaigns*, 453.

Chapter 8

1. Wert, *Sword*, 341.

2. Wert, *Sword*, 331; *OR*, 36, pt. 1, 909; pt. 2, 643; Grant, *Personal Memoirs*, vol. 2, 229.

3. Wert, *Sword*, 331; Lowe, *Meade's Army*, 142; Sears, *Lincoln's Lieutenants*, 626.

4. *OR*, 36, pt. 1, 133, 906, 909, 915; Gallagher, *Spotsylvania Campaign*, 47, 48.

5. *OR*, 36, pt. 1, 909; Warner, *Generals in Blue*, 100; Charles Mills-Mother, May 14, 1864, Mills Papers, AHEC; Agassiz, *Meade's Headquarters*, 116–17.

6. *OR*, 36, pt. 1, 909; Bunker, Memoir, 5, UM; Charles Mills-Mother, May 10, 11, 1864, Mills Papers, AHEC.

7. *OR*, 36, pt. 1, 113, 909; Weld, *War Diary*, 291; Rhea, *Battles*, 218; Charles Mills-Mother, May 14, 1864, Mills Papers, AHEC.

8. *OR*, 36, pt. 1, 113, 909, 928, 935; Weld, *War Diary*, 291; Lord, *History*, 371; Charles Mills-Mother, May 14, 1864, Mills Papers, AHEC.

9. *OR*, 36, pt. 1, 928, 935; Cogswell, *History*, 364; Houston, *Thirty-Second Maine*, 134; *SOR*, vol. 6, 737.

10. *OR*, 36, pt. 1, 935; Jackman, *History*, 243; *SOR*, vol. 6, 721, 738; *SHSP*, vol. 9, 146; *Warrenton Indicator*, October 2, 1867; Rhea, *Battles*, 245; *Monroe Journal*, October 29, 1912.

11. *OR*, 36, pt. 1, 909; *SHSP*, vol. 9, 146, 147; Rhea, *Battles*, 245; Beddall, Diary, AHEC; Burrage, *History*, 165; Albert, *History*, 128.

12. *SOR*, vol. 6, 721; Fox, *Red Clay*, 260, 261; Hall, Diary, LC; Young, *Lee's Army*, 147, 150, 301, 302; Mackowski and White, "Battle," 17, 43.

13. *OR*, 36, pt. 1, 909, 936; Fox, *Red Clay*, 261; *SOR*, vol. 6, 738; Charles Mills-Mother, May 14, 1864, Mills Papers, AHEC; Albert, *History*, 128.

14. *OR*, 36, pt. 1, 936; Hardy, *General Lee's Immortals*, 278; Fox, *Red Clay*, 2612; Hall, Diary, LC.

15. *OR*, 36, pt. 1, 936; *Raleigh Semi-Weekly Standard*, June 7, 1864; Hall, Diary, LC; Hopkins, *Seventh Regiment*, 170; Fox, *Red Clay*, 261.

16. *OR*, 36, pt. 1, 909, 916; Wilkinson, *Mother*, 107; Charles Mills-Mother, May 14, 1864, Mills Papers, AHEC; "Battle of Spotsylvania Court House May 1864," 69, 70, McDowell Papers, PSU.

17. Weld, *War Diary*, 291, 292; *OR*, 36, pt. 1, 909, 1045; "Battle of Spotsylvania Court House May 1864," 70, 72, McDowell Papers, PSU; Wilkinson, *Mother*, 107; Poague, *Gunner with Stonewall*, 92; Bunker, Memoir, 6, UM.

18. *OR*, 36, pt. 1, 909; pt. 2, 677–79; Poague, *Gunner with Stonewall*, 92; Wilkinson, *Mother*, 107, 108; *Statesville Record and Landmark*, September 14, 1893; *SOR*, vol. 6, 707; Mackowski and White, "Battle," 57.

19. *OR*, 36, pt. 2, 677–78; Rhea, *Battles*, 264.

20. *OR*, 36, pt. 1, 111, 112, 128, 198; *Philadelphia Weekly Times*, June 27, 1885; Bowen, *History*, 293; Edwards, Memoir, 143, ALPLM.

21. *OR*, 36, pt. 2, 657; Warner, *Generals in Blue*, 575; Dana, *Recollections*, 191; Rhea, *Battles*, 316.

22. Edwards, Memoir, 143, 144, ALPLM; Warner, *Generals in Blue*, 342–43; Rhea, *Battles*, 93; *OR*, 36, pt. 1, 126n.

23. Hess, *Trench Warfare*, 72; Rhea, *Battles*, 261; Edwards, *Memoir*, 144, ALPLM.

24. Edwards, Memoir, 144, ALPLM; *Philadelphia Weekly Times*, June 27, 1885; *SOR*, vol. 6, 556; John C. Tidball Letter, n.d., Record Group 94, NA; Mackowski and White, "Battle," 47, 54; *Washington Weekly Post*, June 27, 1899.

25. Edwards, Memoir, 144, ALPLM; Tyler, *Recollections*, 179; *Boston Globe*, May 12, 1914; *OR*, 36, pt. 1, 673, 1087; Mackowski and White, "Battle," 15; McAllister, *Civil War Letters*, 419; Gallagher, *Spotsylvania Campaign*, 102.

26. Tyler, *Recollections*, 179, 180; *OR*, 36, pt. 1, 673; Watkins, Memoir, FSNMP; Bowen, *History*, 294; Blight, *When This Cruel War*, 296; Edwards, Memoir, 145, ALPLM.

27. Hess, *Trench Warfare*, 72; *OR*, 36, pt. 1, 684; Rhea, *Battles*, 261, 262; Jacob Seibert-Father, May 14, 1864, Seibert Papers, FSNMP.

28. Hess, *Trench Warfare*, 72; *OR*, 36, pt. 1, 720; Rhea, *Battles*, 262.

29. *OR*, 36, pt. 1, 720; Tyler, *Recollections*, 179; Rhea, *Battles*, 260, 262.

30. *OR*, 36, pt. 1, 359; Holmes, *Touched with Fire*, 116.

31. Lowe, *Meade's Army*, 154; Mackowski and White, "Battle," 44.

32. *OR*, 36, pt. 1, 336, 359, 410, 703; Rhea, *Battles*, 263–64.

33. Rhea, *Battles*, 263; *OR*, 36, pt. 1, 703; Silloway, Diary, FSNMP; *PMHSM*, vol. 4, 254.

34. *OR*, 36, pt. 1, 107, 108, 112, 1023, 1024; Young, *Lee's Army*, 94, 97, 105, 112, 115, 276, 278, 281, 285, 286; Sword, *Southern Invincibility*, 169.

35. Holt, *Mississippi Rebel*, 252, 253; *Columbus Weekly Dispatch*, June 6, 1907.

36. *SOR*, vol. 6, 698; Holt, *Mississippi Rebel*, 253; Yeary, *Reminiscences*, 148; *Columbus Weekly Dispatch*, June 6, 1907; *Galveston News*, July 15, 1893.

37. *SOR*, vol. 6, 698; Yeary, *Reminiscences*, 148; Holt, *Mississippi Rebel*, 253.

38. Nathaniel Harris-General, August 2, 1866, Harris Letter, FSNMP; *OR*, 36, pt. 1, 1091; Holt, *Mississippi Rebel*, 253; *SHSP*, vol. 8, 107; *Yazoo Sentinel*, July 19, 1900.

39. Pfanz, *Richard S. Ewell*, 386; Rhea, *Battles*, 268; *Mobile Advertiser and Register*, June 1, 1864; Scott, "Memoirs," VHS.

40. Scott, "Memoirs," VHS; *Mobile Advertiser and Register*, June 1, 1864; *OR*, 36, pt. 1, 1057; Hess, *Trench Warfare*, 70; William S. Shockley-Eliza, May 4, 1864, Shockley Papers, DU; Rhea, *Battles*, 266, 268.

41. Scott, "Memoirs," VHS; Roche, "Bloody Angle"; Rhea, *Battles*, 268; Young, *Lee's Army*, 156, 303.

42. Roche, "Bloody Angle"; Scott, "Memoirs," VHS; Rhea, *Battles*, 268, 269.

43. Roche, "Bloody Angle"; Davis, *Confederate General*, vol. 5, 19; Clark, *Glance Backward*, 51; *Richmond Dispatch*, May 16, 1864; *Fayetteville Semi-Weekly Observer*, June 16, 1864; *Jackson Clarion-Ledger*, June 11, 1864.

44. Roche, "Bloody Angle"; Rhea, *Battles*, 269; Clark, *Glance Backward*, 52; Gallagher, *Spotsylvania Campaign*, 90.

45. Roche, "Bloody Angle"; Clark, *Glance Backward*, 52; Dunlop, *Lee's Sharpshooters*, 467–68; Rhea, *Battles*, 269.

46. Nathaniel Harris–General, August 2, 1866, Harris Letter, FSNMP; *SHSP*, vol. 8, 105; *Natchez Weekly Democrat*, May 18, 1868; Evans, *16th Mississippi*, 252; Roche, "Bloody Angle."

47. Nathaniel Harris–General, August 2, 1866, Harris Letter, FSNMP; *SOR*, vol. 6, 698; Yeary, *Reminiscences*, 148; *Meridian Daily Clarion*, June 13, 1864; Holt, *Mississippi Rebel*, 255; *Richmond Dispatch*, June 8, 1902; Roche, "Bloody Angle."

48. *SHSP*, vol. 8, 107; vol. 14, 531; Nathaniel Harris–General, August 2, 1866, Harris Letter, FSNMP; Brown, *Colonel*, 271; Evans, *16th Mississippi*, 253; *Wilmington Morning Star*, May 7, 1880.

49. Davis, *Confederate General*, vol. 3, 65, 66; Gallagher, *Spotsylvania Campaign*, 93; *Vicksburg Evening Post*, August 31, 1900.

50. Young, *Lee's Army*, 246; Roche, "Bloody Angle"; Evans, *16th Mississippi*, 256; *OR*, 36, pt. 1, 1091, 1092.

51. Evans, *16th Mississippi*, 256; Roche, "Bloody Angle"; Krick, *Lee's Colonels*, 40; *Vicksburg Daily Times*, November 23, 1866.

52. *OR*, 36, pt. 1, 1092; *SOR*, vol. 6, 698; Dobbins, *Grandfather's Journal*, 194; Ott, "Civil War Diary," 193; *Jackson Clarion-Ledger*, June 13, 1864; Gallagher, *Spotsylvania Campaign*, 93.

53. *OR*, 36, pt. 1, 1092; Nathaniel Harris–General, August 2, 1866, Harris Letter, FSNMP; *Jackson Clarion-Ledger*, June 13, 1864; Evans, *16th Mississippi*, 256; Washburn, *Complete Military History*, 72.

54. Nathaniel Harris–General, August 2, 1866, Harris Letter, FSNMP; Roche, "Bloody Angle"; Yeary, *Reminiscences*, 148; Gallagher, *Spotsylvania Campaign*, 99.

55. *OR*, 36, pt. 1, 1092; Hinton, *Historical Sketch*, 66; Roche, "Bloody Angle"; Gallagher, *Spotsylvania Campaign*, 99; Rhea, *Battles*, 271; Mackowski and White, "Battle," 45.

56. *Meridian Daily Clarion*, June 13, 1864; *SOR*, vol. 6, 700; *Richmond Enquirer*, May 17, 1864; Hinton, *Historical Sketch*, 66.

57. *Richmond Times-Dispatch*, May 22, 1904; Gallagher, *Spotsylvania Campaign*, 98; Pfanz, *Letters*, 298.

58. *OR*, 36, pt. 1, 1092; Nathaniel Harris–General, August 2, 1866, Harris Letter, FSNMP; Hinton, *Historical Sketch*, 66.

59. *OR*, 31, pt. 1, 1093; Caldwell, *History*, 140; *Newberry Herald and News*, July 16, 1909; Rhea, *Carrying the Flag*, 175; Gallagher, *Spotsylvania Campaign*, 95; *CV*, vol. 33, 376.

60. Davis, *Confederate General*, vol. 3, 41–43; Brown, *Colonel*, 93; *CV*, vol. 33, 376.

61. Gallagher, *Spotsylvania Campaign*, 99; Rhea, *Carrying the Flag*, 86, 88; Davis, *Confederate General*, vol. 4, 122–23; Tedards, *Orr's Rifles*, 48.

62. *Anderson Intelligencer*, July 17, 1895.

63. *OR*, 36, pt. 1, 1093; *Augusta Chronicle*, August 14, 1898; Gallagher, *Spotsylvania Campaign*, 95; Rhea, *Battles*, 273; Young, *Lee's Army*, 246.

64. *Augusta Chronicle*, August 14, 1898; *OR*, 36, pt. 1, 1093; Brown, *Colonel*, 94; Caldwell, *History*, 1140–41; Gallagher, *Spotsylvania Campaign*, 95; Rhea, *Battles*, 273.

65. *Augusta Chronicle*, August 14, 1898; *OR*, 36, pt. 1, 1093; Caldwell, *History*, 141; Rhea, *Carrying the Flag*, 207, 208; *Anderson Intelligencer*, May 4, 1882.

66. Caldwell, *History*, 141; *OR*, 36, pt. 1, 1093; *Newberry Herald and News*, July 16, 1909; *Augusta Chronicle*, August 14, 1898; *Anderson Intelligencer*, May 4, 1882.

67. Gallagher, *Spotsylvania Campaign*, 99; Rhea, *Carrying the Flag*, 210, 211; Krick, *Lee's Colonels*, 92; *Augusta Chronicle*, August 14, 1898; *Newberry Herald and News*, July 16, 1909; Rhea, *Battles*, 274.

68. Brown, *Colonel*, 127; *Yorkville Enquirer*, May 25, 1864; *Abbeville Press and Banner*, May 10, 1876; Krick, *Lee's Colonels*, 66; Craig, *Upcountry*, 133.

69. *Abbeville Press and Banner*, May 10, 1876.

70. Rhea, *Carrying the Flag*, 211, 214; Gallagher, *Spotsylvania Campaign*, 102; Caldwell, *History*, 141; *Charleston Daily Courier*, May 28, 1864.

71. *Charleston Daily Courier*, May 28, 1864; Caldwell, *History*, 143.

72. Brown, *Colonel*, 121, 122, 137; *Laurens Advertiser*, August 6, 1895; Gallagher, *Spotsylvania Campaign*, 100.

73. Brown, *Colonel*, 95, 96, 122; Charles E. Whilden–[Brother], May 14, 1864, Whilden Papers, SCHS; Krick, *Lee's Colonels*, 345; Caldwell, *History*, 146, 149; *Charleston Daily Courier*, May 28, 1864; *Anderson Intelligencer*, May 4, 1882.

74. Rhea, *Carrying the Flag*, 72, 80, 215; *Yorkville Enquirer*, May 22, 1879; Gallagher, *Spotsylvania Campaign*, 99.

75. Rhea, *Carrying the Flag*, 216; Gallagher, *Spotsylvania Campaign*, 99, 100.

76. Gallagher, *Spotsylvania Campaign*, 100; *Augusta Chronicle*, August 14, 1898.

77. Harry Hammond–My Dear Wife, May 15, 1864, Hammond-Bryan-Cumming Family Papers, USC; *Manning Times*, June 1, 1904; Caldwell, *History*, 145.

78. Best, *History*, 144; Keiser, Diary, AHEC; *OR*, 36, pt. 1, 669, and pt. 2, 642; Ward, *96th Pennsylvania*, 248.

79. *OR*, 36, pt. 1, 669; Emory Upton–My dear Colonel, April 26, 1879, Upton Papers, BU; Ward, *96th Pennsylvania*, 248; Best, "Through the Wilderness," UM.

80. *OR*, 36, pt. 1, 669; Rhea, *Battles*, 275–76.

81. *OR*, 36, pt. 1, 669; Emory Upton–My Dear Colonel, April 26, 1879, Upton Papers, BU; Ward, *96th Pennsylvania*, 248; *Marion Star*, October 6, 1896.

82. *OR*, 36, pt. 1, 669; *Marion Star*, October 6, 1896; Rhea, *Battles*, 276.

83. Rhea, *Battles*, 276; Edwards, Memoir, 155, ALPLM; Roe, *Tenth Regiment*, 276–77.

84. *OR*, 36, pt. 1, 669; Edwards, "War Reminiscences," BHS; *Herkimer County Journal*, June 2, 1864; *Bethel News*, June 9, 1897; Best, "Through the Wilderness," UM; Keiser, Diary, AHEC; Rhea, *Battles*, 276–77; Luckenbill, Diary, AHEC.

85. *OR*, 36, pt. 1, 669; Best, "Through the Wilderness," UM; Ward, *96th Pennsylvania*, 248; *Herkimer County Journal*, June 2, 1864; Morse, *Personal Experiences*, 89–90; *Muncie Star Press*, September 3, 1911.

86. *OR*, 36, pt. 1, 661; Hess, *Trench Warfare*, 72; Rhea, *Battles*, 267, 277

87. *OR*, 36, pt. 1, 144, 661; *SOR*, vol. 6, 612; Chadwick, *Brother*, 227; Baquet, *History*, 124; Haines, *History*, 174–76.

88. *Akron Daily Democrat*, June 4, 1895; Haines, *History*, 176, 178.

89. *OR*, 36, pt. 1, 411, 416, 421, 425, 669; Rhea, *Battles*, 267, 277; Muffly, *Story*, 902; Best, *History*, 145.

90. John C. Tidball Letter, n.d., Record Group 94, NA; *SOR*, vol. 6, 556; *OR*, 36, pt. 1, 509, 524, 765, 767, 770, 771, 772; Mackowski and White, "Battle," 56–57.

91. *OR*, 36, pt. 1, 537, 539, 669; Best, "Through the Wilderness," UM; Baquet, *History*, 124; Best, *History*, 145; *Muncie Star Press*, September 3, 1911.

92. Edwards, Memoir, 155, ALPLM; *Jackson Clarion-Ledger*, June 13, 1864; Washburn, *Complete Military History*, 72.

Chapter 9

1. Wert, *Sword*, 335, 336, 338, 345.

2. Wert, *Sword*, 329, 330; Warner, *Generals in Blue*, 541–42.

3. Lowe, *Meade's Army*, 356.

4. Wert, *Sword*, 320–21, Livermore, *Days and Events*, 304.

5. Rhea, *Battles*, 58, 59, 65, 129–30; Judson, *History*, 199.

6. *OR*, 36, pt. 2, 638, 661, 662, 666, 667; Rhea, *Battles*, 282.

7. *OR*, 36, pt. 2, 662; Rhea, *Battles*, 283; Wert, *Brotherhood*, 298.

8. *OR*, 36, pt. 1, 562, 1066; Rhea, *Battles*, 283.

9. Rhea, *Battles*, 284; *OR*, 36, pt. 1, 1066, and pt. 2, 663.

10. Rhea, *Battles*, 284.

11. Humphreys, *Virginia Campaign*, 101; Howe, *Touched with Fire*, 116.

12. *OR*, 36, pt. 2, 663, 664.

13. Small, *Road*, 139.

14. Small, *Road*, 139; *OR*, 36, pt. 1, 554; Bennett, *Sons*, 437; Cassedy, *Dear Friends*, 463.

15. Cassedy, *Dear Friends*, 463; *OR*, 36, pt. 1, 1066; *SHSP*, vol. 8, 548; Bennett, *Sons*, 437.

16. *OR*, 36, pt. 2, 669, 670; Rhea, *Battles*, 287, 288.

17. Wert, *Brotherhood*, 298; *OR*, 36, pt. 1, 611, 620, 625; Chamberlin, *History*, 238.

18. Chamberlin, *History*, 237, 238; Rhea, *Battles*, 287; Davis, *Three Years*, 340; *OR*, 36, pt. 1, 611.

19. *OR*, 36, pt. 2, 664, 671.

20. *SHSP*, vol. 20, 547–48; Krick, *Parker's Virginia Battery*, 248; *OR*, 36, pt. 1, 1057; Hagood, Memoirs, 152, USC.

21. Humphreys, *Virginia Campaign*, 101n3; *OR*, 36, pt. 1, 541; Jordan, "Happiness," 151–52.

22. *OR*, 36, pt. 2, 654.

23. *OR*, 36, pt. 1, 68, 360, 541; pt. 2, 665.

24. OR, 36, pt. 1, 68.

25. Grant, *Personal Memoirs*, vol. 2, 216, 232; Porter, *Campaigning with Grant*, 108.

26. Rhea, *Battles*, 289–90.

27. Rhea, *Battles*, 289; Wert, *Sword*, 343, 354.

28. *OR*, 36, pt. 1, 112, 128, 198; Young, *Lee's Army*, 244–46; Ricketts, Diary, MNBP.

29. Lowe, *Meade's Army*, 155; Warner, *Generals in Blue*, 403–4.

30. Lowe, *Meade's Army*, 155.

31. *OR*, 36, pt. 1, 146; Ricketts, Diary, MNBP; *Cincinnati Enquirer*, May 16, 1914.

32. *Washington National Tribune*, October 20, 1887; Ricketts, Diary, MNBP; *OR*, 36, pt. 1, 749.

33. *OR*, 36, pt. 1, 725; Ricketts, Diary, MNBP; Peter Vredenburgh–My Dear Father, May 15, 1864, Vredenburgh Letters, MCHA; Edwin C. Hall-Parents, May 17, 1864, Hall Papers, VHS.

34. *New York Times*, May 18, 1864; Walker, *General Hancock*, 200; Seymour, *Civil War Memoirs*, 126.

35. Silliker, *Rebel Yell*, 157; Francis E. Rew–My dear Parents, May 12, 1864, Rew Civil War Letters, RNBP; Hess, *Union Soldier*, 22.

36. Reid-Green, *Letters Home*, 20; Faust, *This Republic*, 32.

37. Faust, *This Republic*, 33, 35, 37, 41, 59; Carmichael, *War*, 72, 135, 149.

38. Silliker, *Rebel Yell*, 157; Wert, *Sword*, 111.

39. Lane, "Some Recollections," SANC; William R. Rutherford–My own Darling, May 16, 1864, Rutherford Papers, USC; Caldwell, *History*, 143.

40. *OR*, 36, pt. 1, 669, 679; Stevens, *Three Years*, 334; Brown, *Colonel*, 248; *PMHSM*, vol. 4, 268, 269; *Abbeville Press and Banner*, September 25, 1878; *Edgefield Advertiser*, June 1, 1864; Edwards, Memoir, 146, 147, ALPLM.

41. *Boston Globe*, May 12, 1914.

42. *Anderson Intelligencer*, August 18, 1897.

43. Hyde, *Following the Greek Cross*, 201; Jones, *Lee's Tigers*, 206.

44. Caldwell, *History*, 145.

45. *Columbia Guardian*, May 26, 1864; *Newberry Herald and News*, January 9, 1903; *Anderson Intelligencer*, May 4, 1882; Brown, *Colonel*, 122.

46. Michael F. Rinker–Father and Mother, May 17, 1864, Rinker Letter, VMI.

47. *Montpelier Morning Journal*, July 2, 1910; Coffin, *Battered Stars*, 175; *Springfield Reporter*, February 16, 1894.

48. *OR*, 36, pt. 1, 684, 685; Ward, *96th Pennsylvania*, 253; Watkins, Memoir, FSNMP; Keiser, Diary, AHEC; *Jackson Clarion-Ledger*, June 13, 1864.

49. *Boston Globe*, September 3, 1911; Stevens, *Three Years*, 335, 336; *OR*, 36, pt. 1, 669.

50. Adams, *Memorial*, 148; *OR*, 36, pt. 1, 669; Watkins, Memoir, FSNMP.

51. Watkins, Memoir, FSNMP.

52. Coffin, *Battered Stars*, 175; Brown, *Colonel*, 285; Edwards, Memoir, 148, 149, ALPLM.

53. Roche, "Bloody Angle."

54. *Wilmington Journal*, November 8, 1867; *Abbeville Press and Banner*, September 25, 1878; Muffly, *Story*, 262; *Columbia Democrat*, July 2, 1864.

55. Chase, Memoirs, 105–6, FSNMP; Francis Asbury Wayne Jr.–Mother, May 17, 1864, Atkinson Collection, UNC.

56. McAllister, *Civil War Letters*, 420; Cudworth, *History*, 471.

57. *Philadelphia Weekly Times*, February 20, 1886; *OR*, 36, pt. 1, 491; Charles E. Whilden–[Brother], May 15, 1864, Whilden Papers, SCHA.

58. *Philadelphia Weekly Times*, February 20, 1886.

59. *Anderson Intelligencer*, May 4, 1882.

60. *Anderson Intelligencer*, May 4, 1882, May 31, 1905.

61. *Wilmington Journal*, November 8, 1867; Tyler, *Recollections*, 192; Williams, *From Spotsylvania*, 6; Nathaniel Harris–General, August 2, 1866, Harris Letter, FSNMP; *Port Gibson Weekly Standard*, November 18, 1865.

62. Tyler, *Recollections*, 177; Benson, *Berry Benson's Civil War Book*, 77.

63. Mackowski and White, "Battle," 57; Muffly, *Story*, 262, 860; Bowan, Diary, AHEC.

64. Bruce, *Twentieth Regiment*, 378; Robertson, *Personal Recollections*, 105; *OR*, 36, pt. 1, 371.

65. Simons, *Regimental History*, 208; Ward, *History*, 250; Ernsberger, *Paddy Owen's Regulars*, vol. 2, 814.

66. Ernsberger, *Paddy Owen's Regulars*, vol. 2, 814; Lash, *"Duty Well Done,"* 392–93; Waitt, *History*, 310.

67. Waitt, *History*, 309.

68. Waitt, *History*, 310.

69. Waitt, *History*, 308, 309, 312; Wheelan, *Bloody Spring*, 213.

70. Galwey, *Valiant Hours*, 212.

71. Welch, *Boy General*, 119.

72. Memoir, Kirk Papers, MSU.

73. Muffly, *Story*, 708, 718.

74. *OR*, 36, pt. 1, 379; *SHSP*, vol. 32, 213, 214; Mackowski and White, "Battle," 58.

75. Waitt, *History*, 310; *SHSP*, vol. 32, 213; Riggs, *13th Virginia Infantry*, 49.

76. *SHSP*, vol. 32, 207; *Richmond Times-Dispatch*, December 11, 1904.

77. Worsham, *Foot Cavalry*, 138–39.

78. Stephens, *Intrepid Warrior*, 396.

79. John C. Tidball Letter, n.d., Record Group 94, NA; *OR*, 36, pt. 1, 534, 1045; *SOR*, vol. 6, 567; Mackowski and White, "Battle," 59; *Pittsburgh Post-Gazette*, May 12, 1914; Rhodes, *History*, 282, 284.

80. *OR*, 36, pt. 1, 1045, 1087; Gallagher, *Fighting For*, 376; Personal Diary of Movements kept from June 1st 1863 to May 4, 1865, Alexander Papers, UNC.

81. Memoir, vol. 9, Alexander Papers, UNC; *SOR*, vol. 6, 542.

82. Caldwell, *History*, 143; *Jackson Clarion-Ledger*, June 11, 1864; Rhea, *Carrying the Flag*, 223; *OR*, 36, pt. 1, 373; Brown, *Colonel*, 100–101, 104–5; *Pickens Keowee Courier*, August 31, 1910.

83. Caldwell, *History*, 144; Tedards, *Orr's Rifles*, 57, 58; Morse, *Personal Experiences*, 90, 91; *Anderson Intelligencer*, July 17, 1895; *Laurens Advertiser*, August 6, 1895.

84. Roche, "Bloody Angle"; Gallagher, *Spotsylvania Campaign*, 107–8.

85. Rhea, *Battles*, 296; James H. Lane–Sir, October 6, 1904, Carrington Manuscript, DU.

86. Alexander, Memoir, 1, SANC; Hardy, *General Lee's Immortals*, 280.

87. Alexander, Memoir, 1, SANC; Hardy, *General Lee's Immortals*, 280, 281; *Monroe Journal*, October 29, 1912.

88. Alexander, Memoir, 1–2, SANC; Lane's Report, September 16, 1864, Lane Papers, LC; Hardy, *General Lee's Immortals*, 281, 282.

89. Lane's Report, September 16, 1864, Lane Papers, LC; *Monroe Journal*, October 29, 1912; *SHSP*, vol. 9, 147; Rhea, *Battles*, 296; Young, *Lee's Army*, 246; *OR*, 36, pt. 1, 113, 114, 915.

90. Lane's Report, September 16, 1864, Lane Papers, LC; *Warrenton Indicator*, October 2, 1867; *SHSP*, vol. 9, 147, 149; James H. Lane–Sir, October 6, 1900, Carrington Manuscript, DU.

91. *OR*, 36, pt. 1, 944; pt. 2, 679; Scott, *Forgotten Valor*, 520.

92. *OR*, 36, pt. 1, 909, 910; Rhea, *Battles*, 295.

93. *OR*, 36, pt. 1, 910, 944; Charles Mills–Dearest Mother, May 15, 1864, Mills Papers, AHEC.

94. *OR*, 36, pt. 1, 939, 941, 944, 954, 973; Sauers, *Civil War Journal*, 202.

95. Lane's Report, September 16, 1864, Lane Papers, LC; *SHSP*, vol. 9, 148; *OR*, 36, pt. 1, 950, 958.

96. *OR*, 36, pt. 1, 950, 958; *SHSP*, vol. 9, 148; *Lake Geneva Herald*, May 31, 1895.

97. *OR*, 36, pt. 1, 950, 964; Sauers, *Civil War Journal*, 202–4; Parker, *History*, 548.

98. *SHSP*, vol. 9, 148, 149; Clark, *Histories*, vol. 2, 667; Rhea, *Battles*, 298.

99. Lane Report, September 16, 1864, Lane Papers, LC; *OR*, 36, pt. 1, 939, 941.

100. Floyd, Memoir, 11, VHS; Lane Report, September 16, 1864, Lane Papers, LC; *Richmond Dispatch*, May 16, 1864; *Monroe Journal*, October 29, 1912; *SHSP*, vol. 9, 150; Lane, Memoir, FSNMP.

101. Lane Report, September 16, 1864, Lane Papers, LC; *SOR*, vol. 6, 741; *OR*, 36, pt. 1, 969; Frederick Lehman–Parents, May 15, 1864, Lehman Family Papers, UM; *Camden Confederate*, June 8, 1864.

102. Rhea, *Battles*, 299; Sale, Diary, FSNMP; Bernard, *Civil War Talks*, 223.

103. Crater, *History*, 56–57; *Camden Confederate*, June 8, 1864.

104. *OR*, 36, pt. 1, 969; Bernard, *Civil War Talks*, 223; Henderson, *41st Virginia Infantry*, 61; Phillips, Memoir, 48, VHS; Trask, *61st Virginia Infantry*, 21; Krick, *Lee's Colonels*, 291.

105. Rhea, *Battles*, 299; *SOR*, vol. 6, 743, 745; Young, *Lee's Army*, 298, 304; *OR*, 36, pt. 1, 944.

106. *Statesville Record and Landmark*, September 14, 1893.

107. *Statesville Record and Landmark*, September 14, 1893; *Charlotte Observer*, September 3, 1893.

108. Major Joseph A. Engelhard–Col., May 20, 1864, Lane Papers, AU; Lane's Report, September 16, 1864, Lane Papers, LC; James H. Lane–Sir, October 6, 1900, Carrington Manuscript, DU; *SOR*, vol. 6, 744; William Mahone–Col., May 20, 1864, Wilcox Papers, LC; Clark, *Histories*, vol. 4, 475.

109. Rhea, *Battles*, 299; Battle of Spotsylvania Court House May 1864, 69, McDowell Papers, PSU; Bunker, Memoir, 7, UM; Charles Mills–Mother, May 15, 1864, Mills Papers, AHEC.

110. Rhea, *Battles*, 302; Grant, *Personal Memoirs*, vol. 2, 232.

Chapter 10

1. *Edgefield Advertiser*, June 1, 1864; *OR*, 36, pt. 1, 122, 128, 198; Young, *Lee's Army*, 245, 246.

2. Steplyk, *Fighting*, 7, 8, 53; Hess, *Union Soldier*, 108; Carmichael, *War*, 141, 149.

3. Hess, *Union Soldier*, 94, 95, 111, 114, 197, 223.

4. *Edgefield Advertiser*, June 1, 1864.

5. Holt, *Mississippi Rebel*, 262.

6. *Charleston Daily Courier*, May 28, 1864.

7. Nathaniel Harris–General, August 2, 1866, Harris Letter, FSNMP; Krick, *Civil War Weather*, 129.

8. *SHSP*, vol. 7, 537; vol. 32, 208–9; *Richmond Times-Dispatch*, December 11, 1904; Phillips, Civil War Diary, VMI.

9. *OR*, 36, pt. 1, 555, 611; pt. 2, 665.

10. *OR*, 36, pt. 1, 555, 611; pt. 2, 656; Rhea, *Battles*, 302; Grant, *Personal Memoirs*, vol. 2, 229, 223; Lowe, *Meade's Army*, 155, 157; Porter, *Campaigning with Grant*, 109; John Cummings–Author, June 26, 2021, electronic message, Wert, Personal Collection.

11. Grant, *Personal Memoirs*, vol. 2, 233, 234; Porter, *Campaigning with Grant*, 109; Lowe, *Meade's Army*, 156.

12. *OR*, 36, pt. 2, 656, 673; Holmes, *Touched with Fire*, 115.

13. *OR*, 36, pt. 1, 611, 612, 617, 625, 626, and pt. 2, 674.

14. *OR*, 36, pt. 1, 611, 612, 617, 625, 626, and pt. 2, 674, 675; Rhea, *Battles*, 303.

15. *OR*, 36, pt. 1, 4.

16. *OR*, 36, pt. 1, 4, 1003; Gallagher, *Spotsylvania Campaign*, 101; Greiner et al., *Surgeon's Civil War*, 188.

17. Cudworth, *History*, 471; *Glimpses*, vol. 4, 306; Wiggins, "Some Incidents," SANC.

18. *Richmond Times-Dispatch*, March 19, 1905; *OR*, 36, pt. 1, 1092; Murphey, "Sketch," 55, BPL; Hess, *Union Soldier*, 69; *Raleigh State Chronicle*, May 19, 1891.

19. Welch, *Confederate Surgeon's Letters*, 96; Washburn, *Complete Military History*, 73.

20. Silliker, *Rebel Yell*, 153; King et al., *History*, 73; Marvel, *Race*, 216; newspaper article, n.d., Edwards Papers, FSNMP; *Indiana Weekly Messenger*, August 21, 1919.

21. Holt, *Mississippi Rebel*, 259; Gallagher, *Spotsylvania Campaign*, 92.

22. Porter, *Campaigning with Grant*, 110; Robertson, *Personal Recollections*, 106; Weygant, *History*, 325; *OR*, 36, pt. 1, 1094; *Vermont Union*, January 18, 1896.

23. Porter, *Campaigning with Grant*, 110; Benson, *Berry Benson's Civil War Book*, 77; Battle of Spotsylvania Court House May 1864, 68, McDowell Papers, PSU; *Southern Watchman*, June 1, 1864.

24. Craig and Baker, *As You May Never See*, 78; *Philadelphia Times*, December 17, 1891; Benson, *Berry Benson's Civil War Book*, 76; Benjamin Brown–Sir, May 24, 1905, Confederate Veteran Papers, DU.

25. Johnston, *Civil War Letters*, 28.

26. Craig and Baker, *As You May Never See*, 78; Evans, *16th Mississippi*, 262; McAllister, *Civil War Letters*, 419; Jones, *Campbell Brown's Civil War*, 255.

27. Wallace, *5th Virginia Infantry*, 138; Mackowski and White, *Season*, 93.

28. Wheelan, *Bloody Spring*, 216.

29. Walker, *History*, 474; *Burlington Free Press*, July 2, 1892; Muffly, *Story*, 819.

30. *Greensboro Record*, August 6, 1903; George Ring–My Own Darling, May 15, 1864, Ring Papers, TU.

31. Bowen, *History*, 296, 297; Keiser, Diary, AHEC.

32. *Monongahela Valley Republican*, July 7, 1887; *Boston Globe*, September 3, 1911; Westbrook, *History*, 198.

33. *OR*, 36, pt. 1, 1092; *SOR*, vol. 6, 699, 700; Yeary, *Reminiscences*, 149; Dobbins, *Grandfather's Journal*, 194, 195; Clark, *Glance Backward*, 53.

34. Phillips, Civil War Diary, VMI; *SOR*, vol. 6, 522.

35. *Monongahela Valley Republican*, July 7, 1887; Hess, *Union Soldier*, 78; Holt, *Mississippi Rebel*, 260.

36. Caldwell, *History*, 147; Brown, *Colonel*, 98.

37. *OR*, 36, pt. 2, 660; Ernsberger, *Paddy Owen's Regulars*, vol. 2, 818; Daniel L. Bovee–Friends, June 9, 1864, Bovee Letter, AHEC; *CV*, vol. 34, 8; *Muncie Star Press*, September 3, 1911; Washburn, *Complete Military History*, 72.

38. *OR*, 36, pt. 1, 112, 620, 626; Edwards, Memoir, 150–54, ALPLM; Rhea, *Battles*, 305, 306; *Muncie Star Press*, September 3, 1911.

39. Edwards, Memoir, 152, 153, ALPLM; Rhea, *Battles*, 305.

40. Brown, *Colonel*, 98; *SOR*, vol. 6, 522; Parrish, *Wiregrass*, 185; Caldwell, *History*, 147; *Montpelier Examiner*, June 27, 1896.

41. Bowen, Diary, FSNMP.

42. Rhea, *Battles*, 92, 109; Benjamin Brown–Sir, May 24, 1905, Confederate Veteran Papers, DU; *New Bern Times*, November 10, 1865; *Abbeville Press and Banner*, September 25, 1878; *Opelousas Courier*, December 2, 1878; *CV*, vol. 22, 473; vol. 33, 128; Bloodgood, *Personal Reminiscences*, 255; *Richmond Examiner*, June 1, 1864.

43. Dunn, *Harvestfields*, 240; Chesson, *Journal*, 152.

44. Gallagher, *Spotsylvania Campaign*, 82; Charles M. Miller–My Dear Sir, February 23, 1905, Daniel Papers, UVA; *Buffalo Sunday Morning News*, May 19, 1912; Johnston, *Civil War Letters*, 29; Casler, *Four Years*, 213.

45. Casler, *Four Years*, 213, 214.

46. *PMHSM*, vol. 4, 237; Graham, "Report," FSNMP.

47. Cadmus Wilcox–Brother, December 17, 1864 [?], Wilcox Papers, LC; Swisher, *Warrior in Gray*, 181; Gales, Diary, FSNMP; Caldwell, *History*, 147.

48. *Columbus Weekly Dispatch*, June 6, 1907; Holt, *Mississippi Rebel*, 257; Johnston, *Civil War Letters*, 28.

49. Evans, *16th Mississippi*, 262; *Augusta Chronicle*, August 14, 1898.

50. Tazewell, *Clinch Valley News*, May 6, 1921.

51. Rhea, *Battles*, 308, 309; *OR*, 36, pt. 2, 724.

52. *OR*, 36, pt. 2, 724; Dana, *Recollections*, 197.

53. Rhea, *Battles*, 310; *OR*, 36, pt. 2, 703, 704.

54. *OR*, 36, pt. 1, 448; pt. 2, 704; Cowtan, *Services*, 256, 270; Murphey, *History*, 159; Sawyer, *Military History*, 168.

55. *OR*, 36, pt. 2, 704, 713, 724; Rhea, *Battles*, 310.

56. *OR*, 36, pt. 1, 337, 541; pt. 2, 705, 717, 718, 726; Rhea, *Battles*, 310.

57. Keiser, Diary, AHEC; Tyler, *Recollections*, 195–96.

58. *New York Times*, May 18, 1864; *Southern Watchman*, June 1, 1864; Ward, *96th Pennsylvania*, 255; Longacre, *To Gettysburg*, 205; *Harrisburg Daily Independent*, July 18, 1895.

59. *PMHSM*, vol. 4, 256, 262, 270, 271; Muffly, *Story*, 263; Peter Vredenburgh–My Dear Father, May 15, 1864, Vredenburgh Letters, MCHA; Best, "Through the Wilderness," UM; Blight, *When This Cruel War*, 296.

60. *Boston Globe*, May 13, 1914; William White–My Darling Wife, May 17, 1864, White Correspondence, VTHS; Luckenbill, Diary, AHEC; Muffly, *Story*, 175.

61. Howe, *Touched with Fire*, 116, 117; Morse, *Personal Experiences*, 92; *Philadelphia Weekly Times*, February 2, 1886; Mackowski and White, "Battle," 49; Edward "Ned" Russell–My dear sisters, May 15, 1864, Russell Letters, FSNMP.

62. *OR*, 36, pt. 1, 360; Chase, Memoirs, 106, FSNMP; *Indiana Democrat*, March 10, 1897; Oestreich, *Journal*, 48, AHEC.

63. Amos B. Stanton–My own Dear wife, May 12, 1864, Stanton Letter, FSNMP; Welch, *Boy General*, 121; Lowe, *Meade's Army*, 156; *Muncie Star Press*, September 3, 1911; Ward, *96th Pennsylvania*, 255; Corby, *Memoirs*, 91; *Lexington Herald-Leader*, September 3, 1911.

64. McAllister, *Civil War Letters*, 420; Riggs, *13th Virginia Infantry*, 49; *Mobile Advertiser and Register*, May 28, 1864; Roche, "Bloody Angle."

65. Allan, Memoir, vol. 9, Allan Papers, UNC; Brown, *Colonel*, 256; Smith, *Anson Guards*, 239; Nichols, *Soldier's Story*, 156; Mackowski and White, "Battle," 64; *Richmond Enquirer*, May 20, 1864; *Anderson Intelligencer*, February 7, 1906; Robert Dunlap–Mother, May 20, 1864, Dunlap Family Letters, VMI; *Washington Weekly Post*, June 27, 1899.

66. Gallagher, *Spotsylvania Campaign*, 114; Coffin, *Battered Stars*, 181; Samuel Brooks–My Dear Wife, May 20, 1864, Brooks Correspondence, AHEC.

67. Edward "Ned" Russell–My dear sisters, May 15, 1864, Russell Letters, FSNMP; *Sheffield and Rotterdam Independent*, June 4, 1864; G. W. Holstein–My dear Abby, May 22, 1864, Holstein Papers, HSMC.

68. *OR*, 36, pt. 1, 230, 231; Woolsey, *Hospital Days*, 150; Bunker, Memoir, 7–8, UM.

69. *OR*, 36, pt. 1, 230, 231.

70. Woolsey, *Hospital Days*, 150; *Fremont Weekly Journal*, May 27, 1864; G. W. Holstein–My dear Abby, May 22, 1864, Holstein Papers, HSMC.

71. The calculation of Union casualties is based on *OR*, 30, pt. 1, 137–49, 246, and pt. 2, 661; *PMHSM*, vol. 4, 251; Rhea, *Battles*, 311; Walker, *History*, 475, 476.

72. Young, *Lee's Army*, 235–36, 244–305; Rhea, *Battles*, 176, 312; Osborne, *Civil War Diaries*, 138; *Jackson Clarion Ledger*, June 13, 1864; Wiggins, "Some Incidents," SANC; *Montgomery Daily Advertiser*, May 30, 1864; *Wilmington Journal*, July 12, 1867; Diary, Ardrey Papers, DU; *Milledgeville Southern Recorder*, June 14, 1864.

73. *Salisbury Watchman*, May 30, 1864.

Chapter 11

1. Catton, *Grant Takes Command*, 239.
2. Gallagher, *Spotsylvania Campaign*, 82.

3. *PMHSM*, vol. 4, 257, 276; *OR*, 36, pt. 1, 635.

4. *PMHSM*, vol. 4, 249.

5. *PMHSM*, vol. 4, 249, 258; Rhea, *Battles*, 314.

6. Wheelan, *Bloody Spring*, 219; Mackowski and White, "Battle," 50; Rhea, *Battles*, 314.

7. *PMHSM*, vol. 4, 258.

8. Lowe, *Meade's Army*, 155–56; *PMHSM*, vol. 4, 258; Cozzens, *B&L*, vol. 5, 490.

9. Cozzens, *B&L*, vol. 5, 490.

10. Matter, *If It Takes All Summer*, 345; Rhea, *Battles*, 314.

11. Lowe, *Meade's Army*, 155; Rhea, *Battles*, 315.

12. Rhea, *Battles*, 315, 316; Wert, *Sword*, 357.

13. Wert, *Sword*, 357; Wheelan, *Bloody Spring*, 219; Rhea, *Battles*, 316; Lowe, *Meade's Army*, 155; *OR*, 36, pt. 2, 656–59.

14. Rhea, *Battles*, 316; *PMHSM*, vol. 4, 258.

15. Rhea, *Battles*, 315; Dana, *Recollections*, 191; Wert, *Sword*, 357.

16. *OR*, 36, pt. 2, 643, 654; Wert, *Sword*, 357; Rhea, *Battles*, 316.

17. *OR*, 36, pt. 2, 643, 677–80; Rhea, *Battles*, 317; Wert, *Sword*, 357; Grant, *Personal Memoirs*, vol. 2, 232.

18. *OR*, 36, pt. 1, 339; pt. 2, 703; Warner, *Generals in Blue*, 338; Rhea, *Battles*, 319.

19. Warner, *Generals in Blue*, 33, 42, 46, 73, 139, 183, 212, 323, 466, 520; John M. Lovejoy–My Dear Mother, May 17, 1864, Lovejoy Letters, CU.

20. Wert, *Sword*, 357; Rhea, *Battles*, 317, 318.

21. *OR*, 36, pt. 1, 18, and pt. 2, 695; Warner, *Generals in Blue*, 317, 644; Meade, *Life and Letters*, vol. 2, 197; Rhea, *Battles*, 318; Wert, *Sword*, 357.

22. Swinton, *Campaigns*, 453, 454; Wilkeson, *Recollections*, 87; Gallagher, *Spotsylvania Campaign*, 183, 184; Wert, *Sword*, 357, 358; William White–My blessed one, May 16, 1864, White Correspondence, VTHS.

23. *Charlotte Democrat*, May 24, 1864.

24. Carmichael, *Audacity*, 59; Hess, *Trench Warfare*, 68.

25. Rhea, *Battles*, 220; *SHSP*, vol. 33, 24; Gallagher, *Spotsylvania Campaign*, 87.

26. *Edgefield Advertiser*, June 1, 1864; *Mobile Advertiser and Register*, May 28, 1864; *National Tribune Scrapbook*, 70.

27. William D. Rutherford–My own darling, May 16, 1864, Rutherford Papers, USC; Long, *Memoirs*, 344.

28. *Richmond Dispatch*, May 16, 1864; *Richmond Times-Dispatch*, March 19, 1905; Robert D. Johnston–Dear Senator Daniel, June 30, 1905, Daniel Papers, UVA.

29. See chapters 6–10.

30. Brown, *Colonel*, 271; Hinton, *Historical Sketch*, 67–68; *PMHSM*, vol. 4, 65.

31. Harry Hammond–My Dear Wife, May 15, 1864, Hammond-Bryan-Cumming Family Papers, USC; Krick, *14th South Carolina Infantry*, 22; *Wilmington Journal*, November 8, 1867.

32. Kundahl, *Bravest*, 220, 221; Bryan Grimes–My Dearest Wife, May 14, 1864, Grimes Papers, UNC; Gallagher, *Stephen Dodson Ramseur*, 112.

33. Davis, *Confederate General*, vol. 5, 75, 108, 109; *Richmond Times-Dispatch*, May 22, 1904

34. John Gordon–John Daniel, n.d., Daniel Papers, UVA; Freeman, *Lee's Lieutenants*, vol. 3, xxxiv, xl, 448.

35. Freeman, *Lee's Lieutenants*, vol. 3, 407, 409; Krick, *Lee's Colonels*, passim; Davis, *Confederate General*, vol. 3, 47; Wert, *Glorious Army*, 278.

36. Gallagher, *Spotsylvania Campaign*, 90; Gallagher, *Lee*, 11.

37. Gallagher, *Spotsylvania Campaign*, 16, 17; Allan, Memoir, vol. 9, Allan Papers, UNC; Gallagher, *Lee*, 11.

38. Gallagher, *Spotsylvania Campaign*, 17; Pfanz, *Richard S. Ewell*, 393; Jones, *Campbell Brown's Civil War*, 248, 258, 259.

39. *OR*, 36, pt. 1, 1074; pt. 3, 846, 863; Gallagher, *Spotsylvania Campaign*, 17–18; Allan, Memoir, vol. 9, Allan Papers, UNC.

40. Robertson, *General A. Hill*, 272, 273.

41. Overton Steger–Miss Cordelia, May 16, 1864, Steger Letters, AHEC; Clark, *Histories*, vol. 1, 723, 727.

42. Both Richmond newspapers quoted in, respectively, *Dublin Irish People*, July 30, 1864; *New York Herald*, June 2, 1864.

43. Tower, *Lee's Adjutant*, 160.

44. *OR*, 36, pt. 1, 69, 543, 658, and pt. 2, 720, 721, 728, 729, 756, 757.

45. *OR*, 36, pt. 1, 670, and pt. 2, 658, 762, 763.

46. *OR*, 36, pt. 1, 19, 337, 910, 911, and pt. 2, 864–65; Krick, *Civil War Weather*, 123–25.

47. *OR*, 36, pt. 1, 337, 1073; Mackowski and White, *Season*, 149.

48. *OR*, 36, pt. 1, 336, 337, 1073; Mackowski and White, *Season*, 149; Pfanz, *Richard S. Ewell*, 393.

49. *OR*, 36. Pt. 1, 149; Young, *Lee's Army*, 236; *New York Times* article reprinted in *New Orleans Daily True Delta*, May 22, 1864.

50. Gallagher, *Spotsylvania Campaign*, 177–188; Rhea, *Battles*, 5; *L'Anse Sentinel*, May 26, 1922.

51. Mackowski and White, "Battle," 46; Best, *History*, 147; Galwey, *Valiant Hours*, 210; Haines, *History*, 172.

52. *Harrisburg Daily Independent*, July 18, 1895; Jedediah Hotch-kiss–My Dear Wife, May 13, 1864, Hotchkiss Papers, LC; Clark, *Glance Backward*, 53.

53. Power, *Lee's Miserables*, 33; Craig and Baker, *As You May Never See*, 75; Azariah Bostwick–Sister, June 5, 1864, Bostwick Letters, FSNMP.

54. Gordon, *Reminiscences*, 283, 285; *Anderson Intelligencer*, April 24, 1915.

55. R. T. Owen–Archie, April 8, 1894, McLendon Collection, MDAH; Hess, *Union Soldier*, 159.

56. Brown, *Colonel*, 261; *Richmond Times*, February 3, 1899; Mackowski and White, *Season*, 96; Warner, *Generals in Blue*, 323.

57. St. Georges Parish, Spotsylvania County, Va., 79, 1860 Census; Mackowski and White, *Season*, 148.

58. *Harrisburg Daily Independent*, July 18, 1895; *Alexandria Gazette*, February 17, 1897; Mackowski and White, *Season*, 75; *Washington Weekly Post*, June 27, 1899.

59. *Eutaw Whig and Observer*, March 7, 1895; *Dayton Herald*, June 8, 1906; *Roanoke Times*, March 18, 1902; *Winston-Salem Journal*, March 13, 1921.

60. Mackowski and White, *Season*, 96–97; Brown, *Colonel*, 261; *Richmond Times*, February 3, 1899; *Richmond Dispatch*, September 2, 1900; *Richmond Times-Dispatch*, October 19, 1941.

61. Mackowski and White, *Season*, 96–97; Brown, *Colonel*, 261, *Richmond Times*, February 3, 1899.

62. *Philadelphia Weekly Times*, February 20, 1886; *Opelousas Courier*, November 7, 1878; Mackowski and White, *Season*, 98; *Winchester Star*, July 20, 1920.

63. Henry W. Slocum–Commissary 20th Army Corps, May 14, 1865, Sanford Family Papers, LVA; *Fort Wayne Daily Gazette*, December 28, 1865; Mackowski and White, "Battle," 64.

64. Mackowski and White, "Battle," 64; *New Orleans Times-Picayune*, June 8, 1866; *Wilmington Journal*, September 20, 1866; *Columbia Daily Phoenix*, November 10, 1866; *Richmond Times-Dispatch*, November 14, 1903; *Anderson Intelligencer*, February 7, 1906; Davis, *Confederate General*, vol. 5, 19.

65. Hess, *Union Soldier*, 186.

66. *PMHSM*, vol. 4, 237–38; Newell, *"Ours,"* 268.

67. *Alexandria Gazette*, May 31, 1889; *Abbeville Press and Banner*, January 14, 1891; *Dayton Herald*, June 8, 1906; *Winston-Salem Journal*, March 13, 1921; Mackowski and White, *Season*, 147.

68. *Yorkville Enquirer*, October 6, 1881; *Harrisburg Daily Independent*, July 18, 1895; *Winston-Salem Journal*, March 13, 1921.

69. *Philadelphia Inquirer*, December 7, 1930; *Hartford Courant*, May 26, 1932; Mackowski and White, *Season*, 98.

70. "Vermont Veterans," 5; *Richmond Times*, March 10, 1898; *Harrisburg Daily Independent*, July 18, 1895; *Winston-Salem Journal*, March 13, 1921.

71. *Carlisle Valley Sentinel*, September 2, 1881; *Dayton Herald*, June 8, 1906; *Montgomery Advertiser*, December 13, 1931.

72. *New Philadelphia Daily Times*, May 20, 1909; *Cincinnati Enquirer*, May 16, 1914; Mackowski and White, *Season*, 63.

73. *Dayton Herald*, June 8, 1906.

Bibliography

Unpublished Sources

Abraham Lincoln Presidential Library and Museum, Springfield, Ill.
  Edwards, Oliver. Memoir. Edward-Johnston Family Papers.
Alabama Department of Archives and History, Montgomery
  Purifoy, John. Memoir.
Atlanta Historical Society, Kenan Research Center, Atlanta History Center,
      Atlanta, Ga.
  Simms Family Papers. MSS 11.
Auburn University, Special Collections and Archives Library, Auburn, Ala.
  Lane, James H. Papers.
Bethel Historical Society, Bethel, Maine
  Edwards, Clark S. "War Reminiscences."
Boston Public Library, Boston, Mass.
  Murphey, Josiah F. "Sketch of My Life in the Army during the Late War
      of the Rebellion."
  Whittier, Charles A. "Reminiscences of the War, 1861–1865, or Egotistic
      Memoirs, C.A.W., Feb. 13, 1888 M. Milit. Hist. S." Typescript.
Boston University, Boston, Mass.
  Massachusetts Military Historical Society Collection.
      Anderson, Richard H. Papers.
      Upton, Emory. Papers.
Bowdoin College, George L. Mitchell Department, Special Collections and
      Archives, Hawthorne-Longfellow Library, Brunswick, Maine
  Emery, Edwin, Diaries and Memoirs, 1863–1942.
Cornell University, Division of Rare and Manuscript Collections, Carl A.
      Kroch Library, Ithaca, N.Y.
  Gail and Steven Rudin Collection of Civil War Letters, #4696
      Lovejoy, John M. Letters.
Duke University, David M. Rubenstein Rare Book and Manuscript Library,
      Durham, N.C.
  Ardrey, William E. Papers.
  Bradbury, Samuel. Collection.
  Carrington, I. H. Manuscript. William Patterson Smith Papers.
  Confederate Veteran Papers.
  Daniel, John Warwick. Papers.
  Dillard, John James. Papers.
  Dula, A. J. "Civil War Incidents as Told by an Old Veteran from Memory."

Harden, Edward. Papers.

Longstreet, James. Papers.

Munford-Ellis Family Papers.

Scott, Irby G. Papers.

Shockley, William S. Papers.

Emory University, Special Collections, Stuart A. Rose Manuscript,
Archives, and Rare Book Library, Atlanta, Ga.

Gourdin, Robert Newman. Papers.

Longstreet, James. Papers.

Fredericksburg and Spotsylvania National Military Park, Library,
Fredericksburg, Va.

Alston, P. G. Letter to *Asheville Courier*.

Ames, Albert N. Papers.

Apple, Richard L. Letters.

Bostwick, Azariah. Letters.

Bowen, Charles T. Diary.

Chase, Stephen P. Memoirs.

Cross, Frederick. "Historic People and Places in Chancellorsville,
Wilderness, Spotsylvania C. H. Region."

Davis, William Fish. Memoir.

Edwards, Clark S. Papers.

Gales, Seaton E. Diary.

Graham, Ruth. "Report of Field Investigation of the Chancellorsville
Campaign."

Harris, Nathaniel. Letter.

Keiser, Henry. Diary.

Kepner, John Price. Diary for 1864, typescript.

Kersh, George P. Letters.

Lane, James H. Memoir.

McNeill, Alexander. Letters.

Newman, William B. Recollections.

Parmelee, Samuel Spencer, and Uriah N. Parmelee. Papers.

Russell, Edward K. Letters.

Sale, John F. Diary.

Seibert, Jacob. Papers.

Silloway, Henry F. Diary.

Snider, Joseph C. Diary.

Stanton, Amos B. Letter.

Walter, Franklin G. Diary and Letters.

Watkins, Thomas. Memoir.

Hamilton College Library, Archives, Clinton, N.Y.
  Brown, Morris J. Collection.
Handley Regional Library, Stewart Bell Jr. Archives, Winchester, Va.
  Barton, Randolph. Recollections 1861–1865.
  Hite, John P. Diary. Charles J. Lillis Collection.
  McCown, James L. Memoirs. Typescript. Ben Ritter Collection.
  Miller, Abram S. Papers. James A. Miller Collection.
Historical Society of Montgomery County, Archives. Norristown, Pa.
  Holstein, G. W. Papers.
Indiana University, Lilly Library, Bloomington
  Orr, William. Papers.
Library of Congress, Washington, D.C.
  Doyle, Thomas S. "Memoir of Thomas S. Doyle, Lt., Co. E, 33rd Virginia
    Infantry."
  George, Harold C. Papers.
  Hall, George W. Diary
  Hanna-McCormick Family Papers.
  Hotchkiss, Jedediah. Papers.
  Hunt, Henry J. Papers.
  Lane, James H. Papers.
  Thompson, Gilbert. "My Journal, 1861–1865."
  Wilcox, Cadmus. Papers.
Library of Virginia, James I. Robertson Jr. Civil War Sesquicentennial
    Legacy Collection, Richmond
  Hoover Family Papers.
  McMurran, Joseph. Memorandum Book.
  Munford, Thomas T. Letter, May 9, 1864.
  Sanford Family. Papers.
Louisiana State University Archives, Hill Memorial Library, Baton Rouge
  Bachelor, Albert A. Papers.
Manassas National Battlefield Park, Library, Manassas, Va.
  Ricketts, James B. Diary & Movements of the 3rd Div, 6th AC.
Massachusetts Historical Society, Boston
  Lyman, Theodore. Papers.
Michigan State University, Special Collections Library, East Lansing
  Kirk, Newton T. Papers. #1397.
Mississippi Department of Archives and History, Jackson
  Crawford, John Berryman. Letters.
  Lomax, Alexander A. Notebook.
  McLendon, Elizabeth Spencer. Collection.

Monmouth County Historical Association, Library and Archives, Freehold, N.J.
    Vredenburgh, Peter. Letters.
National Archives, Washington, D.C.
    Records Group 94
        Tidball, John C. Letter.
Navarro College, Pearce Civil War Collection, Pearce Museum, Corsicana, Tex.
    Spafford, A. Papers.
Ohio State University, Thompson Rare Books and Manuscripts Library, Columbus
    Ricksecken, Rufus. Letters.
Pennsylvania State University, Eberly Family Special Collections Library, University Park
    McDowell, Mary Gyla. 100th Pennsylvania Volunteer Infantry Regiment Papers (HCLA1648).
Richmond National Battlefield Park, Library, Richmond, Pa.
    Hardaway, Robert A. Letter.
    Rew, Francis E. Civil War Letters.
South Carolina Historical Society, Charleston
    Whilden, Charles E. Papers.
South Portland Public Library, South Portland, Maine
    Kaler, James Otis Collection.
        Weeks, John H. "152nd New York Vol. Inf. At Spotsylvania."
State Archives of North Carolina, Raleigh
    Civil War Collection, Military Collection.
        Albright, Henry Clay. Papers.
        Alexander, A. P. Memoir.
        Stikeleather, John Alexander. Reminiscences.
        Wallace, Jasper L. Reminiscences.
    George Holland Collection
        Lane, Daniel. "Some Recollections of Battle of Spotsylvania, May 12, 1864."
    Lowry Shuford Collection
        Bone, John W. "My War Story."
    Private Collections.
        Blair, Albert W. Letters.
        Lefever, Isaac. Letters.
        Pearsall, George W. Letters.
        Wiggins, Thomas Medicus. "Some Incidents in the Campaign of 1864."
        Wright, John Collection

State Historical Society of Wisconsin, Madison

Anderson, James S. Papers. Edited by Dennis R. Moore.

Tennessee State Library and Archives

Brown-Ewell Papers.

Tulane University, Howard-Tilton Memorial Library, New Orleans, La.

Ring, George P. Papers. Louisiana Historical Association Collection.

United States Army Heritage Education Center, Archives, Carlisle, Pa.

Civil War Documents Collection

Andrews, John Oliver. "War Record of John Oliver Andrews."

Barnes, John L. Letter, March 25, 1864.

Beddall, Samuel A. Diary.

Blackford, Eugene. Letters.

"Bobbie." Letter.

Bovee, Daniel B. Letter, June 9, 1864.

Bowan, George A. Diary.

Brooks, Samuel. Correspondence.

Corbin, Elbert. Diary.

Halsey, Edmund D. Papers.

Harris, Avery. Reminiscences.

Hoffman, B. H. Letters.

Howard, Francis Marion. Letter.

Keiser, Henry. Diary. Typescript.

Law Family. Papers. Typescript.

Luckenbill, Lewis. Diary.

Mills, Charles. Papers.

Oestreich, Maurus. Journal.

Randolph, Thomas H. Letters.

Seibert, Jacob M. Letters.

Soule, Horatio S. Diary.

Steger, Overton. Letters.

VanAernum, Henry. Papers.

Webb, John G. Letters.

Wyman, Arthur B. Papers.

University of Georgia, Hargrett Rare Book and Manuscript Library, Athens

Duggan, Ivy W. Papers.

LaRoque, John G. Letters to Nannie M. LaRoque, 1862–1864.

University of Michigan, Ann Arbor

Lehman Family. Papers. Bentley Historical Library.

James S. Schoff Civil War Collection. William L. Clements Library.

Best, Isaac O. "Through the Wilderness with Grant."

Bunker, Nathaniel W. Memoir.

University of North Carolina, Wilson Library, Southern Historical
    Collection, Chapel Hill

Alexander, Edward Porter. Papers.

Allan, William. Papers.

Atkinson, E. K. Collection.

Claiborne, John Francis Hamtramck. Papers.

Green, James E. Diary.

Greene, Ambrose George. Papers.

Grimes, Bryan. Papers.

Moore, Samuel J. C. Papers.

Pendleton, William Nelson. Papers.

Polk-Brown-Ewell Papers.

Ramseur, Stephen Dodson. Papers.

Shaffner, John Francis. Papers.

Walker, James A. Papers.

University of South Carolina, Special Collections, South Carolinian Library,
    Columbia

Hagood, James R. Memoirs of the First South Carolina Regiment of
    Volunteer Infantry in the Confederate War for Independence from
    April 12, 1861 to April 10, 1865.

Hammond-Bryan-Cumming Family. Papers.

Rutherford, William Drayton. Papers.

University of Southern Mississippi, McCain Library and Archives, Special
    Collections, Hattiesburg

Dickson, Hugh Carroll. Civil War Letters.

University of Texas, Austin, Briscoe Center for American History

Crockett, Edward Richardson. Papers.

University of Utah, Special Collections, J. Willard Marriott Library, Salt
    Lake City

Ottinger, George Martin. Journal.

University of Virginia, Albert and Shirley Small Special Collections Library,
    Charlottesville

Daniel, John Warwick, and the Daniel Family. Papers. #158.

McCabe, W. Gordon. Papers. #10568.

Vermont Historical Society, Montpelier

White, William. Correspondence.

Virginia Historical Society, Richmond

Bolton Family Papers.

Dinwiddie, Harman. Papers.

Dunn Family Papers.

Fairfax, John Walter. Papers.

Floyd, Augustus Evander. Memoir. Typescript.

Hall, Edwin C. Papers.

Lee, Fitzhugh. "Report of Major General Fitzhugh Lee of the Operations of His Cavalry Division A.N.V. from May 4th 1864 to September 19th 1864."

Phillips, James Eldred. Papers.

Randolph Family Papers.

Scott, Alfred L. "Memoirs of Service in the Confederate Army."

Sorrel, G. Moxley. Diary.

Taylor, Erasmus. "War Reminiscences of Major Erasmus Taylor, C.S.A., Written For His Children."

Venable, Charles Scott. Papers.

Virginia Military Institute, Archives, Preston Library, Lexington

Brooke, Samuel S. Papers. Typescript. #221.

Dunlap Family Letters, 1864. #0373.

Garibaldi, John. Correspondence, 1862–1864, typescript. #284.

Phillips, Charles C. Civil War Diary and Signal Message Book, 1864. #0327.

Rinker, Michael F. Letter, 1864. #0381.

Washington and Lee University, Special Collections, James B. Leyburn Library, Lexington, Va.

Barclay, Alexander Tedford. Correspondence.

Lee-Jackson. Collection.

Wert, Jeffry D. Personal Collection

West Virginia University, West Virginia and Regional History Center, Morgantown

Reynolds, Powell. Letters. West Virginia Collection.

Newspapers

Abbeville (S.C.) Press And Banner

Abingdon (Va.) Virginian

Akron (Ohio) Beacon Journal

Akron (Ohio) Daily Democrat

Alexandria (Va.) Gazette

Alexandria (La.) Weekly Town Talk

Anderson (S.C.) Intelligencer

Atlanta (Ga.) Constitution

Augusta (Ga.) Chronicle

Augusta (Ga.) Constitutionalist

Baltimore (Md.) Sun

Beckley (W. Va.) Post-Herald

Bellevue (La.) Bossier Banner

Bethel (Maine) News

Bloomsburg (Pa.) Columbia Democrat

Bloomsburg (Pa.) Star of the North
Boston (Mass.) Globe
Buffalo (N.Y.) Sunday Morning News
Burlington (Vt.) Free Press
Burlington (Vt.) Weekly Free Press
Camden (S.C.) Confederate
Camden (S.C.) Journal
Carlisle (Pa.) Valley Sentinel
Charleston (S.C.) Daily Courier
Charlotte (N.C.) Democrat
Charlotte (N.C.) Observer
Charlotte (N.C.) Western Democrat
Chicago (Ill.) Tribune
Cincinnati (Ohio) Enquirer
Columbia (S.C.) Daily Phoenix
Columbia (S.C.) Democrat
Columbia (S.C.) Guardian
Columbus (Miss.) Weekly Dispatch
Confederate Union (Milledgeville, Ga.)
Coudersport (Pa.) Potter Enterprise
Daily Confederate (Raleigh, N.C.)
Dayton (Ohio) Herald
Dublin (Ireland) Irish People
Edgefield (S.C.) Advertiser
Eutaw (Ala.) Whig and Observer
Fayetteville (N.C.) Semi-Weekly
    Observer
Fitchburg (Mass.) Sentinel
Fort Wayne (Ind.) Daily Gazette
Fredericksburg (Va.) Free Lance
Fremont (Ohio) Weekly Journal
Galveston (Tex.) News
Greensboro (Ala.) Record
Greenwood (Miss.) Commonwealth
Greenwood (S.C.) Index-Journal
Harrisburg (Pa.) Daily Independent
Hartford (Conn.) Courant
Herkimer (N.Y.) County Journal
Indiana (Pa.) Democrat
Indiana (Pa.) Weekly Messenger

Indianapolis Journal
Island Pond (Vt.) Essex County
    Herald
Jackson (Miss.) Clarion-Ledger
Janesville (Wis.) Weekly Gazette
L'Anse (Mich.) Sentinel
Lake Geneva (Wash.) Herald
Lancaster (S.C.) Ledger
Lancaster (Pa.) New Era
Lauren (S.C.) Advertiser
Lexington (S.C.) Dispatch-News
Lexington (Va.) Gazette
Lexington (Ky.) Herald-Leader
Logan (Ohio) Hocking Sentinel
London (England) Examiner
Manning (S.C.) Times
Mansfield (Ohio) News-Journal
Marion (Ohio) Star
McConnellsburg (Pa.) Fulton
    Democrat
Meridian (Miss.) Daily Clarion
Milledgeville (Ga.) Southern
    Recorder
Mobile (Ala.) Advertiser and Register
Mobile (Ala.) Evening News
Monongahela (Pa.) Valley
    Republican
Monroe (N.C.) Journal
Montgomery (Ala.) Advertiser
Montgomery (Ala.) Daily Advertiser
Montpelier (Idaho) Examiner
Montpelier (Vt.) Examiner
Montpelier (Vt.) Morning Journal
Morrisville (Vt.) News and Citizen
Muncie (Ind.) Star Press
Natchez (Miss.) Weekly Democrat
New Bern (N.C.) Our Living and Our
    Dead
New Bern (N.C.) Times
Newberry (S.C.) Herald and News

BIBLIOGRAPHY

New Orleans (La.) Daily True Delta
New Orleans (La.) Republican
New Orleans (La.) Times-Picayune
New Philadelphia (Ohio) Daily Times
New York (N.Y.) Daily News
New York (N.Y.) Herald
New York (N.Y.) Times
Opelousas (La.) Courier
Philadelphia (Pa.) Inquirer
Philadelphia (Pa.) Times
Philadelphia (Pa.) Weekly Press
Philadelphia (Pa.) Weekly Times
Pickens (S.C.) Keowee Courier
Pittsburgh (Pa.) Post-Gazette
Pittston (Pa.) Gazette
Plymouth (Ind.) Democrat
Port Gibson (Miss.) Weekly Standard
Portland (Maine) Transcript
Raleigh (N.C.) Confederate
Raleigh (N.C.) Daily Confederate
Raleigh (N.C.) Daily Conservative
Raleigh (N.C.) News and Observer
Raleigh (N.C.) Semi-Weekly
    Standard
Raleigh (N.C.) State Chronicle
Randolph (Kans.) Enterprise
Reading (Pa.) Times
Richmond (Va.) Daily Dispatch
Richmond (Va.) Daily Enquirer
Richmond (Va.) Dispatch
Richmond (Va.) Enquirer
Richmond (Va.) Examiner
Richmond (Va.) Sentinel
Richmond (Va.) Times
Richmond (Va.) Times-Dispatch
Roanoke (Va.) Times
Rockbridge County (Va.) News
Salisbury (N.C.) Daily Gazette
Salisbury (N.C.) Watchman
Savannah (Ga.) Morning News

Selma (Ala.) Daily Reporter
Selma (Ala.) Times
Sheffield (England) Sheffield and
    Rotterdam Independent
Southern Watchmen
Springfield (Vt.) Reporter
St. Albans (Vt.) Daily Messenger
Statesville (N.C.) Record And
    Landmark
Staunton (Va.) News Leader
Staunton (Va.) Spectator and
    Vindication
Syracuse (N.Y.) Daily Courier and
    Union
Tazewell (Va.) Clinch Valley News
Vergennes (Vt.) Middlebury Record
Vermont (Vt.) Union
Vicksburg (Miss.) Daily Times
Vicksburg (Miss.) Evening Post
Warrenton (N.C.) Indicator
Washington (D.C.) Evening Star
Washington (D.C.) National Tribune
Washington (D.C.) Post
Washington (D.C.) Weekly Post
White Oaks (N. Mex.) Eagle
Wilkes-Barre (Pa.) Times Leader
Wilmington (N.C.) Daily Dispatch
Wilmington (Vt.) Deerfield Valley
    Times
Wilmington (N.C.) Journal
Wilmington (N.C.) Morning Star
Wilmington (N.C.) Semi-Weekly
    Advertiser
Winchester (Va.) Star
Winnsboro (S.C.) Tri-Weekly News
Winston-Salem (N.C.) Journal
Wisconsin State Journal
Wytheville (Va.) Dispatch
Yazoo (Miss.) Sentinel
Yorkville (S.C.) Enquirer

Government Publications

U.S. Bureau of the Census. St. Georges Parish. Spotsylvania County, Va., 1860.

———. Non-population Schedules. 1850–1880.

———. Slave Schedules. St. Georges Parish. Spotsylvania County, Va. 1860.

U.S. War Department. *The War of the Rebellion: A Compilation of the Official Records of the Union and Confederate Armies*, 128 vols. Washington, D.C.: U.S. Government Printing Office, 1880–1902.

Published Books and Articles

Adams, John R. *Memorial and Letters of Rev. John R. Adams, DD.* Cambridge, Mass.: University Press, John Wilson and Son, 1890.

Agassiz, George R., ed. *Meade's Headquarters, 1863–1865: Letters of Colonel Theodore Lyman from the Wilderness to Appomattox.* Boston: Atlantic Monthly Press, 1922.

Albert, Allen D., ed. *History of the Forty-Fifth Regiment Pennsylvania Veteran Volunteer Infantry 1864–1865.* Williamsport, Pa.: Grit Publishing Company, 1912.

Allardice, Bruce S. *Confederate Colonels: A Biographical Register.* Columbia: University of Missouri Press, 2008.

Armstrong, Richard L. *25th Virginia Infantry and 9th Battalion Virginia Infantry.* Lynchburg, Va.: H. E. Howard, 1990.

Ashcraft, John M. *31st Virginia Infantry.* Lynchburg, Va.: H. E. Howard, 1988.

Aubrecht, Michael. "Due Credit: Spotsylvania Grunts Get Their Say," *America's Civil War* 31, no. 6 (January 2019).

Bandy, Ken, and Florence Freeland, eds. *The Gettysburg Papers*, 2 vols. Dayton, Ohio: Press of Morningside Bookshop, 1978.

Baquet, Camille. *History of the First Brigade, New Jersey Volunteers from 1861 to 1865.* Reprint, Gettysburg, Pa.: Stan Clark Military Books, 1991.

Bean, W. G. *The Liberty Hall Volunteers: Stonewall's College Boys.* Charlottesville: University Press of Virginia, 1964.

———. *Stonewall's Man: Sandie Pendleton.* Reprint, Wilmington, N.C.: Broadfoot, 1987.

Bennett, Brian A. *Sons of Old Monroe: A Regimental History of Patrick O'Rorke's 140th New York Volunteer Infantry.* Dayton, Ohio: Morningside House, 1999.

Benson, Berry. *Berry Benson's Civil War Book: Memoirs of a Confederate Scout and Sharpshooter*, edited by Susan Williams Benson. Athens: University of Georgia Press, 1992.

Bernard, George S. *Civil War Talks: Further Reminiscences of George S. Bernard & His Fellow Veterans*, edited by Hampton Newsome, John Horn, and John G. Selby. Charlottesville: University of Virginia Press, 2012.

Best, Isaac O. *History of the 121st New York State Infantry*. Reprint, Baltimore, Md.: Butternut & Blue, 1996.

Bingham, Henry H. "Memoirs of Hancock." 1872. William P. Palmer Collection, Western Reserve Historical Society, Cleveland, Ohio.

Blight, David W., ed. *When This Cruel War Is Over: The Civil War Letters of Charles Harvey Brewster*. Amherst: University of Massachusetts Press, 1992.

Bloodgood, John D. *Personal Reminiscences of the War*. New York: Hunt & Eaton, 1893.

Bond, Natalie Jenkins, and Osmun Latrobe Coward, eds. *The South Carolinians: Colonel Asbury Coward's Memoirs*. New York: Vantage Press, 1968.

Bowen, James L. *History of the Thirty-Seventh Regiment Mass. Volunteers in the Civil War of 1861–1865*. Holyoke, Mass.: Clark W. Bryan & Company, 1884.

Boyd, David French. *Reminiscences of the War in Virginia*, ed. T. Michael Parrish. Austin, Tex.: Jenkins, 1989.

Brown, Henri LeFevre, ed. *History of the Third Regiment Excelsior Brigade 72d New York Volunteer Infantry 1861–1865*. Jamestown, N.Y.: Journal Printing Co., 1902.

Brown, Varina D. *A Colonel at Gettysburg and Spotsylvania*. Reprint, Baltimore, Md.: Butternut & Blue, n.d.

Bruce, George A. *The Twentieth Regiment of Massachusetts Volunteer Infantry 1861–1865*. Reprint, Baltimore, Md.: Butternut & Blue, 1988.

Buck, Samuel D. *With the Old Confeds: Actual Experiences of a Captain in the Line*. Reprint, Staunton, Va.: Lot's Wife Publishing, 2007.

Burr, Frank A. *Life and Achievements of James Addams Beaver: Early Life, Military Services and Public Career*. Philadelphia, Pa.: Ferguson Bros. & Co., 1882.

Burrage, Henry S. *History of the Thirty-Sixth Regiment Massachusetts Volunteers, 1862–1863*. Boston: Press of Rockwell and Churchill, 1884.

Caldwell, J. F. J. *The History of a Brigade of South Carolinians, Known First as "Gregg's" and Subsequently as "McGowan's Brigade."* Reprint, Marietta, Ga.: Continental Book Company, 1951.

Caldwell, Willie Walker. *Stonewall Jim: A Biography of James A. Walker, C.S.A.* Elliston, Va.: Northcross House, 1990.

Cannan, John. *Bloody Angle: Hancock's Assault on the Mule Shoe Salient May 12, 1864*. Cambridge, Mass.: DaCapo Press, 2002.

Carmichael, Peter S., ed. *Audacity Personified: The Generalship of Robert E. Lee*. Baton Rouge: Louisiana State University Press, 2004.

———. *The War for the Common Soldier: How Men Thought, Fought, and Survived in Civil War Armies*. Chapel Hill: University of North Carolina Press, 2018.

Carr, Benjamin B. *History of Co. E, 20th N.C. Regiment 1861-'65*. Goldsboro, N.C.: Nash Brothers Book and Commercial Publishers, 1906.

Casler, John O. *Four Years in the Stonewall Brigade*. Reprint, Dayton, Ohio: Press of Morningside Bookshop, 1971.

Cassedy, Edward K., ed. *Dear Friends at Home: The Civil War Letters and Diaries of Sergeant Charles T. Bowen Twelfth United States Infantry First Battalion 1861-1864*. Baltimore, Md.: Butternut & Blue, 2001.

Catton, Bruce. *Grant Takes Command*. Boston: Little, Brown, 1969.

Chadwick, Bruce, ed. *Brother against Brother: The Lost Civil War Diary of Lt. Edmund Halsey*. Bel Air, Calif.: Birch Lane Press, 1997.

Chamberlin, Thomas. *History of the One Hundred and Fiftieth Regiment Pennsylvania Volunteers, Second Regiment, Bucktail Brigade*. Reprint, Baltimore, Md.: Butternut & Blue, 1986.

Chapla, John D. *50th Virginia Infantry*. Lynchburg, Va.: H. E. Howard, 1997.

———. *48th Virginia Infantry*. Lynchburg, Va.: H. E. Howard, 1989.

———. *42nd Virginia Infantry*. Lynchburg, Va.: H. E. Howard, 1983.

Chesson, Michael B., ed. *The Journal of a Civil War Surgeon*. Lincoln: University of Nebraska Press, 2003.

Clark, George. *A Glance Backward: On Some Events in the Past History of My Life*. Houston, Ala.: Press of Rein & Sons, [1914].

Clark, Walter, ed. *Histories of the Several Regiments and Battalions from North Carolina in the Great War 1861-'65*, 5 vols. Reprint: Wendell, N.C.: Broadfoot's Bookmark, 1982.

Coffin, Howard. *The Battered Stars: One State's Civil War Ordeal during Grant's Overland Campaign*. Woodstock, Vt.: Countryman Press, 2002.

Cogswell, Leander W. *A History of the Eleventh New Hampshire Regiment Volunteer Infantry in the Rebellion War 1861-1865*. Concord, N.H.: Republican Press Association, 1891.

Colt, Margaretta Barton. *Defend the Valley: A. Shenandoah Family in the Civil War*. New York: Orion Books, 1994.

Confederate History Symposium. Hillsboro, Tex.: Hill Junior College, 1984.

Confederate Veteran Magazine, 40 vols. Reprint, Wilmington, N.C.: Broadfoot, 1987-88.

Corby, William. *Memoirs of Chaplain Life: Three Years Chaplain in the Famous Irish Brigade, "Army of the Potomac."* Notre Dame, Ind.: Scholastic Press, 1891.

Cowtan, Charles W. *Services of the Tenth New York Volunteers (National Zouaves) in the War of the Rebellion.* New York: Charles H. Ludwig, 1882.

Cozzens, Peter, ed. *Battles and Leaders of the Civil War*, vols. 5 and 6. Urbana: University of Illinois Press, 2002–4.

Craig, Joel, and Sharlene Baker, eds. *As You May Never See Us Again: The Civil War Letters of George and Walter Battle 4th North Carolina Infantry.* Reprint, Wake Forest, N.C.: Scuppernong Press, 2010.

Craig, Tom Moore, ed. *Upcountry South Carolina Goes to War: Letters of the Anderson, Brockman, and Moore Families 1853–1864.* Columbia: University of South Carolina Press, 2009.

Crater, Lewis. *History of the Fiftieth Regiment, Penna. Vet. Vols., 1861–65.* Reading, Pa.: Coleman Printing House, 1884.

Cudworth, Warren H. *History of the First Regiment (Massachusetts Infantry), From the 25th of May 1861 to the 25th of May 1864.* Boston: Walker, Fuller, and Company, 1866.

Cutrer, Thomas W., ed. *Longstreet's Aide: The Civil War Letters of Major Thomas J. Goree.* Charlottesville: University Press of Virginia, 1995.

Dame, William Meade. *From the Rapidan to Richmond and the Spotsylvania Campaign.* Reprint, Richmond, Va.: Owens, 1987.

Dana, Charles A. *Recollections of the Civil War.* New York: D. Appleton and Company, 1899.

Davis, Charles E., Jr. *Three Years in the Army: The Story of the Thirteenth Massachusetts Volunteers from July 16, 1861, to August 1, 1864.* Boston: Estes and Lauriat, 1894.

Davis, Oliver Wilson. *Life of David Bell Birney: Major-General United States Volunteers.* Reprint, Gaithersburg, Md.: Ron R. Van Sickle Military Books, 1987.

Davis, William C., ed. *The Confederate General*, 6 vols. Gettysburg, Pa.: National Historical Society, 1991.

Dawson, Francis W. *Reminiscences of Confederate Service, 1861–1865*, edited by Bell I. Wiley. Baton Rouge: Louisiana State University Press, 1980.

Dobbins, Austin C., ed. *Grandfather's Journal: Company B, Sixteenth Mississippi Infantry, Harris' Brigade, Mahone's Division, Hill's Corps, A.N.V.* Dayton, Ohio: Morningside House, 1988.

Douglas, Henry Kyd. *I Rode With Stonewall.* Chapel Hill: University of North Carolina Press, 1940.

Dowdey, Clifford, and Louis H. Manarin, eds. *The Wartime Papers of R. E. Lee.* Boston: Little, Brown, 1961.

Dozier, Graham T., ed. *A Gunner in Lee's Army: The Civil War Letters of Thomas Henry Carter.* Chapel Hill: University of North Carolina Press, 2014.

Driver, Robert J., Jr. *52nd Virginia Infantry.* Lynchburg, Va.: H. E. Howard, 1986.

Dunlop, W. S. *Lee's Sharpshooters; or, the Forefront of Battle.* Reprint, Dayton, Ohio: Morningside House, 1988.

Dunn, Craig L. *Harvestfields of Death: The Twentieth Indiana Volunteers of Gettysburg.* Carmel: Guild Press of Indiana, 1999.

Ernsberger, Don. *Paddy Owen's Regulars: A History of the 69th Pennsylvania "Irish Volunteers,"* 2 vols. Bloomington, Ind.: Xlibris Corporation, 2004.

Evans, Clement A., ed. *Confederate Military History, Volume 3.* Reprint, Dayton, Ohio: Press of Morningside Bookshop, 1975.

Evans, Robert G., ed. *The 16th Mississippi Infantry: Civil War Letters and Reminiscences.* Jackson: University Press of Mississippi, 2002.

Faust, Drew Gilpin. *This Republic of Suffering: Death and the American Civil War.* New York: Alfred A. Knopf, 2008.

Favill, Josiah Marshall. *The Diary of a Young Officer Serving with the Armies of the United States during the War of the Rebellion.* Reprint, Baltimore, Md.: Butternut & Blue, 2000.

Fox, John J., III. *Red Clay to Richmond: Trail of the 35th Georgia Infantry Regiment, C.S.A.* Winchester, Va.: Angle Valley Press, 2004.

Frederick, Gilbert. *The Story of a Regiment Being a Record of the Military Services of the Fifty-Seventh New York State Volunteer Infantry in the War of the Rebellion 1861–1865.* Chicago: C. H. Morgan Co., 1895.

Freeman, Douglas Southall, ed. *Lee's Dispatches: Unpublished Letters of General Robert E. Lee, C.S.A., to Jefferson Davis and the War Department of the Confederate States of America.* With additional dispatches and foreword by Grady McWhiney. New York: G. P. Putman's Sons, 1957.

———. *Lee's Lieutenants: A Study in Command,* 3 vols. New York: Charles Scribner's Sons, 1942–44.

Frye, Dennis E. *2nd Virginia Infantry.* Lynchburg, Va.: H. E. Howard, 1984.

Gaff, Alan D. *On Many a Bloody Field: Four Years in the Iron Brigade.* Bloomington: Indiana University Press, 1996.

Gallagher, Gary W. *The Confederate War.* Cambridge, Mass.: Harvard University Press, 1997.

BIBLIOGRAPHY

——. ed. *Fighting for the Confederacy: The Personal Recollections of General Edward Porter Alexander.* Chapel Hill: University of North Carolina Press, 1989.

——. *Lee and His Army in Confederate History.* Chapel Hill: University of North Carolina Press, 2001.

——. ed. *Lee: The Soldier.* Lincoln: University of Nebraska Press, 1996.

——. ed. *The Spotsylvania Campaign.* Chapel Hill: University of North Carolina Press, 1998.

——. *Stephen Dodson Ramseur: Lee's Gallant General.* Chapel Hill: University of North Carolina Press, 1985.

——, ed. *The Wilderness Campaign.* Chapel Hill: University of North Carolina Press, 1997.

Gallagher, Gary W., and Carolina E. Janney, eds. *Cold Harbor to the Crater: The End of the Overland Campaign.* Chapel Hill: University of North Carolina Press, 2015.

Galwey, Thomas Francis. *The Valiant Hours,* edited by W. S. Nye. Harrisburg, Pa.: Stackpole Company, 1961.

Gannon, James P. *Irish Rebels, Confederate Tigers: The 6th Louisiana Volunteers, 1861–1865.* Mason City, Iowa: Savas, 1998.

Garnett, Theodore S. *Riding with Stuart: Reminiscences of an Aide-de-Camp,* edited by Robert J. Trout. Shippensburg, Pa.: White Mane, 1994.

Gilson, John H. *Concise History of the 126th Regiment Ohio Volunteer Infantry.* Salem, Ohio: Walton Steam Jobs and Label Printer, 1883.

Glatthaar, Joseph T. *General Lee's Army: From Victory to Collapse.* New York: Free Press, 2008.

Glimpses of the Nation's Struggle: M.O.L.L.U.S., Minnesota, 6 vols. Reprint, Wilmington, N.C.: Broadfoot, 1992.

Gordon, John B. *Reminiscences of the Civil War.* Reprint, Gettysburg, Pa.: Civil War Times Illustrated, 1974.

Gould, Joseph. *The Story of the Forty-Eighth.* Philadelphia, Pa.: Alfred M. Slocum Co., 1908.

Grant, Ulysses S. *Personal Memoirs of U. S. Grant,* 2 vols. New York: Charles L. Webster & Company, 1885–86.

Green, William H. "From the Wilderness to Spotsylvania," *War Papers, MOLLUS, Maine,* vol. 2. Reprint, Wilmington, N.C.: Broadfoot, 1992.

Greiner, James M., Janet L. Coryell, and James R. Smither, eds. *A Surgeon's Civil War: The Letters and Diary of Daniel M. Holt, M.D.* Kent, Ohio: Kent State University Press, 1994.

Grimes, Bryan. *Extracts of Letters of Major-General Bryan Grimes to His Wife*, ed. Gary W. Gallagher. Reprint, Wilmington, N.C.: Broadfoot, 1986.

Grimsley, Mark. *And Keep Moving On: The Virginia Campaign, May–June 1864*. Lincoln: University of Nebraska Press, 2002.

Gwynne, S. C. *Hymns of the Republic: The Story of the Final Year of the American Civil War*. New York: Scribner, 2019.

Haines, Alanson A. *History of the Fifteenth Regiment New Jersey Volunteers*. Reprint, Gaithersburg, Md.: Butternut Press, 1987.

Hardy, Michael C. *General Lee's Immortals: The Battles and Campaigns of the Branch-Lane Brigade in the Army of Northern Virginia, 1861–1865*. El Dorado Hills, Calif.: Savas Beatie, 2018.

Harsh, Joseph L. *Confederate Tide Rising: Robert E. Lee and the Making of Southern Strategy, 1861–1862*. Kent, Ohio: Kent State University Press, 1998.

Hayes, Patrick J., ed. *The Civil War Diary of Father James Sheeran: Confederate Chaplain and Redemptorist*. Washington, D.C.: Catholic University of America Press, 2016.

Hays, Gilbert Adam. *Under the Red Patch: Story of the Sixth Third Regiment Pennsylvania Volunteers 1861–1864*. Pittsburgh, Pa.: Press of Market Review, 1908.

Henderson, William D. *41st Virginia Infantry*. Lynchburg, Va.: H. E. Howard, 1986.

Hess, Earl J. *Field Armies & Fortifications in the Civil War: The Eastern Campaigns, 1861–1864*. Chapel Hill: University of North Carolina Press, 2005.

———. *Lee's Tar Heels: The Pettigrew-Kirkland-MacRae Brigade*. Chapel Hill: University of North Carolina Press, 2002.

———. *The Rifle Musket in Civil War Combat: Reality and Myth*. Lawrence: University Press of Kansas, 2008.

———. *Trench Warfare Under Grant and Lee: Field Fortifications in the Overland Campaign*. Chapel Hill: University of North Carolina Press, 2007.

———. *The Union Soldier in Battle: Enduring the Ordeal of Combat*. Lawrence: University Press of Kansas, 1997.

Hinton, Isaac T. *A Historical Sketch: Quitman Guards, Company E, Sixteenth Mississippi Regiment, Harris' Brigade*. Reprint, Middletown, Del.: n.p., 2018.

Holmes, Oliver Wendell, Jr. *Touched with Fire: Civil War Letters and Diary of Oliver Wendell Holmes, Jr. 1861–1864*, edited by Mark DeWolfe Howe. Cambridge, Mass.: Harvard University Press, 1946.

Holt, David. *A Mississippi Rebel in the Army of Northern Virginia: The Civil Memoirs of Private David Holt,* edited by Thomas D. Cockrell and Michael B. Ballard. Baton Rouge: Louisiana State University Press, 1995.

Hopkins, William P. *The Seventh Regiment Rhode Island Volunteers in the Civil War 1862–1865.* Providence, RI: Snow & Farnham, 1903.

Houghton, Edwin B. *Campaigns of the Seventeenth Maine.* Portland, Maine: Short & Loving, 1866.

Houston, Henry C. *The Thirty-Second Maine Regiment of Infantry Volunteers: An Historical Sketch.* Portland, Maine: Press of Southworth Brothers, 1903.

Howard, McHenry. *Recollections of a Maryland Confederate Soldier and Staff Officer under Johnston, Jackson, and Lee.* Reprint, Dayton, Ohio: Press of Morningside Bookshop, 1975.

Humphreys, Andrew A. *The Virginia Campaign of '64 and '65: The Army of the Potomac and the Army of the James.* New York: Charles Scribner's Sons, 1903.

Hyde, Thomas W. *Following the Greek Cross; or Memories of the Sixth Army Corps.* Boston, Mass.: Houghton Mifflin, 1894.

Jackman, Lyman. *History of the Sixth New Hampshire Regiment in the War for the Union.* Concord, N.H.: Republican Press Association, 1891.

Johnson, Robert Underwood, and Clarence Clough Buel, eds. *Battles and Leaders of the Civil War,* 4 vols. Reprint, New York: Thomas Yoseloff, 1956.

Johnston, Hugh Buckner, ed. *The Civil War Letters of George Boardman Battle and of Walter Raleigh Battle of Wilson, North Carolina.* Wilson, N.C.: n.p., 1953.

Jones, Terry L., ed. *Campbell Brown's Civil War: With Ewell and the Army of Northern Virginia.* Baton Rouge: Louisiana State University Press, 2001.

———. *Lee's Tigers: The Louisiana Infantry in the Army of Northern Virginia.* Baton Rouge: Louisiana State University Press, 1987.

Jordan, David M. *"Happiness Is Not My Companion": The Life of General G. K. Warren.* Bloomington: Indiana University Press, 2001.

Judson, Amos M. *History of the Eighty-Third Regiment Pennsylvania Volunteers.* Foreword and notes by John J. Pullen. Dayton, Ohio: Morningside, 1986.

Kepler, William. *History of the Fourth Regiment Ohio Volunteer Infantry in the War of the Rebellion.* Reprint, Huntington, W. Va.: Blue Acorn Press, 1992.

King, David H., A. Judson Gibbs, and Jay H. Northup, compilers. *History of the Ninety-Third Regiment, New York Volunteer Infantry 1861–1865.* Milwaukee, Wis.: Swain & Tate, Printers, 1895

King, John R. *My Experience in the Confederate Army and in Northern Prisons*. Clarksburg, W. Va.: United Daughters of Confederacy, Chapter No. 1333, 1917.

Kleese, Richard B. *49th Virginia Infantry*. Lynchburg, Va.: H. E. Howard, 2002.

Koonce, Donald B., ed. *Doctor to the Front: The Civil War Journal of Thomas Fanning Wood, M.D. 1861–1865*. Greenville, S.C.: Spectrum Communications, 1997.

Krick, Robert E. L. *Staff Officers in Gray: A Biographical Register of the Staff Officers in the Army of Northern Virginia*. Chapel Hill: University of North Carolina Press, 2003.

Krick, Robert K. *Civil War Weather in Virginia*. Tuscaloosa: University of Alabama Press, 2007.

———. *The 14th South Carolina Infantry Regiment of the Gregg-McGowan Brigade, Army of Northern Virginia*. Wilmington, N.C.: Broadfoot, 2008.

———. *Lee's Colonels: A Biographical Register of the Field Officers of the Army of Northern Virginia*, 5th ed. Wilmington, N.C.: Broadfoot, 2009.

———. *Parker's Virginia Battery C.S.A.* Berryville, Va.: Virginia Book Company, 1975.

Kundahl, George G., ed. *The Bravest of the Brave: The Correspondence of Stephen Dodson Ramseur*. Chapel Hill: University of North Carolina Press, 2010.

Laboda, Lawrence R. *From Selma to Appomattox: The History of the Jeff Davis Artillery*. New York: Oxford University Press, 1996.

Lash, Gary G. *"Duty Well Done": The History of Edward Baker's California Regiment (71st Pennsylvania Infantry)*. Baltimore, Md.: Butternut & Blue, 2001.

Laswell, Mary, ed. *Rags and Hope: The Recollections of Val C. Giles, Four Years with Hood's Brigade, Fourth Texas Infantry 1861–1865*. New York: Coward-McCann, 1961.

Livermore, Thomas L. *Days and Events, 1860–1866*. Boston: Houghton Mifflin, 1920.

Long, A. L. *Memoirs of Robert E. Lee: His Military and Personal History*. New York: J. M. Stoddard, 1886.

Longacre, Edward G. *To Gettysburg and Beyond: The Twelfth New Jersey Volunteer Infantry, II Corps, Army of the Potomac, 1862–1865*. Hightstown, N.J.: Longstreet House, 1988.

Lord, Edward O., ed. *History of the Ninth Regiment New Hampshire Volunteers in the War of the Rebellion*. Concord, NH: Republican Press Association, 1895.

Lowe, David W., ed. *Meade's Army: The Private Notebooks of Lt. Col. Theodore Lyman*. Kent, Ohio: Kent State University Press, 2007.

Mackowski, Chris, and Kristopher D. White. "The Battle of the Bloody Angle, or 'Mule Shoe' Spotsylvania Court House, May 12, 1864," *Blue & Gray Magazine* 26, no. 1 (2009).

———. *A Season of Slaughter: The Battle of Spotsylvania Court House, May 8–21, 1864*. El Dorado Hills, Calif.: Savas Beatie, 2013.

Mahood, Wayne. *"Written in Blood": A History of the 126th New York Infantry in the Civil War*. Hightstown, N.J.: Longstreet House, 1997.

Marbaker, Thomas D. *History of the Eleventh New Jersey Volunteers from Its Organization to Appomattox*. Reprint, Hightstown, N.J.: Longstreet House, 1990.

Marvel, William. *Race of the Soil: The Ninth New Hampshire Regiment in the Civil War*. Wilmington, N.C.: Broadfoot, 1988.

Matter, William D. *If It Takes All Summer: The Battle of Spotsylvania*. Chapel Hill: University of North Carolina Press, 1988.

McAllister, Robert. *The Civil War Letters of General Robert McAllister*, edited by James I. Robertson Jr. New Brunswick, N.J.: Rutgers University Press, 1965.

McDermott, Anthony W. *A Brief History of the 69th Regiment Pennsylvania Veteran Volunteers, From Its Formation Until Final Muster Out of the United States Service*. Philadelphia, Pa.: D. J. Gallagher, 1889.

McDonald, Archie P., ed. *Make Me a Map of the Valley: The Civil War Journal of Stonewall Jackson's Topographer*. Dallas, Tex.: Southern Methodist University Press, 1973.

Meade, George. *The Life And Letters of George Gordon Meade*, 2 vols. Reprint, Baltimore, Md.: Butternut & Blue, 1994.

Menge, W. Springer, and J. August Shimrak, eds. *The Civil War Notebook of Daniel Chisholm: A Chronicle of Daily Life in the Union Army, 1864–1865*. New York: Orion, 1989.

Michie, Peter S. *The Life and Letters of Emory Upton: Colonel of the Fourth Regiment of Artillery, and Brevet Major-General, U.S. Army*. New York: D. Appleton and Company, 1885.

Miller, Richard F. *Harvard's Civil War: A History of the Twentieth Massachusetts Volunteer Infantry*. Hanover, N.H.: University Press of New England, 2005.

Mixson, Frank M. *Reminiscences of a Private*. Columbia, S.C.: State Company, 1910.

Morrison, James L., Jr., ed. *The Memoirs of Henry Heth*. Westport, Conn.: Greenwood Press, 1974.

Morse, Francis W. *Personal Experiences in the War of the Great Rebellion, From December, 1862, to July, 1865*. Albany, N.Y.: printed but not published, 1866.

Muffly, J. W., ed. *The Story of Our Regiment: A History of the 148th Pennsylvania Vols*. Reprint, Baltimore, Md.: Butternut & Blue, 1994.

Mulholland, St. Clair A. *The Story of the 116th Regiment, Pennsylvania Volunteers in the War of the Rebellion*, ed. Lawrence Frederick Kohl. Reprint, New York: Fordham University Press, 1996.

Murphey, Thomas G. *The History of The First Regiment of Delaware Veteran Volunteers*. Philadelphia, Pa.: James C. Claxton, 1866.

Musselman, Homer D. *The Carolina Light, Parker and Stafford Light Virginia Artillery*. Lynchburg, Va.: H. E. Howard, 1992.

Myers, Irvin G. *We Might As Well Die Here: The 53d Pennsylvania Veteran Volunteer Infantry*. Shippensburg, Pa.: White Mane Books, 2004.

National Tribune Scrapbook: Stories of the Camp, March, Battle, Hospital and Prison Told by Comrades. Washington, D.C.: National Tribune, n.d.

Neese, George M. *Three Years in the Confederate Horse Artillery*. Reprint, Dayton, Ohio: Press of Morningside Bookshop, 1983.

Nevins, Allan, ed. *A Diary of Battle: The Personal Journals of Colonel Charles S. Wainwright, 1861–1865*. Reprint, Gettysburg, Pa.: Stan Clark Military Books, 1993.

Newell, Joseph Keith. *"Ours": Annals of the 10th Regiment, Massachusetts Volunteers in the Rebellion*. Springfield, Mass.: C. A. Nichols, 1875.

Newsome, Hampton, John Horn, and John G. Selby, eds. *Civil War Talks: Further Reminiscences of George S. Bernard and His Fellow Veterans*. Charlottesville: University of Virginia Press, 2012.

Nichols, G. W. *A Soldier's Story of His Regiment (61st Georgia)*. Reprint, Kennesaw, Ga.: Continental Book Company, 1961.

Nolan, Alan T. *Lee Considered: General Robert E. Lee and Civil War History*. Chapel Hill: University of North Carolina Press, 1991.

Nosworthy, Brent. *The Bloody Crucible of Courage: Fighting Methods and Combat Experience of the Civil War*. New York: Carroll & Graf Publishers, 2003.

Osborne, Seward R., ed. *The Civil Diaries of Col. Theodore B. Gates, 20th New York State Militia*. Hightstown, N.J.: Longstreet House, 1991.

Ott, Eugene Matthew, Jr. "The Civil War Diary of James J. Kirkpatrick, Sixteenth Mississippi Infantry, C.S.A." M.A. thesis, Texas A & M University, 1984.

Page, Charles A. *Letters of a War Correspondent*. Reprint, n.p.: Palala Press, n.d.

Page, Charles D. *History of the Fourteenth Regiment, Connecticut Vol. Infantry*. Meriden, Conn.: Horton Printing, 1906.

Papers of the Military Historical Society of Massachusetts, 15 vols. Reprint, Wilmington, N.C.: Broadfoot, 1989–90.

Parker, Thomas H. *History of the 51st Regiment of P.V. and V.V.* Reprint, Baltimore, Md.: Butternut & Blue, 1998.

Parrish, James W. *Wiregrass to Appomattox: The Untold Story of the 50th Georgia Infantry Regiment, C.S.A.* Winchester, Va.: Angle Valley Press, 2009.

Pfanz, Donald C., ed. *The Letters of General Richard S. Ewell, Stonewall's Successor*. Knoxville: University of Tennessee Press, 2012.

———. *Richard S. Ewell: A Soldier's Life*. Chapel Hill: University of North Carolina Press, 1998.

Poague, William Thomas. *Gunner with Stonewall: Reminiscences of William Thomas Poague*, edited by Monroe F. Cockrell. Jackson, Tenn.: McCowat-Mercer Press, 1957.

Porter, Horace. *Campaigning with Grant*. Reprint, New York: Bonanza, 1961.

Powell, William H. *The Fifth Army Corps (Army of the Potomac): A Record of Operations During the Civil War in the United States of America, 1861–1865*. Reprint, Dayton, Ohio: Press of Morningside Bookshop, 1984.

Power, J. Tracy. *Lee's Miserables: Life in the Army of Northern Virginia from the Wilderness to Appomattox*. Chapel Hill: University of North Carolina Press, 1998.

Priest, John Michael, ed. *One Surgeon's Private War: Doctor William W. Potter of the 57th New York*. Shippensburg, Pa.: White Mane, 1996.

Pryor, Elizabeth Brown. *Reading the Man: A Portrait of Robert E. Lee through His Private Letters*. New York: Viking, 2007.

Rafuse, Ethan S. *Robert E. Lee and the Fall of the Confederacy, 1863–1864*. Lanham, Md.: Rowman & Littlefield, 2008.

Rankin, Thomas M. *37th Virginia Infantry*. Lynchburg, Va.: H. E. Howard, 1987.

———. *23rd Virginia Infantry*. Lynchburg, Va.: H. E. Howard, 1985.

Ray, Fred L. *Shock Troops of the Confederacy: The Sharpshooter Battalions of the Army of Northern Virginia*. Asheville, N.C.: CFS Press, 2006.

Raymer, Jacob Nathaniel. *Confederate Correspondent: The Civil War Reports of Jacob Nathaniel Raymer, Fourth North Carolina*, edited by E. B. Munson. Jefferson, N.C.: McFarland, 2009.

Reidenbaugh, Lowell. *27th Virginia Infantry*. Lynchburg, Va.: H. E. Howard, 1993.

Reid-Green, Marcia, ed. *Letters Home: Henry Matrau of the Iron Brigade*. Lincoln: University of Nebraska Press, 1993.

Rhea, Gordon C. *The Battle of the Wilderness, May 5-6, 1864*. Baton Rouge: Louisiana State University Press, 1994.

———. *The Battles for Spotsylvania Court House and the Road to Yellow Tavern, May 7-12, 1864*. Baton Rouge: Louisiana State University Press, 1997.

———. *Carrying the Flag: The Story of Private Charles Whilden, the Confederacy's Most Unlikely Hero*. New York: Basic Books, 2004.

Rhodes, John H. *The History of Battery B, First Regiment Rhode Island Light Artillery in the War to Preserve the Union 1861-1865*. Reprint, Baltimore, Md.: Butternut & Blue, 1996.

Rhodes, Robert Hunter, ed. *All for the Union: The Civil War Diary and Letters of Elisha Hunt Rhodes*. New York: Orion Books, 1985.

Riggs, David F. *13th Virginia Infantry*. Lynchburg, Va.: H. E. Howard, 1988.

Riggs, Susan A. *21st Virginia Infantry*. Lynchburg, Va.: H. E. Howard, 1991.

Robertson, James I., Jr. *4th Virginia Infantry*. Lynchburg, Va.: H. E. Howard, 1982.

———. *General A. P. Hill: The Story of a Confederate Warrior*. New York: Random House, 1987.

———. *The Stonewall Brigade*. Baton Rouge: Louisiana State University Press, 1963.

Robertson, Robert Stoddart. *Personal Recollections of the War: A Record of Service with the Ninety-third New York Vol. Infantry*. Cincinnati: Henry C. Sherick, 1884.

Robson, John S. *How a One-Legged Rebel Lives: Reminiscences of the Civil War*. Reprint, Gaithersburg, Md.: Butternut Press, 1984.

Roche, Thomas T. "The Bloody Angle," Philadelphia *Weekly Times*, September 3, 1881.

Roe, Alfred S. *The Tenth Regiment Massachusetts Volunteer Infantry 1861-1864*. Springfield, Mass.: Tenth Regiment Veteran Association, 1909.

Rosenblatt, Emil and Ruth Rosenblatt, eds. *Hard Marching Every Day: The Civil War Letters of Private Wilbur Fisk, 1861-1865*. Lawrence: University Press of Kansas, 1992.

Royall, William L. *Some Reminiscences*. Reprint, Columbia, S.C.: n.p., 2018.

Ruffner, Kevin C. *44th Virginia Infantry*. Lynchburg, Va.: H. E. Howard, 1987.

Samito, Christian G., ed. *"Fear Was Not in Him": The Civil War Letters of Major General Francis C. Barlow, U.S.A.* New York: Fordham University Press, 2004.

Sauers, Richard A., ed. *The Civil War Journal of Colonel William J. Bolton 51st Pennsylvania April 20, 1861–August 2, 1865.* Conshohocken, Pa.: Combined Publishing, 2000.

Sauers, Richard A., and Peter Tomasak. *Ricketts' Battery: A History of Battery F, 1st Pennsylvania Light Artillery.* n.p.: Luzerne National Bank, 2001.

Sawyer, Franklin. *A Military History of the 8th Regiment Ohio Vol. Inf'y: Its Battles, Marches and Army Movements.* Reprint, Huntington, W. Va.: Blue Acorn Press, 1994.

Schaff, Morris. *The Battle of the Wilderness.* Reprint, Gaithersburg, Md.: Butternut Press, 1986.

Scott, Robert Garth, ed. *Fallen Leaves: The Civil War Letters of Major Henry Livermore Abbott.* Kent, Ohio: Kent State University Press, 1991.

——. ed. *Forgotten Valor: The Memoirs, Journals, and Civil War Letters of Orlando B. Willcox.* Kent, Ohio: Kent State University Press, 1999.

Scott, W. W. *A History of Orange County, Virginia.* Reprint, Baltimore: Regional, 1974.

Sears, Stephen W. *Lincoln's Lieutenants: The High Command of the Army of the Potomac.* Boston: Houghton Mifflin Harcourt, 2017.

Seville, William P. *History of the First Regiment, Delaware Volunteers.* Reprint, Hightstown, N.J.: Longstreet House, 1998.

Seymour, William J. *The Civil War Memoirs of Captain William J. Seymour: Reminiscences of a Louisiana Tiger,* edited by Terry L. Jones. Baton Rouge: Louisiana State University Press, 1991.

Sheehan-Dean, Aaron. *Why Confederates Fought: Family and Nation in Civil War Virginia.* Chapel Hill: University of North Carolina Press, 2007.

Silliker, Ruth L., ed. *The Rebel Yell and the Yankee Hurrah: The Civil War Journal of a Maine Volunteer.* Camden, Maine: Down East Books, 1985.

Simons, Ezra D. *A Regimental History: The One Hundred and Twenty-fifth New York State Volunteers.* New York: Judson Printing, 1888.

Small, Harold A., ed. *The Road to Richmond: The Civil War Memoirs of Major Abner R. Small of the Sixteenth Maine Volunteers.* New York: Fordham University Press, 2000.

Smith, John Day. *The History of the Nineteenth Regiment of Maine Volunteer Infantry 1862–1865.* Minneapolis, Minn.: Great Western Printing, 1909.

Smith, John L. *History of the Corn Exchange Regiment: 118th Pennsylvania Volunteers, from Their First Engagement at Antietam to Appomattox.* Philadelphia: J. L. Smith, 1905.

Smith, Mark M. *The Smell of Battle, the Taste of Siege: A Sensory History of the Civil War.* New York: Oxford University Press, 2015.

Smith, Stuart W., ed. *Douglas Southall Freeman on Leadership.* Shippensburg, Pa.: White Mane, 1993.

Smith, W. A. *The Anson Guards: Company C, Fourteenth Regiment North Carolina Volunteers 1861–1865.* Reprint, Wendell, N.C.: Broadfoot's Bookmark, 1978.

Sommers, Richard J. *Richmond Redeemed: The Siege at Petersburg.* El Dorado Hills, Calif.: Savas Beattie, 2014.

Sorrel, G. Moxley. *Recollections of a Confederate Staff Officer,* edited by Bell Irvin Wiley. Jackson, Tenn.: McCowat-Mercer Press, 1958.

Southern Bivouac, 6 vols. Reprint, Wilmington, N.C.: Broadfoot Publishing Company, 1992, 1993.

Southern Historical Society Papers, 52 vols. Reprint, Wilmington, N.C.: Broadfoot, 1990–92.

Steere, Edward. *The Wilderness Campaign.* Reprint, Gaithersburg, Md.: Olde Soldier Books, 1987.

Stephens, Robert Grier, ed. *Intrepid Warrior: Clement Anselm Evans Confederate General from Georgia, Life, Letters, and Diaries of the War Years.* Dayton, Ohio: Morningside House, 1992.

Steplyk, Jonathan M. *Fighting Means Killing: Civil War Soldiers and the Nature of Combat.* Lawrence: University Press of Kansas, 2018.

Stevens, George T. *Three Years in the Sixth Corps.* Reprint, Alexandria, Va.: Time-Life Books, 1984.

Stewart, Robert Laird. *History of the One Hundred and Fortieth Regiment Pennsylvania Volunteers.* Philadelphia, Pa.: Franklin Bindery, 1912.

Stiles, Robert. *Four Years under Marse Robert.* Reprint, Dayton, Ohio: Press of Morningside Bookshop, 1977.

Stocker, Jeffrey D., ed. *From Huntsville to Appomattox: R. T. Coles's History of 4th Regiment, Alabama Volunteer Infantry, C.S.A., Army of Northern Virginia.* Knoxville: University of Tennessee Press, 1996.

Styple, William B. *Generals in Bronze: Interviewing the Commanders of the Civil War.* Kearny, N.J.: Belle Grove, 2005.

———, ed. *Writing & Fighting the Confederate War: The Letters of Peter Wellington Alexander Confederate War Correspondent.* Kearny, N.J.: Belle Grove, 2002.

Supplement to the Official Records of the Union and Confederate Armies, 95 vols. Wilmington, N.C.: Broadfoot, 1994–99.

Swinton, William. *Campaigns of the Army of the Potomac*. Reprint, Secaucus, N.J.: Blue & Gray Press, 1988.

Swisher, James K. *Warrior in Gray: General Robert Rodes of Lee's Army*. Shippensburg, Pa.: White Mane Books, 2000.

Sword, Wiley. *Southern Invincibility: A History of the Confederate Heart*. New York: St. Martin's Press, 1999.

Tankersley, Allen P. *John B. Gordon: A Study in Gallantry*. Atlanta: Whitehall Press, 1955.

Tate, Thomas K., ed. *Col. Frank Huger, C.S.A.: The Civil War Letters of a Confederate Artillery Officer Frank Huger*. Jefferson, N.C.: McFarland, 2011.

Tedards, Rosalind Todd. *Orr's Rifles*. Wilmington, N.C.: Broadfoot, 2017.

Thomas, Mary Warner and Richard S. Sauers,, eds. *The Civil War Letters of First Lieutenant James B. Thomas Adjutant, 107th Pennsylvania Volunteers*. Baltimore, Md.: Butternut & Blue, 1995.

Tompkins, Daniel A. *Company K, Fourteenth South Carolina Volunteers*. Charlotte, N.C.: Observer Printing and Publishing House, 1897.

Toney, Marcus G. *The Privations of a Private: The Campaign under Gen. R. E. Lee; The Campaign under Gen. Stonewall Jackson. . . .* Nashville, Tenn.: M. E. Church, 1905.

Tower, R. Lockwood, ed. *Lee's Adjutant: The Wartime Letters of Colonel Walter Herron Taylor, 1862–1865*. Columbia: University of South Carolina Press, 1995.

Trask, Benjamin H. *16th Virginia Infantry*. Lynchburg, Va.: H. E. Howard, 1986.

——. *61st Virginia Infantry*. Lynchburg, Va.: H. E. Howard, 1988.

Trask, Kerry A. *Fire Within: A Civil War Narrative from Wisconsin*. Kent, Ohio: Kent State University Press, 1995.

Trudeau, Noah Andre. *Bloody Roads South: The Wilderness to Cold Harbor, May–June 1864*. Boston: Little, Brown, 1989.

Tucker, Glenn. *Hancock the Superb*. Indianapolis, Ind.: Bobbs-Merrill Company, 1960.

Tyler, Mason Whiting. *Recollections of the Civil War*. New York: G. P. Putnam's Sons, 1912.

Ural, Susannah F. "A Little Body of Malcontents," *Civil War Times* 53, no. 3 (June 2014).

"Vermont Veterans Visit Virginia 25 Years after the War," *On the Skirmish Line: Central Virginia Battlefields Trust* 21, no. 4 (Fall 2017).

Wadsworth, Mike. *The 13th South Carolina Volunteer Infantry C.S.A.* Wilmington, N.C.: Broadfoot, 2008.

Waitt, Ernest Linden, compiler. *History of the Nineteenth Regiment Massachusetts Volunteer Infantry 1861–1865.* Salem, Mass.: Salem Press, 1906.

Walker, Francis A. *General Hancock.* New York: D. Appleton, 1894.

———. *History of the Second Army Corps in the Army of the Potomac.* Reprint, Gaithersburg, Md.: Olde Soldier Books, n.d.

Wallace, Lee A., Jr. *5th Virginia Infantry.* Lynchburg, Va.: H. E. Howard, 1986.

Ward, David A. *The 96th Pennsylvania Volunteers in the Civil War.* Jefferson, N.C.: McFarland, 2018.

Ward, Joseph R. C. *History of the One Hundred and Sixth Regiment Pennsylvania Volunteers 2d Brigade, 2d Division, 2d Corps 1861–1865.* Philadelphia: F. McManus, Jr., 1906.

Warner, Ezra J. *Generals in Blue: Lives of the Union Commanders.* Baton Rouge: Louisiana State University Press, 1981.

"War's Hardening Hand," *Civil War Monitor* 9, no. 2 (Summer 2019).

Washburn, George H. *A Complete Military History and Record of the 108th Regiment N. Y. Vols. from 1862 to 1894.* Rochester, N.Y.: Press of E. R. Andrews, 1894.

Waters, Zack C. and James C. Edmonds. *A Small but Spartan Band: The Florida Brigade in Lee's Army of Northern Virginia.* Tuscaloosa: University of Alabama Press, 2010.

Weigley, Russell F. *A Great Civil War: A Military and Political History, 1861–1865.* Bloomington: Indiana University Press, 2000.

Welch, Richard F. *The Boy General: The Life and Careers of Francis Channing Barlow.* Madison, N.J.: Fairleigh Dickinson University Press, 2003.

Welch, Spencer Glasgow. *A Confederate Surgeon's Letters to His Wife.* Reprint, Marietta, Ga.: Continental Book Company, 1954.

Weld, Stephen Minot. *War Diary and Letters of Stephen Minot Weld.* Boston: Massachusetts Historical Society, 1979.

Wert, Jeffry D. *A Brotherhood of Valor: The Common Soldiers of the Stonewall Brigade, C.S.A., and the Iron Brigade, U.S.A.* New York: Simon & Schuster, 1999.

———. *Cavalryman of the Lost Cause: A Biography of J. E. B. Stuart.* New York: Simon & Schuster, 2008.

———. *Custer: The Controversial Life of George Armstrong Custer.* New York: Simon & Schuster, 1996.

BIBLIOGRAPHY

———. *From Winchester to Cedar Creek: The Shenandoah Valley Campaign of 1864.* Carlisle, Pa.: South Mountain Press, 1987.

———. *General James Longstreet: The Confederacy's Most Controversial Soldier—A Biography.* New York: Simon & Schuster, 1993.

———. *Gettysburg: Day Three.* New York: Simon & Schuster, 2001.

———. *A Glorious Army: Robert E. Lee's Triumph, 1862–1863.* New York: Simon & Schuster, 2011.

———. *The Sword of Lincoln: The Army of the Potomac.* New York: Simon & Schuster, 2005.

Westbrook, Robert S. *History of the 49th Pennsylvania Volunteers.* Reprint, Baltimore, Md.: Butternut & Blue, 1999.

Wexler, Fred C. *The Tammany Regiment: A History of the Forty-Second New York Volunteer Infantry, 1861–1864.* Bloomington, Ind.: iUniverse, 2016.

Weygant, Charles H. *History of the One Hundred Twenty-Fourth Regiment, N.Y.S.V.* Reprint, Celina, Ohio: Ironclad, 2002.

Wheelan, Joseph. *Bloody Spring: Forty Days That Sealed the Confederacy's Fate.* Boston: DaCapo Press, 2014.

Wilkeson, Frank. *Recollections of a Private Soldier in the Army of the Potomac.* New York: G. P. Putnam's Sons, 1887.

Wilkinson, Warren. *Mother, May You Never See the Sights I Have Seen: The Fifty-Seventh Massachusetts Veteran Volunteers in the Army of the Potomac 1864–1865.* New York: Harper & Row, 1990.

Williams, Ben Ames, ed. *A Diary from Dixie.* Boston: Houghton Mifflin, 1949.

Williams, Richard Brady, ed. *Stonewall's Prussian Mapmaker: The Journals of Captain Oscar Hinrichs.* Chapel Hill: University of North Carolina Press, 2014.

Williams, Sidney S. *From Spotsylvania to Wilmington, N.C. by Way of Andersonville and Florence.* Providence, RI: Rhode Island Soldiers and Sailors Historical Society, 1899.

Wilson, Arabella M. *Disaster, Struggle, Triumph: The Adventures of 1000 "Boys in Blue," from August, 1862 to June, 1865.* Albany, N.Y.: Argus Company, 1870.

Winik, Jay. *April 1865: The Month That Saved America.* New York: Harper Collins, 2001.

Wise, Jennings Cropper. *The Long Arm of Lee: The History of the Artillery of the Army of Northern Virginia.* Reprint, New York: Oxford University Press, 1959.

Woolsey, Jane Stuart. *Hospital Days.* New York: D. Van Nostrand, 1870.

Worsham, John H. *One of Jackson's Foot Cavalry*, edited by James I. Robertson Jr. Jackson, Tenn.: McCowat-Mercer Press, 1964.

Wyckoff, Mac. *A History of the 3rd South Carolina Regiment: Lee's Reliables.* Wilmington, N.C.: Broadfoot, 2008.

Yeary, Mamie, ed. *Reminiscences of the Boys in Gray 1861–1865.* Dallas, Tex.: Smith & Lamas, 1912.

Young, Alfred C., III. *Lee's Army during the Overland Campaign: A Numerical Study.* Baton Rouge: Louisiana State University Press, 2013.

Index

Page numbers in italics signify maps.

Bratton, John, 143, 144
Braxton, Carter M., 117
Brewster, William R., 74, 92
Bristoe Campaign (October 1863), 3, 13, 77
Brockman, Benjamin T., 134
Brock Road, 22, 44; Confederate assault along, 27, 28, 32; Union march along, 26, 33–34, 47
Brooke, John R., 71, 74, 90, 126, 138, 188
Brooks, John S., 103
Brooks, Samuel, 181
Brown, B. F., 132–33
Brown, Charles B., 155
Brown, G. Campbell, 55, 110, 171
Brown, Hamilton A., 90
Brown, Henry (Confederate private), 17
Brown, Henry W. (Union brigade commander), 137–38
Brown, Hiram L., 74, 90, 91, 108
Brown, Joseph N., 27, 42, 132, 134, 173, 191, 192
Brown, Morris, Jr., 91
Brown (John and Elizabeth) farmhouse, 58–59, 72–73, 83, 168
Buck, Samuel, 105–6
Bunker, Nathaniel, 182
burials, 179–81
Burnside, Ambrose, 43, 45, 59, 69, 120, 143; criticisms and failings of, 123, 160, 165, 187; Grant designation of, 14; and May 12 Mule Shoe assault, 60, 116, 119, 120, 123, 160; and May 18 attack, 194; and The Wilderness, 23, 119
Butler, Benjamin F., 14

Caldwell, James F. J., 134, 136, 149, 150; on Bloody Angle struggle, 158, 173, 174, 176
Caldwell, John, 69
Carrington, James M., 62–63, 79, 95, 96

Carroll, Samuel S., 74, 95, 178–79, 188
Carter, Thomas H., 16, 63, 82, 101, 117; and May 12 Mule Shoe assault, 96–97; on weakness of salient position, 42–43
Carter, William Page, 82, 89
Casler, John, 174, 176
casualty figures, 56–57, 87, 110, 163; at Gettysburg, 5, 7; in Spotsylvania campaign, 182–83, 195; at The Wilderness, 18, 19, 24, 28, 182
Catharpin Road, 34–35, 36, 38
cavalry: Confederate, 32, 38, 72; Union, 13, 14, 32, 34, 36, 45
Chancellorsville, Battle of (April 3–May 6, 1863), 5, 10, 30, 51, 67, 70; Hancock at, 65; The Wilderness as battlefield in, 18, 19, 24
Chase, Stephen P., 93, 153
Chisholm, Daniel, 107
Christ, Benjamin C., 160, 188
Clyburn, Thomas F., 133–34
Coiner, Cyrus, 109
Coiner, Joseph S., 109
Coleman, Charles, 89
Compton, William A., 107
Compton, William C., 129
Comstock, Cyrus B., 59, 60, 119, 160
Conerly, Buxton Reives, 130, 176
Confederate Army, 15–17; assessment of during Spotsylvania campaign, 187–95; cavalry, 32, 38, 72; decimation of officer ranks in, 7, 28, 77, 79, 192; defensive tactics of, 7, 8; desertions from, 3; morale in, 16–17, 117; reenlistments in, 3, 12, 102–3; winter camps of, 3. See also casualty figures; specific battles and campaigns
Confederate Army units: First Corps, 15, 19, 24, 26, 35–36, 158; Second Corps, 1, 19, 39, 42, 62, 80; Third Corps, 19, 23, 80, 121,

132, 158; Alabama regiments and brigades, 54–55, 111, 125, 127–29, 144; Georgia regiments and brigades, 37, 53–55, 57, 102, 106, 107, 108–9, 121–22, 126, 145, 156; Louisiana regiments and brigades, 38, 78, 79–80, 83, 91–93, 102; Mississippi regiments and brigades, 36–37, 127, 129–32, 152, 169–70; North Carolina regiments and brigades, 54–55, 57, 80, 90, 94–95, 102–4, 111–14, 121–22, 125, 127, 159–62; South Carolina regiments and brigades, 36–37, 133–36, 150–51, 152–53, 169; Stonewall Brigade, 43, 54, 62, 78–79, 82, 92, 93–94, 96; Texas Brigade, 26, 28; Virginia regiments and brigades, 53, 54, 79, 80, 81, 83, 87, 88, 90, 92, 93, 94, 102, 105–6, 107, 108–10, 111, 126, 156–57, 159–60, 163

Congressional Joint Committee on the Conduct of the War (1864), 10, 67

Coons, John, 108

Cowan, Robert Van Buren, 122, 159–60, 163

Crawford, Daniel, 87

Crawford, John Berryman, 170

Crawford, Samuel, 51, 144, 146

Crittenden, Thomas L., 122, 123, 160; about, 120

Crocker, John S., 74, 92, 93, 170

Crockett, Edward R., 49

Cross, Nelson, 137–38

Curtin, Andrew Gregg, 155

Curtin, John I., 120, 121

Cutler, Lysander, 144, 145, 167–68, 169

Cutshaw, Wildred E., 62

Dale, Richard C., 107

Dana, Charles, 123, 146, 178, 187

Dance, Willis J., 117

Daniel, Junius, 54, 78, 94–95, 102, 127; and Confederate counterattack, 111, 112; death of, 192

Davenport, W. W., 151

Davis, Jefferson, 4, 7, 19–20

Davis, Thomas H., 108

Dawes, Rufus, 9, 145

Deas, William J., 89

Delph, Wallace I., 176

Denoon, Charles E., 162

desertion, 3

Dillard, John J., 110

Dolan, F., 172

Doles, George, 53, 54, 57

Doles's Salient, 53–54, 55–56, 82, 111

Donnelly, James, 107

Doubleday, Abner, 10–11, 67

Douglas, Henry Kyd, 82

Doyle, Thomas, 93, 94

Dubose, Dudley M., 145

Dugal, L., 200

Dunlop, William S., 133

Dyer, Frank, 66

Early, Everett, 157

Early, Jubal, 35, 43, 49; assigned command of Third Corps, 38, 100, 192–93; and May 12 combat, 80, 160, 179

Ebright, Aaron W., 148

Edwards, Oliver, 124, 137, 173, 188

Ellis, William, 151

Emery, Edwin, 92

Engelhard, Joseph A., 121

Eustis, Henry, 137–38

Evans, Clement, 11, 17, 82, 105, 154, 157; about, 106; Confederate counterattack by, 109–10, 111, 117, 190; distinguished himself, 192; and Upton assault, 54–55

Ewell, Richard S., 40–41, 78, 79, 101, 127, 129, 133; and Bloody Angle combat, 167, 169, 191; and Confederate fieldworks, 43, 61, 174, 179; Lee criticisms of, 16,

116–17; Meade on, 8, 9; and Meade's command, 9–10, 188; Mule Shoe campaign assessment by, 188; as obstinate and relentless, 9, 14, 47, 49, 143; personal habits of, 9; Spotsylvania campaign strategy of, 18–19; and The Wilderness, 23, 29; troops' confidence in, 13–14, 58

Gregg, David, 34

Gregg, Maxcy, 132

Griffin, Charles, 37, 144, 168

Griffin, Simon G., 120–21

Grimes, Bryan, 61, 112–13, 114, 191

Hager, Billy, 87

Haigh, Charles T., 161

Haines, Alanson A., 196

Haines, William, 95

Haley, John W., 83, 93, 108, 149, 170

Halleck, Henry W., 11, 47, 58

Halsey, Edmund, 138

Hamilton, A. T., 180

Hancock, Asbury W., 172

Hancock, Winfield Scott, 13, 33, 43, 45, 126, 179; about, 65–66, 186; and Bloody Angle combat, 138, 168, 169, 173, 178–79; and Confederate prisoners, 97–98; failings of, 187; at Gettysburg, 65, 66, 141, 186; Landrum farmhouse headquarters of, 126, 168, 197; and May 10 Mule Shoe assault, 49; and May 12 Mule Shoe assault, 59, 66–67, 70–71, 72–73, 74–75, 83, 97, 184, 186; and May 12 stalemate, 116, 123; and May 18–19 clashes, 194, 195; Spotsylvania campaign assessment by, 186; and The Wilderness, 22–23

Harbaugh, T. C., 200

Hardaway, Robert A., 62, 63, 117

Hardin, Thomas J., 131

Harper, John W., 199

Harris, Nathaniel H.: about, 129; and Bloody Angle combat, 152, 154, 167, 169, 172, 176, 190; Confederate counterattack by, 127, 129–32, 136; praises for, 190–91, 192

Harris farm engagement (May 19, 1864), 194–96

Harrison (Edgar and Ann Maria) farmhouse, 61, 81, 101, 104, 105, 124, 167, 178, 199; about, 42

Hartranft, John F., 160

Hawes, S. Horace, 82, 89

Hays, Alexander, 28

Hays, Harry T., 38, 77–78

Henagan, John W., 36

Heth, Henry, 43, 80; and Heth's Salient, 159; and Lee, 7, 45, 49, 63; and The Wilderness, 23, 28

Heth's Salient, 159, 160, 162, 163

Hill, Ambrose Powell "A. P.," 69, 79; illness of, 38, 43, 193; and Lee, 16, 63, 64, 193; and The Wilderness, 19, 22–23, 28

Hite, John P., 93

Hoffman, John S., 82, 101, 105, 126, 154; about, 106; Confederate counterattack by, 108, 111, 117, 190

Holmes, Oliver Wendell, Jr., 56, 143–44, 168, 197

Holt, David, 126–27, 167, 176

Hooker, Joseph, 11, 126

Hotchkiss, Jedediah, 40, 76, 96, 196

Howard, McHenry, 80, 81

Humphrey, Benjamin G., 36

Humphrey, William, 160, 162

Humphreys, Andrew A., 13, 168–69, 173; and May 12 Laurel Hill assault, 143–44, 145–46, 147

Hunt, Isaac, 134

Hunter, Robert W., 81–82, 88, 117–18

Iron Brigade, 50, 70, 149

Iverson, Alfred, 103

Jackson, Asbury, 60
Jackson, Stonewall, 15–16, 28, 79
Jackson, Thomas J., 79
Jenkins, Micah, 26, 28
Johnson, Edward, 1, 35, 39–40, 42, 121; about, 87–88; and Bloody Angle combat, 174, 182; distinguished himself, 192; at Gettysburg, 76–77; and May 12 Mule Shoe, assault, 96, 126, 184; as prisoner, 88, 97–99; and removal of Confederate artillery, 63, 75–76, 81–82
Johnston, Joseph E., 32
Johnston, Robert D., 38, 54–55, 102; about, 103; Confederate counterattack by, 103–4, 190
Jones, Ben, 87
Jones, John M., 28, 77, 80
Judson, Amos M., 142
Justice, George C., 138

Kearny, Philip, 67, 75
Kelly, Thomas, 155
Kershaw, Joseph, 24, 27, 39, 110
Kirk, Newton T., 156
Kirkpatrick, James, 130
Kurtz, George Washington, 94

Landrum, Edward, 197, 200
Landrum, Willis, 161, 197
Landrum (Willis and Lucy) farmhouse, 59, 83, 97–98, 168; later history of, 197, 199–200
Lane, James H., 80, 102, 121; and Heth's Salient combat, 159–60, 161, 163
Lane, Oscar, 159–60
Laurel Hill, 34; May 8 assault on, 36–38, 142; May 10 assault on, 49–51, 56, 142; May 12 assault on, 142–47
LaVilla, 42, 199. *See also* Harrison farmhouse
Leasure, Daniel, 122, 165

Lee, Fitzhugh, 34, 36, 37
Lee, Robert E., 19, 79, 134, 194; advance on Spotsylvania by, 34–35, 38; boldness and aggressiveness of, 4–5, 20, 27, 29, 32, 45, 64, 106, 117; and Confederate fieldworks, 61, 159, 174; counterattacks ordered by, 57, 158–59, 189–90; defensive strategy and tactics of, 7, 8; Ewell criticized by, 16, 104–5, 192; at Gettysburg, 16; on Grant, 63; Grant on, 29, 32; headquarters established by, 46; health of, 4; and Hill, 16, 63, 64, 193; and Laurel Hill action (May 8), 35–36, 38; and May 10 Union assault, 55, 56–57; miscalculation in withdrawing artillery, 61–62, 189; personal staff of, 4; positioning of troops by, 41, 49, 61–62, 127, 159, 178; response to May 12 crisis by, 100, 101, 104–5, 106, 117, 118; strategic considerations of, 7–8; and The Wilderness, 19–20, 22, 23, 24, 26, 27, 28–29; troops commended by, 163, 189, 191, 193; troops' concern for safety of, 55, 57, 106–7, 129; troops' confidence in, 4, 15; withdrawal from Mule Shoe by, 179
Lee, William H. F. "Rooney," 61
Lester, William, 154
Levan, James, 162
Lewis, David, 182
Lincoln, Abraham, 7; and Grant, 8, 10, 12, 58; and Meade, 10, 11, 12
Lipps, Jonas A., 88
Long, Andrew, 93, 171
Long, Armistead L., 61, 63, 82, 106, 190
Longstreet, James, 35; as tactician, 15–16; and The Wilderness, 19, 23, 24, 26, 27, 28

Luce, Constant, 161
Lyman, Theodore, 56, 69, 99, 125, 199; assessment of Spotsylvania Campaign by, 185; on Birney, 67, 68; on Black troops, 119–20; on Confederate fieldworks, 176; on Crittenden, 120; on Gibbon, 70; on Grant, 9, 13–14, 32; and Hancock, 66, 116; on Ricketts, 147; on Warren, 141; on Webb, 107; on Wright, 52

Macgill, Charles, 174
Mackenzie, Ranald S., 52
Mahone, William, 43, 127, 159; and May 10 combat, 45, 49; and May 12 combat, 163, 182
Manly, Matt, 114
Marshall, Charles, 4, 55
May, Benjamin, 162
McAllister, Robert, 57, 74, 92, 114, 153, 188
McClellan, George B., 9, 12, 29, 75
McClenahan, Charles, 172
McCoull (Neill, Eliza, Mary, and Mildred) house and farm, 103, 104, 129, 133, 178, 190; about, 38–39; Confederate dead buried at, 199; later history of, 197–98
McCown, James L., 93–94
McCreary, Camillus W., 135
McDow, Francis Marion, 109
McGowan, Samuel, 170; about, 132; Confederate counterattack by, 132–34, 136, 152; praised, 191, 192
McGuire, Hunter H., 94, 193
McLaurin, William H., 163
McMahon, Martin T., 44, 53
McParlin, Thomas A., 182
Meade, George G., 34, 43, 98–99, 125, 126; and army reorganization, 13; and Bloody Angle combat, 167, 168, 178, 179;
conduct of at Gettysburg, 10–12; congressional attacks on, 10–11, 67; on Grant, 8, 9; and Grant command, 9–10, 188; Grant instructions to, 14, 30, 32, 59–60; Grant views of, 10, 23; and Lincoln, 10, 11, 12; and May 10 Mule Shoe assault, 49–50, 52; and May 12 Mule Shoe assault, 59–60, 116–17, 142, 143–44; and McClellan, 12, 29; and Mine Run Campaign, 3, 11–12; mistakes and failings of, 19, 29, 186; personal traits of, 12, 45; promotions of, 12, 188; and Sheridan, 45; and Spotsylvania campaign strategy, 18–19; and Stanton, 11, 13; and The Wilderness, 23; and Warren, 142, 143–44, 146, 147, 187
Mendell, George H., 71
Merriam, Waldo, 73
Merritt, Wesley, 34
Metcalf, Richard, 140
Miles, Nelson A., 71, 197, 198; distinguished himself, 188; and May 12 Mule Shoe assault, 74, 87, 109
Miller, Abram, 87–88
Mills, Charles, 120, 160, 165
Milroy, Robert, 147
Mine Run Campaign (November 1863), 7, 13, 18, 77, 141–42; Lee in, 19, 20; Meade in, 3, 11–12
Mitchell, William G., 60, 125
Mixon, Alexander, 131
Monaghan, William, 78, 94, 102, 111, 113
Montgomery, Charles R., 89
Morgan, Charles H., 60, 71
Mott, Gershom, 52, 111, 136, 153; demotion of, 188; and May 12 Mule Shoe assault, 70, 72, 75, 92, 94, 102, 124; and Upton assault on salient, 55–56, 58–59
Muffly, Joseph W., 156

Mule Shoe salient: assessments of battle at, 184–87; battle at eastern face of salient, 119, 126, 154–56, 159; battle at Heth's Salient (May 12), 160–64; casualties from fighting at, 56–57, 87, 110, 182–83, 195; Confederate counterattacks at (May 12), 103–4, 107–14, *115*, 121–22, 128, 130–31, 134–35, 152, 159–62, 190–91; Confederate defensive positions at, 1, 40–41, 60–64, 77–83, 102, 105–6, 116; Confederate leadership assessed at, 189–95; Confederate officers killed at, 192; Confederate prisoners taken at, 56, 87–88, 90–91, 97–99, 114, 116, 121, 148, 151, 161, 184; Confederate reinforcements sent to, 127, 129–30, 132–33; Confederate withdrawal from (May 13), 178–79; Confederate withdrawal of artillery from (May 11–12), 61–63, 75–76, 81–82, 189; crisis for Confederate Army at (May 12), 100, 117–18, 158–59, 184, 189; dead and wounded gathered from, 179–81; fieldworks and entrenchments at, 41–43, 61, 154, 156, 174, 176; Lee's leadership at, 61–63, 100, 101, 104–5, 106–7, 117–18, 158–59, 189–90; maps of battle at, *86*, *115*, *139*, *164*, *175*, *177*; nature of combat at, 124–25, 128–32, 134–36, 140, 147–58, 162, 165–67, 169–74, 184, 191, 196; significance of battle at, 196–97; as site for visitors and reunions, 199–200; situation of wounded at, 171–72, 181–82; size of competing forces in, 147; tactical stalemate in, 114–15, 116–17, 123, 136, 185; traverses at, 154, 156; Union assault on (May 10), *48*, 49–57, 185; Union assault on (May 12, morning), 58–60, 66–67, 70–75, 83–85, 87–97, 101–2, 119, 120–21, 184, 186; Union assaults (May 12, afternoon), 123–26, 136–38, 142–47, *164*, 165, 168–69; Union leadership assessed at, 186–89; Union officers distinguishing themselves at, 188; Union soldiers taken prisoner at, 108, 114, 131, 152, 161, 163; western angle as key point of struggle at, 140. *See also* Spotsylvania Campaign

Munford, Thomas T., 41

Neill, Thomas H., 53, 136, 173; about, 123–24; loses nerve, 44, 124
Nelson, William, 62, 117, 122
New York Times, 118, 179, 195
Nichols, G. W., 106, 109–10
Nicholson, William T., 159
Niemeyer, William F., 162–63
Noyes, Wallace W., 151

Old, William W., 40
Old Court House Road, 34, 36
Orange Plank Road, 19, 20, 32, 34, 119; about, 18; and The Wilderness, 22, 23, 26–27
Orange Turnpike, 32, 35–36, 119; about, 18; Union troops' march along, 19, 20, 22, 33
Orr, William, 13
Owen, Joshua T., 74, 95

Page, Richard C. M., 62, 82, 88–89, 96
Palmer, William, 24
Parker, Peter A., 162
Parsons, Joseph B., 137
Patterson, John, 170
Pattison, Alexander B., 170
Pearce, Holden, 172
Peck, William, 78
Pegram, John, 28, 105
Pegram, William, 122

Pendleton, Alexander S. "Sandie," 17, 79
Pendleton, William N., 16, 34, 62, 145, 157
Peninsula Campaign (July 1862), 67, 68
Penrose, William, 180
Perrin, Abner, 127–28, 181, 190, 192, 199
Perry, Edward A., 28
Perry, William F., 37, 144
Phillips, James E., 162
Pitzer, Andrew L., 68
Pleasanton, Alfred, 13, 14
Poague, William T., 122, 123
Po River skirmish (May 10), 49
Porter, Horace, 30, 33, 59, 116, 170
Potter, Robert B., 120–21, 122, 123
Prescott, George L., 143
prisoners: Confederate soldiers taken, 56, 87–88, 90–91, 97–99, 114, 116, 121, 148, 151, 161, 184; Union soldiers taken, 108, 114, 131, 152, 161, 163
public opinion, 7–8
Purifoy, John, 89–90

Ramseur, Stephen Dodson, 54, 124–25, 127; about, 111–12; and Bloody Angle combat, 152, 171, 190; called a hero, 191; Confederate counterattack by, 112–14
Rapidan River crossing, 2, 19, 77
Rappahannock Station, 51
Rawlins, John A., 116, 147, 187
Raymer, Jacob Nathaniel, 183
Reams, John, 90
reenlistments, 3, 12, 102–3
Reese, William J., 89, 91, 95
religious beliefs, 149, 166
Rhea, Gordon, 63, 185
Ricketts, James B., 124, 147–48
Riggs, David, 95
Robertsons, Robert, 196
Robinson, John C., 37

Robinson, William, 188
Roche, Thomas T., 129, 130, 181
Rodes, Robert, 38, 39, 57, 127, 129, 133, 182; and Confederate counterattack, 111, 112; considered hero, 191; position of in salient, 40, 42, 110; and removal of artillery, 61, 63
Roebling, Washington, 146
Rosecrans, William S., 120
Rugg, Orrin P., 151
Russell, David A., 124, 136, 137, 173, 188; and Upton assault on salient, 51–52, 53, 56
Russell, Edward, 98
Russell, Ned, 44, 45

Sale, John F., 162
salients: tactical weaknesses of, 41. *See also* Mule Shoe salient
Sanford, Joseph, 198
Saunders, John C. C., 128
Saunders, William, 192
Saunders's Field, 10, 20, 22, 27
Scales, Alfred, 121
Schall, John W., 148
Scott, William D., 53
Second Manassas, Battle of (August 29–30, 1862), 4, 5, 69, 162
Seddon, James, 56
Sedgwick, John, 13, 33, 43; about, 44; death of, 44–45, 123; and The Wilderness, 22, 23, 26–27
Seven Days Campaign (1862), 5, 75
Seymour, William, 91–92
Shady Grove Church, 36, 38, 43
Sheridan, Philip H., 14, 32, 34; and Meade, 45
Sherman, William T., 14, 188
Shimer, Cornelius C., 138
Shooter, Evander C., 135
Shooter, Washington P., 135
Sickles, Daniel, 10–11, 13, 67
Sigel, Franz, 13, 14
Skinner, James H., 109

Union Army, 8–15; assessment of during Spotsylvania campaign, 187–89; Burnside as commander of, 60, 119; cavalry of, 13, 14, 32, 34, 36, 45; Confederate prisoners of, 56, 87–88, 90–91, 97–99, 114, 116, 121, 148, 151, 161, 184; Grant command of, 8, 9–10, 188; McClellan command of, 9, 12, 29, 75; morale of, 14, 33; Rapidan River crossing by, 2, 19, 77; reorganization of, 13; winter campsites of, 12. *See also* casualty figures; *specific battles and campaigns*

Union Army units: First Corps, 13; Second Corps, 13, 22, 23, 24, 38, 50–51, 59, 65, 66–67, 74–75, 83, 85, 95, 100, 123–26, 132, 141, 167; Third Corps, 13, 92; Fifth Corps, 13, 19, 20, 22, 24, 33, 37, 49, 50–51, 141, 144–46, 165, 167–68; Sixth Corps, 13, 19, 22, 24, 27, 33, 38, 43, 52–56, 123–26, 136–37, 146, 150, 167–68; Ninth Corps, 14, 19, 23, 24, 43, 59, 80, 158, 159, 160, 165; Delaware regiments and brigades, 74, 95; Indiana regiments and brigades, 69, 108; Iron Brigade, 50, 70, 149; Maine regiments and brigades, 53, 93, 96, 120, 137, 151, 160–61; Massachusetts regiments and brigades, 44, 120, 124, 125, 143; Michigan regiments and brigades, 87, 161–63; New Hampshire regiments and brigades, 120; New Jersey regiments and brigades, 44, 95, 105, 138, 173; New York regiments and brigades, 53, 74, 85, 92, 107, 120, 125, 137–38, 160–61; Ohio regiments and brigades, 148, 155–56; Pennsylvania regiments and brigades, 49, 53, 56, 74, 87, 97, 101, 105, 120, 122, 125, 137–38, 142–43, 145, 155, 162; Rhode Island regiments and brigades, 120, 124; United States Colored Troops, 119–20; Vermont regiments and brigades, 53, 120, 126, 138, 140, 148, 151; Wisconsin regiments and brigades, 53, 69

United States Colored Troops (USCT), 119–20

Upton, Emory, 194; about, 51; distinguished himself, 188; May 10 attack on salient by, 51–53, 54, 56, 185; and May 12 combat, 136–37, 151, 173

Upton's attack on salient (May 10), 51–57

Van Dyke, William S., 156

Venable, Charles S., 4, 127, 129, 131, 190, 191; on Lee's reactions, 15, 41, 104; and The Wilderness, 23, 24, 26

Vredenburgh, Peter, 179

Wadsworth, James, 28

Wagner, William, 155

Walker, Francis A., 49, 57

Walker, James (Union captain), 138

Walker, James A. (Confederate brigadier general), 40, 61, 78, 79, 92, 93; about, 79

Ward, J. H. Hobart, 74, 92, 108

Warner, Charles P., 152

Warren, Gouverneur K., 13, 33, 43, 116; about, 141–42; and Bloody Angle combat, 167, 179; errors and misjudgments by, 50, 187; Grant fed up with, 141, 146–47, 165, 187; and May 10 attack, 49–50; and May 12 assault, 59, 142–44, 145, 146; Meade criticisms of, 142, 143–44, 146, 147, 187; relieved of command, 146–47, 187; and The Wilderness, 20, 23, 26–27

Washburne, Elihu B., 58